W9-ANM-141

Richard Brinsley Sheridan

a reference guide

A
Reference
Publication
in
Literature

Arthur Weitzman
Editor

Richard Brinsley Sheridan
a reference guide

JACK D. DURANT

G. K. HALL & CO.

70 LINCOLN STREET, BOSTON, MASS.

PR
3683
D88

Copyright © 1981 by Jack D. Durant

Library of Congress Cataloging in Publication Data

Durant, Jack Davis, 1930-
  Richard Brinsley Sheridan, a reference guide.

  (A Reference guide to literature)
  Bibliography: p.
  Includes index.
  1. Sheridan, Richard Brinsley Butler, 1751-1816—
Bibliography. I. Title. II. Series: Reference
guides to literature.
Z8816.D87 [PR3683] 016.822′6 80-28053
ISBN 0-8161-8146-2

This publication is printed on permanent/durable acid-free paper
MANUFACTURED IN THE UNITED STATES OF AMERICA

Contents

THE AUTHOR: Jack D. Durant is Professor of
English at North Carolina State University.
His publications include articles on Otway,
Vanbrugh, Fielding, and Sheridan, and a book
about Sheridan in Twayne's English Authors
Series.

Preface

This reference guide lists essays and books written about Richard
Brinsley Sheridan since 1816, the year of his death. The items come
mainly from the standard reference and serial indexes (through the
listings available to me for 1979), but I have tried, too, to gather
titles from within the writings themselves and from the footnotes
and bibliography lists attaching to them.

It is not an exhaustive list. Given the innumerable amateur and
provincial stagings of Sheridan's plays, it is easy to imagine the
hundreds, even thousands, of newspaper reviews in print within the
English-speaking world, items not recorded in comprehensive indexes
and therefore not included here. For this list, I have screened
only two newspaper indexes, the Times (London) and the New York
Times. Furthermore, I cannot offer a complete list of the introduc-
tions and prefaces to Sheridan's plays. Many issues of his plays
were assumed from the outset to be ephemeral publications.
Indexes may list them, but libraries no longer shelve them, and they
are now out of reach. Should time have given value to such publications they are now often held in treasure collections and will not
circulate through interlibrary loan. For this reason I have not
seen Edmund Gosse's introduction to The School for Scandal in
Heinemann's Favourite Classics Series (1905) or Carl van Doren's
introduction to this same play in the Oxford Limited Editions Club
Series (1934). My annotation of prefatory criticism, then, is
incomplete and is even selective within the incompleteness. That is,
I have not attempted to see issues of Sheridan's plays which make no
apparent claim to worth or durability. By way of suggesting the
scope of continuing interest in Sheridan, I have placed before the
bibliography itself a list of the Sheridan texts, a selective list
but, I think, a representative one. The body of the bibliography is
selective in one other respect: the annotation of literary histories
and general reference works.

I need to emphasize, finally, that the subject index--the items
set out in the index under Sheridan's own name--is incomplete in the
significant sense that it does not reflect systematic subject analysis of general and encyclopedic studies of Sheridan. Such works
should be consulted whatever the specific subject pursued.

Preface

I take pleasure in thanking Ann Smith, the Director of Interlibrary Loan Services at the D. H. Hill Library (North Carolina
State University) and her staff for contributing immeasurably to the
preparation of this book. I also give sincere thanks to Charlene
Turner, who typed the manuscript with patience and skill.

Introduction

When Sheridan died in 1816 he left behind him a legacy of confusion concerning both his character and his contribution. Comment about him since his death, then, takes form as a sustained effort to resolve his riddles. In chronicling his life and career, biographers have sought to wrest from his complex personality a reliable center of unity and integrity. Textual editors have confronted no less exacting a task in trying to ascertain his texts, for he did very little to point them on their way. And critics have encountered every perplexity in placing him properly in the history of drama and in locating the sources of his enduring appeal. Of these three categories of persistent inquiry--biography, textual study, and criticism--only the second has, with the publication in 1973 of Sheridan's Dramatic Works as edited by Cecil Price (see 1973.11), achieved a large measure of definitive resolution. Recent critical books by John Loftis and Mark S. Auburn (1977.4 and 1977.2) have brought new clarity to the historical place and distinctive character of Sheridan's dramatic art. But the basic biographical problem, the enigma of Sheridan's character, persists even yet.

Biography

This enigma persists because the very real ambiguity of Sheridan's character fell prey from the outset to moral and political biases from which it had constantly to be rescued. On the day following his death the London Times published an influential and much-reprinted obituary admiring the accomplishments of his genius but deploring his weakness of character and denying him any real claim to greatness (1816.6). In 1817 the first full-length biography of him, that of John Watkins (1817.4), not only cast doubts upon his artistic integrity, hinting that he might have stolen The School for Scandal, but also justified itself upon largely negative terms: that his life was a lesson in how not to be. At the same time, however, obituary notices and biographical sketches were insisting that his reputation for indolence did not discredit his legacy, that he was a man more sinned against than sinning (1816.5, 17, 19; 1817.1), and this line of sentiment extended itself into the second full-length biography of him (the first documented one), that of Thomas Moore in 1825 (1825.9), an effort, in significant

part, to rescue his name from the injustices done against it by
John Watkins and other early detractors.

Moore's rescue effort failed for at least two reasons. In the
earnestness of its cause, it gave Sheridan's personality too little
opportunity to demonstrate itself freely, and, in identifying
Sheridan with Moore's own powerful political biases, it thrust him
into the center of political controversy. The first of these
deficiencies gave rise to the anecdotal biography Sheridaniana
(1826.9), a declared attempt to liberate Sheridan from the bonds
Moore had placed upon his personality. The second denied Sheridan
the advantage of objective evaluation and gave his character back to
the moralists, who ferreted from it further negative examples.

William Smyth, a Cambridge don who had once served as governor
to Sheridan's son Tom, saw in it the lesson that happiness comes
only of self-control (1840.2). Margaret Oliphant saw in it a neglect of progeny, to whom he might have given fortune and title
(1883.7). Percy Fitzgerald, eager to deflate Moore's too facile
praise of it, saw it as worthy of admiration only on the lowest
levels of excellence (1886.3); and when, at the urging of the
marquess of Dufferin and Ava (Sheridan's great-grandson), Fraser
Rae published a biography praising his subject warmly (1896.15),
Fitzgerald struck back vehemently. Feeling himself slighted by
remarks made in Lord Dufferin's introduction to Rae's books, he
reinforced in two thin but virulent pamphlets (both based upon
separately published articles) his attack upon Sheridan the man
(1897.7 and 10). Since all along Sheridan had retained a committed
band of defenders--e.g., William Earle, the "Octogenarian," who
drew upon personal memoirs (1859.1), and George Gabriel Sigmond
(1852.3), who drew heavily upon Moore--he presented himself to the
twentieth century a sadly divided image, one polarized by the
effusions of Rae on the one hand and the fulminations of Fitzgerald
on the other.

This dilemma seems to have given him to the twentieth century
less as a man than as a conundrum, a crux to be resolved by one or
another ingenious theory of conduct. Generally candid in acknowledging his failings, his twentieth-century biographers have sought
to recruit sympathy for him by showing that he was not fully to
blame, that he was the natural product of a complex and contradic-
tory age (Sichel, 1909.5), or that he was the victim of forces outside his control: of vicious calumniators (DNB, 1921.1), of his own
morbid and self-destructive psychology (Butler, 1931.1), of class
prejudices (Rhodes, 1933.8), of jealousy (Cove, 1947.1), of human
nature itself (Sherwin, 1960.10). Others have preserved sympathy
for him by largely dismissing the most controversial parts of his
life (Darlington, 1933.5), or separating his achievements from his
character (Foss, 1939.2), or idealizing his humanitarian principles
(Glasgow, 1940.5), or celebrating the merits of his defects
(Bingham, 1972.5). He is no longer the treacherous idler some

Victorians would have him to be, but he is not yet really accessible either, not as a man to be taken seriously.

Biography has provided a fascinating image of him to be sure: a brilliant Irish scapegrace, a wit, a romantic, an enigma disguised by outward levity, a paradox of careless deeds and impeccable principles. Little wonder that fiction and popular essay have sought him out (see 1863.1; 1915.2; 1926.3; 1940.7; 1960.20). What he deserves, however, and what the study of him yet needs is a biography cleared of the inclination to rescue him from earlier misconceptions, an objective presentation freed of political and moral bias and of behavioral theory, a documented exposition of his relationships with other people and of the conduct of his several careers. Until such a service is done him, Thomas Moore's biography, despite its political stridency, will likely remain the best one, the one amplest in factual substance and solid literary information.

Texts

Sheridan left his texts in a confused state not because of his indolence but because he wanted to protect his claims upon them as income-producing properties and because he could never fully satisfy himself that they were ready for publication. Copyright law aggravated the first of these restraints. It held that a play once printed was available for presentation anywhere (see 1928.12). In controlling stage rights over his plays, then, Sheridan withheld them from publication, with the result that vamped and pirated and otherwise badly corrupted versions of them came into print while authorized versions did not. He intended to publish them eventually, and he even made arrangements with several booksellers to do so; but, in trying to satisfy his own exacting taste, he could never bring the project to completion, and he left it unfinished at his death. He did go on record as approving the 1781 edition of The Critic, but no other of his dramatic texts, not even the "corrected" third edition of The Rivals (1776), was authorized by him. (For a full account of these textual backgrounds see 1973.11.)

At his death his manuscripts apparently came into the charge of Samuel Rogers, the "friend" mentioned in the Scots Magazine for July 1816 (1816.10), who planned to collect the scattered works of Sheridan and publish them by subscription for the benefit of his family. When this project came to fruition, however, it was not what it announced itself to be: it was not based upon manuscripts owned by the Sheridan family, nor was it edited by Thomas Moore. Published under the aegis of three London booksellers (John Murray, James Ridgway, and Thomas Wilkie), all of whom had legitimate rights to publish Sheridan (see 1973.11), it reprinted a variety of unauthorized texts (including The Rivals, St. Patrick's Day, The Duenna, A Trip to Scarborough, The School for Scandal, Pizarro, and The Camp). Thomas Moore suppled only an "advertisement" (1821.1),

explaining why he had not written a biographical preface, but the
collection came to be known popularly as the "Moore" edition; and,
possibly because it was promoted at the outset by false advertising,
it carried enormous influence until 1902. In that year Fraser Rae,
again sponsored by Lord Dufferin, who had sponsored his biography of
Sheridan, published the play manuscripts long in the possession of
the Sheridan family. His book, while certainly no model of editorial scholarship, attacked the failings of the Murray text of 1821
and provided a footing for G. H. Nettleton's careful edition of
Sheridan's Major Dramas (i.e., The Rivals, The School for Scandal,
and The Critic) in 1906. In 1926 Iolo A. Williams published seven
of the plays (those in the Murray edition, excluding The Camp)
freshly edited from good sources, and in 1928 came Crompton Rhodes's
edition of The Plays and Poems of Richard Brinsley Sheridan, which
restored The Camp to the canon and printed or commented upon every
work properly associated with Sheridan's theatrical career. It also
provided the first reliably edited collection of his poems.

The Williams and Rhodes editions gave rise in 1928 to a concentrated flurry of comment upon the Sheridan texts, especially the
text of The School for Scandal. In offering a kind of bibliographical supplement to the Williams edition, Rhodes had published early
in 1927 (1927.8) an essay approving of the copy texts chosen by
Williams and identifying Williams's source for The School for
Scandal as the best one available for the play. It was Thomas
Moore's collation, done more than a century before, of two reliable
sources, the Dublin edition of 1799 (presumably based upon a copy
of the play given by Sheridan to his sister Alicia LeFanu) and a
manuscript copy given by Sheridan to his friend Mrs. Crewe in 1777.
Discovered by Rhodes himself in the library of the Royal Irish
Academy in Dublin, with the help of W. J. Lawrence, this collation
provided, said Rhodes, the one reliable text of the play. He saw
it as supplanting all other basic texts. But M. J. Ryan, writing
in the Times Literary Supplement, challenged this claim for it
(1928.17 and 18). He argued that the Dublin edition of 1799, a
slipshod and incorrect text, could not logically be thought the
first printing of the LeFanu MS. Nor could the Crewe MS represent
Sheridan's final thinking on his play since, by his own confession,
he was not ready even nineteen years later to surrender the play to
the printer. Furthermore, many discrepancies between Williams's
text and the source claimed for it indicated that the Williams
edition did not in fact follow the Dublin edition of 1799 as
emended by Moore in conformity with the Crewe MS. When, in the
Times Literary Supplement a month later (1928.13), Rhodes explained
these discrepancies as corrections and restorations occasioned by
lapses in the Moore collation, Ryan acceded to the basic value of
the collation, provided it be thus corrected and restored. But,
meantime, other of his reservations about Rhodes's editorial knowledge had excited in the Times Literary Supplement a curious debate
about printing and manuscript conventions in the late eighteenth
century--the use of the round s in printing and the "ye" contraction in handwriting--conventions by which manuscripts of The School

for Scandal and early printed piracies of it might be dated.   (see
1928.3-4, 10, 14-16.)

The Times Literary Supplement again provided the forum when, in
1929, F. W. Bateson charged that Williams and Rhodes had chosen the
wrong basic texts for their editions of both The Rivals and The
School for Scandal.   The best text of The Rivals, he argued
(1929.4), is an abbreviated version printed in Elizabeth Inchbald's
The British Theatre (1808).   It copies an authorized promptbook and
possibly reflects the last of the three revisions mentioned by
Sheridan (in ambiguous French) in a letter of 1816 to his translator
and adapter Agricole Chateauneuf.   The best text of The School for
Scandal is not the 1799 Dublin edition as emended by Moore.   It is
the Murray edition of 1821, the text probably supplied to Murray by
James Ridgway, who had bought the copyright from Sheridan and had,
in 1799, advertised imminent publication of the authorized text.
If the Crewe MS used by Moore in his collation is that of 1777 (and
not a Crewe MS of later date), it is a much earlier version of the
play than the one presumably printed in the Murray edition and is
therefore less likely than the Murray text to reflect Sheridan's
latest thinking on his play.   So argued Bateson (1929.5).   But he
won no converts, least of all Rhodes, who answered him confidently,
and, after a series of responses and counterresponses (see 1929.10,
12, 14; 1930.1, 7, 9) the debate fell to silence in 1930.

The decade of the thirties, however, was to see two major devel-
opments in the study of Sheridan texts.   The first, in 1935, was
the publication of the Larpent MS of The Rivals (see 1935.4), and
the text approved by the lord chamberlain's office for performance
at Covent Garden.   When compared to the first edition of 1775 and
the third edition corrected of 1776, it offers a valuable record of
Sheridan's practices of revision.   The second significant development was the discovery of the Crewe MS of The School for Scandal,
the manuscript against which Moore had emended the Dublin edition
of 1799 in establishing what he considered an authoritative text of
the play (but see 1963.19).   It had dropped from sight during the
time of the Williams and Rhodes editions and was at last traced by
G. H. Nettleton to the collection of a private owner.   Inscribed by
the playwright to Frances Crewe and corrected in his own hand, it
served as the basic text for The School for Scandal as printed in
the valuable anthology British Dramatists from Dryden to Sheridan
(1939.4) edited by Nettleton with Arthur E. Case.

Other textual criticism of the thirties elucidated Sheridan's
share in Benjamin Thompson's The Stranger, an adaptation from
Kotzebue (1930.6), and undertook to establish the first printed
version of the authentic text of The School for Scandal (1935.2;
1936.3).   The forties saw interest focused on the scenario and stage
history of Robinson Crusoe, Sheridan's Drury Lane pantomime (1943.2;
1944.2, 6-8; 1945.5, 6); and, to recognize the bicentennial of
Sheridan's birth, a catalog of the printed issues of The School for

Scandal, issues of the spurious text published up to 1782, appeared
in the early fifties (1951.9; 1953.11). In the fifties, too, Cecil
Price took up the study of Sheridan. Preparing himself to write a
comprehensive critical-biographical sketch of the playwright, he
first set himself the task of editing the Sheridan letters (which
appeared in three volumes in 1966); then, having mined the textual
sources more intensively than any of his predecessors--and having
published a scattering of valuable textual essays along the way
(see 1959.5; 1961.12; 1962.19; 1963.19; 1966.11; 1967.16-17; 1969.7;
1972.17)--he published the Dramatic Works of Sheridan in 1973, an
edition given authority not only by its thoroughgoing textual apparatus but also by an editorial principle through which Sheridan
himself, whose own editorial practices Price adopts, participates
in the textual decisions.

The status of Sheridan's letters and his dramatic texts is now
an excellent one. Presumably, too, Price will eventually provide
standard editions of other Sheridan documents. Since little
improvement can be expected in the status of the speeches, most of
which survive only in corrupted forms, the vexed issue of the
Sheridan texts now stands virtually resolved, having enjoyed through
the years the ministrations of exacting critical minds.

Criticism

Sheridan's work, like his life, has always been easy game for
detractors. Much traditional thinking holds, for example, that
while his speeches display fluency and wit, they carry little
thought or conviction. By received view, too, his Pizarro represents a prostitution of his powers, and even his comedies, the base
of his literary fame, boast little more than a facile and shallow
brilliance (1816.8; 1853.1; 1832.1; 1837.3; 1883.8; 1884.5; 1917.1;
1955.2; 1957.5). Hollow of moral substance, they render human
nature on only the most superfical plane and rise only slightly
above the level of farce (1826.8; 1880.4; 1920.1; 1946.4; 1955.2).
In general, they reflect the theatrical opportunism by which
Sheridan gratified his great eagerness to please, an eagerness much
greater than his commitment to art (1972.14; 1973.10). These kinds
of reservations touch the minds even of his admirers as they consider the persistent popularity of his comedies, and much of the
criticism about him takes the form of explaining his extraordinary
durability, why it is that his comedies should enjoy a popularity
second only to Shakespeare's (1826.5; 1896.15; 1930.11; 1931.3)
while evincing no recognizable Shakespearean virtue, no poetry, no
searching psychological reality, no troubling moral ambiguity.

Among the explanations offered, one is that the comedies succeed
for their exuberance and physical fun, the sheer boisterous vigor of
them (1820.1; 1914.6; 1917.1; 1935.1; 1954.1; 1968.8; 1972.8). The
play of language also participates in the phenomenon, not just the
sound of language, however important that may be (1961.13; 1963.1;

1963.9; 1963.23), but also the tension of rhetoric (1966.10; 1974.3;
1974.13), the excitement of wit (1874.7; 1877.1; 1961.14; 1972.8),
the exhilaration of parody (1917.2; 1949.10). About Sheridan's
comedies, too, there is an irresistible warmth, a sympathy that
reassures without deceiving, that attacks sentimentality without
defeating benevolence (1899.5; 1956.8; 1962.14; 1967.5; 1972.7;
1974.10), and while moral ambivalence may not figure prominently in
the dramatic effects, the plays do not elude moral issues entirely.
Beneath their glitter often liew a tinge of pathos (1830.5; 1923.1;
1953.1). They root themselves in doctrines deeply felt, if not profoundly conceived (1920.5; 1923.1; 1927.11; 1973.3; 1974.6), and, for
all their liveliness, they often evoke instructive and reflective
laughter (1967.10; 1953.7; 1970.11). Moreover, they are the work of
a redoubtable theatrical craftsman, the son of theatrical parents,
a playwright of impeccable instincts. Through their language and
interpretive possibilities they have established themselves as
vehicles for great actors (1962.8; 1964.9). Choosing not to follow
Shakespeare's path into the depths of the human comedy, Sheridan
chose to bring the comedy of manners to its highest pitch. In
doing so he brought fresh gaiety to the English stage, and he should
no more be faulted for his choice than Beaumarchais should be
faulted for not being Molière (1931.3).

Until quite recently Sheridan was credited with efforts to
reform the comedy of his day, to banish the sentimental muse and
restore laughter to its rightful place, a courageous but futile
crusade (1915.1). In 1972, however, Robert Hume demonstrated that
no such reforming crusade was necessary in the 1770s, that laughter
had never really left the English stage (see 1972.10), and five
years later John Loftis and Mark Auburn (1977.4 and 1977.2)
demonstrated that Sheridan generally worked within the conventions
of his own theater. Not an innovative reformer at all, he drew
freely upon earlier traditions and current practices and made it
his distinction that he applied the conventions better than other
playwrights, not that he made up new ones. The contexts of
Sheridan's comedies, and his achievements within them, now have a
stability not available to them before.

Comment upon The Rivals, in addition to that celebrating its
vitality and geniality (1820.1; 1830.4; 1948.8; 1954.5; 1960.2;
1961.13; 1968.8) and that acknowledging its essential innocence of
theme (1905.1; 1913.4; 1942.5), has centered upon its sources,
especially the sources of its characters (1903.1; 1928.6; 1960.9;
1970.2). That it is basically a comedy of character appears,
according to Mark Auburn, in its American stage history, a history
demonstrating that extravagant formal changes, changes made in
behalf of character, do not diminish its comic effects (1975.1),
and John Loftis recognizes it as being a comedy of character in the
tradition of Congreve, a play closely similar to those of Congreve
in character types and character relationships (1977.4). St.
Patrick's Day, too, for all its lugubriousness (1975.4), is in

Introduction

Auburn's view, principally a comedy of character (1977.2).

The Duenna has given rise to musicological comment (1961.6; 1970.10; 1973.4; 1976.2) and has earned admiration for its intricate fabric of comic ironies (1975.4). But its chief pleasures derive, says Auburn, from its complex plot (1977.2). In John Loftis's view, it is a comedy of action, a play subordinating character to plot in the manner of the Spanish intrigue plays of the Restoration (1977.4).

While A Trip to Scarborough has attracted little sustained comment, it has provided an index to Sheridan's Georgian ethos, as opposed to the late Restoration one of Vanbrugh's The Relapse, the play from which it is adapted (1928.11; 1962.12; 1975.4); and Professor Loftis sees it as reflecting neoclassical standards of form and thematic attitude very similar to those governing its great successor, The School for Scandal (1977.4).

As the play generally held to be Sheridan's masterpiece, The School for Scandal has commanded more critical comment than any other of his works and emerges in his posthumous reputation as a kind of microcosm of the man and his art. Critics have deplored its ethical slightness (1826.17; 1850.1; 1914.6; 1952.3; 1954.5; 1957.5; 1960.2) and have seen in it a sentimentality verging on anti-intellectualism (1945.1). In 1874, one illustrious critic, Henry James, labeled it lifeless and ghostly, the hallmark of an impoverished stage (1874.4). In 1896 another of them, Bernard Shaw, forecast its imminent demise (1896.17). Bit it has prevailed not only for features irresistible in it--wit, vigor, plot, intrigue, satire, sophistication--but also, as Mark Auburn indicates, for the complexity it achieves within its received conventions, the combination of such familiar comic types as punitive comedy of exposure, comedy of self-adjustment, and comedy of merit rewarded (1977.2). By the interplay of these types, and by the combination of satiric and affective attitudes, it achieves a universality of appeal while also establishing itself as a play fully representative of its own time.

Perhaps because of its character as an afterpiece and because of its topical limitations, The Critic has not enjoyed so lively a stage history as The Rivals and The School for Scandal. It has enjoyed, however, a level of critical approval consistently higher than that given the earlier two plays. In its own time it breathed new life into the tradition of theatrical burlesque (see 1872.1; 1879.1; 1905.1), and in later times it gained admiration for over-coming the ephemerality of mere burlesque, of sustaining at one and the same time a timeliness and a timelessness (1908.2; 1946.7; 1963.15; 1965.1; 1966.8; 1974.1). Criticism has come more and more to see this phenomenon as resulting from a mixture of modes within the play, not just dramatic modes of comedy and satire and burlesque (1975.4; 1977.4; 1975.13) but nondramatic modes as well, the satiric apologia in the manner of Pope's Epistle to Dr. Arbuthnot (1977.4) and the self-reflexive narrative which, like Sterne's Tristram Shandy, controls multiple perceptions of reality (1974.9). Mark Auburn sees The Critic as answering more fully to Sheridan's skills than any other of his plays because it provided him with a structure into which he could pack all the comic techniques he had developed in his earlier works (1977.2).

Although popular as a Victorian acting piece, Sheridan's last play, Pizarro, has not often commanded serious interest as dramatic art. Instead, critics have derided it for displaying the very offenses attacked so brilliantly by Sheridan in The Critic. While having no illusions about its values as art, however, recent commentary has turned to it for a representative instance, in the character of Rolla, of the romantic hero who responds with innate high passion to the cruelties of an illogical world (1970.6). And Professor Loftis, declining to regard it as a lapse in the dramatic powers of Sheridan, sees it instead as a new departure for him, a dramatization of his own political principles and a dramatic attack against the policies of the majority under Pitt, especially the policies sustaining the slave trade (1975.6 and 1977.4).

Many students of parliamentary oration have described Sheridan's oratorical skills--his gifts for ridicule and witty rejoinder, his favorite rhetorical schemes and tropes (see 1822.3; 1852.2; 1853.1; 1942.4)--but a detached and objective account of his political career has yet to be written, that of Michael Sadleir being at best only a sketch (1912.4). Also to be written is a comprehensive and closely documented account of his career as a theatrical manager. Some clarification is needed, too, of his thought. A deep thinker he probably was not; but he was a man of deeply felt conviction, and the body of conviction underlying his work needs some kind of coherent elucidation. It is perhaps no longer true that he is the most neglected of major literary figures, but the range and basis of his achievement yet invite many kinds of close examination.

The Sheridan Texts

The items listed below reflect (through the first list) the gradual
standardization of Sheridan's texts and (through the six lists
following) the persistent popularity of Sheridan's dramatic works.
Annotations explain the selections made for the first list (the
list of "Major Collections"). Choices for the next six lists turn
upon such considerations as (1) frequency of reissue, (2) identity
of editor, (3) textual source, (4) types of readership. These
considerations perhaps demonstrate Sheridan's continuing avail-
ability to classrooms and libraries and his appeal to book
collectors, theatrical directors, graphic illustrators, literary
and theatrical aficionados both professional and lay. What has to
be emphasized is that texts appearing before 1939--i.e., before
those included in British Dramatists from Dryden to Sheridan
(edited by G. H. Nettleton and A. E. Case [Boston: Houghton
Mifflin, 1939])--are not properly received as standard. Most
others, especially those published between 1821 and 1906, derive
from the John Murray edition of 1821 (see "Major Collections"
below), or, when not based wholly upon the John Murray text,
represent incomplete collations. Texts now recognized as authoritative, in addition to those edited in 1939 by Nettleton and Case,
are those edited by Cecil Price, John Loftis, and Alan Downer (as
given in the lists below). Those edited by Price are standard and
are properly preferred for research. Price's edition of Sheridan's
letters (also given below) is considered standard; but no reliable
text of Sheridan's speeches exists, except, perhaps, that of his
second speech against Warren Hastings, a speech given in
Westminster Hall in 1788 and published from shorthand transcriptions
by Sir E. A. Bond in Speeches of the Managers and Counsel of the
Trial of Warren Hastings (1859). While, as suggested by the lists
given below, The Rivals, The School for Scandal, and The Critic
have the most vigorous publication history, The Duenna is represented in the National Union Catalogue by fifty-six issues between
1775 and 1925 and Pizarro is represented by fifty-five issues
between 1799 and 1910. Individual issues of the remaining plays are
not numerous.

Even though the National Union Catalogue, upon which the present
selected lists are based, includes about a thousand entries under

Sheridan's name, it is by no means a complete list. Among its
entries (again presumably incomplete) appear about sixty translations: one or more of Sheridan's plays rendered into Arabic,
Scandinavian, Dutch, French, German, Greek, Italian, Portugese,
Russian, Slavic, and Spanish. By far the most frequently translated
of them is The School for Scandal, and perhaps no translations
carry more interest than those of Agricole Chateauneuf, whose
French adaptations of The Rivals and The School for Scandal
(published in 1824) elicited comment from Sheridan himself in one
of his last letters. (See letter no. 937 in Cecil Price's edition
of Sheridan's letters. Also see item 1929.4 in the body of this
bibliography.) The National Union Catalogue also lists some
twenty adaptations of Sheridan's plays: shortened versions,
modernized versions, musical versions. Perhaps the most interesting
of these is a setting of The Duenna announced by Sergei Prokofiev in
1941 and given its premiere in Moscow in 1959. (See 1941.1 and
1959.2.)

Major Collections

1821 The Works of the Late Right Honourable Richard Brinsley
Sheridan. 2 vols. John Murray, 1821.
Purports (in public announcements) to print the plays
from authentic and original copies but actually reprints
them from a variety of unauthorized texts, those for A
Trip to Scarborough and The School for Scandal containing
many doubtful variants and those for St. Patrick's Day and
The Camp deriving from Dublin piracies. The issue gathers
influence not only from the announcements misrepresenting
its texts but also from a widespread presumption that
Thomas Moore had edited it. Actually, Moore supplied
only an "advertisement" devoted principally to explaining
why he had not supplied the expected biographical preface.
(See 1821.1.)

1902 Sheridan's Plays Now Printed As He Wrote Them. And His
Mother's Unpublished Comedy, "A Journey to Bath." Edited
by W. Fraser Rae. London: David Nutt, 1902, 358 pp.
Prints from manuscripts then in the possession of
Sheridan's great-grandson (The marquess of Dufferin and
Ava) the texts of St. Patrick's Day, The Duenna, The
School for Scandal, and The Critic. The Rivals, for which
no manuscript existed at Frampton Court, follows the text
of the first edition of 1775, "Sheridan's own acting
version of his comedy" (p. xiv). Where gaps appear in the
manuscripts, they are filled out with materials from "the
current versions" (p. xxxv), but these versions are not
identified, nor are variant readings supplied. The
edition does not purport to arrive at Sheridan's final
judgments on his texts. (See 1902.7.)

1906   The Major Dramas of Richard Brinsley Sheridan. The Rivals,
        The School for Scandal, The Critic. Edited by George
        Henry Nettleton. Boston: Ginn, 1906, 448 pp.
            Draws basic texts from the Rae edition of 1902 but adds
        textual apparatus showing collations with certain early
        printed texts (viz., the first three editions of The
        Rivals and the 1781 edition of The Critic). Other
        apparatus includes a bibliographical note on early
        collected issues of Sheridan's plays, together with lists
        of these issues and of the three plays as published
        separately before the appearance of the John Murray
        edition of 1821. The introduction continues to be valu-
        able for its extensive critical and historical information.
        (See 1906.3.)

1926   The Plays of Richard Brinsley Sheridan. Edited by Iolo A.
        Williams. New York: Lincoln MacVeagh, The Dial Press,
        1926, 384 pp.
            Bases six of Sheridan's seven major plays upon respect-
        able texts--i.e., the first edition of The Rivals (1775),
        a Dublin edition of St. Patrick's Day (1788), an edition
        of The Duenna authorized in 1794 by Thomas Harris, to whom
        Sheridan had sold the copyright in 1775, the first edition
        of The Critic (1781), an acting text of A Trip to
        Scarborough (1781), the first edition of Pizarro (1799)--
        but prints a text of The School for Scandal provided by R.
        Crompton Rhodes, whose own edition of Sheridan's Plays
        and Poems (listed below) was to appear in 1928. The text
        of The School for Scandal is purported to follow Thomas
        Moore's alterations of the Dublin edition of 1799,
        alterations based upon a manuscript copy of the play given
        by Sheridan to Mrs. Crewe. The claims made by Rhodes for
        this text cannot be substantiated under scrutiny. (See
        1926.16; see also 1927.8; 1928.13, 17-19.)

1928   The Plays and Poems of Richard Brinsley Sheridan. Edited by
        R. Crompton Rhodes. 3 vols. Oxford: Blackwell, 1928.
        Reprint ed., New York: Russell & Russell, 1962.
            Selects for Sheridan's major plays the basic texts
        chosen by Iolo A. Williams for his edition of 1926 (see
        above), except that the third edition corrected of 1776
        replaces the first edition of 1775 as the basic text of
        The Rivals, and the Moore-Crewe text of The School for
        Scandal draws conflations from an issue of the play
        printed in 1826 by John Cumberland (presumed based upon a
        Drury Lane promptbook) rather than from the Murray text
        (assumed edited by Moore) used in developing the Williams
        edition. Going much beyond Williams, Rhodes provides
        extensive textual apparatus (including bibliographic

citation of all the early texts known to him). He also
provides the first reliably edited collection of
Sheridan's poems, returns The Camp to the Sheridan canon,
and prints texts of (and/or comments upon) every work he
could properly associate with Sheridan's theatrical and
literary careers. While still valuable for its critical
commentary (both that provided by the editor and that
extracted from contemporary sources) the edition fails of
definitiveness both because authoritative Sheridan
materials have since come to light (e.g., the Larpent
manuscript of The Rivals and several new manuscripts of
The School for Scandal) and because the editorial judgment is sometimes misdirected. (It is Rhodes's conviction, for example, that the third edition corrected
represents Sheridan's own finally approved text of The
Rivals and that the Moore-Crewe collation is the authoritative text of The School for Scandal.) (See 1928.11.)

1973   The Dramatic Works of Richard Brinsley Sheridan. 2 vols.
        Edited by Cecil Price. Oxford English Text Series.
        Oxford: Clarendon Press, 1973.
            Provides standard texts and/or authoritative comment
        upon all the dramatic work known or thought to be
        Sheridan's (either wholly or in part, finished or
        unfinished). Recalling that the first edition of The
        Critic (1781) was the only printed issue of any one of his
        comedies approved by Sheridan, Price compares it to
        several manuscripts and a prompt copy of the play and
        deduces thereby the principles governing Sheridan's own
        editorial practice. This deduction indicates that
        Sheridan took special pains to provide a good reading
        version of his work, one not necessarily identical to
        current acting versions. It also indicates his tendency
        to restore for print passages excised from acting texts
        and to print topical references current at the time the
        play was introduced, even though such references might
        change in later productions. These and other principles
        assist Price in making editorial choices of which
        Sheridan would himself approve. For copy texts, Price
        has "usually accepted authorized first editions," but when
        they are not available he has "fallen back on the author's
        manuscript or the theatre copy prepared for the Lord
        Chamberlain's examination" (p.32). Prefaces to the
        individual plays provide accounts of composition and
        explain editorial decisions. Contemporary newspaper
        comment, especially that elucidating textual changes,
        accompanies each play, as does extensive bibliographic and
        textual apparatus. (See 1973.11.)

1975   Sheridan's Plays. Edited by Cecil Price. Oxford Standard
       Authors Series. London: Oxford University Press, 1975,
       473 pp.
           Reproduces the texts but not the textual apparatus of
       Price's 1973 edition. (See 1975.11.)

Selected Other Collections

1840   The Dramatic Works of Richard Brinsley Sheridan. With a
       Biographical and Critical Sketch. Edited by Leigh Hunt.
       London: E. Moxon, 1840, 168 pp. Reissued 1846, 1865. (See
       1840.1.)

1848   Dramatic Works: with a Memoir by G[eorge] G[abriel] S[igmond].
       Bohn's standard Library. London: Henry G. Bohn, 1848,
       571 pp. Reissued 1852, 1854, 1857, 1861; Bell and Daldy,
       1866, 1870, 1872, 1878; G. Bell and Sons, 1898, 1901;
       Samuel Bagster, 1902; New York: J. Pott, 1902; G. Bell and
       Sons, 1915. (See 1852.3.)

1863   The Dramatic Works of Richard Brinsley Sheridan. Edited by
       Richard Grant White. 3 vols. London: Nirmo, 1863.
       Reissued 1883; New York: Dodd, Mead, 1883. (See 1883.8.)

1873   The Works of the Right Honourable Richard Brinsley Sheridan,
       with a Memoir by James P. Browne, M.D., Containing
       Extracts from the Life by Thomas Moore. 2 vols. London:
       Bickers and Son, 1873. Reissued Philadelphia:
       Lippincott, 1873; Bickers, 1884; Ward, Lock, Bowden, 1891.
       (See 1873.1.)

1874   The Works of Richard Brinsley Sheridan; Dramas, Poems,
       Translations, Speeches, and Unifinished Sketches. With a
       Memoir of the Author, a Collection of Ana, and Ten Chalk
       Drawings. Edited by F. Stainforth. London: Chatto and
       Windus, 1874, 664 pp. Reissued 1875, 1876?, 1879, 1883?,
       1886, 1890, 1897, 1899, 1901, 1913; New York: Routledge,
       1874. (See 1874.6.)

1883   The Plays of Richard Brinsley Sheridan; with an Introduction
       by Henry Morley. Morley's Universal Library. London: G.
       Routledge, 1883, 320 pp. Reissued 1884, 1885, 1886, 1887,
       1888, 1889, 1890, 1892. (See 1883.6.)

1900   The Plays of Sheridan. With a Bibliographical Note. Edited
       by A. W. Pollard. Library of English Classics. London:
       Macmillan, 1900, 463 pp. Reissued 1901, 1903, 1908, 1920,
       1925. (See 1900.5.) Edited by Clayton Hamilton for
       Macmillan's Modern Reader's Series, 1926, 1929, 1941.

(See 1926.5.)

1906   The Dramatic Works of Richard Brinsley Sheridan, with an
       Introduction and Notes by Joseph Knight. The World's
       Classics no. 79. London: Oxford University Press, 1906,
       515 pp. Reissued 1910, 1915, 1921, 1923, 1924, 1925,
       1926, 1927, 1930, 1931, 1939, 1944, 1946, 1949, 1951
       ("reset from newly collated text"), 1956, 1960, 1964.
       (See 1906.1.)

1906   The Plays of Richard Brinsley Sheridan. Edited by Ernest
       Rhys. Everyman's Library, no. 95. London: J. M. Dent,
       1906, 495 pp. Reissued 1907, 1908, 1911, 1913, 1915,
       1917, 1924, 1928, 1931, 1937, 1949. Edited by Walter
       Cove (Pseud. Lewis Gibbs) 1956, 1960. (See 1956.4.)

                    Selected Partial Collections

1885   Sheridan's Comedies: The Rivals and The School for Scandal.
       Edited by Brander Matthews. Boston: J. R. Osgood, 1885,
       333 pp. Reissued 1891. New York: T. Y. Crowell, 1904.
       (See 1885.1.)

1886   The Rivals and The School for Scandal by Richard Brinsley
       Sheridan. Edited by Henry Cassell. Cassell's National
       Library. New York: Cassell, 1886, 191 pp. Reissued 1904,
       1905, 1909 (in Cassell's Little Classics), 1914.

1896   The School for Scandal and The Rivals. Edited by Augustine
       Birrell. London: Macmillan, 1896, 392 pp. Reissued 1908,
       1926, 1930. (See 1896.4.)

1907   The Rivals and The School for Scandal. Edited by Will David
       Howe. Macmillan's Pocket American and English Classics.
       New York, London: Macmillan, 1907, 352 pp. Reissued 1910,
       1912, 1916, 1917, 1922, 1923, 1925, 1929, 1933. (See
       1907.1.)

                    Selected Individual Issues

The Rivals

1820   The Rivals, a Comedy by R. B. Sheridan. With Prefatory
       Remarks . . . Faithfully Marked with Stage Business and
       Stage Directions. As It Is Performed at the Theatres
       Royal. By W. Oxberry, Comedian. Oxberry's New English
       Drama, no. 2. London: W. Simpkin and R. Marshall, 1820,
       86 pp. Boston: Wells and Lilly, 1822, 117 pp. (See
       1820.1.)

182_   The Rivals: a Comedy, in Five Acts. Printed from the Acting
        Copy with Remarks . . . by D[aniel] G[eorge[. . . Added
        . . . The Costume . . . and the Stage Business. London:
        Cumberland, 182?, 76 pp. Reissued 1824?, 1826 (as
        Cumberland's British Theatre no. 10), 1829[?].

1846?   The Rivals: a Comedy, in Five Acts. French's Standard Drama
        no. 31. New York: S. French and Son, [1846?], 72 pp.
        Reissued 185-?, 1855, 1864:, 187-, 1874. Eight other
        issues undated.

1889   The Rivals, by Richard Brinsley Sheridan. Illustrated by
        Frank M. Gregory. New York: White and Allen, 1889, 81 pp.
        Reissued London: S. Low, 1890; New York: Dodd, Mead, 1893,
        1895, 1896; Barse and Hopkins, 189-.

1897   The Rivals; a Comedy Written by Richard Brinsley Sheridan.
        Edited by G. A. Aitken. The Temple Dramatists. London:
        J. M. Dent, 1897, 177 pp. Reissued 1900, 1902, 1904,
        1910, 1912, 1921, 1925, 1928, 1961; Philadelphia: McKay,
        19--. (See 1897.1.)

1902   The Rivals, A Comedy by Richard Brinsley Sheridan. With an
        Introduction from the Autobiography of Joseph Jefferson.
        New York: Century, 1902, 233 pp. Reissued 1906. (See
        1902.5.)

1905   The Rivals, with an Introduction by Edmund Gosse. Favourite
        Classics. London: W. Heinemann, 1905, 117 pp. (See
        1905.2.)

1907   The Rivals, by Richard Brinsley Sheridan, with an Introduction
        by Brander Matthews. New York: T. Y. Crowell, 1907, 167
        pp. (See 1907.2.)

1910   The Rivals; a Comedy by Richard Brinsley Sheridan, with an
        Introduction and Notes by Joseph Quincy Adams, Jr. The
        Riverside Literature Seires, no. 196. New York: Houghton
        Mifflin, 1910, 155 pp. (See 1910.1.)

1913   The Rivals. Edited by Thomas Balston. Oxford: Clarendon
        Press, 1913, 110 pp. Reissued 1916, 1921, 1925, 1955,
        1960. (See 1913.4.)

1920   The Rivals, by Richard Brinsley Sheridan. Edited by William
        Lyon Phelps. Living Literature Series. New York: Gregg
        Publishing, 1920, 129 pp. (See 1920.3.)

1929   The Rivals. With Introduction and Notes by Robert Herring.

. .

English Literature Series, no. 119. London: Macmillan,
1929, 131 pp. Reissued 1931, 1933, 1936, 1938, 1939,
1940, 1944, 1945, 1948, 1950, 1951, 1952, 1955, 1956,
1965. (See 1929.7.)

1930   The Rivals by Richard Brinsley Sheridan. Edited by Will
       David Howe and revised by H. Y. Moffett. New Pocket
       Classics. New York: Macmillan, 1930, 186 pp. Reissued
       1935, 1937, 1947, 1959. (See 1907.1.)

1935   The Rivals, a Comedy. As It Was First Acted at the
       Theatre-Royal in Covent Garden. Written by Richard
       Brinsley Sheridan. Edited from the Larpent MS by Richard
       Little Purdy. Oxford: Clarendon Press. 1935, 194 pp.
       (See 1935.4.)

1939   "The Rivals" in British Dramatists from Dryden to Sheridan.
       Edited by G. H. Nettleton and A. E. Case. New York:
       Houghton Mifflin, 1939, pp. 791-830. 2d ed. (prepared by
       George Winchester Stone, Jr.), 1969; reissued by
       Southern Illinois University Press, 1976. (See 1939.4.)

1953   The Rivals. Edited by Alan S. Downer. Crofts Classics. New
       York: Appleton-Century-Crofts, 1953, 90 pp. (See 1953.7.)

1953   The Rivals, a Comedy. With an Introduction by John Mason
       Brown and Illustrations by René Ben Sussan. London:
       Printed for Members of the Limited Editions Club at the
       Curwen Press, 1953, 170 pp.

1958   The Rivals. Edited by Vincent F. Hopper and Gerald B. Lahey.
       With a note on the staging by George L. Hersey. Theatre
       Classics for the Modern Reader. Great Neck, N.Y.:
       Barron's Educational Series, 1958, 176 pp. (See 1958.2.)

1958   The Rivals. Edited by Thomas Crehan. London English
       Literature Series. London: University of London Press,
       1958, 144 pp.

1967   The Rivals, by Richard Brinsley Sheridan. Macmillan's
       English Classics, New Series. Edited by A. Norman
       Jeffares. London: Macmillan; New York: St. Martin's
       Press, 1967, 144 pp. (See 1967.9.)

1968   The Rivals by Sheridan. Edited by C[ecil] J[ohn] L[ayton]
       Price. London: Oxford University Press, 1968, 140 pp.
       (See 1968.8.)

1968   The Rivals. Edited by Arthur E. McGuinness. San Francisco:

Chandler Publishing, 1968, 107 pp. (See 1968.4.)

1973   The Rivals, 1775. Edited by A. Norman Jeffares. Ilkley:
        Scolar Press, 1973, 116 pp. A facsimile issue. (See
        1973.7.)

The School for Scandal

1823   The School for Scandal: a Comedy. By Richard Brinsley
        Sheridan. London: John Murray, 1823, 156 pp.

1826?   The School for Scandal. A Comedy in Five Acts. By Richard
        Brinsley Sheridan. Printed from the Acting Copy, with
        Remarks . . . As Now Performed at the Theatres-Royal,
        London. Cumberland's British Theatre, no. 95. London: J.
        Cumberland, 1826?, 88 pp. Reissued 1827, 1829?, 1830.

1846?   The School for Scandal; a Comedy, in Five Acts. French's
        Standard Drama, no. 8. New York: Samuel French, 1846?,
        86 pp. Reissued 1848?, 185-, 1855?, 1860, 187-; As
        remodeled and arranged for the Fifth Avenue Theatre by
        Augustin Daly, 72 pp., 1874, 1875, 1880, 1901; With stage
        directions recorded from Sir Herbert Beerbohm Tree at
        His Majesty's Theatre, London, 1909, 69 pp. In a
        privately printed issue, the Daly version also appeared in
        1890 and 1891. (See 1874.3.)

1856   The School for Scandal, a Comedy. Lacy's Acting Edition
        Plays. London: T. H. Lacy, 1856, 85 pp. Four undated
        issues, probably all earlier than 1856, also appear in
        the National Union Catalogue.

1873?   The School for Scandal. A Comedy, in Five Acts. Dicks'
        Standard Plays, no. 2. London: J. Dicks, 1873?, pp. 385-
        410. Reissued 1883? An additional issue is undated.

1892   The School for Scandal; a Comedy by Richard Brinsley Sheridan.
        Illustrated by Frank M. Gregory. New York: Dodd, Mead,
        1892, 169 pp. Reissued 1895.

1897   The School for Scandal. Edited by G. A. Aitken. The Temple
        Dramatists. London: J. M. Dent, 1897, 165 pp. Reissued
        1902, 1905, 1911, 1951. Philadelphia: D. McKay, n.d.
        (See 1897.3.)

1905   The School for Scandal, with an Introduction by Edmund Gosse.
        Favourite Classics. London: W. Heinemann, 1905. Reissued
        1920.

1917   The School for Scandal. Edited by Hanson Hart Webster.
        Riverside College Classics. Boston: Houghton Mifflin,
        1917, 161 pp. Reissued 1918.

1927   The School for Scandal. Edited by Robert Herring. English
        Literature Series. London: Macmillan; New York: St.
        Martin's Press, 1927, 168 pp. Reissued 1929, 1935, 1938,
        1940, 1942, 1945, 1946, 1947, 1950, 1959, 1961, 1963,
        1964. (See 1927.4.)

1928   Sheridan's School for Scandal. Edited by E. M. Jebb. Oxford:
        Clarendon Press, 1928, 112 pp. Reissued 1931, 1939, 1943,
        1946, 1947, 1950, 1959, 1961, 1965. (See 1928.8.)

1930   The School for Scandal. Edited by Will David Howe, revised
        by H. Y. Moffett. The New Pocket Classics. New York:
        Macmillan, 1930, 181 pp. Reissued 1937.

1930   The School for Scandal, by Richard Brinsley Sheridan. Edited
        by R. Crompton Rhodes. Oxford: Printed for the
        Shakespeare Head Press by Basil Blackwell, 1930, 172 pp.
        (See 1930.8.)

1934   The School for Scandal, a Comedy, by R. B. Sheridan; with an
        Introduction by Carl Van Doren and Hand-Coloured Etchings
        by René Ben Sussan. Oxford: Printed for the Members of
        the Limited Editions Club, 1934, 150 pp.

1939   "The School for Scandal." In British Dramatists from Dryden
        to Sheridan. Edited by G. H. Nettleton and A. E. Case.
        New York: Houghton Mifflin, 1939, pp. 833-76. 2d ed.
        (prepared by George Winchester Stone, Jr.), 1969; reissued
        by Southern Illinois University Press, 1976. (See
        1939.4.)

1949   The School for Scandal, with an Introduction by Sir Laurence
        Olivier and Designs for Decor and Costumes by Cecil
        Beaton. London: Folio Society, 1949, 119 pp. (See
        1949.8.)

1958   The School for Scandal. Edited by Vincent F. Hopper and
        Gerald B. Lahey. With a note on staging by George L.
        Hersey. Theatre Classics for the Modern Reader. Great
        Neck, N.Y.: Barron's Educational Series, 1958, 172 pp.
        (See 1958.3.)

1961   The School for Scandal. Edited by William L. Sharp. Chandler
        Editions in Drama. San Francisco: Chandler Publishing,
        1961, 100 pp. (See 1961.14.)

1966   The School for Scandal. Edited by John Loftis. Crofts
        Classics. New York: Appleton-Century-Crofts, 1966, 126 pp.
        (See 1966.7.)

1967   The School for Scandal. Edited by T[homas] Crehan. London
        English Literature Series. London: University of London
        Press, 1967, 150 pp. (See 1967.6.)

1967   The School for Scandal, by Richard Brinsley Sheridan. Edited
        by A. Norman Jeffares. Macmillan's English Classics, New
        Series. London: Macmillan; New York: St. Martin's Press,
        1967, 181 pp. (See 1967.10.)

1969   The School for Scandal, 1780. Menston: Scolar Press, 1969,
        78 pp. Facsimile reprint of the first edition, Dublin,
        1780. (See 1969.2.)

1971   The School for Scandal. Edited by C[ecil] J[ohn] L[ayton]
        Price. London: Oxford University Press, 1971, 149 pp.
        (See 1971.8.)

The Critic

1820   The Critic; or, Tragedy Rehearsed, a Dramatic Piece by R. B.
        Sheridan. With Prefatory Remarks . . . Faithfully Marked
        with the Stage Business and Stage Directions, as It is
        Performed at the Theatres Royal. By W. Oxberry, Comedian.
        Oxberry's Edition. London: W. Simpkin and R. Marshall,
        1820, 39 pp. (The New English Drama), vol. 9, no. 1.
        Reissued 1830; Boston: Wells and Lilly, 1822, 68 pp.

1827?   The Critic; or, A Tragedy Rehearsed. A Dramatic Piece in Two
        Acts. By Richard Brinsley Sheridan . . . Printed from the
        Acting Copy, with Remarks . . . As Now Performed at the
        Theatres-Royal, London. London: J. Cumberland, 1827?,
        42 pp. Reissued 1831? London: G. H. Davidson, n.d.

185-   The Critic, or, A Tragedy Rehearsed. A Dramatic Piece, in
        Two Acts. French's Standard Drama, no. 56. New York:
        Samuel French, 185-, 46 pp. Reissued 186-, 188-.

1853   The Critic; or, A Tragedy Rehearsed. A Dramatic Piece in Two
        Acts. By Richard Brinsley Sheridan. Lacy's Acting
        Edition, no. 109. London: T. H. Lacy, 1853, 30 pp. Two
        other issues undated.

1897   The Critic; or, A Tragedy Rehearsed, a Farce. Edited by G. A.
        Aitken. The Temple Dramatists. London: J. M. Dent, 1897,
        105 pp. Reissued 1904, 1909, 1920, 1925.

1905   The Critic; with an Introduction by Edmund Gosse.   London: W.
        Heinemann, 1905, 70 pp.   (See 1905.1.)

1908   The Critic; or, A Tragedy Rehearsed; a Dramatic Piece in Two
        Acts by Richard Brinsley Sheridan.   Acting Version of the
        Yale University Dramatic Association, with a Preface by
        William Lyon Phelps . . . and an Introduction by George
        Henry Nettleton.   New Haven: A. A. Gammell, 1908, 64 pp.
        Reissued 1911.   (See 1908.2.)

1939   "The Critic."   In British Dramatists from Dryden to Sheridan.
        Edited by G. H. Nettleton and A. E. Case.   New York:
        Houghton Mifflin, 1939, pp. 878-901.   2d ed.   (prepared by
        George Winchester Stone, Jr.), 1969; reissued by Southern
        Illinois University Press, 1976.   (See 1939.4.)

1949   The Critic; or, A Tragedy Rehearsed.   Edited by J. C. Trewin.
        London: Falcon Educational Books, 1949, 88 pp.   (See
        1949.10.)

1962   The Critic.   Edited by Robert Herring.   English Literature
        Series.   London: Macmillan, 1962, 92 pp.

Selected Nondramatic Works

1816   Speeches of the Late Right Honourable Richard Brinsley
        Sheridan (Several Corrected by Himself).   Edited by a
        Constitutional Friend [Sir John Phillipart?].   5 vols.
        London: P. Martin, 1816.

1819   Clio's Protest; or "The Picture" Varnished.   With Other Poems.
        By the Late Right Honourable R. B. Sheridan.   London:
        Printed for Joseph Arnould, 1819, 60 pp.   (See 1819.1.)

1842   The Speeches of the Right Honourable Richard Brinsley Sheridan.
        With a Sketch of His Life.   Edited by a Constitutional
        Friend.   2d ed.   3 vols.   London: G. Bohn, 1842.   Reissued
        1848; New York: Russell & Russell, 1969.   (See 1842.2.)

1859   Speeches of the Managers and Counsel of the Trial of Warren
        Hastings.   Edited by E. A. Bond.   London: Longman, Brown,
        Green, Longmans, 1859-1861.

1966   The Letters of Richard Brinsley Sheridan.   Edited by Cecil
        Price.   3 vols.   Oxford: Clarendon Press, 1966.   (See
        1966.12.)

Abbreviations

DNB   Dictionary of National Biography

MHRA   Annual Bibliography of English Language and Literature Compiled by Members of the Modern Humanities Research Association

NUC   National Union Catalogue

Writings About Sheridan, 1816 - 1979

<u>1816</u>

1   ANON. <u>Authentic Memoirs of the Life and Death of R. B.</u>
     <u>Sheridan. With an Estimate of His Character and Talents</u>.
     London: W. Hone, 16 pp.
          Recounts Sheridan's life and concludes by reprinting
     1816.6.

2   ANON. "Character of Sheridan." <u>North American Review</u>
          4 (November): 32-38.
              Reprints 1816.6.

3   ANON. "Eloquence of the British Parliament." <u>Port Folio</u>
     5th ser. 1 (1816): 492-99.
          Compares Sheridan as a speaker to Pitt and Fox and finds
     him "though dissimilar to both . . . inferior to neither"
     (p. 493). An "orator" rather than a "debater," he gave to
     his speeches just the right play of imagination and just
     the right touch of humor. "All was forcible, graceful,
     and chaste: nervous without impetuosity; natural without
     carelessness, and earnest without pedantry" (p. 493).

4   ANON. ["Funeral of Sheridan"]. <u>Times</u> (London), 13 July, p. 3.
          Announces the funeral of Sheridan in Westminster Abbey
     "on this day." "He will be followed to the grave by a
     small number of his friends."

5   ANON. <u>The Life of the Right Honourable Richard Brinsley</u>
     <u>Sheridan Containing a Comprehensive Review of His</u>
     <u>Abilities As a Poet, a Statesman, an Orator, and a</u>
     <u>Dramatist with the Remarks of Pitt, Fox, and Burke on</u>
     <u>His Most Celebrated Speeches and Many Curious Anecdotes</u>
     <u>of His Parliamentary, Literary, and Private Career Never</u>
     <u>Before Published, Including His Monody on Garrick, Verses</u>
     <u>to Miss Linley, and a Collection of Fugitive Poetry, &c</u>,
     <u>&c</u>. London: John Fairburn, [1816?], 42 pp.
          Discusses as "hearsay" the stories of indolence and
     improvidence attaching to the later life of Sheridan and

demonstrates through the records of his achievement that
his genius, "shooting like a comet in its eccentric orbit
into the regions of infinite space, astonished the world
by its extraordinary splendour" (p. 33). In any one of
his characters--as poet, statesman, orator, or dramatist--
he would have brought distinction to his country; and to
all his extraordinary "recommendations," he added "the
most consummate personal courage--a courage void of
offense towards man--a courage associated with the most
polished politeness, the most perfect urbanity" (p. 36).
His genius "was not a single star, it was a galaxy of
stars, a combination of matchless excellence never before
presented by the human mind" (p. 36). (The second edition
[also 1816] advertises an account of Sheridan's funeral.)

6   ANON. "Mr. Sheridan." <u>Times</u> (London), 8 July, p. 3.
        Presents Sheridan as a genius who achieved great things
     through his comedies and his speeches but whose full
     promise fell victim to an indolence blighting him from
     youth: "a man who is inveterately thoughtless of
     consequences, and callous to reproof--who knows not when
     he squanders money, because he feels not those obligations
     which constitute or direct its uses--such a man it is
     impossible to rescue from destruction." It cannot be
     said that he friends abandoned him at last because in
     truth he had no friends. He was the "weakest of men,"
     and the term "greatness" has no real application to him.
     His life teaches that "great abilities may emerge from
     the meanest station"; but it also teaches "that great
     vices throw obstacles before the march of ambition, which
     no force nor superiority of intellect can remove." In
     this fact lies the "nobler praise, and purer happiness
     of our moral system."

7   ANON. "Mr. Sheridan's Funeral." <u>Times</u> (London), 15 July, p. 3.
        Describes Sheridan's funeral, mentioning the removal
     of the body from the house of Peter Moore in St. George
     Street to the Abbey and listing the chief mourners, who
     were led in the procession by the dukes of York and
     Sussex.

8   ANON. "Right Hon. Richard Brinsley Sheridan." <u>Gentleman's
     Magazine</u> 86, n.s. 9 (August): 177-82.
        Concludes the obituary essay of the July issue (1816.9)
     by reprinting (as adapted from 1816.1) an account of
     Sheridan's life, a sketch actually begun in the July
     issue with details of his parentage. "It was, perhaps,
     in the knowledge of human nature that he surpassed all
     his contemporaries. His sagacity was particularly

exercised in discovering the character and propensities
of his acquaintances, or of those with whom he had any
business to transact, and he generally succeeded in
converting this kind of knowledge to his own advantage"
(p. 181). With Pizarro, "he degraded his reputation as
the first dramatic writer of the country, and sunk himself
to a level with the Play-wrights of the day, to whom
profit was everything, fame nothing" (p. 182).

9   ANON. "Right Hon. Richard Brinsley Sheridan." Gentleman's
     Magazine 86, n.s. 9 (July): 81-86.
        Reprints, with some added material about Sheridan's
     parentage, 1816.6.

10   ANON. "Sketch of the Life and Character of the Late Right
     Hon. R. B. Sheridan." Scots Magazine and Edinburgh
     Literary Miscellany 78 (July): 522-29.
        Memorializes Sheridan by recalling his parentage, his
     education, and his three careers (as writer, politician,
     and theater manager), then gives in detail an account of
     his final illness, attributing his death to a gradual
     failure of his digestive powers. His last breath was
     received by his widow, and his sickbed was visited, for
     three days before his death, by the bishop of London.
     His friends "design to collect his scattered works, and
     to publish them by subscription. They are chiefly in
     the hands of an eminent literary friend, whose regard
     for his memory will secure to the public a complete
     edition of his writings; and whose labours will be
     further recommended by their being gratuitously exerted
     for the benefit of Mr. Sheridan's family" (pp. 524-35).
     After listing Sheridan's dramatic works (in a list which
     includes "The Tempest, altered" but challenges the
     authority of The Camp), the sketch closes with a
     "character" of Sheridan taken from 1816.6: Sheridan was
     the most richly endowed of geniuses, but his life is a
     history of waste, and his death (deprived of friends)
     reflects the usual friendlessness of an overebullient
     reveler. He was "the weakest of men" (p. 528), and the
     term "greatness" has nothing to do with him. Biographical
     materials derive from 1816.1.

11   [BYRON, GEORGE GORDON, LORD.] "Extracts of A Monody to the
     Memory of the Late Right Hon. R. B. Sheridan, Recited at
     the Opening of Drury-Lane Theatre, Sept. 7, 1816."
     Gentleman's Magazine 86, n.s. 9 (October): 350.
        Evokes the sympathy felt "When all of Genius which can
     perish, dies." (An extract of sixty-nine lines is given.)
     (Cf. 1816.12.)

1816

12   _____. Monody on the Death of the Right Honourable R. B.
      Sheridan, Written at the Request of a Friend, to Be
      Spoken at Drury Lane Theatre. London: Printed for John
      Murray, 12 pp.
          Evokes (in heroic couplets) an atmosphere of melancholy
      in which to recall Sheridan's talents, shame his enemies,
      and taunt his peers. A tribute of glory is properly his
      despite the calumnies of vain and jealous detractors; and
      it now remains for orators, playwrights, and wits to
      emulate if they can his high standards of achievement.
      "Nature formed but one such man / And broke the die--in
      moulding Sheridan!" (p. 12).

13   CONCANEN, M[ATTHEW]. "Invocation to Friendship." London:
      Morning Chronicle , ½ p.
          Shares an engraved page with Thomas Moore's "Lines
      . . . on the Death of the Late R. B. Sheridan, Esq.".
      (1816.17) and complains, with Moore, against the supposed
      "friends," including the prince regent, who apparently
      abandoned Sheridan in his final need. The poem consists
      of three quatrains.

14   GENT, THOMAS. Monody to the Memory of the Right Hon. H. B.
      Sheridan. London: Longman, Hurst, Rees, Orme, and Brown,
      15 pp.
          Credits Sheridan with restoring decency to the comic
      stage and with defending his country in a selfless and
      courageous way. His heroic stand against the naval
      mutinies and against the ambitions of Napoleon receive
      special commendations. The entire eulogy is in Hammond
      Measure.

15   [HUNT, LEIGH.] "The Late Mr. Sheridan." Examiner, 446,
      14 July, pp. 433-36.
          Sketches the life of Sheridan and puts down "the
      general impressions he has left upon one who admired
      without knowing him, and often without applauding"
      (p. 433). As a playwright, Sheridan did his bit toward
      keeping alive "a certain softness and sociality of spirit,
      without which, among other helps, a nation might relapse
      into brutality" (p. 435). As to character he was careless
      and improvident, but his origins ameliorate his offenses.
      In sum, "he was a man of wit, a lively and elegant
      dramatist, a winning and powerful orator, a sound
      politician, a lover of real freedom, a careless liver; an
      Irishman, in short, with much of the worst, and more of
      the best of his light-hearted but unfortunate countrymen.
      His worst can affect but few;--his best will redound to
      the good of his country and the delight of thousands to
      come" (p. 436).

16   _____ . "Literary Notices. No. 12." Examiner, 456,
        22 September, pp. 602-3.
             Quotes Bryon's "Monody on the Death of the Right
        Honourable R. B. Sheridan" (1816.12) and finds it "too
        general and too uniformly grave" (p. 603), of indifferent
        execution and given to insupportable exaggerations: "Mr.
        Sheridan was an excellent orator undoubtedly: and he was
        undoubtedly a wit; but as a genius, generally speaking,
        that is to say, as an original or as something complete
        of his kind, he has been surpassed ad infinitum; and
        though he wrote charming prose dialogue, and verses full
        of social wit, yet in the real sense of the word poet,
        we will venture to say he was none at all" (p. 603).

17   [MOORE, THOMAS.] Lines on the Death of from the
        Morning Chronicle of Monday August 5, 1816. Ascribed to a
        Personage of the Highest Poetical Talent, and to Gratify
        the Anxious Curiosity of the Public, Re-Published, Without
        Note or Comment. London: W. Hone, 8 pp.
             Excoriates highly placed and privileged people (includ-
        ing the prince regent) who had flattered Sheridan during
        his prime and abandoned him in his final need. Such
        people call to mind a certain large fly said by natural-
        ists to feed upon the brains of living elks and then leave
        them to die. "Oh, Genius! thy patrons, more cruel than
        they, / First feed on thy brains, and then leave thee to
        die" (p. 8). The body of the poem eulogizes Sheridan for
        the brightness and gentleness of his wit and for his deep
        devotion to freedom. (Also issued on a single engraved
        page together with 1816.13.)

*18   PEPPERPOD, PETER [PSEUD.] The Literary Bazaar; or Poet's
        Council. A Grand Historic, Heroic, Serio-Comic,
        Hudabrastic Poem, in Two Cantos. With A Pic-nic Elegy
        on R. B. Sheridan. London: Published for the Author by
        James Harper & Co., J. M. Richardson, and T. and J.
        Allman, 63 pp.
             The British Library copy consulted omits the "Pic-nic
        Elegy."

19   PHILLIPS, CHARLES. A Garland for the Grave of Richard
        Brinsley Sheridan. London: N. Hailes, 15 pp.
             Eulogizes Sheridan (in verse) as a universal genius
        whose greatheartedness and integrity stand equal to his
        art and whose wretched and lonely death brings shame upon
        the whole nation, especially upon the prince who abandoned
        him. When honor at last returns to the land, Sheridan,
        the preeminent Irishman, will lead her band. That he is
        the "human epitome of Ireland" appears (according to the

1816

prefatory note) in the diversity of character he shares
with his homeland: "Who is there that has not traced the
same strange and peculiar characteristics!--the careless
magnificence--the burning passion--the enchanting
eloquence--the ready wit--the generous devotion--the
prompt and thoughtless prodigality of self, that fling
their alternate shade and sunshine over the uncultured
loveliness of his landscape" (pp. 7-8).

20 TAYLOR, JOHN, ESQ. "Lines, Occasioned by the Medical
Attendance on the Late Right Hon. Richard Brinsley
Sheridan." Gentleman's Magazine 86, n.s. 9 (August): 159.
Pays homage, in nine octasyllabic couplets, to the
skill and charity of Sheridan's physician, Dr. Bain, who
held the bailiffs at bay while prolonging as best he
could the failing life of his patient.

21 WALLER, B., A.M. "Epistle to R. B. Sheridan, Esq. Written
in June 1799." Gentleman's Magazine 86, n.s. 9
(November): 445-46.
Fancies (in heroic couplets) a visit from the ghost of
Garrick in which Garrick appeals to Sheridan (through the
poet) to abandon his political career and return to the
neglected muse.

1817

1 ANON. "Life of Sheridan." Port Folio, 5th ser. 3 (June):
469-73.
Concludes the biographical sketch begun in the May
issue (1817.2) and acquits Sheridan of any active enmity
against virtue (however inactive an advocate of it he
might have been). "Upon the whole, if we wish to
contemplate Mr. Sheridan with that favourable regard
which should ever be the portion of departed genius, let
us look to the fairness of his political life--to the
firmness and integrity of his public character--to his
gallantry--his spirit--his generosity--his good-nature--
and, more than all, to the splendid concentration of
talents that adorned his mind" (p. 473).

2 ANON. "Memoirs of the Right Honourable Richard Brinsley
Sheridan." Port Folio, 5th ser. 3 (May): 365-77.
Digests from Watkins's biography of Sheridan (1817.4) a
narrative of the playwright's life (from the beginning to
about 1783). Some credit is given (p. 372) to Watkins's
charge that Sheridan plagiarized The School for Scandal.

3   ANON.   "7.   Richard Brinsley Sheridan."   In The Annual
     Register or a View of the History, Politics, and
     Literature.   For the Year 1816.   London: Baldwin, Cradock,
     and Joy, pp. 218-20.
          Sketches, among the obituary chronicles for 1816, a
     biographical account which includes cryptic assessments
     of Sheridan's work (e.g., The School for Scandal is "a
     comedy which, perhaps more than any other of the modern
     drama, revived the witty age of the English theatre"
     [p. 219]) and describes his decline as follows: "Deeply
     involved in his circumstances, and suffering in his
     private character in consequence of his necessities, with
     a constitution broken by his habits of life, and a
     debilitated mind, he sunk, the melancholy example of
     brilliant talents deprived of almost all their value by
     moral defects" (p. 220).

4   WATKINS, JOHN.   Memoirs of the Public and Private Life of
     The Right Honorable Richard Brinsley Sheridan, with a
     particular Account of his Family and Connexions.   2 vols.
     London: Colburn.
          Presents the life of Sheridan as a caveat to the mighty,
     a just caution to the vain, an object lesson to the
     indolent, and a warning to the improvident and careless.
     Despite the possibility that he stole The School for
     Scandal from a young lady, the daughter of a merchant in
     Thames Street, his contributions to the craft of drama
     were creditable.   But his desire for notice overbore the
     limit of his gifts, and he entered political life to
     gratify his ambition, taking with him an undoubted flair
     for oratory but no real talent for statecraft and an
     indolence and extravagance which had plagued him since
     childhood.   He was "unquestionably a man of acute
     intellectual powers" (2: 390), but, for want of proper
     leadership in youth and because of undisciplined self-
     indulgences, he misdirected his powers; and his memoir
     is now of service only "if it be regarded as a beacon
     pointing out the extreme danger of resting satisfied in
     the possession of splendid talents without applying them
     to any efficient and practical purposes in the great
     business of human life" (2: 398).   Reviewed in 1817.1-2;
     1819.2-3; 1824.2; 1826.4, 7.

                              1818

1   ANON.   "Anecdote of Sheridan."   Port Folio, 5th ser. 5 (May):
     395.
          Gives the story of Sheridan's waggish resourcefulness

1818

in quitting the company of a horsedealer whom he suddenly encountered in the street and to whom he owed money. While, at Sheridan's request, the horsedealer demonstrated the paces of his own mount, Sheridan rode off in the other direction on the horse not yet paid for.

2   ANON. "Sheridan's Debt to Nature." Port Folio, 5th. ser. 5 (May): 397.
    Prints a jingle inspired by Sheridan's celebrated impecuniousness:
    "Dick, pay your debts," a fellow roar'd one day.
    "I will," replied the limb of legislature.
    "Then tell me, Dick, what debt you first will pay?"
        "Why, first I'll pay--I'll pay the debt of Nature!"

1819

1   ANON. "Art. 18. Clio's Protest; or, 'The Picture' varnished With other Poems. By the late Right Honourable R. B. Sheridan." Monthly Review; or, Literary Journal Enlarged, 2d ser. 89 (May): 97-101.
    Reviews the Clio's Protest volume, quoting extracts from the title poem and from "The Ridotto of Bath" with the purpose of demonstrating the quality of Sheridan's early wit. The remaining pieces in the volume--"Lines Addressed to Laura" and the epilogue to Semiramis--give authentic evidence of Sheridan's sense of pathos (in the first instance) and his patriotic spirit (in the second).

2   ANON. "Art. I. Memoirs of the Public and Private Life of the Right Honourable Richard Brinsley Sheridan, with a particular Account of his Family and Connexions. By John Watkins LL.D." Monthly Review; or, Literary Journal Enlarged, 2d ser. 89 (July): 225-35.
    Reports on Watkins's Memoirs by sketching Sheridan's life and making strictures upon it: "His whole career, indeed, furnished a distressing proof of native talent impeded by a want of culture; illustrating both the drama and the senate for a season, but falling into the shade at the time when continued exertion would have bought it forth in augmented splendor. How different is this from the account we had occasion to render some years ago (MR. vol. lxxx) of the progress of Gibbon" (p. 233). Watkins himself wins no high praise. His political bias against Sheridan is obvious, and his selection of source materials is so undiscriminating as to lack all force.

3   ANON. "Art. II.--Memoirs of the Public and Private Life

of the Right Honourable Richard Brinsley Sheridan, with
a particular Account of his Family and Connexions. By
John Watkins, LL.D." Analectic Magazine 14 (1819):
341-50.
    Reprints 1819.2.

4 HAZLITT, WILLIAM. "On the Comic Writers of the Last
   Century." In Lectures on the English Comic Writers.
   London: Taylor and Hessey; Philadelphia: M. Carey and
   Son, pp. 302-43.
       Includes Sheridan in a survey of eighteenth-century
   comic writers and admires especially his ability to give
   dramatic being to character types he might have seen
   insufficiently realized in the work of other people (e.g.,
   Murphy's Malvil, a forerunner of his own Joseph Surface).
   "This is the merit of Sheridan's comedies, that every
   thing in them tells" (p. 335). Blessed with wit,
   ingenuity, action, and incident, they unmask hypocrisy
   even while promoting affection. Similarly, the speeches
   of Sheridan in Parliament show a "manly, unperverted
   good sense, and keen irony" (p. 337). ¡ He was "the last
   accomplished debater in the House of Commons" (p. 338).

                          1820

1 OXBERRY, WILLIAM. "Remarks. The Rivals." In The New
   English Drama. London: W. Simpkin and R. Marshall,
   pp. 32-37.
       Gives warm appreciation to the play and the playwright,
   placing the one among "the most agreeable comedies we
   have" (p. 32) and the other among men "of first-rate
   talents" (p. 36). Sheridan's characters and situations
   may be derivative, but he "was the farthest possible
   from a servile plagiarist" (pp. 35-36). If he did not
   wholly create his characters, "he compared them with
   their prototypes in nature, and understood their bearings
   and qualities, before he undertook to make a different
   use of them" (p. 36). It may be that The School for
   Scandal is superior to The Rivals in "the elegance and
   brilliancy of the dialogue, in a certain animation of
   moral sentiment, and in the masterly denouement of the
   fable," but The Rivals "has more life and action in it,
   and abounds in a greater number of whimsical characters,
   unexpected incidents, and absurd contrasts of situation"
   (p. 32). It is so broad and farcical in its humor that
   it cannot bear up well in an indifferent representation;
   but, if the actors are well prepared in their parts,
   there "is scarcely a more delightful play" imaginable
   (p. 32).

1821

1821

1 MOORE, THOMAS. Advertisement. In The Works of the Late
   Right Honourable Richard Brinsley Sheridan. London:
   John Murray, I: v-xiii.
       Apologizes that a biographical essay does not accompany
   the texts of the plays and explains the omission on
   grounds (1) of the unavailability of the most valuable
   living source of biographical information, (2) the
   necessity of mentioning (with some risk of offense)
   persons yet living, and (3) the need to master the whole
   milieu of the subject (while yet taking care not to get
   too remote from him).

1822

1 ANON. "Death of Mr. Sheridan." Port Folio, 5th ser.
   14 (August): 135-36.
       Observes, in a serialized history of Europe, that the
   death of Sheridan in 1816 was very properly seen as a
   public event, even though Sheridan had for some time
   been outside the legislature and had relaxed all
   disciplines upon his private life. In his sad decline
   resides "a severe, but it may be a salutary lesson, how
   vain it is, with the most splendid endowments and
   successes, to expect true felicity even in this state of
   existence, without fixedness of principle and simplicity
   of life" (pp. 135-36).

2 ANON. "The School for Scandal. Miss Grimani--cum multis
   aliis." London Magazine 5 (May): 481-83.
       Celebrates The School for Scandal as a play in which
   "life seems to have resolved itself into an essence, and
   conversation to have lost all its 'outward limbs and
   flourishes,'" a play in whose characters "all that is
   perfect in wit and spirit is concentrated" (p. 481). In
   a recent revival of the play at Drury Lane, Miss Grimani
   is quite unsuitable as Lady Teazle. She reads the role
   in too sentimental a way. But no one now can hope to
   emulate those earlier performers (Miss Farren as Lady
   Teazle, King as Sir Peter, Palmer as Joseph, etc.) who
   have brought legend to the roles.

3 BUTLER, CHARLES. "Mr. Sheridan--Mr. Dundas." In
   Reminiscences of Charles Butler. 2 vols. London: John
   Murray, 1822-1827.
       Describes the oratorical skill of Sheridan by observing
   that he required considerable preparation in displaying

his talents and was therefore not a brisk debater.
Sometimes, however, he was effective in quick eprigrammatic
replies. Because of his procrastination and indolence,
it was hardly known of him that he did indeed possess
common sense and dignity to an extraordinary degree; he
had little general information and little classical
learning, but he displayed in his speeches very great
powers of mind and a happy turn of ridicule. When he
rose to the serious and severe, his style was magnificent;
but, even at his most eloquent, he inclined a bit too
much to prettiness. He had many failings of character,
but they came to notice because of the larger brightness
of his luster. People not subject to public censure will
most often discover, on self-examination, that they enjoy
such a privilege not because of their superior rectitude
but because of their obscurity. Note: This annotation
is derived from the second American edition of the
Reminiscences, based upon the fourth London edition (New
York: Bliss, White, Collins, Harnay, 1825), pp. 166-68.

4   [LAMB, CHARLES.] "The Old Actors." London Magazine 5 (April):
      305-11.
          Defines "artificial comedy" as a mode of comic action
      situated outside moral judgment, then nominates The School
      for Scandal as an artificial comedy mixed with incompat-
      ible sentimentalities. Only such actors as John Palmer,
      who created the role of Joseph Surface, could splice the
      two modes together. Palmer could so "act" his villainy as
      to give it an extrajudgmental aesthetic appeal. Thus
      he could minimize the too facile contrast between
      Joseph's vice and Charles's virtue. In more recent
      times, even though the casts of the comedy remain good
      ones, audiences and managers require that the artificial
      bouyancy of The School for Scandal give place to
      sentimental moralizing. A brilliance such as Palmer's,
      even if it were available, could not now flourish.

                              1823

1   LAMB, CHARLES. "On the Artificial Comedy of the Last
      Century." In Elia. Essays Which Have Appeared Under
      That Signature in the London Magazine. London: Taylor
      and Hessey, pp. 323-41.
          Reprints 1822.4.

1824

1   ANON. "Art. IV. <u>Memoirs of the Life and Writings of Mrs.</u>
    <u>Frances Sheridan . . . By her Granddaughter, Alicia</u>
    <u>Lefanu</u>." <u>Monthly Review</u> 104 (July): 257-65.
        Considers the most interesting parts of these <u>Memoirs</u>
    to be those treating of R. B. Sheridan. Even so, LeFanu
    offers nothing new about him and spends too much time
    acquitting him of Watkins's calumnies (cf. 1817.4).
    Her book, like Watkins's own, reinforces the conviction
    "that the union of genius and virtue is more frequent in
    Sheridan's life than a few unfortunate instances of their
    divorce might induce a gloomy mind to apprehend" (p. 265).

2   LeFANU, ALICIA. <u>Memoirs of the Life and Writings of Mrs.</u>
    <u>Frances Sheridan, Mother of the Late Right Hon. Richard</u>
    <u>Brinsley Sheridan . . . with Remarks upon a Late Life of</u>
    <u>the Right Hon. R. B. Sheridan</u>. London: G. and W. B.
    Whittaker, 446 pp.
        Devotes the closing chapter (pp. 392-435) to correcting
    errors made by Watkins in his biography of Sheridan
    (1817.4). Among such errors is the charge that Sheridan
    stole <u>The School for Scandal</u> from the daughter of a
    merchant in Thames Street and that Elizabeth Sheridan,
    the playwright's first wife, died of a stroke after
    discovering that her carriage, in which she was prepared
    to take an outing, had been reclaimed by creditors.
    Authenticated accounts give the lie to these and other
    such fabrications (including Watkins's comments on the
    deaths of the Linley sibling). On occasion, too, the
    <u>Memoirs</u> pause to correct such errors of Watkins as that
    in which he claims that Sheridan made few lasting
    friendships at Harrow (cf. pp. 252-53). Reviewed in
    1824.1.

1825

1   ANON. "Art. VII. <u>Memoirs of the Life of the Right</u>
    <u>Honourable Richard Brinsley Sheridan. By Thomas Moore</u>."
    <u>Monthly Review</u>, 2d ser. 108 (Ctober): 149-62.
        Recognizes the interest contained in the life of
    Sheridan despite the failings which aggravated in him a
    parasitical attachment to the Prince of Wales, a
    persistent improvidence, and an eventual disgraceful
    sottishness. Moore's biography (reviewed here) is
    always overflorid and is tedious in its treatment of
    Sheridan's literary career, but its rendering of his
    political career overrides the tedium. However one

might detest Sheridan's scandalous conduct at the end of
his life, one must share with Moore the friendly feelings
that come of considering the "brilliant talents" that
Sheridan wasted and "the gay and kindly disposition of
heart which long rendered him the charm of private
society" (p. 162).

2   ANON. "Art. VII. Memoirs of the Life of the Right
    Honourable Richard Brinsley Sheridan. By Thomas Moore."
    Westminster Review 4 (October): 371-407.
        Draws from Moore's Memoirs of Sheridan (1825.9) evi-
    dence that "Sheridan was extremely ignorant" and that his
    early jottings on serious subjects (e.g., his scheme of
    female education) were the "vision of a fasting mind." In
    "the provinces of wit and fancy he contrived to do without
    knowledge, but whenever we find him committing himself
    to paper argumentatively on grave subjects we observe a
    lamentable crudity and a lack of bottom." He even
    "flattered himself, it appears, that knowledge could be
    obtained by the mere force of genius working on 'a few
    leading and fixed ideas'" (pp. 379-80). Moore earns
    admiration for illustrating Sheridan's creative processes,
    i.e., for showing that what Sheridan lacked in creative
    invention he compensated for in hard work. Moore also
    earns high praise for his treatment of Sheridan's
    political career, although he fails to treat accurately
    the efforts of the prince to secure for Sheridan a place
    in Parliament after 1812. A sidenote to Moore's comments
    upon the famous rift between Sheridan and Burke on the
    issue of the French Revolution appears in a letter (here
    quoted) of General Richard Fitzpatrick to "the celebrated
    Mrs. Benwell" (p. 399). It suggests that many members
    of the House of Commons found the rift to be a "childish
    affair" (p. 399).

3   ANON. "Kelly's Memoirs." [Colburn's] New Monthly Magazine
    14 (1825): 487-94.
        Reprints with admiration two of Kelly's anecdotes about
    the Sheridan: (1) Sheridan's ordering the music for
    Pizzaro, and (2) his inveigling a new watch from Thomas
    Harris (the manager of Covent Garden Theatre).

4   ANON. "Memoir of the Life of the Right Honourable Richard
    Brinsley Sheridan. By Thomas Moore." Port Folio,
    5th ser. 20 (November): 401-13.
        Reviews Moore's book admiringly but rejects the account
    in it of Sheridan's cruel decline (specifically the
    charges of neglect made by Moore against the Prince of
    Wales) and offers an assessment of Sheridan's political

life and his character much severer than Moore's: "As a
politician, Sheridan vacillated between all parties, and
was trusted by none; and his moral failings were too
great and too obvious to be passed over without strong
animadversion" (p. 413).

5   ANON. "Moore's Life of Sheridan." [Colburn's] New Monthly
    Magazine 14 (1825): 474-84.
        Sees Sheridan's life as dividing itself into three
    segments--the dramatist, the legislator, and the man--and
    credits Moore with giving his happiest passages to the
    first of these. In a fastidiousness to emphasize the
    loftier aspects of his subject's character, Moore has
    robbed Sheridan of his diversity and wit. These features
    receive better treatment in Michael Kelly's
    Reminiscences (see 1826.15). In presenting Sheridan,
    these two books show "how much the biographer infuses
    of himself into his hero, and how, in the very best
    delineations of persons and of things, the resemblance
    takes its colour from the modalities of thought and
    feeling of the artist by whom it is sketched" (p. 474).

6   ANON. "Original Letter from Miss Linley, Afterwards Mrs.
    Sheridan." Gentleman's Magazine 95, n.s. 18 (October):
    287-96.
        Prints a letter signed by "E. Linley" and addressed
    (according to the editorial headnote) to Miss Linley's
    confidential friend Miss Saunders. Dated 2 May 1772
    it describes Miss Linley's troubled affairs of heart in
    those days--her attraction (in spite of herself) to
    Thomas Mathews, his abuses of her, Long's claims upon
    her, Sheridan's arrival for the rescue, the elopement
    with Sheridan to France, the return, and Sheridan's first
    duel with Mathews.

7   ANON. "71. Memoir of the Life of the Right Hon. Richard
    Brinsley Sheridan. By Thomas Moore. 4t0. pp. 719.
    Longman." Gentleman's Magazine 95, n.s. 18 (October):
    345-51.
        Reviews Moore's Memoir most favorably; then concludes
    with the following comment upon Sheridan himself: "Had
    his youthful principles been fixed by judicious and
    steady culture, and his habits regulated by the unremit-
    ting demands of a profession, there would have been less
    room for wayward impulse to act in--less material on
    which it could successfully operate--the life of this
    lamented son of genius might have escaped the most trying
    of its vicissitudes--his moral taste its progressive
    degeneracy--his decent pride its mortifications--and his

political fame the incompleteness of its lustre. As it
is, and at the worst, we must admire--we must forgive
one who, while Literature exists in England, can never
be forgotten" (p. 351).

8   BOADEN, JAMES. Memoirs of the Life of John Philip Kemble,
     Esq. Including a History of the Stage, From the Time of
     Garrick to the Present Period. London: Longman, Hurst,
     Rees, Orme, Brown and Green, 1: 203-4, 409-12.
        Pauses to mention, while chronicling the career of John
     Philip Kemble, Sheridan's lassitude in handling the
     artistic department of Drury Lane Theatre during the
     managerial tenure of Thomas King. "Melancholy proofs of
     this [lassitude] appeared in piles of long forgotten
     tragedies and comedies, which he had promised to consider,
     and had never opened" (1: 204). Petitioners might gather
     at his house; but, when he greeted them, "so cordial were
     his manners, his glance so masterly, and his address so
     captivating, that the people, for the most part, seemed
     to forget what they actually wanted, and went away, as
     if they had come only to look at him" (1: 204). A second
     aside observes that Kemble's authority and responsibility
     in the theater grew in the late 1780s in proportion to
     Sheridan's ever deepening involvement in political matters
     (1: 409-12).

9   MOORE, THOMAS. Memoirs of the Life of the Right Honourable
     Richard Brinsley Sheridan. London: Longman, Hurst, Rees,
     Orme, Brown, and Green, 719 pp.
        Constructs from documents made available by the
     Sheridan family and from private impressions of Sheridan's
     own intellectual and political milieu an assessment of the
     playwright and statesman which sees him rising to eminence
     from a slight foundation of instruction and maintaining
     himself there by dint of great effort and continuous
     preparation. Not only were his plays and speeches
     laboriously premeditated; his conversation, however
     spontaneous it might have seemed, took color too from
     thrusts and sallies prepared and saved for proper
     occasions. In political character he was wholly above
     reproach, never showing slavish dependencies to party.
     public and never showing slavish dependencies to party.
     In moral character he was from his youngest days indolent,
     improvident, and undisciplined in temperament (tendencies
     greatly aggravated by his careers in the theater and in
     Parliament), but, however irregular his habits and
     ruinous his accounts, he never, even in his darkest
     moments, lost his natural good feelings; nor, in fact,
     was he so deeply in debt at the time of his death as he

1825

is widely thought to be. Moreover, any judgment against
his improvidence should be weighed against the thought
that, had he been careless of principle, he might have
died a wealthy and titled man. Reviewed in 1825.1-2, 4-5,
7; 1826.2-5, 7-8, 13-14, 17, 21-22.

10   ____. Memoirs of the Life of the Right Honourable
Richard Brinsley Sheridan. 2d ed. 2 vols. London:
Longman, Hurst, Rees, Orme, Brown and Green.
Reprints 1825.9 in two volumes.

11   ____. Memoirs of the Life of the Right Honourable
Richard Brinsley Sheridan. 2 vols. Philadelphia: H. C.
Carey and I. Lea.
Reprints 1825.10.

12   ____. Memoirs of the Life of the Right Honourable
Richard Brinsley Sheridan. 3d ed. 2 vols. London:
Longman, Hurst, Rees, Orme, Brown and Green.
Reprints 1825.10.

1826

1   ANON. "Art X. Sheridaniana; or, Anecdotes of the Life of
Richard Brinsley Sheridan; his Table-Talk, and Bon Mots."
Monthly Review, 3d ser. 2 (May): 108-11.
Devotes virtually all of a review of Sheridaniana
(1826.9) to extracts from and comments upon the letter
supposedly written by Elizabeth Linley describing her
relationship with Thomas Mathews and the events
surrounding it (see 1825.6). Because Thomas Moore had
neglected to mention the letter in his biography of
Sheridan and because it appears in Sheridaniana, it is
treated thus amply.

2   ANON. "Memoirs of the Life of the Right Honourable Richard
Brinsley Sheridan. By Thomas Moore." Museum of
Foreign Literature and Science 8, n.s. 1 (January): 69-78.
Reprints 1825.1.

3   ANON. "Memoirs of the Life of the Right Honourable Richard
Brinsley Sheridan. By Thomas Moore." United States
Literary Gazette 3 (15 February): 361-67.
Attacks Moore's Memoirs of the Life of Sheridan
(1825.9) for being stylistically overwrought and
politically so biased as to promote Sheridan's reputation
at the expense of Burke's. "Sheridan's fame rests on too
firm a basis to need that Burke's reputation, or that of

any other man, should be pulled down for its support"
(p. 363).

4   ANON. "Memoirs of Sheridan, by Dr. Watkins and Mr. Moore."
     Quarterly Review 33 (March): 561-93.
        Acknowledges the haste, turgidity, and political bias
     of Watkins's memoirs of Sheridan (1817.4) but credits them
     with greater accuracy and pertinence, as regards
     Sheridan's political career, than Moore's. Moore's book
     suffers from the sneering attitude it invariably takes
     against Watkins; it suffers from an overly florid meta-
     phorical style; but most of all it suffers from ingenuous
     use of sources and, therefore, from inaccuracies. In
     recounting Sheridan's elopement, for example, Moore
     neglects use of Miss Linley's own version of the matter,
     as recently printed in the Gentleman's Magazine (1825.6).
     Furthermore, Moore allows confusion as to Sheridan's
     devotion to parliamentary reform. He minimizes the
     implications of Sheridan's desertion of his party in 1812,
     and, in a fatuous way, he nominates Sheridan as the
     author of the regency letter in 1789, even when sound
     evidence identifies Burke as the author. Most
     reprehensibly, however, he maligns the prince for
     neglecting the dying Sheridan even when available reports
     clear the prince of such neglect and when facts presented
     by Moore himself show that the prince could not have had
     early knowledge of Sheridan's distress. In truth, the
     history of Britain could easily be written without the
     mention of Sheridan's name. His profligacy and self-
     indulgence too quickly darkened and degraded his talents.
     His plays and bon mots establish his place in history,
     and to these aspects of his genius Moore does credit.
     Watkins surpasses Moore in representing Sheridan's
     political life. But Michael Kelly's Reminiscences
     (1826.15) surpasses both Moore and Watkins in recounting
     Sheridan's personal manners. (This article has been
     attributed to J. W. Croker and to John Lockhart. See
     1826.12 and 1826.16 below.)

5   ANON. "Moore's Life of Sheridan." Blackwood's Edinburgh
     Magazine 19 (February): 113-30.
        Responds to Moore's biography of Sheridan by reflecting
     on three aspects of Sheridan's life: his political
     career, his character, and his theatrical genius. The
     reversals in his political career resulted infinitely more
     from the hypocrisy of the Whigs than the ingratitude of
     the prince. He was not by any objective standard a great
     orator. In personal character, he never possessed "any
     true, warm, unselfish, and disinterested feeling, such

as endear to us the character of a man for ever, and disposes or rather forces us to sink his many vices even in his few virtues" (p. 118). His reputation as a wit won for his character the benefit of too generous a doubt, for he was (especially early) disarmingly witty. As a wit "He had little or no learning; and was, there-fore, wholly free from pendantry" (p. 119). As a dramatist, "He stands at the head of all comedy since Shakespeare. Tried on the three questions, of plot, character, and dialogue, he is superior to all of France, Spain, and England" (p. 121). By no means a miracle, this genius for drama derives (1) from his genealogy, i.e., his birth into a theatrical family, (2) the creative stimula-tion of his days in Bath, and (3) his intimate knowledge of forgotten farces, which "he plundered without a pang" (p. 122) for characters and plots. In general, Moore's memoir represents him fairly.

6   ANON. "On Cant in Dramatic Criticism. Miss Kelly's Lady Teazle." Blackwood's Edinburgh Magazine 19 (February): 197-205.
     Explodes the cant that innovation is out of place in the performance of well-known dramatic roles and praises Miss Kelly for daring to bring freshness to the part of Lady Teazle. Miss Kelly has perceived that Lady Teazle is "neither a woman of fashion nor a rustic girl, but something between both. She has tasted the poisonous sweets of dissipation, and they have intoxicated her senses; but her heart, though approached by the malady, has escaped it" (p. 204). While adapting the mode of the city, she must retain some traces of the country, and she must betray, as Miss Kelly does in her performance, "an imperfect and ill-tutored hypocrisy" (p. 205). Despite the cant of some dramatic critics, Miss Kelly's Lady Teazle, though perhaps unconventional (i.e., unlike the celebrated performances of Miss Farren), is nonetheless valid and authentic.

7   ANON. "1. Memoirs of the Rt. Hon. R. B. Sheridan. By John Watkins . . . 2. Memoirs of the Rt. Hon. R. B. Sheridan By Thomas Moore . . . 3. Sheridaniana." Museum of Foreign Literature and Science, 9 n.s. 2 (July): 1-16.
     Reprints 1826.4.

8   ANON. "Review of Moore's Life of R. B. Sheridan." Christian Observer 26 (August): 478-94.
     Applies tests of Christian virtue to Sheridan's character and career, as they are represented in Moore's Memoirs (1825.9), and finds Sheridan lacking in most

respects. The richness and variety of characterization
in his plays cannot compensate for "the absence of sound
virtue and Scriptural morality" in them (p. 480), and
his life offers only negative lessons to the reflecting
mind. It teaches "that a naturally kind and amiable
disposition is very compatible with great selfishness,
and disregard of the comfort and happiness of others"
(p. 493), and it illustrates "the influence of carelessness in lowering, and as it were neutralizing, all nobler
qualities of an individual" (p. 493). It demonstrates,
too, that while "Prudence as to pecuniary matters may
be, and indeed is continually apparent, where there is
no influence of true religion," the "influence of true
religion cannot frequently exist without such prudence"
(p. 494).

9   ANON. Sheridaniana; or Anecdotes of the Life of Richard
      Brinsley Sheridan; His Table Talk and Bon Mots. London:
      Henry Colburn, 334 pp.
          Offers to repair some of the deficiencies of Moore's
      biography of Sheridan (1825.9) by collecting instances
      of Sheridan's wit and intellectual vigor, matters too
      much neglected by Moore, who "seems to be far more
      anxious to prove that he can say fine things, than to
      show that Sheridan was in the habit of saying them"
      (p. v). The anecdotes chosen may reveal in Sheridan a
      character motivated by the reckless gaiety but not by
      loose principle; and many of them display his tenderness
      of heart. The bon mots are selected not just from table
      talk but also from unfinished plays and even from the
      canceled passages of finished plays. While little is
      chosen from Sheridan's speeches, his retorts and other
      moments of parliamentary wit are liberally represented,
      as are his pasquinades and society verses. The
      anecdotes are arranged in chronological order throughout
      the years of his life; and afterward are arranged, under
      topical headings, "Miscellaneous Anecdotes and Bon Mots."
      Reviewed in 1826.1, 4, 7, 10.

10   ANON. "Sheridaniana." London Magazine, 2d ser. 5 (May):
      97-103.
          Supplies several anecdotes about Sheridan not included
      in Sheridaniana (1826.9) and corrects several attributions
      falsely applied to him there. E.g., the quip "Sir, pass
      me up that decanter, for I must return to Madeira since
      I cannot double the Cape" (a bon mot uttered when a new
      bottle of Constantia from the Cape of Good Hope was not
      forthcoming as desired) is taken away from Sheridan and
      given to Samuel Foote. But a good retort made by

1826

Sheridan upon Pitt, who had accused him of drunkenness
in the House of Commons, is offered as a proper addendum
to Sheridaniana. Alluding to an instance of Pitt's own
inebriation in the House, Sheridan had recited a jingle
picturing Pitt and Henry Dundas blinded by drink:

> I can't see the Speaker,
> Pray Hal, do you?
> Not see the Speaker, Bill!
> Why I see two.

*11   BRYANT, WILLIAM CULLEN. "The Character of Sheridan."
New York Review and Atheneum Magazine.
Reprinted in 1884.3 and 1964.3. (See 1884.3 for
annotation.)

12   [CROKER, J. W.] "Memoirs of Sheridan, by Dr. Watkins and Mr.
Moore." Quarterly Review 33 (March): 561-93.
This article (annotated under 1826.4 above) is
attributed to Croker in Poole's Index, I, 1190.

13   J. "Memoirs of the Right Honorable Brinsley Sheridan by
Thomas Moore. Philadelphia." Boston Monthly Magazine
1 (January): 438-45.
Bases an account of Sheridan's life upon extracts from
Moore's Memoirs (1825.9), then admires Moore for executing
his task with "a fearless honesty, and a generous
humanity, that does honor to his heart." The book treats
with interest and impartiality a subject who "left
nothing but his fame to posterity, and to his persecutors
the remembrance of his sufferings" (p. 445).

14   [JEFFREY, FRANCIS.] "Art. I. Memoirs of the life of the
Right Honourable Richard Brinsley Sheridan. By Thomas
Moore. Fourth Edition, 2 vols. 8vo. London, Longman &
Co. 1826." Edinburgh Review 45 (December): 1-48.
Admires Moore's book for its balanced and objective
treatment of political history. As for Sheridan himself,
there is nothing really attractive about his life. "We
cannot say that we care much about his family history,
discomforts, or alliances,--and certainly think it time
that the ferocious duels and fraternal rivalries, which
paved the way to his first marriage, should at length
be buried in oblivion. Still less interest, if possible,
can we now feel in the detail of his expedients and
proceedings as a share-holder or manager of one of the
Theatres;--and least of all can we be gratified by the
sad story of his improvidence and pecuniary
embarrassments--the questionable shifts to which he

sometimes descended to relieve them, or the lamentable excesses in which he sometimes tried to drown their recollection" (p. 3). His literary career obviously claims more interest than his private life; but, while brilliant, it was short, and it ended early. Moore's rendering of history, which steers a midcourse between the "intolerant and the thorough Reformers" (p. 40), contains the largest interest of the book. (This article is attributed to Jeffrey in Poole's Index, 1: 1190.)

15   KELLY, MICHAEL. Reminiscences of Michael Kelly of the King's Theatres and Theatre Royal Drury Lane. 2 vols. London: H. Colburn, passim.
      Includes, in passages scattered throughout the latter pages of the book, anecdotes testifying to Sheridan's fear of newspaper criticism, his superstition, his disregard for punctilio (even in keeping an audience with the king), his natural reticence, his alacrity in composition, his unwavering fidelity to friendship, his composure in the face of crisis. Despite malicious rumors to the contrary, he did not die destitute and friendless. His physician and friends ministered carefully to his final needs and felt deeply the pain of his loss. He was a noble-spirited and great-minded man. Reviewed in 1825.3, 5; 1826.4.

16   [LOCKHART, JOHN.] "Memoirs of Sheridan, by Dr. Watkins and Mr. Moore." Quarterly Review 33 (March): 561-93.
      This article (annotated under 1826.4 above) is attributed to Lockhart in 1896.15 (1: 177).

17   [MANGIN, EDWARD H.] A Letter to T. Moore, Esq. on the Subject of Sheridan's "School for Scandal." By the Author of "An Essay on Light Reading." Bath: George Wood, 24 pp.
      Chides Moore for suspending his proper judgment and acceding to mindless popular sentiment in admiring The School for Scandal. Not at all the redoubtable effort Moore claims it to be, the play shows flaws in most features of language, character, plot, and sentiment. It belittles the virtues of justice and prudence and insinuates "that wickedness is not quite such a naughty thing as it is sometimes represented" (p. 22). In praising the play so effusively as he does in his biography of Sheridan, Moore seems to forget the magnitude of his own reputation as a critic and consequently inflicts "lasting injury on society" (p. 24).

1826

*18   METROPOLITAN QUARTERLY MAGAZINE 1 (1826): 203-55.
          Cited in 1890.1 (p. xi). The date is there given as
      1836, but (according to the Union List of Serials) this
      periodical published only in 1826.

 19   MOORE, THOMAS. Memoirs of the Life of the Right Honourable
      Richard Brinsley Sheridan. 4th ed. 2 vols. London:
      Longman, Rees, Orme, Brown, and Green.

 20   R., C. "More Last Words of Sheridan." Blackwood's
      Edinburgh Magazine 19 (March): 351-53.
          Addresses the editor--in response to the editorial
      review of Moore's Memoirs of Sheridan (1826.4)--with the
      purpose of clearing Sheridan's name in two respects: (1)
      against charges of "payability" (i.e., negligence in
      discharging his debts), and (2) against charges of
      hardheartedness in private and public dealings. In fact,
      he lived so in dread of duns that he often paid the same
      debt over and over, yielding first to the most impudent
      claims and afterward to the just ones. His debts at the
      time of his death (about 5000 pounds) were not excessive;
      and, while he was not ostentatious in his private
      liberality (thus obscuring the extent of it), his public
      character certainly displayed nobility at the time of the
      naval mutinies. His greatest political crime "was that
      he got the Whigs thrown out of office, a deed for which
      the Nation should properly admire him."

 21   SENEX. "Reminiscences.--No. III. Richard Brinsley Sheridan
      &c." Blackwood's Edinburgh Magazine 20 (July): 25-41.
          Measures Moore's memoirs of Sheridan against actual
      personal recollections and finds the memoirs in general
      to be biased and unconvincing. For example, Garrick did
      not, as Moore says, revise Mrs. Sheridan's Discovery in
      effort to compete with The Duenna. Sheridan's friendship
      with the Prince of Wales did not, as Moore implies,
      dissipate the force of Sheridan's character. The
      prototype for Charles Surface is not, as Moore would have
      it, Sheridan himself but Charles James Fox. Sheridan was
      not likely to have been, despite Moore's report, an
      impenetrable dunce at Harrow School. Although Moore
      cannot understand why Sheridan chose to revise Vanbrugh's
      Relapse, the reasons are quite clear: the task was easy;
      the play fitted the company of performers; it was an apt
      vehicle for three fine actresses (Mrs. Abington, Mrs.
      Robinson, and Miss Farren). Finally, despite Moore's
      surly judgments against Pizarro, the play deserves credit
      not just as an acting piece but as a repository for noble
      sentiments and fine heroic ideals, ideals perhaps too
      trifling for "such 'heroic dignity' as Tommy Moore's"

(p. 41). It was perhaps Moore's bias against such warmth
of feeling that forbade his printing in the memoirs the
famous extra stanza to the national anthem penned
impromptu by Sheridan to celebrate the king's escape from
an assassin's bullet at Drury Lane Theatre one fateful
evening.

22   _____. "Reminiscences.--No. IV. Richard Brinsley Sheridan
      &c. (Concluded from Last Number.)." <u>Blackwood's</u>
      <u>Edinburgh Magazine</u> 20 (August): 201-214.
        Complains further (see 1826.21) against the political
      bias coloring Moore's memoirs of Sheridan. Having
      misjudged the principles upon which Britain opposed
      independence for the Americans, and having seen the French
      and American revolutions in one distorted light, Moore
      elevated (at the expense of Pitt and Burke) the
      triumvirate of Fox, Sheridan, and Grey to positions of
      unwarranted national honor. In fact, his book should
      properly be called "An Apology for the Rashness,
      Inconsistency and consequent Disappointments of the Whig
      Party, from the Death of the Earl of Chatham to that of
      his son William Pitt, and continued to the Death of
      Richard B. Sheridan, of whose Life and Writings a
      detailed History is also given, by the Author of the
      Fudge Family, the Two-Penny Post-bag, and the Memoirs
      of Captain Rock" (p. 206). In making fair estimation of
      Sheridan's character, "we must steer a middle course,
      between blind admiration of his talents, and unqualified
      reprobation of his faults" (p. 213). Achieving
      prominence through his comedies he acceded to the
      "seductive blandishments, delusive hopes, and patent
      temptations" (p. 214) encouraged in him by highly placed
      political mentors; and, ironically, his greatest enemies
      "were those by whom his ambitious propensities were fed"
      (p. 213). Ironically, too, his fame will at last rest
      upon what he pretended to despise, his reputation as a
      dramatist. A good life of Sheridan has yet to be written.

1827

1   [HAZLITT, WILLIAM.] "On the Want of Money." <u>Monthly</u>
      <u>Magazine or British Register of Literature, Sciences,</u>
      <u>and the Belles-Lettres</u>, n. s. 3 (January): 35-45.
        Instances the melancholy practice of living from
      hand to mouth by recalling the difficulties Sheridan's
      household staff often encountered in scavenging the
      neighborhood for breakfast fixings. A long footnote cites
      other of Sheridan's monetary embarrassments (and his
      efforts to out-countenance them). History affords few

1827

better instances than Sheridan of "that uncertain, casual, precarious mode of existence, in which the temptation to spend remains after the means are exhausted" (p. 35). The one comfort that Sheridan could claim is that "he did not foresee that Mr. Moore would write his Life" (p. 36).

2   MOORE, THOMAS. <u>Memoirs of the Life of the Rt. Honourable Richard Brinsley Sheridan</u>. 5th ed. 2 vols. London: Longman, Rees, Orme, Brown, and Green.

Addresses a new preface (entitled "Preface to the Fifth Edition") to three complaints brought by reviewers against earlier appearances of the book: (1) that Moore had neglected to mention a gift of 4,000 pounds proferred by the prince to Sheridan for the purchase of a seat in Parliament; (2) that Moore had misrepresented the agency by which Sheridan had been released from the sponging house in 1814 (Moore having cited Whitbread as the agent rather than the prince); and (3) that Moore had failed of accuracy in saying that the family of Sheridan had declined a gift of 200 pounds offered them by a sympathetic benefactor while Sheridan was on his deathbed. On the basis of sound documentation Moore reaffirms his original positions on the second and third of these grievances. The first of them (based on an omission made from ignorance not malice) he agrees to correct on examining reliable evidence; and, in an extension of the preface, he reports from trustworthy sources that the prince had indeed sent 3,000-4,000 pounds to Sheridan through an agent but that the gift never reached the beneficiary. The latter part of the preface also provides information intended to vindicate somewhat Whitbread's conduct to Sheridan after the Drury Lane fire and the conduct of those friends and acquaintances who, having neglected to help Sheridan during his hours of need, yet crowded to his funeral. Not only had these latter, in many cases, been invited to the funeral by Sheridan's widow; they had also learned of his distresses too late to help him. For his part, Whitbread, who had seemed to withhold from Sheridan money rightfully his, had been required to do so by legal technicalities and should therefore not be blamed.

1828

1   ANGELO, HENRY. <u>Reminiscences of Henry Angelo, with Memoirs of His Late Father and Friends, Including Numerous Original Anecdotes and Curious Traits of the Most</u>

Celebrated Characters That Have Flourished During the Last
Eighty Years. 2 vols. London: H. Colburn, passim.
    Recalls, from firsthand knowledge of the Sheridans,
Richard's elopement with Elizabeth Linley, his duels with
Captain Mathews, his eventual marriage to Elizabeth
(despite their fathers' earlier objections) thus to bring
to a happy conclusion a potentially Montagu-and-Capulet-
like situation. Passing references to the Sheridans--who
were longtime intimates of the Angelos--occur throughout
the memoir.

1830

1   HUISH, ROBERT. Memoirs of George the Fourth . . . with
    Characteristic Sketches of All the Celebrated Men Who
    Were His Friends and Companions. London: T. Kelly,
    1: 94-98; 2: 236-43.
        Acknowledges that the acquaintance held with Sheridan
    by the Prince of Wales was no doubt capable of
    "enlivening the fancy, and heightening the imagination
    and wit" of the prince but that it also injured "that
    high tone of morals with which the heart of a monarch
    of a Christian country should be especially inspired"
    (1: 95). If indeed the prince declined to assist the
    dying Sheridan, he possibly did so because he had given
    Sheridan 4,000 pounds with which to purchase a seat in
    Parliament, and Sheridan had diverted the money to his
    own uses. The prince therefore felt no obligation to
    assist him again five years later (2: 240-41). While,
    with the death of Sheridan, the prince lost a friend of
    his youth, a companion of his pleasures, and a confi-
    dential servant, he also lost an "abettor of his juvenile
    profligacies" (2: 236).

2   [HUNT, LEIGH.] "The Play-Goer [The Duenna at Covent
    Garden]." Tatler. A Daily Journal of Literature and the
    Stage 1, no. 44 (25 October): 175.
        Reviews the cast of the production (with emphasis given
    to the new singers, Mr. Wilson and Miss Romer) and admires
    them all. "In short, we find ourselves, on this occasion,
    in the rare and happy state of being able to praise all
    the performers."

3   _____. "The Play-Goer [The Duenna at Drury Lane]." Tatler.
    A Daily Journal of Literature and the Stage 1, no. 80
    (6 December): 319-20.
        Acknowledges that The Duenna is not the "cleverest" of
    Sheridan's comedies but holds it to be the "most genial."

1830

It has "the most heartsease and good nature in it; and bears more traces of the gallant lover of Miss Lindley [sic], and less of the tricksome politician and reckless debauchee, than the more finished performances (p. 319). It would probably be more successful, however, if it were played as straight comedy (without the music) or if the songs were duller than they are, for an English opera "will not allow of any real merit in the plot or dialogue." It cannot accommodate an action that divides attention with the music.

4 _____. "The Play-Goer [The Rivals at Drury Lane]." Tatler. A Daily Journal of Literature and the Stage 1, no. 77 (2 December): 307.

Reviews a performance of The Rivals and sets out the desiderata of the major roles (the masculine vigor of Sir Anthony, the "old gentlewomanly staidness" of Mrs. Malaprop, the "lumpish and quivering" cowardice of Acres, the gentlemanliness of Jack, the "comic Luxury" enriching the brogue of Sir Lucius, the "grave insinuation of the ludicrous" in Faulkland, the girlishness of Lydia). "One of the pleasant things in being present at this comedy is to see how Mrs. Malaprop's blunders are hailed by the persons around you. It furnishes a curious insight into the respective amounts of their reading and education."

5 _____. "The Play-Goer [The School for Scandal at Drury Lane]." Tatler. A Daily Journal of Literature and the Stage 1, no. 46 (27 October): 183.

Surmises that Charles Surface, should we see him grown old, would be like Sheridan himself in late years, i.e., hounded even in old age by his proclivity to wine and debt. It is impossible to love even the heartier side of Charles's character because Charles, like most of Sheridan's characters, reflects Sheridan's own uneasy cast of mind. "There is almost always some real pain going on amongst his characters. They are always perplexing, mortifying, or distressing one another; snatching their jokes out of some misery, as if they were playing at snap-dragon. They do not revel in wit for its own sake, like those of Congreve; nor wear a hey-day impudence, for the pleasure of the thing, as in Vanbrugh; nor cultivate an eternal round of airiness and satisfaction, as in good-natured Farquhar. Sheridan's comedy is all-stinging satire. His bees want honey" (pp. 164-65). A performance of the play at Drury Lane on 26 October 1830 did ample credit to it. Macready, as Joseph Surface, did not quite adequately affect the process of betraying himself in his own hypocrisy, but

1832

he was yet a successful Joseph. Other performances were comparably excellent.

6 _____. "The Play-Goer [The School for Scandal at Drury Lane]." Tatler. A Daily Journal of Literature and the Stage 1, no. 70 (24 November): 279-80.
Describes the screen scene and declares it without equal in dramatic literature for "situation and accumulated interest" (p. 279). "We are aware of no scene in the comic drama, that is so heaped up with a succession of positions and perils like this, or is crowned with such a perfect climax. Lady Teazle is kept in the corner like a barrel of gunpowder which you know will sooner or later be fired, and every moment the threat increases, till it comes naturally, though with all the vivacity of abruptness, to a head" (pp. 279-80).

1831

1 HOWARD, ALFRED, ed. The Beauties of Sheridan, Consisting of Selections from His Poems, Dramas, and Speeches. Boston: F. S. Hill, 211 pp.
Provides excerpts of, or selections from, "The Monody on Garrick," "The Love Epistles of Aristaenetus," the fugitive poems, the prologues and epilogues, The Rivals, The School for Scandal, and the speeches.

1832

1 ANON. "Richard Brinsley Sheridan." In The Georgian Era: Memoirs of the Most Eminent Persons, Who Have Flourished in Great Britain, from the Accession of George the First to the Demise of George the Fourth. London: Vizetelly, Branston, 1: 364-76.
Credits Sheridan with considerable charm, wit and eloquence but finds his art to be derivative and his life misdirected. Driven always by ambition and "an insatiable appetite for display" (p. 373), he would not rest until he moved in the first society and enjoyed the applause of the multitude. Consequently, he neglected his private responsibilities while promoting his public character and eventually "beheld, with indifference, his respectability vanish, his pecuniary resources diminish, and his liabilities enormously increase" (p. 373). His patriotism was undoubtedly great, but it could not fully atone "for the injuries he inflicted on many of his fellow-countrymen, by his

1832

reckless profligacy, as an individual" (p. 374).

2   GENEST, JOHN. <u>Some Account of the English Stage from the</u>
    <u>Restoration in 1660 to 1830</u>. 10 vols. Bath: H. E.
    Carrington.
        Contains, scattered throughout volumes 5 through 8,
    notes on the Drury Lane calendar for the period of
    Sheridan's management. Volume 5 also contains
    references (with cast lists and miscellaneous comments)
    to the initial performances at Covent Garden of <u>The</u>
    <u>Rivals</u> and <u>The Duenna</u>.

                        1835

*1   MOORE, THOMAS. <u>Memoirs of the Life of the Right Honourable</u>
     <u>Richard Brinsley Sheridan</u>. Paris: Baudry's European
     Library, 494 pp.
        Reprints 1825.9. Listed in <u>NUC</u> (pre-1956), vol. 393,
     p. 456.

                        1836

1   ANON. "The School for Scandal." <u>Times</u> (London),
    17 February, p. 6.
        Notes that of the original cast of <u>The School for</u>
    <u>Scandal</u> only Miss Hopkins survives and of the original
    cast of <u>The Critic</u> only Jack Bannister survives. Although
    a bit troubled by the gout, Bannister is now cheerfully
    enjoying his seventy-sixth year.

2   WRAXALL, SIR NATHANIEL WILLIAM. <u>Historical Memoirs of His</u>
    <u>Own Time</u>. New ed., rev. 4 vols. London: R. Bentley,
    passim.
        Includes, in a broad account of English political
    history between 1772 and 1784, references to Sheridan's
    maiden speech in the House of Commons and to early events
    in his political career; his motion of censure against
    Lord North's administration, his rise to an under-
    secretaryship of state in the Rockingham ministry, his
    appointment to a secretaryship of treasury in the
    Coalition Ministry of Fox and Lord North. Note: These
    <u>Memoirs</u> first appeared in a two-volume edition in 1815.
    The current annotation derives from a one-volume reprint,
    <u>Historical Memoirs of My Own Time</u> (Philadelphia: Lea and
    Blanchard, 1845, 524 pp.).

3   _____. <u>Posthumous Memoirs of His Own Time</u>. 3 vols. London:

Richard Bentley, 1: 36-56 and passim.
Admires Sheridan as "the most highly endowed man whom
we have beheld in our time" (1: 42) but laments the sad
irony that his ending was so unlike his beginning. As a
young man, he was the flower of Parliament. His wit and
poise in debate held every ear, and no opponent could
best him. But his irregular habits cheated him of his
promise. Had he but disciplined his character he would
surely have risen to ministerial rank. But his weakness
for drink and his elaborate mismanagement of his own
exchequer rendered him unfit for singular public service,
however honorable and honest he invariably was in every
feature of political principle. At the end, his figure
grotesque and his fortunes dissipated, he gave a sad
image to the world, the image of wasted genius and
unfulfilled hopes. Other passages (scattered throughout
volumes 2 and 3) touch Sheridan's contributions to
major political events between 1784 and 1789; e.g.,
his opposition to Pitt's India Bill, his celebrated
speech in the House of Commons against Warren Hastings,
his defense of Mrs. Fitzherbert, his conduct during
the first regency crisis.

1837

1   ANON. "The Abuse of Riches." Waldie's Select Circulating
    Library, part 2, no. 26, 26 December pp. 415-16.
        Prints, with explanatory comment, a sermon supposed
    to have been written by Sheridan for delivery by a
    clergyman visiting him at his country house near
    Osterley. Directed against a gentleman who had offended
    his neighbors by ungenerous conduct to the poor, it
    teaches a lesson of charity.

2   ANON. "Gallery of Illustrious Irishmen.--No. VIII.
    Sheridan.--Part I." Dublin University Magazine
    9 (April): 469-85.
        Presents Sheridan's life as representing a period of
    transition between a simpler, more graceful past, and
    a comfortable, yet less gratifying present. Sheridan
    is "The last of the dramatists, among the last of the
    wits of that elder and purer school" (p. 469). His life
    affords an eventful and instructive history endowed both
    with incentive and warning, and the chronicle of his
    earlier years (through 1777) reveals him to be a man
    schooled not in books but in quickened observation and
    rapid intuition. "Though superficial as a statesman,
    and not very profound as a thinker, he was admirably

1837

versed in the volume of life" (p. 484).

3   ANON. "Gallery of Illustrious Irishmen.--No. VIII.
    Sheridan.--Part II." Dublin University Magazine 9 (May):
    600-615.
        Continues the rendering of Sheridan's life begun in
    the April issue (1837.2) by surveying his major theatrical
    career (the happiest years of his life) and admiring his
    plays for their characterization and satiric wit (however
    shallow and tenuous they are in moral substance). The
    next phase of his life (his earlier political career)
    gives full expression to his highly social character:
    "a pleasing countenance--a general tone of sense--the
    companionable powers of wit and vivacity--the ready
    sympathy, with all the varying moods--the quick rebound
    of mind--the salient wit--the ready repartee-the tone
    of mind equally capable of seriousness and levity, as
    occasion may require" (p. 615). If subject to a
    controlling prudence, such a character can exert broad
    and powerful influence behind the scenes.

4   ANON. "Gallery of Illustrious Irishmen.--No. VIII.
    Sheridan--Part III." Dublin University Magazine
    9 (June): 672-95.
        Concludes the sketch developed through the two
    preceding issues (1837.2, 3) by describing the chief
    moments of Sheridan's political career and accounting in
    general terms for the eventual ruination of his life.
    For a period of years, after the death of his wife in
    1792, he more and more seemed a man for whom nothing
    could be done. Devoted to drink and to bankruptcy, he
    projected a character not compatible with friendship.
    His friends therefore fell away. He was at length
    "degenerated into a confirmed drunkard; and, with all his
    amiability and talent, disqualified for the uses of life,
    as much by this disgusting and debasing propensity, as
    by his total unfitness for affairs" (p. 693). He died
    "an object of pity and regret" (p. 695).

5   ANON. "Memoirs of Sheridan." Bentley's Miscellany
    1 (1837): 419-27.
        Recounts Sheridan's life as an instance of the paradox
    that celebrated wits give rise to melancholy biographies.
    "In nine out of ten cases, what is such a memoir other
    than a record of acute suffering, the almost inseparable
    attendant of that thoughtless and mercurial temperament
    which cannot, or will not, conform to the staid usages of
    society; which makes ten enemies where it makes one
    friend; is engaged in a constant warfare with common

sense, and lives for the day, letting the morrow shift
for itself? (p. 419) Sheridan's case, however, is
fitter subject for regret than indignation. He was given
no early training in order and frugality. Without birth,
profession, or income, he achieved celebrity. He paid
the penalty for his errors and was in truth a man far
worthier in his character than many supposed models of
probity.

6   ANON. "Modern Biography. Sheridan." Southern Literary
    Messenger 3 (August): 470-72.
        Considers biography in general (and Moore's life of
    Sheridan in particular) a damaging enterprise because it
    invades the private life of the subject and vitiates the
    value his memory might have as an example to the young.
    Sheridan's biography reveals a wasted talent. His work
    speaks better for him than his life does, but even it
    (especially his poetry) does not justify the accolades
    given him in his own time. He lived too much among
    mankind and was too much the wit to be a poet; he was
    too ready and graceful a conversationalist and enjoyed
    too fatal a facility with society ever to produce poems
    of permanent merit. "Sheridan was more of an improvisa-
    tore than a poet; and, by the way, it may be curious to
    observe, that nothing yet has come from improvisation"
    (p. 472).

7   CUNNINGHAM, GEORGE GODFREY. "Richard Brinsley Sheridan."
    In Lives of Eminent and Illustrious Englishmen from
    Alfred the Great to the Latest Times. On an Original
    Plan. Glasgow: A. Fullarton, 7: 165-85.
        Recounts Sheridan's life, giving emphasis to his
    political career and quoting liberally from his best
    speeches (most notably the Westminster Hall speech
    against Warren Hastings). If, as a result of
    disappointment, sickness, and improvidence, his political
    conduct at the close of his career is subject to question,
    his literary career in no sense is. It stands above
    reproach. His reputation for warmth, wit, and
    conviviality will also forever claim a high place in
    popular esteem.

1839

1   BROUGHAM, HENRY, LORD. Historical Sketches of Statesmen
    Who Flourished in the Time of George III. 1st ser.
    London: Charles Knight, pp. 211-18.

1839

Pays tribute to Sheridan's great success as an orator,
a success earned even against large odds (e.g., little
classical training, little early association with
political minds, inauspicious social background). Little
admiration belongs, however, to his conduct as a man and
a statesman. "As a statesman, he is without a place in
any class, or of any rank; it would be incorrect and
flattering to call him a bad, or a hurtful, or a
short-sighted, or a middling statesman; he was not
statesman at all" (p. 217). As a man, "his character
stood confessedly low; his intemperate habits, and his
pecuniary embarrassments, did not merely tend to
imprudent conduct, by which himself alone might be the
sufferer; they involved his family in the same fate"
(p. 217). His life is a warning to the virtuous.

1840

1 HUNT, LEIGH, ed. "Biographical and Critical Sketch." In
   The Dramatic Works of Richard Brinsley Sheridan. London:
   Edward Moxon, pp. vii-xv.
       Undertakes to explain the waste of Sheridan's gifts,
   remarking his early habits of delay, his high animal
   spirits, his love of luxury. Characteristic of the
   "mistrusting and artificial habits of his mind," however,
   was "the extreme and constant care" with which his plays
   "were elaborated, and brought to their final state of
   terseness and polish" (p. xiii).

2 SMYTH, WILLIAM. Memoir of Mr. Sheridan. Leeds: J. Cross,
   74 pp.
       Draws upon experiences within the Sheridan household
   (as tutor, between 1792 and 1796, to Sheridan's son Tom)
   to demonstrate that "happiness is connected with
   self-control" (p. 74). Certainly gifted with splendid
   genius and greatness of heart, Sheridan lived a life
   committed by deep affection to family, friends, and
   country; but, lacking self-control from his earliest youth,
   he more and more lost the capacity to deny himself any
   whim, and he died broken by self-indulgence. Despite his
   brilliant mind and charming presence, he abandoned his
   character to great carelessness. "It is not to be
   expressed, the rage and paroxyms [sic] of fury into which
   people who had to do with Mr. Sheridan were often thrown
   (and indeed all of them some time or other), by a conduct
   of this nature. Letters unanswered, promises, engagements,
   the most natural expectations totally disregarded. He
   seemed quite lawless and out of the pale of human

sympathies and obligations" (p. 52). Numerous anecdotes illustrate these failings in Sheridan, and the extra-ordinary way he had of disarming animus in others.

1841

1 [MACAULAY, THOMAS BABINGTON.] "Comic Dramatists of the Restoration." Edinburgh Review 72 (January): 490-528.
    Mentions Sheridan very briefly as a failed imitator of Congreve but as the wittiest English dramatist since Congreve. The Language in Congreve's Old Bachelor "is resplendit with wit and eloquence--which indeed are so abundant that the fools come in for an ample share--and yet preserves a certain colloquial air, a certain indescribable ease, of which Wycherley had given no example, and which Sheridan in vain attempted to imitate" (p. 515). "Wycherley had wit; but the wit of Congreve far outshines that of every comic writer, except Sheridan, who has arisen within the last two centuries" (p. 528).

1842

1 ANON. "Anecdote of Sheridan." Times (London), 24 September, p. 5.
    Recalls Sheridan as saying that the life of a theater manager is like that of a prison ordinary, for both must preside over executions. One oversees the deaths of criminals, the other of aspiring authors. "The number of authors whom he was forced to extinguish was, he said, a perpetual literary massacre, that made St. Bartholomew's altogether shrink in comparison."

2 ANON. "Memoir of the Right Honourable Richard Brinsley Sheridan." In The Speeches of the Right Honourable Richard Brinsley Sheridan. With a Sketch of His Life. Edited by a Constitutional Friend [Sir John Phillipart?]. London: P. Martin, 1: i-xvi.
    Bases a short account of Sheridan's life on the premise that "The source of Sheridan's misfortunes was ambition, or an insatiable appetite for display." But "the same vice which ultimately led to his ruin, was also the cause of his celebrity" (p. xv).

3 ANON. "Richard Brinsley Sheridan." Fraser's Magazine 26 (July): 103-11.
    Provides a "slight sketch" such as one might glimpse on "turning over the leaves of a volume in a cursory

1842

way" (p. 103), a sketch the more authentic for represent-
ing its subject "in his private circle and domestic
society" rather than in his public endeavors. For
example, the experience of an Irish lad who sought
unsuccessfully for many days to see Sheridan in London
illustrates that Sheridan, who had left Ireland at a
young age, was less sensitive to the appeals of
individual Irishmen (in this case a kinsman) than he was
to the larger social causes of the Irish nation.

<u>1843</u>

1   ANON. "The Sheridan Family" <u>Times</u> (London), 4 December,
    p. 5.
        Announces the deaths of Sheridan's son Charles Brinsley
    Sheridan (at age forty-eight) and his grandson, Frank
    Sheridan, son of the playwright's own older son Thomas.

<u>1844</u>

1   ANON. "Charles B. Sheridan, Esq." <u>Gentleman's Magazine</u>
    175, n. s. 21 (April): 433-34.
        Provides an obituary notice--with a brief biographical
    sketch--of Sheridan's second son, who died on 29 November
    1843 at his house in Bolton Street, Piccadilly.

<u>1846</u>

1   HUNT, LEIGH, ed. "Biographical and Critical Sketch." In
    <u>The Dramatic Work of Richard Brinsley Sheridan</u>. London:
    Edward Moxon, pp. vii-xv.
        Reprints 1840.1.

<u>1847</u>

1   BAKER, W. "To the Editor of the Times." <u>Times</u> (London),
    2 December, p. 6.
        Insists, in a letter addressed through the <u>Times</u> to
    Richard Brinsley Sheridan, that one William Stewart
    Sheridan, an accused matricide, was identified to him
    from a reliable source (viz., the sister of the accused)
    as a grandson of the playwright and that reference to the
    playwright's tippling, which had given offense to the
    Sheridan family (see 1847.2) was made for the scientific
    purpose of establishing "hereditary predisposition" in
    the accused. Any pain caused by these reports to the

family of the playwright is much regretted.

2   SHERIDAN, RICHARD BRINSLEY. "To the Editor of the Times."
    Times (London), 30 November, p. 8.
        Addresses through the Times a letter to W. Baker,
    coroner for Middlesex, directing him to contradict
    publicly his false declaration that one William Stewart
    Sheridan, an accused Hackney matricide, was the grandson
    of the celebrated Sheridan and that Sheridan "never spoke
    in the House of Commons without the inspiration of
    half-a-pint of brandy."

3   VERITAS. "Mr. Sheridan and Mr. Baker." Times (London),
    3 December, p. 6.
        Derides W. Baker, the coroner for Middlesex, for taking
    as truth the testimony of a drunken Hackney wanderer that
    she and her brother, an accused matricide, were the
    grandchildren of the celebrated Sheridan. Mr. Baker
    should have taken measures to validate such a story
    before risking insult to a respected family. He might
    simply have asked the Hackney woman who her father had
    been.

                              1848

1   ANON. "Memoir of the Right Honourable Richard Brinsley
    Sheridan." In The Speeches of the Right Honourable
    Brinsley Sheridan. With a Sketch of His Life. Edited
    by a Constitutional Friend [Sir John Phillipart?].
    London: P. Martin, 1: i-xvi.
        Reprints 1842.2. Rev. in 1848.2.

2   WHIPPLE, EDWIN P. "Richard Brinsley Sheridan." North
    American Review 66 (January): 73-110.
        Mentions two new issues of Sheridan's work (Leigh
    Hunt's edition of his plays, and his speeches as edited
    by a "Constitutional Friend"), then recounts his life in
    effort to "set forth the talents of this remarkable
    adept in mystification and Regus Professor of appearances"
    (p. 75). While ambitious, indolent, unprincipled,
    shallow, vain, lascivious, and immoral--one whose "good-
    humored selfishness and . . . graceful heartlessness were
    his best substitutes for virtue" (p. 73)--Sheridan was
    not the most abandoned of rogues. Perhaps his
    intemperance and sloth brought misery to his family, but
    at least he did not, through "bigotry or lust of power"
    (p. 109), ruin or injure his nation. He does not, then,
    deserve complete condemnation, but neither does he merit

1848

sentimental excuses. He achieved more fame than his
moderate powers might reasonably hope to earn for him.
His life enjoyed its share of pleasure. And he had no
right to expect "that the rakes and good-fellows, his
companions of the bottle and the debauch, would be the
bankers of his poverty, or the consolers of his dying
hours" (p. 110).

1850

1 ANON. "Editorial Introduction." In The School for Scandal.
   French's Standard Drama Series. New York: Samuel French,
   2 unnumbered pages.
       Admires the craftsmanship of so young a playwright as
   Sheridan but expresses misgivings about "the moral
   tendencies" of the piece. Charles, for example, is "too
   leniently dealt with" by the playwright. "We could never
   admire that species of generosity, which would rob a
   creditor to lavish money upon one, who might have been in
   no greater want of it than he to whom it was legally due."
   Sir Peter is the least reprehensible character in the
   play, "and even he is disposed to make light of the
   supposed peccadillo of Joseph in the fourth act."

1851

1 WHIPPLE, EDWIN P. "Richard Brinsley Sheridan." In Essays
   and Reviews. 2d ed. Boston: Ticknor, Reed, and Fields,
   2: 250-302.
       Reprints 1848.2.

1852

1 ANON. "Sheridaniana." New-York Daily Times, 3 November,
   p. 5.
       Prints anecdotes illustrating Sheridan's tendency to
   accommodate unto himself other people's ideas, properties,
   and phrases. For example, having pretended not to hear
   Lord Holland repeat to him a colleague's reference to the
   Addington Peace as one "of which everybody is glad, and
   nobody proud," Sheridan used the phrase two hours later
   in one of his own speeches.

2 GOODRICH, CHAUNCEY A[LLEN]. "Mr. Sheridan." In Select
   British Eloquence: Embracing the Best Speeches Entire, of
   Great Britain for the Last Two Centuries; with Sketches

of Their Lives, an Estimate of Their Genius, and Notes,
Critical and Explanatory. New York: Harper & Brothers,
pp. 399-404. Reissued 1853, 1854, 1855, 1856, 1861, 1864,
1868, 1870, 1872, 1874, 1875, 1884. New York: Bobbs-
Merrill, 1963.

Reviews Sheridan's career as a speaker and observes of
it that after the Westminster Hall speech against Warren
Hastings in 1788 (the speech included in this collection),
Sheridan never attempted "that lofty strain of eloquence
which gained him such rapturous applause on this occasion"
(p. 401). Thereafter, good sense and wit characterized
his speaking as did a gift for detecting the weak
arguments of his adversary and subjecting these weaknesses
to a severe raillery. By these devices Sheridan made
himself "much more formidable to Mr. Pitt, during his
long and difficult administration, than many in the
Opposition ranks of far greater information and reasoning
abilities" (p. 402). In general, he neglected close study
of the issues he debated but turned for information to
his colleagues. "And such was the quickness and
penetration of his intellect, that he was able, with
surprising facility, to make himself master of the
information thus collected for his use, and to pour it
out with a freshness and vivacity which were so much the
greater because his mind was left free and unencumbered
by the effort to obtain it" (p. 402).

3   S[IGMOND], G[EORGE] G[ABRIEL.] ed. "Life of Sheidan." In
    The Dramatic Works of the Right Honourable Richard
    Brinsley Sheridan. Bohn's Standard Library. London:
    H. G. Bohn, pp. 1-206.

Seeks to rescue Sheridan from ignominy by remarking
that his celebrated faults were no more severe than the
comparable failings of illustrious contemporaries. The
problem is that his personal weaknesses managed to
overwhelm his later years and color the record of his
life. Of available biographical accounts, Watkins's
reflects a severe political bias against Sheridan; Moore
provides the most reliable narrative. On Moore's Memoirs,
then, Sigmond bases his own detailed biography, providing
discussions of the poems and of the plays (as to
composition and production) and affirming the conviction
that "Probably there never was a dramatist who more
thoroughly understood the exact province of comedy than
did Sheridan" (p. 68). Whatever faults his characters
might exhibit, "they are portrayed so as to instruct our
understanding, but not to shock our feelings" (p. 68).

1853

1 GILFALLEN, GEORGE. "Modern British Orators.--No. II. R. B.
   Sheridan." Hogg's Instructor, 3d ser. 1 (November):
   361-70.
       Judges Sheridan as "one of those moral wrecks over whom
   your grief cannot be profound" (p. 362) and pictures him
   in Parliament "enouncing his false brilliancies of
   sentiment, and his real brilliancies of wit, with the same
   lack-lustre and coarse physiognomy inspired into meaning
   and power by two sparkling, splendid eyes, and in the
   same high, but husky tones, dying away occasionally into
   inglorious hiccups, or into grunts of stifled, but
   irrepressible laughter" 9p. 362). As an orator, Sheridan
   spoke with a thick voice, but his manner was nonetheless
   theatrical and vigorous. He took delight in such
   rhetorical turns as antithesis, apostrophe, and
   exaggeration; his sallies of wit, while not really
   numerous, were often happy; his presence was
   self-possessed, and he evinced (best of all) "a vein of
   strong good sense, which he brought more effectually and
   entirely to bear upon public affairs, as none of it was
   employed upon the care of his private conduct" (p. 364).
   Yet his defects were numerous: he lacked taste and was
   often "tawdry and vulgar" (p. 365). He was given to
   facile "amplifications" of language and text, i.e.,
   "changes are rung too long upon one idea" (p. 365); and
   (worst of all), "He was not deeply in earnest" (p. 366).

2 MOORE, THOMAS. Memoirs, Journal, and Correspondence, edited
   by Lord John Russell, M.P. 8 vols. London: Longman,
   Brown, Green, and Longmans, 1853-1856, passim.
       Devotes many entries--especially between the years 1818
   and 1825--to anecdotal information derived from
   individuals who had known Sheridan and whose acquaintance
   with him might supply Moore with materials for his
   biography of Sheridan. Among those interviewed are Dr.
   Parr, a school master of Sheridan's at Harrow, Lord
   Holland, nephew of Charles James Fox, Sukey Ogle, sister
   of Sheridan's second wife, Dr. Bain, Sheridan's physician,
   William Smyth, once tutor to Sheridan's son Tom. An entry
   for November 1825 finds one of Moore's friends, John
   Wilson, feeling the newly published biography to outshine
   its subject. Note: The present annotation is taken from
   a single-volume issue of the Memoirs edited with some
   abridgment by Lord John Russell (London: Longman, Green,
   Longmans, and Roberts, 1860, 750 pp.)

3 _____. Memoirs of the Life of the Rt. Hon. Richard Brinsley

Sheridan. 2 vols. New York: Redfield.
Reprints 1825.10.

1854

1 GILFALLEN, GEORGE. "Modern British Orators.--No. II. R. B.
   Sheridan." Eclectic Magazine, 31 (January): 19-28.
   Reprints 1853.1.

2 KELLY, WALTER KEATING, ed. Erotica: The Elegies of
   Propertius; the Satyricon of Petronius, and the Kisses of
   Johannes Secundus, Literally Translated, and Accompanied
   by Poetical Versions from Various Sources, to which are
   Added the Love Epistles of Aristaenetus. Translated by
   R. Brinsley Sheridan and Mr. Halhed. London: H. G. Bohn,
   pp. 431-96.
      Prints the poems without comment.

3 PATMORE, PETER GEORGE. "Richard Brinsley Sheridan and Thomas
   Sheridan." In My Friends and Acquaintance, Being
   Memorials, Mind-Portraits and Personal Recollections of
   Deceased Celebrities of the Nineteenth Century with
   Selections from Their Unpublished Letters. London:
   Saunders and Otley, 3: 255-340.
      Confesses no close acquaintance with Sheridan or his
   son but acknowledges their interest to literary history
   and draws upon William Smyth's memoirs (1840.2) to sketch
   the characters of both of them. Later sections of the
   discussion describe three Sheridan manuscripts given to
   the author "About two and twenty years ago" by a "valued
   friend" (p. 266). They include Sheridan's autograph
   corrections on a prompt copy of Thompson's The Stranger,
   the burlesque burletta "Ixion," a full "Fairy Opera" in
   three acts, and a two-act "Musical Afterpiece." The
   manuscripts also include two farces thought to be written
   by Tom Sheridan.

1855

*1 ANON. The Speeches of the Rt. Hon. the Earl of Chatham, the
    Rt. Hon. Richard Brinsley Sheridan, and the Rt. Hon. Lord
    Erskine and the Rt. Hon. Charles James Fox . . . with
    Biographical Memoirs and Introductions and Explanatory
    Notes, edited by a barrister. 2 vols. 4th ed. London:
    Aylott and Co.
       Listed in NUC, 460: 116.

1855

2   C[ALCRAFT], J. W.   "The Dramatic Writers of Ireland.--No. VI.
    Richard Brinsley Sheridan." Dublin University Magazine
    46 (July): 38-55.
        Describes Sheridan's life through matters of fact,
    protesting that his "pretensions as a writer, his
    qualities as a legislator," and "his frailties as a
    man" (p. 55) need no longer be reviewed. "If he had
    possessed a greater share of worldly judgment and
    prudence, with a more limited genius, tempered by a
    methodical mind, his life would have been happier for
    himself, more profitable to his friends, his family, and
    dependants, and the moral lesson it supplies would have
    been less distressing, though, perhaps, not equally
    instructive" (p. 55).

3   [CALCRAFT, J. W.] "Richard Brinsley Sheridan." Eclectic
    Magazine 36 (September): 656-72.
        Reprints 1855.2.

4   HARSHA, DAVIS A[DDISON]. "Sheridan Brinsely Sheridan." In
    The Most Eminent Orators and Statesmen of Ancient and
    Modern Times. Containing Sketches of their Lives,
    Specimens of Their Eloquence, and an Estimate of Their
    Genius. New York: Charles Scribner, pp. 240-55.
        Draws upon such sources as Wraxall (1836.3) and
    Brougham (1839.1) to chronicle Sheridan's political
    career and deduce his gifts as an orator: "The forte of
    Sheridan lay in the powerful effusions of brilliant wit,
    mingled with humor and fun." He "possessed a remarkable
    versatility of talents--extensive knowledge of the human
    heart--great powers of fancy--exuberant stores of wit--a
    deep, clear, mellifluous voice, whose tones were perfectly
    suited to invective, descriptive, pathetic, or impassioned
    declamation--a singularly piercing eye--an animated and
    impressive countenance--a fiery and dauntless spirit that
    never faltered before an antagonist,--and a manner
    altogether striking, admirable and impressive" (p. 251).

1856

1   ROGERS, SAMUEL. Recollections of the Table-Talk of Samuel
    Rogers to Which is Added Ponsoniana, edited by Alexander
    Dyce. London: E. Moxon, pp. 63-71 and passim.
        Includes anecdotes describing some of Sheridan's
    exploits as a prankster: e.g., his playing dead to
    frighten Mrs. Crewe, his having one of Mrs. Crewe's
    tenants introduce himself to her as Joseph Richardson,
    an intimate friend of Sheridan's, his confiscating a

handsome phaeton and driving it off to Vauxhall, etc.
Other anecdotes describe the force of Sheridan's oratory
against Hastings, his infatuation (after the death of
his first wife) with Pamela, the adopted daughter of
Madame de Genlis, the play of his wit while he was
drinking wine, the brilliance of his eyes, the message
sent from his deathbed to Lady Bessborough that his eyes
"will look up to the coffin-lid as brightly as ever"
(p. 70).

1858

1 MOORE, THOMAS. Memoirs of the Life of the Rt. Hon. Richard
   Brinsley Sheridan. 2 vols. New York: Redfield.
      Reprints 1853.3.

2 PEACOCK, T HOMAS L OVE . "Memoirs of Percy Bysshe Shelley."
   Fraser's Magazine 57 (June): 643-58.
      Includes a judgment of Shelley's against comedy in
   general and The School for Scandal in particular: "I
   induced him one evening to accompany me to a representation of the School for Scandal. When, after the scenes
   which exhibited Charles Surface in his jollity, the
   scene returned, in the fourth act, to Joseph's library,
   Shelley said to me,--'I see the purpose of this comedy.
   It is to associate virtue with bottles and glasses, and
   villany [sic] with books.' I had great difficulty to
   make him stay to the end. He often talked of 'the
   withering and perverting spirit of comedy.' I do not
   think he ever went to another" (p. 658).

1859

1 [EARLE, WILLIAM.] Sheridan and His Times By an Octogenarian,
   Who Stood By His Knee in Youth and Sat at His Table in
   Manhood. 2 vols. London: J. F. Hope.
      Declares for itself the aim of correcting earlier
   biography in three ways: (1) presenting Sheridan in his
   own moral milieu, apart from the severer judgments of
   later times, (2) supplying anecdotes fully reflective of
   his character, and (3) endowing his story with an
   intimacy made possible only through personal acquaintance
   with him. "Knowing Sheridan in our boyhood, when we
   stood at his knee--in our manhood when seated with him at
   the festive board--in his night-gown and slippers--in his
   every-day costume--in his every-day nature--in that mental
   deshabille which easily and gracefully displayed its own

powers, fluently and refined--we trust that those who may
do us the honour of running their eye down the following
pages will rise from their task fully satisfied that we
have accomplished our object" (1: 7). Reviewed in 1860.1.

1860

1   T., L. J. "Richard Brinsley Sheridan." Living Age
      64 (31 March): 771-85.
        Condemns the bad treatment given Sheridan by his
biographers and complains that the most recent biographical account (Sheridan and His Times by an Octogenarian,
1859.1) makes no improvement. The book "teems with
tokens of a mind unable either to think clearly or to
express its meaning in straightforward language" (p. 771).
While Sheridan's character must post enigmas to any
biographer, it may certainly be said of him "That he had
many rare and winning gifts of mind and soul; that his
impulses were mainly right and noble; that most of those
who knew him best seem also to have loved him most
dearly; that his ambition, large as it was and growing
with what it fed on, seldom, if ever, out-ran his high-
toned honesty of purpose, or turned his proud self-
reliance into uncharity and overweening self-conceit; that
he loved his political principles, however faulty they may
have been, better than party, and never sacrificed either
to a greed for worldly advancement at any price" (p. 785).
A lengthy sketch of Sheridan's life affirms these
judgments.

*2   _____. "Richard Brinsley Sheridan." Universal Review
      3 (1860): 75-98.
        Reprinted in 1860.1. Cited in 1890.1, p. x.

3   THOMSON, KATHERINE BYERLEY, and THOMSON, JOHN COCKBURN.
      "Richard Brinsley Sheridan." In The Wits and Beaux of
      Society. London: James Hogg and Sons, 2: 97-161.
        Traces the fame of Sheridan to its zenith in the
Westminster Hall speech against Warren Hastings and to
its nadir in the quarrel with Samuel Whitbread after the
destruction of Drury Lane Theatre in 1809. Beginning as
a dunce and ending as a profligate, he aggravated his own
decline by swindling, drinking, and debauching and by
disregarding all that is "right and beautiful in conduct.
If he went down to the grave a pauper and a debtor, he
had made his own bed, and in it he was to lie" (p. 157).
But he claims pity at last because he suffered
abandonment in the hour of his need, "awakening to the

terrible truth of the hollowness of man and the rottenness
of the world"! (p. 99) To imagaine him in this suffering
is to love him despite his faults. (See 1860.4.)

4 WHARTON, GRACE, AND WHARTON, PHILIP [pseud]. "Richard
   Brinsley Sheridan." In The Wits and Beaux of Society.
   London: James Hogg and Sons, 2: 97-161.
       See 1860.3.

1861

1 NORTON, CAROLINE. "Books of Gossip: Sheridan and His
   Biographers." Macmillan's Magazine 3 (January): 173-79.
       Excoriates several "anecdotical" biographers who slay
   Sheridan's character by glibly calling him a criminal,
   an improvident, a gambler, a drunk, a womanizer, and a
   scapegrace. A new biography based upon properly validated
   sources is then promised by Mrs. Norton herself. Singled
   out for special contempt is the treatment of Sheridan in
   The Wits and Beaux of Society (1860.3.), a work based
   upon unvalidated anecdotes. Biographical books and
   sketches by Watkins (1817.4), Moore (1825.9), Earle
   (1859.1), and Leigh Hunt (1840.1) also come under attack.

1862

1 FRY, ALFRED A[UGUSTUS]. A Lecture on the Right Honourable
   R. Brinsley Sheridan Delivered at Constantinople.
   Constantinople: [Schimpff?], 32 pp.
       Summarizes the life of Sheridan in such a way as to
   conclude that he was a man of unparalleled intellectual
   power, one who waved the wand of enchantment over the
   theater, the legislature, and the supper table. To his
   character, however, there was a darker side. The full
   moral of Sheridan's life must take into account his lack
   of self-control. But even so, it should be said of
   Sheridan as Sterne says of Lefevre (in Tristram Shandy)
   "That when the Accusing Spirit inscribes the follies of
   such men in the Register of Heaven's Archives, the
   Recording Angel blots out the record with a tear" (p. 32).

1863

1 ANON. "English Manners Upon the French Stage." Times
   (London), 29 April, p. 10.
       Summarizes the plot of a French comedy called Un Homme

1863

de Rien (by Aylic Langlé) in which Sheridan, the central
figure, displays a natural gallantry and scorn of money.
For the sake of gallantry he throws away a diamond worth
2,000 pounds, and, gallant to the end, he bests by wit and
graciousness the jealous aristocrats who would embarrass
and belittle him.

2   BETA; J. C.; AND De MESCHIN, THOMAS. "Sheridan and Lord
    Belgrave's Greek." Notes and Queries, 3d ser. 3
    (11 April): 294-95.
        Offers three responses to the query raised by
    Fitzhopkins (1863.3) about Sheridan's correcting Lord
    Belgrave's Greek. Beta quotes an account of the episode
    given in Thomas De Quincey's Autobiographic Sketches but
    feels the most reliable account of the matter to come from
    the parliamentary history. De Meschin mentions a version
    of the affair in Sheridaniana (1826.9). J. C. quotes with
    belief a note appended to the satirical poem the Pursuits
    of Literature (1797) in which Sheridan is actually
    credited with having a better command of the passage
    quoted from Demosthenes than Belgrave has.

3   FITZHOPKINS. "Sheridan's Greek." Notes and Queries, 3d ser.
    3 (14 March): 209.
        Seeks a reliable source for an anecdote, quoted here
    from Anecdotes of Impudence (London, 1827), p. 108, in
    which Sheridan, in responding to a speech given in the
    House of Commons by Lord Belgrave, presumes to correct
    Belgrave's Greek.

4   LLOYD, GEORGE. "Sheridan's Greek." Notes and Queries, 3d
    ser. 3 (16 May): 395.
        Declares Sheridan fully capable of braving the House of
    Commons with impudence and quotes yet another version
    (see 1863.2; 3) of the anecdote in which he corrects Lord
    Belgrave's Greek. In this version Sheridan found, upon
    entering the House of Commons, a paper on which the Greek
    passage had been written. He committed the passage to
    memory (not knowing how he might use it) and seized the
    opportunity, when he had it, to correct Lord Belgrave's
    mistake.

5   S., B. "Sheridan and Lord Belgrave's Greek." Notes and
    Queries, 3d ser. 3 (25 April): 329-30.
        Agrees with the earlier correspondent J. C. (1863.2)
    that Sheridan corrected Lord Belgrave's faulty Greek. It
    is not likely that Sheridan sought to dupe the sitting
    House with gibberish. In further proof of Lord Belgrave's
    blunder, B. S. quotes an unpublished lampoon, in his own

possession, presumably written by Sheridan, alluding to
the episode.

1864

1   JACOX, FRANCIS. "Sheridan's Faulkland: Typically
     Considered." [Colburn's] New Monthly Magazine
     132 (December): 414-21.
        Rejects the popular sentiment that Faulkland's
     character is dull to play and to contemplate. In truth,
     Faulkland's subtle psychological malady places him in a
     literary tradition peopled by such fascinating (if
     troubled) lovers as Addison's Will Wormwood, Prior's
     Henry, Goethe's own fantastic youth, Peacock's Scythrop
     (of Nightmare Abbey), George Eliot's Philip Wakem (of The
     Mill on the Floss), and the mad lover of Tennyson's Maud
     (among yet others).

1866

1   MORLEY, HENRY. "Miss Herbert as Lady Teazle." In The
     Journal of a London Playgoer from 1851 to 1866. London:
     G. Routledge, pp. 381-83.
        Comments admiringly (in the entry for 10 February
     1866) upon Miss Herbert's performance of Lady Teazle at
     the St. James Theatre, a performance blending city and
     country manners in proper proportions. The play itself,
     which endures because it spends its wit not just on
     passing follies but upon the vices of society, also
     merits admiration. "The lightest wit, if it be true wit,
     is durable as granite when it deals with the essentials
     of human nature, and not with the mere accidents of
     passing fashion" (p. 381). (The Journal is reissued
     among Morley's Books and Papers in 1891 by Routledge.)

1867

1   RAE, W[ILLIAM] F[RASER]. "Richard Brinsley Sheridan."
     Fortnightly Review 8, n. s. 2 (1 July - 1 Decmeber):
     310-32.
        Judges Sheridan as one who "wrote, as he lived, for
     the sake of effect" (p. 320). He was not a man of genius;
     as a writer he achieved only the second rank. Had he
     lived at a later time, he would have formed his ambitions
     after goals very different from those he actually chose.
     He would "drink less claret; he would write articles

1867

instead of comedies, and he might not aspire to manage
Drury Lane Theatre. His speeches in Parliament would be
quite as powerful without being at all flowery; they
would contain more sarcasms than tropes. To be the boon
companion of the Prince of Wales would not appear to him
the greatest object of his ambition" (p. 332). But,
being a child of his age, he determined to be precisely
what he was, succeeding (much like Dryden) through force
of will rather than through native genius. Despite the
follies laid at his door by later generations, he fully
earned (in the context of his own time) the famous
encomium given him by Lord Byron.

2   _____. "Richard Brinsley Sheridan." Living Age 95
       (12 October): 102-15.
          Reprints 1867.1.

3   [THORNBURY.] "Old Stories Re-Told: Sheridan's Duels with
          Captain Mathews." All the Year Round 18 (3 August) 128-36.
          Draws heavily upon Elizabeth Linley's supposed letter
       to her friend (see 1825.6) to recount the two duel
       episodes. Young Sheridan figures here as the romantic
       hero of "our old love story" and Mathews as "an Iago," who
       "spread his web" about Miss Linley and "arranged his
       pitfalls with Satanic subtlety" (p. 228). The narrative
       mentions several of Miss Linley's "bowing and grimacing
       lovers" (p. 227), beginning with Walter Long and
       including Charles Sheridan and Nathaniel Halhed. It ends
       with an image of Sheridan in 1816: "a worn-out, drunken,
       friendless, impoverished, disgraced man, who had
       recklessly thrown away his genius, expired in the
       extremest poverty, the sheriff's officers eager to carry
       him to die in a Cursitor Street sponginghouse" (p. 233).
       (The author is identified as "Mr. Thornbury" in 1871.2.)

4   _____. "Sheridan's Duels with Captain Mathews." Every
       Saturday 4 (24 August): 227-33.
          Reprints 1867.3.

                              1869

1   HERON, D. C. "Sheridan." In The Afternoon Lectures on
          Literature and Art. Delivered in the Theatre of the
          Royal College of Science. S. Stephen's Green, Dublin, in
          the Years 1867 and 1868. Dublin: W. McGee, pp. 213-34.
          Recounts the life of Sheridan and pays homage to him as
       a gifted playwright, a brilliant orator, an accomplished
       wit, an Irish phenomenon, and a credit to his Irish

heritage. Since "caution and calculation were impossible to be combined with the other qualities existing in Sheridan's character" (p. 233), it is for history to forgive his errors and revel in his accomplishments.

*2 ZINCK, AUGUST GEORG LUDVIG. Congreve, Vanbrugh, og Sheridan. En Skildrig til Belysning af de sociale Forhold og det aandelige Liv i England fra Carl den Andens Tid og til henimod den franske Revolution. Copenhagen.
   Listed in 1890.1, p. x.

1870

1 ANON. "Richard Brinsley Sheridan. [Colburn's] New Monthly Magazine, n. s. 148 (June): 705-15.
   Demonstrates that Sheridan worked not from inspiration and spontaneity but deliberation and artifice, taking careful artistic measures to hide his art. He contrived to have it thought that he learned without effort and composed impromptu. But his impromptu efforts, both spoken and written, were (as his letters attest) "generally poor and pointless" (p. 195). In preparing speeches he worked out his arguments systematically, leaving amplification and adornment for the moment of presentation. But these adornments, too, he prepared for ready use, jotting them on cards and scraps of paper. He had a penchant for springing as if spontaneously a practiced mot held ready for the proper moment. His plays seem to grow under his hands, a collection of discrete scenes finally molded into form. As the form develops, lines of dialogue might move from one character to another. He liked to work at night under a "profusion of lights" (p. 198), and he thought wine to be a great aid to composition.

1871

1 ANON. "Richard Brinsley Sheridan. [Colburn's] New Monthly Magazine, n.s. 148 (June): 705-15.
   Celebrates Sheridan as the paragon of literary Irishmen: a wag industrious only in his pleasures, dashing, romantic, reckless, hopelessly improvident, never so resourceful as when eluding creditors, so vicious in his idleness as to injure not just his own interests but the interests of others as well, but irresistibly a genius and a great man. Sheridan was "very nearly the biggest giant in an age of giants," and "Those only who

1871

have his genius ought to possess the privilege of
animadverting on his errors" (p. 715). In appreciating
genius, the generality of mankind must dismiss its errors,
remembering that greatness implies not just accomplishments but also heightened moral sensibilities. To a man
of genius "remorse is a terrible abstraction—a live,
baleful shape that lacerates his mind, that squeezes his
heart" (p. 415). Since genius "avenges upon itself" the
wrongs it has committed, it stands above the harsh
judgment lesser minds might make upon it.

2 FITZGERALD, PERCY. "The Loves of Famous Men. No. VII.
Sheridan." Belgravia 14 (April): 163-75.
Describes the courtship of Sheridan and Elizabeth
Linley (the many rival suitors, the emotional excesses
and fainting spells, the elopement, the duels) as
resembling a romantic novel played out in Bath during
the city's most romantic era. Against such a narrative,
The Rivals takes on a decidedly autobiographical color.
Lydia Languish is a comic fictionalization of Elizabeth
Linley, Jack Absolute of Richard Sheridan, Sir Anthony
of Thomas Sheridan, Sir Lucius of Captain Thomas
Mathews. And, like the real story, the fictional
rendering is set in Bath.

1872

1 MATHEWS, CHARLES. "Sheridan's 'Critic.'" Tinsley's
Magazine 11 (November): 414-18.
Insists (on the testimony of long experience in the
role of Puff) that acts 2 and 3 of The Critic draw much
of their comedy from local (i.e., topical) humor and
that actors and managers have free license to bring this
local comedy up to date by adding jokes of their own.
Sheridan approved of such practices in his own time and
would approve of them again in later times.

1873

1 BROWNE, JAMES P., M.D. Introduction to The Works of the
Right Honourable Richard Brinsley Sheridan. London:
Bickers and Son, 1: i-xli.
Provides an introductory memoir of the playwright's
life based upon Thomas Moore (1825.9) from whose
biography numerous long extracts are drawn.

1874

1   ANON. "An Old Westminster Election." Times (London),
        20 February, p. 8.
        Quotes from the Evening Post for 18 November 1806 the
        report of a speech given from the hustings by Sheridan to
        the Westminster electorate on 15 November 1806. In the
        speech, Sheridan appeals to his supporters not in his own
        behalf but in behalf of the constitution. Their continued
        zeal will seat him in Commons for Westminster.

2   ANON. "Sheridan's Works." Saturday Review 38 (17 October):
        505-6.
        Attacks Stainforth's new edition of Sheridan's Works
        (see 1874.6) not only for supplying an unneeded book but
        also for bringing to light subliterary efforts (such as
        the Love Epistles of Aristaenetus) which ought to be left
        to oblivion. In truth, Sheridan has little to boast.
        "His speeches and his plays are of much the same quality,
        and both are marked by audacious but successful hits, and
        by gross and amazing blunders. He had no self-respect to
        restrain him from committing himself to any escapade
        either in literature or politics, and was always ready to
        take his chance of hit or miss in pursuit of those
        sensational effects which flattered his vanity and
        gratified his love of excitement. . . . He was, in short,
        a rather plodding, and heavy Beaumarchais, with all the
        tricks, but without the genuine brightness and originality
        of the Frenchman" (p. 506).

3   DALY, AUGUSTIN, adapter. Editorial Introduction to The
        School for Scandal, by Sheridan. American Academy of
        Dramatic Arts Edition of Standard Plays, no. 2. New York:
        Samuel French, pp. 3-4.
        Prints a promptbook text prepared for presentation at
        the Fifth Avenue Theatre. The "Editorial Introduction"
        sees this version as becoming "the future standard and
        universal prompt-book wherever and whenever again the
        School for Scandal is acted" (p. 4). The introduction
        also acknowledges flawed moral tendencies in the play:
        "We could never admire that species of generosity which
        [in Charles Surface] would rob a creditor to lavish money
        upon one who might have been in no greater want of it than
        he to whom it was legally due" (p. 3). Only Sir Peter
        is above reproach, and even he makes light of Joseph's
        "supposed peccadillo" in act 4. The play suffers from
        too much ornamental dialogue and too little warmth of
        feeling. But its dazzling wit compensates for its
        defects. (Cf. 1850.1.)

1874

4   [JAMES, HENRY.] "The Drama" ["The School for Scandal at
     Boston"]. Atlantic Monthly 34 (December): 754-57.
          Attributes to a "commendably natural" performance at
     the Boston Museum the impression that The School for
     Scandal, "in spite of the traditional glamour that
     surrounds it," is in fact a "strangely lifeless and
     ghostly" play (p. 756). "Its ideas, in so far as it
     has any, are coarse and prosaic, and its moral atmosphere
     uncomfortably thin. . . . It has hardly a ray of fancy,
     of the graceful or the ideal, and even its merit--its
     smartness and smoothness and rapidity--has something hard
     and metallic" (p. 756). Its great popularity rests,
     presumably, upon its wit, which the whole world can
     understand while feeling itself clever to do so, and
     upon the "average sense of fair play" hit by it. It also
     claims a "robustness and smoothness of structure" and an
     "extreme felicity and finish of style" (p. 757). That
     it should have enjoyed so continuous a popularity,
     however, testifies at last to "the poverty of the English
     stage" (p. 756).

5   RAE, W[ILLIAM] F[RASER]. "Richard Brinsley Sheridan." In
     Wilkes, Sheridan, Fox: The Opposition Under George the
     Third. London: W. Isbister, pp. 141-245.
          Presents admiring descriptions of Sheridan's life, his
     literary style, his parliamentary career, his oratorical
     gifts (both as to composition and delivery), his social
     manner, and his moral character. "His career, which is as
     much a romance as that of any personage in fiction, has
     but one parallel in our history, the career of the
     attorney's clerk of Hebrew race who has risen to be Prime
     Minister of the United Kingdom. Both Sheridan and Mr.
     Disraeli first made their mark as men of extraordinary
     wit; both failed in their first attempt to make the House
     of Commons accept them at their own valuation, and both
     occupy places in the first rank among parliamentary
     orators" (p. 244). Like Burke, Pitt, and Fox, "Sheridan
     is one of the immortals ruling 'our spirits from their
     urns'" (p. 245).

6   STAINFORTH, F., ed. "Life of Richard Brinsley Sheridan." In
     The Works of Richard Brinsley Sheridan. London: Chatto &
     Windus, pp. 1-84.
          Demonstrates, through a general biographical survey,
     that throughout his life Sheridan "but too consistently
     acted upon the principles which the first Lord Holland
     used playfully to impress upon his son:--'Never do to-day
     what you can possibly put off till to-morrow, nor ever
     do, yourself, what you can get any one else to do for

you'" (pp. 14-15). As an artistic craftsman, however,
he exemplifies "the difficult art of combining ease with
polish, and being, at the same time, idiomatic and
elegant" (p. 49). As a politician, nothing brings
greater credit to Sheridan's life than "his services to
freedom during the stormy period between 1793 and 1801"
(p. 62).

7 TAINE, H. A. History of English Literature, translated by
   H. Van Laun. New York: Henry Holt, 1: 524-31.
   Translates Taine's Histoire de la littérature anglaise
   (Paris, 1863-1864) which includes a comprehensive account
   of Sheridan's life and an assessment of his comic art: "A
   piquant style, and perfect machinery; pungency in all the
   words, and animation in all the scenes; a super-abundance
   of wit, and marvels of ingenuity; over all this a true
   physical activity, and the secret pleasure of depicting
   and justifying oneself, of public self-glorification:
   here is the foundation of The School for Scandal, here the
   source of the talent and the success of Sheridan"
   (p. 524), and upon these attributes he succeeds even
   though his comedies are "merely comedies of society"
   (p. 526), The Rivals a collection of exaggerated
   caricatures and The School for Scandal a distillation from
   two characters by Fielding (Blifil and Tom Jones) and two
   plays by Molière (Le Misanthrope and Tartuffe).

1875

1 HARVEY, FRANCIS. Genealogical Table of the Families of
   Sheridan, Lefanu and Knowles, Compiled by F. H. London:
   Privately printed for James McHenry, 2 pp.
   Includes the genealogical tables announced in the title
   together with a "Key" to these tables providing brief
   notes on the more illustrious members of the three
   families. The entry for Sheridan lists his plays and
   several other titles either known or thought to be his.
   The tables are intended to "illustrate the life of James
   Sheridan Knowles, a descendant of the playwright's aunt,
   Frances Sheridan Knowles.

1876

1 ANON. "Literary Gossip." The Athenaeum, no. 2514
   (1 January): 24.
   Announces the discovery in the British Museum of a
   holograph copy of Mrs. Sheridan's "Trip to Bath" (among a

1876

collection of plays once belonging to Sheridan and given
to the Museum by Coventry Patmore in 1864). A very slight
comparison of this piece with The Rivals "leaves no doubt
whatever" that Sheridan found in his mother's play the
source of his own and that in drawing Mrs. Malaprop he
borrowed blunders from Frances Sheridan's Mrs. Tryfort
"without any alteration whatever."

1877

1 MATTHEWS, J. BRANDER. "'The School for Scandal.'"
Appleton's Journal, n.s. 2 (June): 556-62.
    Acknowledges the centennial of The School for Scandal
by commenting upon "its time, its author, its first
performance, its success in England, in America, and in
other than English-speaking lands, its construction, its
character, and its wit" (p. 556). Its time was propitious
in that contemporary taste had created a void for it to
fill. Its author brought to his task experience,
theatrical success, and authorial industry. Carefully
supervised rehearsals and impeccable casting aided its
initial success, and it has endured in England even
despite some irreverent treatment (e.g., Macready's
reducing it to a three-act afterpiece) and some vile
productions. It came immediately to America and was held
throughout colonial and Federalist times to be a
touchstone of excellence. In translations and adaptations
it quickly found its way to Paris, Vienna, and Venice.
Its debts to other plays, often cited and muttered at, are
generic and inconsequential. While obviously compounded
of two separate embryonic fragments, it is well enough
unified, and it asserts its greatness through its wit,
a wit not emanent from the characters' minds but from
Sheridan's own brilliance. Sheridan resides with the
second class of dramatists, those "who can say one thing
in many ways" (p. 561). The thing he has to say is "wit,"
and of this he is master in all its forms.

*2 MOORE, THOMAS. Memoirs of the Life of the Right Honourable
Richard Brinsley Sheridan, by Thomas Moore. To Which Are
Added the Autograph Letters Printed in That Work and Many
Others Unpublished; Fragments of Essays; Unfinished Plays
and Poems; and other Manuscripts of Sheridan and Many
Portraits of Himself and His Contemporaries Collected and
Arranged by His Grandson, Richard Brinsley Sheridan.
4 vols. Frampton, Dorset.
    Listed in NUC, 393: 456. The unique copy is in the
collection of Yale University.

1 BAKER, H. BARTON. "Richard Brinsley Sheridan." Gentleman's
   Magazine 243, 6th n.s., 21 (September): 304-20.
       Recounts Sheridan's life by way of illustrating that in
   rare cases (such as the playwright's own) great creative
   talent is handed down from generation to generation. Not
   only did Sheridan inherit great talent; he also transmitted
   it to his descendants.

2 [DOWE, W.] "The Sheridans--A Rare Literary Family."
   National Quarterly Review 36 (January): 117-34.
       Describes the literary achievements of the Sheridan
   family from Denis Sheridan's translation of the Bible into
   Irish (published in 1649) to Lord Dufferin's Yacht Voyage
   to Iceland (1873). Intervening titles of special interest
   include Opera Horarum Subsecivarum (MS) by Thomas Sheridan
   D.D. (Dublin, 1723), A Complete Dictionary of the English
   Language by Thomas Sheridan, M.A. (London, 1780), The
   School for Scandal by Richard Brinsley Sheridan (London,
   1780), Revolutions in Sweden by Charles Francis Sheridan
   (Dublin, 1815), Songs of Greece (from the Romaic) by
   Charles Brinsley Sheridan (London, 1825), Memoirs of Mrs.
   Frances Sheridan by Alicia LeFanu (London, 1824), The
   Hunchback, a play, by James Sheridan Knowles (London,
   1836), and The Lady of Goraye, a novel, by the Hon. Mrs.
   Caroline Norton (London, 1860). The discussion includes a
   comprehensive sketch of R. B. Sheridan's life and career.

1879

1 MATTHEWS, J. BRANDER. "Sheridan's 'Critic.'" Lippincott's
   Magazine of Popular Literature and Science 24 (November):
   629-35.
       Gives The Critic biographical and historical contexts by
   identifying it as the last of Sheridan's real contributions
   to drama: the successor of Buckingham's The Rehearsal and
   an extension of the burlesque burletta Ixion, on which
   Sheridan had worked with his school friend N. B. Halhed.
   Generous quotation from an account written by C. J.
   Mathews, one of the best early interpreters of Puff,
   indicates that stage business in The Critic was handed
   down from one generation of performers to another and
   that topical allusions were added or altered to fit the
   times (cf. 1872.1). Grotesque buffoonery, furthermore,
   was from the outset a hallmark of the piece. While
   certainly farcical, The Critic testifies, as do all of
   Sheridan's plays, to the playwright's quintessential wit,

1879

"a wit which had power to assume whatever pleasant shape
might be best fitted to charm the ear and the understanding" (p. 630).

<u>1880</u>

1 ANON. "Sheridan." <u>Temple Bar</u> 60 (December): 488-503.
        Bases a brief biographical sketch on the premise that
   Sheridan was "A wit rather than a humourist, an orator
   more than a statesman, a brilliant writer of comedy and
   farce." Although he "stood in the first rank in society
   and in the House of Commons," he "died poor, worn out by
   debauchery, and with bailiffs about him." At last,
   however, he was buried in the Abbey "in recognition of
   the purity of his political life" and "in admiration of
   his splendid talents" (p. 488).

2 MATTHEWS, J. BRANDER. "'Pinafore's' Predecessor." <u>Harper's</u>
   <u>New Monthly Magazine</u> 60 (March): 501-8.
        Responds to a current American craze for English comic
   opera by recalling that the leading precursors of the
   form include <u>The Beggar's Opera</u> and <u>The Duenna</u>, both
   ballad operas, i.e., operas in which the music is
   secondary to the plot and is usually adapted from popular
   ballad melodies. <u>The Duenna</u> fails to approximate <u>The</u>
   <u>Rivals</u> and <u>The School for Scandal</u> in wit and
   characterization (though it shows sporadic excellence in
   both these respects), but its style of broad humor
   anticipates the comic manner of W. S. Gilbert: Sheridan's
   Father Paul, for example, clearly foreshadows Gilbert's
   Sir Joseph Porter (in <u>H. M. S. Pinafore</u>). And despite its
   artistic failings, <u>The Duenna</u> offers eminently singable
   songs. It demonstrates the playwright's fine musical
   instincts and earns distinction as the best theatrical
   work of its kind.

3 _____. "Sheridan's 'Rivals.'" <u>Scribner's Monthly</u>
   21 (December): 182-89.
        Celebrates Joseph Jefferson's revival of <u>The Rivals</u> by
   describing the play's origins and early history and
   admiring its wit and vitality. A product of inspired
   (and needy) youth, it lacks sharp insight into human
   nature, and it panders (through the Julia-Faulkland
   business) to unworthy contemporary tastes. But it is
   brilliantly crafted, and it testifies to Sheridan's true
   comic sense. So authentic is this sense that it
   aggravates charges of plagiarism. But none of these
   charges really bears close examination. In writing <u>The</u>

Rivals, Sheridan owes no significant debt to Steele, or
Smollett, or Prior, or Theodore Hook, or Frances Sheridan,
nor does he draw heavily upon his own youthful experience.
The Rivals is the work of an untrammeled bright
imagination.

4 NICOLL, HENRY JAMES. Great Orators. Burke, Fox, Sheridan,
Pitt. Edinburgh: Macniven & Wallace, pp. 149-204.
Surveys Sheridan's literary and political careers,
placing them in contexts of his family and milieu. His
plays are recognized as having a superficial excellence
derived principally from the representation of a single
narrow walk of life. His political career is seen as
achieving its zenith with the Westminister Hall speech
against Hastings but as failing of statesmanly excellence
because of the "faults of his character, and his habitual
laziness" (p. 196). In general, however, his "public life
was on the whole a much better one than his private"
(p. 197). It is chiefly because of the latter that "the
moral of his career is written in letters too legible to
be enforced by any words of ours" (p. 204).

1881

1 ANON. "Sheridan." Living Age 148 (15 January): 131-40.
Reprints 1880.1.

2 ANON. "Sheridan's 'Rivals.'" Monthly Reference Lists
[Providence Public Library], 1 (April): 15.
Lists references to the play (as to text and comment)
and to the playwright. For example, "The text of the
play is in Sheridan's 'Dramatic works.' See also, the
study of it in Hazlitt's 'English comic writers,'
p. 211-18. . . . On Sheridan himself, see his 'Memoirs' by
Thomas Moore. Also, Brougham's 'Statesmen of the time of
George III,' v. 1."

3 ANON. "Tom Sheridan." All the Year Round, n.s. 28
(12 November): 232-36.
Laments the lack of information about Sheridan's son
Tom and offers to repair the lack a bit by citing
anecdotes testifying to Tom's charm and by placing Tom's
character alongside his father's. Rivaling his father's
spendthrift ways, Tom pursued a reckless and extravagant
life. Nor was he more regular than his father in
managing Drury Lane Theatre. Like his father he looked
upon the theater as a "bank or bill-discounting
establishment" (p. 234), and like him he constantly

harrassed the treasurer, Peake, for ready money. Dying on 12 September 1817 at the Cape of Good Hope (where he was colonial paymaster), he left his family quite unprovided for. But his daughters met with excellent fortune: one became the brilliant Caroline Norton, another Lady Dufferin, and the third duchess of Somerset.

4 [MATTHEWS, J. BRANDER.] "Richard Brinsely Sheridan: I." American 1 (8 January): 205-6.
Insists, despite the misconceptions fostered by Moore's Life and the detractions of pedants and sober moralists, that Sheridan was a brilliant and ready wit, a wit in conversation, poetry, drama, and oratory. Perhaps he borrowed sallies and tropes from other people, but he made them distinctively his own; and, while he may have stored up quips for quick delivery, he always delivered them fresh and with all the character of spontaneity.

5 _____. "Richard Brinsley Sheridan: II." American 1 (15 January): 221-22.
Continues to defend Sheridan as a wit (see 1881.4) by insisting that while some of his witticisms might have been prepared (as would be entirely proper for parliamentary presentation), he was certainly capable of impromptu sallies. In his natural laziness, he repeated and reworked certain good quips; but he never did so to ill-advantage, and it is the greatest tribute to the vitality of his wit that were he living today, he would still be a successful and famous man. Such a claim cannot readily be made about most famous men of the past.

1882

1 FITZGERALD, PERCY. "Our Play-Box: 'The School for Scandal.'" Theatre, 3d ser. 5 (1 March): 171-74.
Attributes the perennial freshness of The School for Scandal to Sheridan's art in choosing topics and characters common to all sorts and conditions of men. By failing to do so, Congreve and Wycherley limited the appeal of their plays. The School for Scandal is a play best acted on a stage large enough to allow the characters to move freely and group themselves comfortably, and it should be performed in a wry and insinuating tone, one not giving too serious a turn to the witty maxims but yet not fully obscuring the seriousness of their content. A revival of the comedy at the Vaudeville Theatre on 4 February 1882 proved highly satisfactory in these respects.

*2   MOORE, THOMAS. <u>Memoirs of the Life of the Right Honourable</u>
     <u>Richard Brinsley Sheridan</u>. 2 vols. in 1. New York: P.J.
     Kenedy.
          Listed in <u>NUC</u>, 393: 456.

3   WEDMORE, FREDERICK. "The Revival of 'The School for
     Scandal.'" <u>Academy</u> 21 (11 February): 109-10.
          Compares a revival of <u>The School for Scandal</u> at the
     Vaudeville Theatre with earlier revivals (some ten years
     before) at the Vaudeville and at the Prince of Wales.
     The latest production surpasses that at the Prince of
     Wales in costume and setting. It retains many excellences
     in staging and casting achieved by the earlier Vaudeville
     production. In general, however, the earlier production
     is the better. The current Lady Teazle, for example,
     lacks some of the bouyancy, vivacity, and spontaneity of
     the earlier. In that her role is "no exacting intellectual
     study" (p. 110), it depends directly upon the personality
     of the actress performing it. The current Maria,
     furthermore, projects "only too much intelligence."
     Maria, after all, is "an ingenue more French than English"
     (p. 110).

1883

1   ANON. "<u>English Men of Letters</u>.--Sheridan. By Mrs. Oliphant."
     <u>Athenaeum</u>, no. 2913 (25 August): 234-36.
          Feels the attitude of Mrs. Oliphant's biography of
     Sheridan to be ill-judged and the facts occasionally to
     be less than accurate. In complaining against Sheridan's
     dissipations and improvidences (the extent of which she
     exaggerates), Mrs. Oliphant neglects almost entirely the
     cause of his durability and fame. Overwhelmed by his
     minor vices, she seems unimpressed by what really matters
     about him: "a name in literature which will long
     survive, a reputation in Parliament which is almost
     unique, and a heritage of intellect which his descendants
     have shown to be a precious and enviable possession"
     (p. 236).

2   ANON. "Mr. White on Shakespeare and Sheridan." <u>Atlantic</u>
     <u>Monthly</u> 52 (October): 566-70.
          Admires two recent products of Richard Grant White's
     critical mind: an edition of Shakespeare's works (Boston:
     Houghton Mifflin, 1883) and an introduction to Sheridan's
     plays (see 1883.8). The former is admirable as a model
     of exacting textual criticism; the latter earns admiration
     as a "general survey of poor human nature" (p. 568). By

1883

well-chosen anecdotes (in one of which Sheridan steals a
pair of boots in Bristol; in another his corpse is
arrested for debts), White elucidates Sheridan's character
as a wastrel and scamp. White's comprehensive assessment
of Sheridan's work is "just and final" (p. 569) in seeing
it as brilliant, shallow, lacking in wisdom, dull of
insight, slight of imagination, devoid of poetic feeling,
morally empty (except for some bland social satire), the
products of a surface man, himself a blending of his own
Surface brothers.

3   ANON. "Mrs. Oliphant on Sheridan." Saturday Review 56
     (22 September): 379-80.
          Deplores the immaturity and inaccuracy of Mrs.
     Oliphant's treatment of Sheridan, agreeing with her that
     his brilliance is overpraised and that he never really
     swayed public opinion but disagreeing with her assessment
     of his art, especially with her presumption in contrasting
     him to Shakespeare. His literary forebears are properly
     seen to be Wycherley and Congreve, playwrights who, while
     currently little mentioned (and apparently unknown to
     Mrs. Oliphant), are in fact greater comedians of manners
     than he.

4   ANON. "Sheridan." The Month 49, n.s. 30 (1883): 281-86.
          Acknowledges the publication of Mrs. Oliphant's
     Sheridan and condenses from it a sketch of the playwright's
     life.

5   CAINE, T. HALL. "Sheridan. By Mrs. Oliphant." Academy
     24 (15 September): 171-72.
          Complains that Mrs. Oliphant, in her Sheridan (1883.7),
     treats her subject too narrowly and judgmentally, failing
     to give proper credit to the extraordinary range of his
     success. He was not, in fact, the imprudent chucklehead
     his grandfather had been. As a man of the world he made
     no serious slips, and his life is rendered problematic
     only by its duration. Had he died at thirty-seven, the
     author of three brilliant comedies, the most gifted orator
     in Commons, his memory would suffer no taint. But he
     lived to be old, to be stymied by Whitbread, to be
     abandoned by Prince and party, to be plagued by infirmity.
     It is old age that renders him "a characterless prodigal
     of genius" (p. 172). Mrs. Oliphant needs reminding that
     Sheridan "was a great man" (p. 171).

6   MORLEY, HENRY. Introduction to The Plays of Richard Brinsley
     Sheridan. Morley's Universal Library. London: George
     Routledge and Sons, pp. 5-8.

Provides a sketch of the playwright's life, concluding that his creditable career ended in 1780: thereafter "Thirty-six years of carelessly overburdened social and political life remained to Sheridan" (p. 8). Despite the general carelessness of his mind, he "acquired full mastery over one form of the play of thought," responding in his work to "the reaction against insincerity and formalism" then developing in Europe (p. 8).

7   OLIPHANT, MARGARET. Sheridan. English Men of Letters Series. London: Macmillan, 207 pp.
    Presents the life and work of Sheridan in such a way as to demonstrate that his "view of life was not a profound one. It was but a vulgar sort of drama, a problem without any depths--to be solved by plenty of money and wine and pleasure, by youth and high spirits, and an easy lavishness which was called liberality, or even generosity as occasion served. But to Sheridan there was nothing to find out in it, any more than there is anything to find out in the characters of his plays" (pp. 107-108). No sooner had he "gained the highest successes which the theatre could give than he abandoned that scene of triumph for a greater one; and when--on that more glorious stage--he had produced one of the most striking sensations known to English political life, his interest in that also waned, and a broken, occasional effort now and then only served to show what he might have accomplished had it been contin- uous. If he had been free of the vices that pulled him to earth, and possessed of the industry and persistency which were not in his nature, he would, with scarcely any doubt, have left both fortune and rank to his descendants. As it was in everything he did, he but scratched the soil" (pp. 197-98). Reviewed in 1883.1, 3-5; 1884.1-2, 5-6.

8   WHITE, RICHARD GRANT. Introduction to The Dramatic Works of Richard Brinsley Sheridan. New York: Dodd, Mead, 1: v-xliii.
    Sees Sheridan's fame as resting on two of the plays, The Rivals and The School for Scandal, of which the latter is inferior to the former in characterization and dramatic interest but superior in wit and stage effect. Sheridan's political career lacks distinction, being progressively dulled by his intemperance, and his oratory rarely merits preservation, being elaborate, not strong, witty, not thoughtful, vehement, not earnest. Although the most witty of dramatists, he is almost wholly lacking in humor, his nearest approach to it appearing in the character of Bob Acres. Reviewed in 1883.2.

1884

1 ANON. "Mrs. Oliphant's Sheridan." Literary World 15
     (January): 22-23.
       Admires the vigor and spirit of Mrs. Oliphant's
     Sheridan (1883.7) but complains that the strictures made
     there against Sheridan's shallowness are beside the point.
     "If Sheridan's characters had not been in a great degree
     true to nature, the world would have found it out before
     this, and would have had none of them. It is not an
     important message, that Sheridan was not a Shakespeare"
     (p. 22).

2 ANON. "Mrs. Oliphant's 'Sheridan.'" Spectator 57
     (26 January): 124-25.
       Deplores the biographical and critical license by which
     Mrs. Oliphant blames Sheridan for being someone he was not
     and by which she slights his art for missing targets it
     did not aim at. "In plays written, as Sheridan's were, to
     amuse and delight audiences who required nothing better
     than to be amused and delighted, profound views of life
     would be out of place; and as these plays have, after the
     lapse of more than a century, lost nothing of their
     attractiveness, we may take it for granted, that if this
     author's view of life was superficial, his knowledge of
     human nature was profound" (p. 125).

3 BRERETON, AUSTIN. "The First Cast of 'The Rivals.'"
     Theatre, 4th ser. 3 (2 June): 281-89.
       Summarizes the careers of the actors who first performed
     in The Rivals and suggests that the failure of the
     first-night performance was probably not due to the
     ineptness of Lee as Sir Lucius (despite traditions to the
     contrary). "It is easy to imagine that when the pompous
     Mr. Lee found the audience objected to the character of
     Sir Lucius, he resigned the part, for no man likes to be
     hissed, even for the author of the play. It was not the
     actor to whom the audience objected, but the character"
     (pp. 282-83).

4 BRYANT, WILLIAM CULLEN. "The Character of Sheridan." In
     Prose Writings of William Cullen Bryant, edited by Parke
     Godwin. New York: D. Appleton, 2: 365-69.
       Distils from Moore's Life a severe (yet sympathetic)
     characterization of Sheridan, seeing him to be endowed
     with high animal spirits and engaging good nature, a man
     frank and open in character but incapable of resolution
     in labor and given to shallow feelings and facile
     convictions. "Everything with him was planned for effect;

1884

his comedies, his operas, his speeches, are all brilliant,
showy, and taking" (p. 367.) Even his frankness and
openness reflect his lassitude. "Had the practice of
deceit been as easy as that of integrity, we are not sure
that Sheridan would not have fallen into it . . . for it
seems that he had not sufficient firmness of principle
to resist the temptations of many other vices" (p. 369).

5   [DICEY, A. V.] "Sheridan. By Mrs. Oliphant." <u>Nation</u>
        39 (14 August): 136-37.
        Sets Mrs. Oliphant aside, after expressing contempt for
     her book, and attempts then to explain Sheridan as a
     public phenomenon: he "possessed in the highest degree
     all the qualities of a brilliant wit and rhetorician."
     His plays and speeches have it in common that they display
     "extreme brilliancy without any great depth of insight"
     (p. 137). But he wrote and spoke at a time when it was
     proper and necessary to influence people's generous
     feelings, not their minds. His brilliance, then, provided
     good footing for his political career, and he can be seen
     as one of the last great patriotic political adventurers,
     a breed not able to flourish on the current political
     scene.

6   MATTHEWS, BRANDER. "Richard Brinsley Sheridan and His
        Biographers." <u>Princeton Review</u>, n.s. 13 (May): 292-303.
        Attacks most of Sheridan's biographers for having
     abused their subject mercilessly and declares with
     indignation that to discern the true Sheridan is to sift
     through the shambles made of his character by the
     biographers: "They have been ignorant and careless like
     the latest of them--Mrs. Oliphant; or hostile and careless
     like the earliest--Dr. Watkins; or they have thought more
     of themselves and their living friends than of their dead
     subject--like Moore" (p. 293). Their failings teach us,
     in any case, that Sheridan's character is a composite of
     complex variables. It cannot be read offhand and at
     random. "Briefly, I am inclined to think that it is to be
     found in the uncommon conjunction in Sheridan of two
     irreconcilable things, a very high standard of morals
     with an absence of training and discipline, the latter
     failing vitiated by the former virtue" (p. 302). Because
     of their "injudicious indolence" (p. 303), Sheridan's
     biographers have not perceived or rendered the complexity
     of his character.
        In surveying the work of Sheridan's biographers,
     Matthews quotes a letter written in 1840 by Sheridan's
     daughter-in-law, C. H. Sheridan, complaining to William
     Smyth of the shabby treatment given the Sheridan family

in his Memoir of Mr. Sheridan (1840.2). The letter is
therefore printed here for the first time. He acknowledges Fraser Rae's sketch of Sheridan in his Wilkes, Fox,
and Sheridan (1874.5) to be the best short treatment of the
playwright, and he predicts that Moore's Memoirs
(1825.9), with all its faults, will always be the
standard biography of Sheridan.

1885

1 MATTHEWS, BRANDER, ed. "Richard Brinsley Sheridan. A
Biographical Sketch." In Sheridan's Comedies: The Rivals
and The School for Scandal. Boston: James R. Osgood,
pp. 13-59.
Introduces Sheridan and his two plays in such a way as
to defend the playwright from detractors, especially those
who charge him with extensive plagiarism. Although
Sheridan was a wit and little else, he went "As far as
mere wit could carry him" (p. 14). His wit draws upon
common sense and not, as Shakespeare's does, upon
informed imagination, but it is true to life and is
nowhere derivative and cheating. Reviewed in 1891.3.

1886

1 ANON. "Some Famous Plays. IV. Sheridan's 'Rivals' and
'School for Scandal.' In Two Parts. Part I." All the
Year Round, n.s. 38 (24 July): 541-47.
Prepares for a discussion of Sheridan's plays by
describing Bath as it was in 1770, by placing the
Sheridans and Linleys in their roles there, and by
recounting details of young Sheridan's life, especially
his elopement with Elizabeth Linley and his two duels with
Mathews. Sheridan's early life needs telling "because of
the influence it subsequently bore upon his productions,
many scenes of which reflect incidents and characters
which had come within his personal experience" (p. 547).

2 ANON. "Some Famous Plays. IV. Sheridan's 'Rivals' and
'School for Scandal.' In Two Parts. Part II." All the
Year Round, n.s. 38 (31 July): 557-60.
Tells the story of Sheridan's introduction into London
society, his unwillingness to let his wife perform in
public, his literary false starts, and his eventual
success with The Rivals, a success achieved after the
"second representation" (p. 558) of the piece.
Biographical narrative also covers Sheridan's purchase

of the Drury Lane patent, his opening campaign as manager
of the theater, the careful composition of The School for
Scandal, and the stunning success of the play, a success
documented here from contemporary press accounts and
memoirs. The play quickly found its way to provincial
and continental theaters (Dublin, Edinburgh, Bath, Paris,
and Vienna), and, while Sheridan's biographer Watkins
raised a question as to its authorship (mentioning as the
true author a young lady in Thames Street), Sheridan's
notes and drafts prove it to be his own.

3   FITZGERALD, PERCY. The Lives of the Sheridans. 2 vols.
       London: R. Bentley and Son.
          Undertakes to represent Sheridan objectively by pulling
       him off the pedestal built for him by Thomas Moore, his
       first major biographer. Since his record really
       demonstrates no large self-sacrifice in behalf of country
       or cause, he does not deserve, as might Nelson or Fox,
       that his faults be minimized or his achievements
       idealized. In managing his affairs he was improvident;
       his public policy, almost wholly partisan, was influenced
       by men not measures. Only on lower standards of
       excellence does he merit admiration. A good-natured,
       jovial, and pleasure-loving character cannot be denied him.
       Nor can a bright wit and clever ingenuity. From small
       resources he accomplished large effects, and he maintained,
       despite setbacks, a bouyant and irrepressible spirit.
       Whatever his personal failings, he gave to the world two
       brilliant and enduring comedies. (In addition to chapters
       on Sheridan and his ancestors, the book gives accounts of
       his most notable descendants.) Reviewed in 1887.1-3.

4   _____. "Sheridan and His Wives." Gentleman's Magazine 260,
       36th n.s., 6 (January): 42-61.
          Selects anecdotes to illustrate that Sheridan was
       "anything but a kind husband" (p. 48) to his first wife,
       that his feverish concern for his young son Tom was "no
       more than an unreasoning selfishness which could not bear
       a moment's uneasiness or be disturbed about anything"
       (p. 55), that he won his second wife through a series of
       deceits (having sent her, for example, some of the same
       love letters he had written to his first wife), and that
       "there was no one with whom he had dealings that he did
       not destroy or at least wreck" (p. 60).

1887

1   ANON. "The Lives of the Sheridans. By Percy Fitzgerald."

1887

Athenaeum, no. 3101 (2 April): 443-44.
Notes ways in which Percy Fitzgerald's book misrepre-
sents Sheridan. It judges him harshly in the light of
contemporaries no better than he (viz., Pitt and Fox).
It gives undue emphasis to his career as a theater
manager, the career by which Sheridan not only ruined the
theater but was ruined by it. It arbitrarily labels as
faults practices in Sheridan's public speaking which, by
any objective standard, would be thought conventional and
well managed. It fails to keep in mind that "we have to
take Sheridan with his failings as well as his excellences,
and that moralizing will not alter facts" (p. 444). If
Sheridan "had always kept his word and his appointments,
had been a pattern of sobriety and died a millionaire, he
would have been a better subject for a tract upon getting
on in life" (p. 444).

2   ANON. "The Lives of the Sheridans." Saturday Review 63
    (12 March): 381.
        Expresses wonder, in reviewing Fitzgerald's Lives of
    the Sheridans (1886.3), at the accomplishments of the
    Sheridan family but finds Richard Sheridan, in the hands
    of this present biographer, to be anything but a "great"
    personality. "A continuous strand of shiftiness, of
    shameless time-serving, of selfish expediency, seems
    traceable through Sheridan's whole career, 'e'en from his
    boyish days,' when as a lad at Harrow he got lesser lads
    to steal his stock of apples."

3   ANON. "Sheridan and His Family." Spectator 60 (23 April):
    562-63.
        Counters Percy Fitzgerald's detractions upon Sheridan's
    character and accomplishments--in The Lives of the
    Sheridans (1886.3)--by declaring that Sheridan (whose
    failings were not singular) deserves praise for standing
    by his political principles, for championing liberal
    causes, for winning and keeping Elizabeth Linley, for
    disallowing, even when he needed money, the continuation
    of her singing career. Fitzgerald did his best to spoil
    his subject, but "the subject was too good to be spoilt"
    (p. 562).

4   ANON. "Sheridan 'In Barrel.'" Saturday Review 63 (7 May):
    652-53.
        Chides the editors of the English Illustrated Magazine
    for printing, without authenticating the data, a story
    describing the contents of a barrel supposed to contain
    effects saved from the Drury Lane fire in 1809 and only
    recently come to light. Casting suspicion on the whole

mass of these materials is the discovery among them of
a letter of Elizabeth Linley's known to be a forgery.
Other letters found in the barrel and attributed to her
are probably letters written to Sheridan by "notorious
cyprians of the town" (p. 653) and addressed for reasons
of discretion to the theater rather than to his lodgings.
(Statements in 1897.7 and 10 suggest that this essay is
by Percy Fitzgerald.)

5   OLIPHANT, MARGARET. Sheridan. English Men of Letters
    Series. New York: Harper & Brothers, 207 pp.
    Reprints 1883.7.

6   STOKER, MATILDA. "Sheridan and Miss Linley." English
    Illustrated Magazine 8 (April): 491-511.
    Bases on the testimony of letters supposed to have been
saved from the Drury Lane fire (and hidden for sixty
years in a cellar near the theater) the argument that
Elizabeth Sheridan's affections for her husband remained
strong throughout their marriage, despite charges to the
contrary made by a recent biographer (presumably 1886.3).
The letters, which had been found in a barrel, cover a
twenty-year period (from 1772 to 1792). The ones
printed here give emphasis to the latter part of this
period and are accompanied by an account of Sheridan's
marriage to Elizabeth: the meeting, the elopement, the
honeymoon, the years of theatrical and political life.
"He loved her always, and for that she forgave him all."
Nor would she have changed her "Dearest Dick," with all
his faults, "for the most immaculate of husbands"
(p. 510).

1888

1   ANON. "'The Rivals' at the Fifth Avenue." Critic 10, n.s.
    13 (10 November): 233.
    Takes occasion, while admiring the performances of
Joseph Jefferson (Acres), John Gilbert (Sir Anthony) and
Mrs. John Drew (Mrs. Malaprop), to consider whether or not
Jefferson's Acres is authentic to Sheridan's intent.
The question at last has no real importance. "If Mr.
Jefferson has raised Acres to a far higher plane than
any of his predecessors, and has made him more human,
natural and sympathetic, without losing one particle of
his humor, the gain is great from every point of view.
It is certain that Sheridan himself would be the last
man to complain of that wonderfully delicate execution
which represents his own conception in a light at once
more truthful and more brilliant. The triumph of the

1888

player consists in the fact that he has lifted the part out of farce into comedy and proved that broad fun is not wholly dependent on horseplay."

2 ANON. "Sheridan's Grandchildren." New-York Times, 23 May, p. 6.
Announces the death of Sheridan's grandson, Richard Brinsley Sheridan of Frampton Court, Dorset, and gives the details of his parentage, family, and career.

3 BAHLSEN, LEOPOLD. Kotzebue und Sheridan. Kotzebues Peru-Dramen und Sheridans Pizarro, ein Beitrag zur Geschichte der Beziehungen zwischen deutscher und englischer Literatur. In Herrigs Archiv fur das Studium der neuren Sprachen und Literaturen, no. 42. Braunschweig: George Westermann, 32 pp.
Suggests that the popularity of German drama in England begins with and is caused by Kotzebue's Peru-plays. In adapting Pizarro, Sheridan identified Kotzebue's sentimental spirit with English patriotic zeal, exciting in English audiences a profound sympathy for Kotzebue. Consequently, and despite the complaints of such British literary figures as Byron and Sir Walter Scott, Kotzebue's works found even wider acceptance and more extensive translation in England than did the sublimer art of Goethe and the more romantically profound work of Schiller.

4 HARTMANN, HERMANN. Über die Vorlagen zu Sheridans Rivals. Insterburg: K. Wilhelmi, 61 pp.
Locates the literary sources of The Rivals in Steele's The Tender Husband, where Sir Harry Gubbin anticipates Sir Anthony Absolute, Captain Clerimont anticipates Captain Absolute, Humphry Gubbin anticipates Acres, Aunt Tipkin anticipates Mrs. Malaprop, and Bridget Tipkin anticipates Lydia Languish. Autobiographical sources for The Rivals derive from young Sheridan's early courtship and from his duels with Captain Mathews. Faulkland represents Sheridan himself; Julia Melville represents Elizabeth Linley; and Sir Lucius O'Trigger represents an Irish poet, a friend of Mathews, named Barnett.

5 WEISS, KURT. Richard Brinsley Sheridan als Lustspieldichter. Leipzig: Otto Conrad, 110 pp.
Discovers in Sheridan's comedies (and elucidates at length) extensive debts to Dryden, Wycherley, Congreve, Vanbrugh, Centlivre, Behn, Cibber, Steele, Foote, Shakespeare, and especially Molière. In plot construction,

characterization, and motivation, Sheridan's comedies reflect their Restoration antecedents. And in wit, situation, satire, and humor, they are more sensible (verständig) and Molière-like than fanciful and Shakespeare-like. In fact, Sheridan earns for himself the right to shine in the history of drama as one of the more important disciples (bedeutenderer Jünger) of Molière.

1889

1 ANON. "Minor Notices of Holiday Publications." Critic 12, n.s. 15 (7 December): 282.

Includes a complaint against the illustrations prepared by Frank Gregory for a new issue of The Rivals (from White and Allen). Some of the pictures catch the characters aptly; others of them, such as that of Sir Lucius, are "totally misconceived." Taken collectively the illustrations are "uneven in merit."

2 ANON. "Relics of Sheridan and Burns." Critic 12, n.s. 15 (26 October): 207.

Describes mementos of Sheridan purchased by a collector (Mr. Bouton) during a recent trip to Europe. Attached to the album containing these "relics" is a hitherto unpublished poem by Thomas Moore (see 1816.17) deploring the supposed neglect to which the prince regent had subjected the dying Sheridan. It begins "And thou, too, whose life, a sick epicure's dream." The remaining seventy-two items, "mounted on tinted cardboard with linen guards," include a miniature of Elizabeth Linley done by R. Westall, some nautical sketches done by Richard Brinsley Tickell, a nephew of Sheridan's killed at Trafalgar, several "valuable and curious autographs," including a letter written by Admiral Nelson from the Victory (dated 10 March 1805), and a second poem, in the poet's autograph, by Thomas Moore.

3 CLAYDEN, P[ETER] W[ILLIAM]. Rogers and His Contemporaries. London: Smith, Elder, 1: 139-44, 273-75.

Describes several legal documents giving proof of Samuel Rogers's concern for Sheridan's troubled financial affairs during the dark days of the playwright's declining health. Later pages (1: 273-75) quote passages from Thomas Moore's diary in which Sheridan is said to have told Rogers of experiences in France during his elopement there with Elizabeth Linley in 1772 (how he faced down with bluff gestures two French officers who were flirting with Miss Linley) and of his decision years later not to prepare a love scene in The School for

1888

Scandal for Charles and Maria because the actors playing
these parts could not do justice to such a scene.
Accounts of Sheridan's practical joking with Richard
Tickell are also extracted here from Moore's diary.
(See 1853.2).

4   JEFFERSON, JOSEPH. The Autobiography of Joseph Jefferson.
     New York: Century, pp. 397-403.
        Justifies on the basis of Sheridan's own precedent the
     liberties taken by Jefferson in staging his own much cut
     and reformulated version of The Rivals. Colleagues such
     as William Warren and John Gilbert had chided him for his
     effrontery. But, encouraged by the warmth and variety of
     the Acres character and by the realization that one could
     reshape The Rivals without distorting its comic spirit (a
     license not allowed by The School for Scandal), he
     proceeded to his project, discovering justification for
     it after the fact in Sheridan's adaptation of Vanbrugh's
     The Relapse.

5   PHILIPPSTHAL, ROBERT. "Richard Brinsley Sheridan." Archiv
     für das Studium der Neuren Sprachen und Litteraturen 86
     (1889): 241-60.
        Emphasizes the irony that while Sheridan's career in
     Parliament (particularly his performance as a speaker)
     was much longer than his career as a playwright and was
     made the more prominent by his literary talents, it is
     virtually lost to history while his plays continue to
     delight the generations. His wit was so original, his
     eye for human weakness so sharp, his sense of the
     ridiculous so keen that he could not confine his talents
     to the theatrical stage. But in displaying them on the
     larger stage of politics, he condemned them to the same
     ephemerality that he foresaw for actors in his monody on
     Garrick.

1890

1   ANDERSON, JOHN P. "Bibliography." In Life of Richard
     Brinsley Sheridan, by Lloyd C. Sanders, Great Writers
     Series. London: Walter Scott, pp. i-xi.
        Lists printed editions of Sheridan's collected works,
     his dramatic works, his speeches, selections from his
     works, and single works of his. An appendix lists books
     and articles about Sheridan, both biography and criticism,
     published between 1789 and 1886.

2   SANDERS, LLOYD C. Life of Richard Brinsley Sheridan. Great

Writers Series. London: Walter Scott, 177 pp.
   Acknowledges that Sheridan the man was certainly a
riddle. Much of his conduct suggests that he was careless
and shallow, but his literary tastes, showing preferences
for Spenser and Dryden, and his discomfort with
metaphyscical discussions suggest that "the secret of his
reckless moods may well have been a desire to silence the
promptings of a gloomy and restless imagination" (p. 116).
While possibly not of the first rank, his accomplishments
merit him respect and admiration. As a dramatist, "he is
a wit, but not a poet" (p. 65). Respected for his
resourcefulness in theatrical production, he was not, as a
theater manager, "ambitious to raise the tone of the stage
by the production of new plays of merit" (p. 135). After
the Hastings trial, he did not greatly distinguish himself
as a statesman; but, throughout his political career, "he
was entirely incorrupt" (p. 160). Whatever detraction
may say of him, "his remains a great name in the annals of
the House of Commons" (p. 160) and in the history of
dramatic literature. Reviewd in 1891.2.

1891

1   ANON. "A Little Case of Borrowing." Atlantic Monthly 67
       (January): 141-43.
       Demonstrates that in writing The Rivals Sheridan very
   likely knew his mother's play "A Journey to Bath," a copy
   of which (in unfinished state) resides among the Sheridan
   papers in the British Museum. In the misuse of such words
   as "progeny," "contagious," "illiterate," and
   "punctuation," Mrs. Malaprop directly recalls the Mrs.
   Tryfort of Frances Sheridan's play. Sir Lucius's speech
   about the fortunes of Blunderbuss Hall closely parallel
   Sir Jeremy Bull's account of Bull Hall in "A Journey to
   Bath" (the mansion house having slipped through the
   fingers but the family pictures still intact). In
   general ways, furthermore, Mrs. Sheridan's Mrs. Tryfort
   shows debts to Congreve's Lady Wishfort (of The Way of the
   World). Hence Congreve's character figures in the
   background of Mrs. Malaprop.

2   ANON. "Sheridan Once More." Saturday Review 71 (10 January):
       55-56.
       Takes occasion, in commenting upon Lloyd Sanders's life
   of Sheridan for the Great Writers Series (1890.2), to
   mention an echo not before cited by Sheridan's commentators, one cited here "with all the more pleasure because
   it is in the highest degree improbable that Sheridan, who

was not specially bookish, had ever met with it" (p. 56).
It finds in a Satire on the Modern Translators (1684) a
notion corresponding to Sir Fretful's remark, in The
Critic, that literary thieves might disfigure thoughts, as
gypsies do children, to make them pass for their own.

3   ANON. "'Sheridan's Comedies.'" Critic 19, n.s. 16
     (14 November): 258-59.
         Reviews a reissue of Brander Matthews's edition of The
     Rivals and The School for Scandal (see 1885.1), in general
     admiring the editorial work but reducing the most
     elaborate part of Matthews's introduction, that explaining
     how Sheridan raised money to buy Drury Lane Theatre, to
     two sentences as follows: "Put in the shortest form it is
     that the money was not raised at all, but that the
     transaction was simply one of shifted pecuniary
     responsibility. Sheridan was honest personally, but he
     never could discern the difference between raising money
     and incurring a new obligation."

4   WINTER, WILLIAM. "A Few Remarks on The School for Scandal."
     In The School for Scandal Remodelled and Arranged by
     Augustin Daly. Souvenir Edition. N.p.: Printed privately
     by Augustin Daly, pp. iii-xxi.
         Puts the play in a broad historical framework (going
     back to Restoration precursors) and explains it in terms
     of several auspicious circumstances: Sheridan's lucky
     parentage, the artificial London society, the critical
     encouragements of David Garrick. Also sketches the stage
     history of the play, listing stellar casts (between 1777
     and 1891) and famous interpretations of the major roles.
     The text, remodeled an arranged by Augustin Daly, is
     the prompter's copy of a production staged at Daly's
     Theatre on 29 January 1891, reviving a production staged
     at the Fifth Avenue Theatre on 12 September 1874. (See
     1874.3.)

1892

1   KLAPPERICH, J[OSEPH]. Zur Sprache des Lustspieldichters
     Richard Brinsley Sheridan. Elberfeld: S. Lucas, 24 pp.
         Establishes Sheridan's preeminence among British
     playwrights of his own and later times, then, in response
     to Thomas Moore's admiration of the playwright's prose
     style (in 1825.9), analyzes selected features of his
     practice: e.g., his use of articles, substantives,
     pronouns, adjectives, adverbs, double negatives, verbs,
     prepositions, interjections, and vulgarisms. In matters

of changing usage, Sheridan seemed to favor older forms.
But he was able to accommodate conventions of language to
the local demands of his dialogue.

2   PRICE, W. T. The Techniques of the Drama. New York:
    Brentano's, pp. 46-51, 183-88.
        Draws upon The School for Scandal to demonstrate that
    the art of the dramatist overrides conventionality of
    motives in drama. The action of The School for Scandal
    evinces "many needless inconsistencies" (p. 48). For
    example, Sir Peter's suspicions of his wife with Charles
    Surface have no dramatic motive; the scandal scenes have
    little to do with the dramatic resolution of the play; Sir
    Benjamin's announced affection for Maria has no dramatic
    purpose. All these inconsistencies, however, are
    "overcome by the unflagging interest that is sustained by
    the glow of wit" (p. 48). This "saving vitality is a kind
    of action in itself" (p. 49). A later passage in the book
    (pp. 183-88) cites Joseph Jefferson's version of The
    Rivals as a happy instance of adaptation, one that
    diminishes the "disturbing artificialities of the plot"
    and adds material apposite to modern audiences but
    entirely in character.

1893

1   ANON. "The School for Scandal." Saturday Review 76
    (18 November): 566-67.
        Likens Augustin Daly's "emasculated" version of The
    School for Scandal (see 1874.3) to "champagne decanted to
    flatness" (p. 566).

2   SMITH, SYDNEY, AND SHERIDAN, R. B. Bon-Mots of Sydney Smith
    and R. B. Sheridan, edited by Walter Jerrald with
    grotesques by Aubrey Beardsley. London: J. M. Dent,
    192 pp.
        Collects in separate sections (a section on Smith and
    anyone else'" [p. 185].) In general, these quips reflect
    the attitudes held by the two men toward wit. Smith felt
    performer he liked best in a certain piece, he replied,
    'The prompter; for I saw less and heard more of him than
    anyone else'" p. 185 .) In general, these quips reflect
    the attitudes held by the two men toward wit. Smith felt
    that it should be spontaneous, "a quick conception and an
    easy delivery" (p. 11). Sheridan felt that "A
    true-trained wit lays his plan like a general" (p. 11).
    Even so, Sheridan was capable of spontaneity. "His wit
    was an incessant flame.--He sometimes displayed a kind of

1893

serious and elegant playfulness, not apparently rising to
wit, but unobservedly saturated with it, which was
unspeakably pleasing.--His wit is the wit of common
sense" (p. 12).

1894

1 [DEMPSTER, C. L. H.] "The Sheridans." Edinburgh Reivew
   180 (October): 433-46.
        Takes occasion, in a review of Helen Dufferin's Poems
   and Verses (see 1894.2), to chronicle the Sheridan family
   and to quote from a word portrait of Sheridan written by
   the son of Helen Dufferin (i.e., Sheridan's own great-
   grandson), the marquess of Dufferin and Ava, whose
   "Account of the Sheridan Family" [sic] accompanies his
   mother's Poems and Verses. This portrait, pleasing though
   it is, understates Sheridan's political disinterestedness.
   He cared little for place and title, and it is further
   to his credit that he acquiesced in the influence of such
   splendid women as his mother and his first wife. It is to
   be said of the Sheridans in general that their literary
   works number into the hundreds. "Novels, poems, songs,
   comedies, pamphlets, memoirs, tales, addresses, speeches,
   lectures, ballads, letters, translations, farces,
   grammars, sermons, histories, prologues, and elegies,
   nothing came amiss to them" (p. 440).

2 DUFFERIN AND AVA, marquess of. "A Sketch of My Mother." In
   Songs, Poems, and Verses by Helen, Lady Dufferin
   (Countess of Gifford). London: John Murray, pp. 1-104.
        Includes, in a biography of Sheridan's granddaughter,
   a sketch of the playwright showing, in general, how
   unfortunate he had been in his biographers and how
   essentially worthy his character had been. Despite the
   misimpressions given by biased and petty biographers, who
   overemphasized their subject's failings, the character of
   Sheridan was gracious, brilliant, and high principled.
   "Succeeding generations of his countrymen may well afford,
   therefore, to forget the pathetic infirmities which
   dimmed the splendour of Sheridan's later years, out of
   respect for one of the greatest speakers that has ever
   entranced the House of Commons, and in gratitude for the
   gift his genius has bequeathed them in his two immortal
   commedies, and the incomparable Critic" (p. 17).

3 HUNT, LEIGH. "The School for Scandal." In Dramatic Essays,
   edited by William Archer and Robert W. Lowe. London:
   Walter Scott, pp. 164-67.

72

Reprints 1830.5.

1895

1   ANON. "Court.--'The Rivals.' By Sheridan." Athenaeum,
    no. 3551 (16 November): 689-90.
        Notices that the younger actors have little flair for
    performing artificial comedy and that current
    inadequacies foreshadow the loss of the art. Seasoned
    actors like William Farren, in the role of Sir Anthony,
    yet preserve an instinct for comedy of manners, but young
    performers lack the bearing and the distinction necessary
    to the form. They are impeded even by the stage
    properties, the canes, swords, and snuff boxes, given
    them to use.

2   [DEMPSTER, C. L. H.] "The Sheridans." Living Age
    205 (18 May): 420-29.
            Reprints 1894.1.

3   RAE, W. F[RASER]. "'Story of a Forgery': A Letter of Miss
    Linley in the Gentlemen's Magazine for September, 1825."
    Athenaeum 105 (26 January): 120.
        Declares the supposed letter of Elizabeth Ann Linley to
    her friend Miss Saunders (see 1825.6) to be a forgery. It
    makes statements of fact not possibly belonging to Miss
    Linley's experience; it is addressed to a lady about whom
    nothing is known and who is nowhere mentioned in the
    authentic correspondence of the Linley family; it is
    written in a handwriting not resembling that of Miss
    Linley; and it is signed in a manner unusual to her.

1896

1   ANON. "A New Life of Sheridan." New York Times, 15 June,
    p. 10.
        Observes, in reviewing Fraser Rae's Sheridan: A
    Biography (1896.15), that there is no distinct public
    demand for such a work. "The curiosity of most readers
    is assuaged by the biographical notices in the
    encyclopedias." Since, however, Sheridan's descendants
    were dissatisfied with all earlier biographies of their
    famous ancestor, they cleared the way for a new one, and
    Rae has fulfilled their hopes amply.

2   ANON. "Lyceum.--'The School for Scandal.'" Athenaeum,
    no. 3583 (27 June): 852.

1896

Marvels that The School for Scandal rivals even Hamlet
in persistent popularity when it can boast none of the
earlier play's depth and moral purpose. "It is destitute
of sympathy. . . . It is, in fact, a mere comedy of manners
of a world brilliant, cold, heartless, artificial . . .
and in which the characters are as inconsistent as they
are insincere." Perhaps the reason for Sheridan's
durability is that wit and satire gain "sparkle and aroma"
with time while sentiment loses them.

3   ANON. "Sheridan." London Quarterly and Holborn Reivew 87,
    n.s. 27, no 2 (1896?): 230--47.
        Admires Fraser Rae's recently published biography of
    Sheridan and constructs, on the basis of Rae's narrative,
    a sad account of Sheridan's lapsed promise, a lapse made
    the more melancholy by the fact that Sheridan realized at
    the end his own self-destructive indolence and knew, too,
    that he lacked the resolution to correct it. In this
    respect his story is comparable to that of Robert Burns,
    another genius who had not cared to learn, until it was
    too late, "the ruin that lurked in the preference of
    Pleasure to Duty" (p. 245). But, if Sheridan paid so
    heavy a penalty for his neglect of the humbler duties of
    life, "much less may those hope to escape a like penalty
    for like offences who have not the excuse of his
    dangerous endowments, his ruinous success, his position of
    strong temptation" (p. 247).

4   BIRRELL, AUGUSTINE, ed. Introduction to The School for
    Scandal and The Rivals, by Sheridan. London: Macmillan,
    pp. vi-xxii.
        Takes the occasion of the recent publication of W.
    Fraser Rae's Sheridan: A Biography (1896.15) to complain
    that Sheridan has not received kind treatment from his
    biographers: not from Rae himself, who attempts to shatter
    all the traditions surrounding him, nor from Moore
    (1825.9) who encrusted his character with Whig gossip.
    Whatever else might be said about him, Sheridan was an
    honest man and an affectionate one. Traditions may
    obscure his personal identity, but his comedies are his
    true tradition, and their place is secure, so long as
    they are perceived for what they are--and for what he
    himself perceived them to be--pure comedy: "No! the real
    risk to which The School for Scandal is more and more
    exposed as the years roll by, is lest it may be found
    trespassing on the borderlands of truth and reality, and
    evoking genuine feeling. . . . It was all comedy to
    Sheridan, and if it ever ceases to be all comedy to us,
    it will be the first blow this triumphant piece has ever

received" (pp. xx-xxi). Reviewed in 1898.4.

5   DUFFERIN AND AVA, marquess of. "Introduction by Sheridan's
     Great-Grandson." In Sheridan: A Biography, by W. Fraser
     Rae. London: Richard Bentley and Sons, 1: vii-xvi.
         Complains that Sheridan's earlier biographers--specific-
     ally Watkins (1817.4), Moore (1825.9), and Smyth
     1840.2)--had misrepresented Sheridan badly. With the full
     confidence of Sheridan's descendants, and with full access
     to the Sheridan documents, W. Fraser Rae has set the
     record straight, treating his subject with scrupulous
     fairness and drawing upon such important new sources as
     the correspondence between the young Sheridan and his yet
     younger friend Thomas Grenville. The myths nurtured by
     biographers before Rae had found footing in the
     circumstances of Sheridan's birth: though of highbred
     stock, his family enjoyed no status in England. His life
     therefore suffered unusual disappointments and his memory
     fell subject to abuse.

6   ELLIOT, A. R. D. "Sheridan." Edinburgh Review 184 (July):
     57-81.
         Condenses from Rae's Sheridan (1896.15) an account of
     Sheridan's life and concludes that Rae, in writing his
     book, "has done excellent work in preventing the many
     noble qualities of his hero from being smothered under
     'good stories,' often preposterously exaggerated or
     entirely untrue" (p. 81).

7   [FITZGERALD, PERCY.] "Sheridan in Barrel--Once Again!"
     Saturday Review 82 (25 July): 83-85.
         Takes Fraser Rae to task for refusing to identify the
     source of several letters credited in his biography of
     Sheridan (1896.15) to Elizabeth Linley and said there to
     have been "temporarily" in Rae's own possession. To
     persevere in such "mystery" is to claim once again
     (cf. 1887.6) to have found Sheridan documents in a
     barrel, especially when only a superficial examination of
     the letters (as to style and circumstances of composition)
     proves them to be fabrications.

8   _____. "Sheridan in Barrel. II." Saturday Review 82
     (8 August): 130-31.
         Continues to demonstrate the spuriousness of letters
     said by Fraser Rae to be written by Elizabeth Linley (see
     1896.7) and questions as well the authenticity of yet
     another Sheridan document, two acts of The School for
     Scandal presumed by Rae to have been edited by Sheridan
     for the eventual publication of his comedy. By remaining

silent about the source of this document, Rae seems once
again to be dipping into the mythological "barrel" of
Sheridan wares. "Though Mr. Fraser Rae was specially
secured by Lord Dufferin to 'whitewash' his ancestor, he
has discharged the office so blindly and with such an
absence of tact that he has succeeded in damaging his
reputation in a way that no one has attempted before"
(p. 131).

9   GLADSTONE, W. E. "Sheridan." Living Age 210 (25 July):
     234-37.
          Reprints 1896.10.

10   _____. "Sheridan." Nineteenth Century 39 (June): 1037-42.
          Finds in the publication of Rae's Sheridan (1896.15)
     occasion to second Rae in rectifying the misjudgments
     made by history upon Sheridan's political career. The
     record suggests that Sheridan was looked to by his party
     to perform the most delicate operations (e.g., those in
     behalf of the prince and Mrs. Fitzherbert, those helping
     to resolve the mutinies at Portsmouth and the Nore); and,
     while he shared the errors of his party in such matters
     as the commercial treaty with France, he was not the
     author of such policies. Nor did he teach, as did Fox,
     that France is the natural enemy of Britain. In his
     devotion to the Irish Union, moreover, he proved himself
     a statesman of heroic worth. Why he did not receive
     just dues from his countrymen it is impossible to say,
     for his claims to recognition are manifest, as witness
     the affection felt for him by his family, especially by
     the sainted Elizabeth Linley.

11   HUTCHINSON, THOMAS. "Sheridan. A Biography. By Fraser Rae."
     Academy 49 (6 June): 461-63.
          Admires the practice in Fraser Rae's biography of
     letting the documents speak for themselves. Rae's method
     is then illustrated through generous quotations from
     Halhed's letters to Sheridan, from the Sheridan-Grenville
     correspondence, and from the letters of Elizabeth Linley
     to young Sheridan. The best worth of Rae's work resides
     thus in his objective presentations of unvarnished facts.
     Only through this kind of objectivity can Sheridan's
     character escape distortion.

12   J[OHNSON], E. G. "Richard Brinsley Sheridan." Dial
     21 (1 July): 11-13.
          Takes occasion, in a review of Rae's Sheridan (1896.15),
     to examine into the causes of Sheridan's tainted reputa-
     tion and to bring Sheridan's character into proper focus.

Early biographers such as Watkins (1817.4), Moore
(1825.9), and Smyth (1840.2) have certainly given the
playwright less than his dues, and the myths generated
by them about him have even found their way onto the
stage, in such travesties as Langle's "Un Homme de Rein,"
which enjoyed a long run in Paris during 1863, amusing
audiences with a dramatization of Sheridan as a reckless
gallant. Rae has righted the record somewhat. He has
exploded many myths about Sheridan and has upheld the
view of him as "an essentially honest (if often culpably
heedless) man, the life-long dupe of dishonest men; an
unbought politician in an age when venality was the rule"
(p. 13).

13   KRAUSE, GUSTAV. "Der wahre Sheridan." Anglia. Beiblatt:
      Mitteilungen aus dem Gesamten Gebiete der Englischen
      Sprache und Litteratur 7 (July): 81-85.
          Remarks the inadequacy of early biographies of
      Sheridan--especially those by Watkins (1817.4) and Smyth
      (1840.2)--and subscriges to the view that Fraser Rae's
      biography (1896.15) presents at last the "true" Sheridan,
      a man who deserved the highest admiration and thanks of
      his countrymen but who failed to receive his full dues
      because, as Mr. Gladstone has remarked (1896.10), he was
      the son of an untitled Irish actor.

14   MILTON, H. A. "The Real Sheridan." Theatre, 4th ser.
      27 (1 June): 332-37.
          Attributes the injustices done in biography to
      Sheridan's character to an unwillingness on the part of
      the British to let a person be highly gifted in more than
      one respect. "Sheridan, in point of fact, has suffered
      less for his failings than for the advantages which
      nature bestowed upon him--his adaptability, his quick,
      ready wit. He has been blamed not so much for his faults
      as for what really were his excellences" (p. 335).
      Although whimsical prejudices will not change over night,
      Fraser Rae's new biography of Sheridan will do its part to
      restore some sanity to the assessment of the playwright's
      character and achievements.

15   RAE, W. FRASER. Sheridan: A Biography. 2 vols. London:
      Richard Bentley.
          Laments the irony that Sheridan, endowed with every
      gift of brilliance, should have inherited as well his
      "grandfather's levity and thriftlessness and all his
      father's ill-luck" (1: 63). Enjoying, in any case, the
      "fine and praiseworthy traits" of his mother's "noble
      and beautiful mind" (1: 58), he pursued his high aims.

"He was always dissatisfied and he was often imprudent; but there is an imprudence which is sublime as well as a discontent which is noble, and their manifestation in his person constitutes one of his titles to esteem" (1: 346-47). In no wise was he excessive for his time, and the physical symptons easily mistaken for drunkenness in him were in fact "an affection of the skin which is just as common among those who drink nothing but water, as among those who drink little except alcohol in various forms" (2: 213-14). He was "The greatest dramatist since Shakespeare and the greatest orator who ever addressed the House of Commons. Unaffected by detraction and indifferent to praise, he now moves among the Immortals, as he formerly did among the great ones of earth, an equal among his equals" (2: 382). The appendix to volume 1 prints "Hernan's Miscellany. No. 1," the single essay of a periodical publication planned by Sheridan in youth, and reprints from the Athenaeum (1895.3) Rae's article "The Story of a Forgery," discrediting a letter falsely attributed to Elizabeth Linley. The appendix to volume 2 prints Sheridan's 1794 speech against Warren Hastings. Reviewed in 1896.3, 6-8, 10-14; 1897.6-10, 15.

16   _____. "Sheridan in Barrel." Saturday Review 82 (29 August): 219-20.
        Responds, in a letter to the editor, to charges made in two earlier issues of the Saturday Review (see 1896.7-8), charges rooted in the mystery surrounding several documents used by Rae in writing his biography of Sheridan (viz., some letters said written by Elizabeth Linley and two acts of The School for Scandal said corrected by Sheridan himself for publication). Although the sources of these documents are here identified (the letters as belonging to Augustin Daly of New York, the corrected acts of The School for Scandal as residing among the Sheridan papers at Frampton Court), the editor of the Saturday Review (in an appendage to Rae's letter) judges Rae's response to be weak because it ignores "the inconsistencies pointed out" (p. 220) in the articles directed against Rae.

17   S[HAW], G[EORGE] B[ERNARD]. "The Second Dating of Sheridan." Saturday Review 81 (27 June): 648-50.
        Advances the theory that since manners change faster than morals and since morals change faster than instincts and passions, a work of literature undergoes several phases of "dating." If its moral substance is deep and authentic, it will survive the first phase of dating,

that of manners. If its rendering of passions and
instincts is sound, it will survive the second phase of
dating, that of morals. Having survived the first phase
of dating, The School for Scandal has now (in 1896)
proceeded to the second one and is not faring well. Lady
Teazle's conduct in the Screen Scene supposes a double
standard of morality for men and women. Since now the
same standard applies to the conduct of both sexes, the
moral posture of the play is "dated" in an unfortunate
way. Its further survival is subject to question.

1897

1   AITKEN, G. A., ed. Introduction to The Rivals, by Sheridan.
    Temple Dramatists Series. London: J. M. Dent, pp. v-viii.
        Credits The Rivals with bringing to an end the "reign
    of the sentimental or genteel comedy" (p. v). The
    "origins" of the play include such antecedents as Frances
    Sheridan's A Journey to Bath, Fielding's Joseph Andrews,
    and Smollett's Humphry Clinker. Lydia Languish recalls
    Steele's Biddy Tipkin (of The Tender Husband) and Lydia
    Melford (of Humphry Clinker). Bob Acres recalls
    Shakespeare's Sir Andrew Aguecheek (however remotely),
    and, in some touches, Acres recalls Congreve's Sir
    Joseph Wittol of The Old Bachelor. A life of Sheridan
    is condensed from Aitkens's edition in the Temple
    Dramatists Series of The School for Scandal (1897.3).

2   _____. Preface to The Critic, by Sheridan. Temple
    Dramatists Series. London: J. M. Dent, pp. v-xi.
        Provides background as to the history of the play, its
    theatrical forerunners, and the playwright's life
    (condensed from Aitkens's edition of The School for
    Scandal; 1897.3). Giving color to its history is the
    tradition that Sheridan was locked in the green room
    until he finished writing it. Its forerunners include
    Beaumont and Fletcher's Knight of the Burning Pestle,
    Fielding's Tom Thumb, and Garrick's A Peep Behind the
    Curtain, but especially the duke of Buckingham's The
    Rehearsal. Several moments in Sheridan's play recall
    similar ones in Buckingham's. (Some are instanced here.)
    "But such occasional reminiscences of the earlier play
    are far from justifying a charge of plagiarism.
    Sheridan's indebtedness does not extend beyond the
    general idea of a satire on bad plays through the
    medium of a rehearsal" (pp. ix-x).

3   _____. Preface to The School for Scandal, by Sheridan.

1897

Temple Dramatists Series. London: J. M. Dent, pp. v-x.
Sketches Sheridan's life and comments briefly upon
(1) the early history of the play, (2) Sheridan's place in
the history of drama (which is "more akin to the work of
the so-called Restoration dramatists than to those of
his immediate predecessors" [pp. viii-ix]), and (3)
Sheridan's supposed debts to his predecessors (which do
not constitute plagiarism but give "interest, life and
action, or, in other words, its dramatic being, to the
cruder ideas which he found ready to his hand" [p. x]).
Reviewed in 1897.4.

4   ANON. "The School for Scandal. Edited with a Preface and
     Notes by G. A. Aitken." Athenaeum, no. 3646
     (11 September): 364.
        Credits the Aitken edition with being a better addition
     to the Temple Dramatists Series (Dent and Company) than
     was Augustin Birrell's introduction and edition of
     Sheridan's complete plays (1896.4). Here, too, however,
     the text is flawed and the introduction contains minor
     errors of fact. Moreover, the poem addressed to Mrs.
     Crewe, "A Portrait," appears here in a form not approved
     by Sheridan.

5   ANON. "Sheridan." Living Age 212 (13 March): 726-35.
     Reprints 1896.3.

6   FITZGERALD, PERCY. "The Real Sheridan." New Century Review
     1 (May): 395-403.
        Responds to Lord Dufferin's attack against him and
     other of Sheridan's biographers (in 1896.5) by complaining
     that the biography approved by Lord Dufferin, that of W.
     Fraser Rae (1896.15), shamelessly whitewashes its subject.
     It builds credit for him by adopting questionable sources,
     such as the Sheridan-Linley love letters, and by ignoring
     detractions made upon him even by members of his own
     family. Comments made by his father, his first wife, his
     widow, and close associates of his family justify
     impressions of him as an impecunious scapegrace and
     womanizer.

7   _____. The Real Sheridan. A Reply to Mr. Fraser Rae's
     "Sheridan a Biography." London: Francis J. Griffiths,
     43 pp.
        Reprints as a continuous essay the arguments of 1896.7,
     8 and 1897.6, 8, 9.

8   _____. "The Real Sheridan." Saturday Review 84 (10 July):
     38.

80

Responds to Lord Dufferin's comment--in a recent speech--that four distinguished people (the duke of Wellington, the marquis of Lansdowne, Lord John Russell, and Mrs. Tom Sheridan) had expressed high admiration for the character of Sheridan. It is a matter of record that all four of these people had, earlier in their lives, made serious detractions upon him.

9   _____. "The Real Sheridan. II." New Century Review 1 (June): 503-8.
   Amasses further evidence (cf. 1897.6) of Sheridan's doubtful character by selecting comments attributed to his son Tom and to others in association with him at Drury Lane Theatre. These comments testify that Sheridan began his career as a theater manager by bilking his debts. Thereafter he made an art of cheating his actors, his playwrights, and his colleagues, even though some of the latter (viz., the Linleys) were members of his own family. In truth, "this new 'real Sheridan' of Lord Dufferin and Mr. Fraser Rae is still no more than the old, real Sheridan we have been so long accustomed to, with all his impecuniosity, his drink, shiftiness, and tricks" (p. 508).

10   _____. Sheridan Whitewashed: an Examination of the New Life by Mr. Fraser Rae: with an Account of the Linley Letters--Said to Have Been Found in Barrels in Drury Lane. London: Downey and Co., 67 pp.
   Continues his attack upon the marquess of Dufferin and Ava and upon W. Fraser Rae by repeating arguments given earlier in the Saturday Review (1896.7, 8) and in the New Century Review (1897.6, 8, 9) that the marquess had misjudged Sheridan's earlier biographers (especially Fitzgerald himself) in his "Introduction" (1896.5) to Rae's Sheridan: a Biography (1896.15) and that Rae had misrepresented Sheridan not only by whitewashing his character (as the marquess would have him do) but also by drawing information from spurious sources: i.e., letters supposed to be written by Elizabeth Linley but actually resurrections of forgeries once said to have been found in a barrel and long ago discredited. Evidence of style and circumstance (here copiously presented) proves the spuriousness of the letters. Evidence of Sheridan's flawed character derives from no source so impressive as the testimony of his own family and associations (also here copiously presented). Rae chooses to ignore or explain away anything detrimental to Sheridan's character.

1897

11   GRAHAME, JAMES. "Sheridan." <u>Eclectic Magazine</u> 129 n.s. 66
        (September): 416-22.
              Reprints 1897.12.

12   _____. "Sheridan." <u>Westminister Review</u> 147 (May): 515-23.
              Admires Fraser Rae's recently published <u>Sheridan</u>
        (1896.15) and distils from it an account of Sheridan's
        life, emphasizing Sheridan's good fortune in being a
        playwright--since playwrights share with musicians and
        portrait artists the distinction of having their art
        "observed" (i.e., scrutinized and/or performed) in later
        times--and acknowledging three great political moments in
        Sheridan's career: the Irish Act of Union, the American
        War of Independence, and the trial of Warren Hastings. In
        Sheridan's life (as Rae renders it) "there thrills a
        strong, passionate, exalted soul, and there shines an
        intellect as brilliant as it is unique" (p. 523).

*13   SAYOUS, EDOUARD. <u>Les discours de Sheridan au temps du</u>
        <u>Directoire et de Napoléon</u>. Paris.
              Cited in 1962.12, p. 563.

14   TRELAWNEY, GEOFFREY. "To the Editor of the Saturday Review."
        <u>Saturday Review</u> 84 (31 July): 115.
              Suggests that Lord Dufferin, one of Sheridan's
        descendents, should know more about his famous ancestor
        than Mr. Percy Fitzgerald does. And, while it is possible
        to cite anecdotes detracting from Sheridan's character, it
        is certainly also possible to cite them in admiration of
        it. He is said, for example, to have given five pounds
        to an orange woman in Covent Garden when he noticed her
        poverty to be greater than his own. (In a responding
        note, the editor rejects the view that Lord Dufferin
        knows more about Sheridan than Percy Fitzgerald does:
        "we think that Mr. Fitzgerald has shown that he knows
        something of Sheridan, whereas Lord Dufferin has
        laboriously shown that he knows nothing.")

1898

1   ANON. "Mr. Jefferson in the Rivals." <u>Critic</u> 30, n.s.
        33 (November): 373-74.
              Judges Jefferson's performance as Acres to be "in some
        respects the most interesting" event of the past month
        and Jefferson himself to be "the most delightful and the
        most distinguished of living American actors" (p. 373).
        Called before the curtain on opening night at the Fifth
        Avenue Theatre, he took occasion to say of the actor's

art that it must be exhibited while it is still imperfect. The finishing touches must be added while the actor is before his audience.

2   OLIPHANT, MARGARET,. <u>Sheridan</u>. English Men of Letters Series. New York: Harper & Brothers, 207 pp.
        Reprints 1883.7.

3   RAE, W. FRASER. "More About Sheridan." <u>Nineteenth Century</u>
        43 (February): 256-65.
        Collects letters and other documents demonstrating, for example, the causes of Sheridan's failure in Stafford in 1812, his earnest efforts to have his son Tom appointed to a lucrative and responsible place (one within political gift but outside the vicissitudes of party), and his role in the retention of the Tories under the new regency in 1811, when Lords Grey and Grenville hoped to bring the Whigs to power. While some feel that Sheridan was cheated of cabinet rank in the ministry of "All the Talents" in 1806, he himself expressed no displeasure with the appointment given him (that of treasurer of the navy), a distinguished and highly compensated position. His only concern was for his son. And while his alienation from Lords Grey and Grenville at the time of the regency made him vulnerable to charges of disloyalty, the real reason for the continuation of the Tories (as Lord Grenville acknowledges in an unpublished letter to his brother Thomas) lay in the prince's distaste for the Whig leadership.

<u>1899</u>

1   DEVONSHIRE, GEORGIANA, duchess of. "Selections from the Letters of Georgiana Duchess of Devonshire." <u>Anglo-Saxon Review</u> 2 (September): 31-89.
        Contains an account given by the duchess herself (in writing to Countess Spencer on 30 October 1779) of <u>The Critic</u>: "It is vastly good,--the first act of the farce is quite charming it occasion'd peals of laughter every minute: The other two, in which the tragedy is rehears'd (to ridicule the insipid tragedys <u>d'aujourdhui</u>) are very good but not so entertaining and rather too long, there is a very pretty french song and an italian one introduc'd in the first act, in the second a view of Tilbury fort and the river which is vastly well done and in the last a sea fight which was too very pretty . . ." (p. 38). The collection also contains a letter from Sheridan to the duchess (dated 19 September 1780) thanking her for the

assistance she gave him in winning election at Stafford
(pp. 46-47). Other reference to Sheridan mentions his
winning a wager with the duke of Hare in 1786 (p. 84),
his wife's displeasure at being a house guest of Mrs.
Crewe (p. 84), and his shooting for a silver arrow at
Weirstay in 1787 (p. 88).

2   RAE, W. FRASER. "Sheridan's Sisters." Temple Bar 118
    (September): 45-63.
        Provides biographical accounts of Sheridan's sisters
    in the understanding that "Both Alicia and Elizabeth
    Sheridan possess the greater interest for us now because
    they were the sisters of Richard Brinsley. The elder
    was, however, a woman of note in her own day, being
    endowed with a large measure of the Sheridan talent.
    The younger had no pretension to literary merit, yet
    the 'journal letters,' as she called them, in which she
    narrated her experiences for her sister's information,
    have supplied the very moral and instructive incidents
    and statements which form the gist of this article"
    (p. 63).

3   _____. "Sheridan's Sons." Temple Bar 116 (March): 407-26.
        Adds particulars about Sheridan's sons to those given
    in Rae's own Sheridan: A Biography (1896.15). These
    particulars (developing the lives and characters of the
    two sons, Thomas and Charles Sheridan) justify the
    conclusion that "Both of Sheridan's sons loved him and
    were proud of having had such a father." Moreover, they
    both "were worthy of such a parent" (p. 426). Charles
    died unmarried in 1843, but Thomas, who died in 1817,
    "left behind him children who, as well as their progeny,
    have added fresh lustre to their race and name" (p. 426).

4   REED, THOMAS B. "Richard Brinsley Sheridan." Cosmopolitan
    26 (March): 534-36.
        Dismisses as facile nonsense the popular view that
    Sheridan was "a genius who accomplished great things
    without labor, and who might have compassed the world
    had he but submitted himself to harness and taken the
    common roadways to fame" (p. 534). In fact, Sheridan's
    accomplishments derived from hard work. Even The Rivals,
    though not the product of a conventionally bookish mind,
    reflects a store of studied observation. Records show
    that the other plays were also carefully made. In all
    his pursuits, Sheridan was "an independent, self-respect-
    ing man who did his work, and deserves a fame more
    substantial than has yet been accorded to him" (p. 536).
    His reputation suffers because the glow of his

brilliance outshines his commitment to deep and serious
principles and because history likes to amuse itself with
the myth of easy success and disappointed promise.

5   SCOTT, CLEMENT WILLIAM. <u>The Drama of Yesterday and To-day</u>.
London: Macmillian, 1: 568-80.
      Includes remarks on <u>The School for Scandal</u> as staged at
the Prince of Wales Theatre in April 1874, remarks
especially admiring of the quality of the production:
"The same profound respect and admiration for art which
inspire the performances of Molière and Corneille and
Racine at the Francais" (p. 580) are here given to
Sheridan with the result that the performance is a
showcase of late eighteenth-century manners, both visually
and histrionically. All the roles display the manners and
gestures appropriate to the highly authenticated settings,
but especially memorable is the performance of Mr.
Coghlan as Charles Surface. "How admirable is the touch
when Sir Oliver, anxious to become the purchaser of his
own picture, the young man kneels on the settee before it
and is lost in reverie of old days and old kindnesses"!
(p. 579) It is a gesture rife with suggestions.

1900

1   [BEERBOHM], MAX. "Acting Good and Evil." <u>Saturday Review</u>
89 (7 April): 424-25.
      Admires a revival of <u>The Rivals</u> chiefly on the grounds
that the miming is not overly mannered and the role of
Lydia Languish is properly played. While most actors
give broad flourish to eighteenth-century deportment, it
is probably that gesture and presence in the eighteenth
century "for all its greater elaborateness, tended more
than ours to an effect of repose" (p. 424). And, while
audiences favor the roles of Sir Anthony, Jack Absolute,
Bob Acres, and Mrs. Malaprop, Lydia "is the salt of the
play," for she "is the flawless incarnation of a type";
she is "incarnate girlhood--one of the eternal verities,
and not the least delightful of them" (p. 424).

2   _____. "Don Juan's Last Wager." <u>Saturday Review</u> 89
(10 March): 295-96.
      Mentions, in a review devoted principally to a play
called "Don Juan's Wager" (translated from Zorilla by
Mrs. Cunninghame Graham), a revival of <u>The Rivals</u> at the
Lyceum Theatre. It is a play that "needs 'go' in its
interpreters rather than imagination" (p. 296), and for
that reason it fares rather better in this production

1900

than does the Hamlet that alternates evenings with it at
the Lyceum.

*3   BRONTIN, AUSTIN. A Short History of the Rivals, The School
      for Scandal and She Stoops to Conquer. London, 23 pp.
          Cited in 1962.12, p. 551.

4   HARTMANN, HERMANN. Sheridan's School for Scandal. Beiträge
      zur Quellenfrage. Konigsberg: Hartungsche Buchdruckerei,
      46 pp.
          Reconsiders the works mentioned by Moore and others as
      possible sources for The School for Scandal, viz.,
      Fielding's Tom Jones, Murphy's Know Your Own Mind,
      Frances Sheridan's Sidney Bidulph, Molière's Misanthrope,
      Wycherley's The Plain Dealer. No one of these works
      makes clear claims as a source. A brief sketch of
      Sheridan's life, a close summary (scene by scene) of The
      School for Scandal, and an account of the early forms of
      the play precede these considerations of source.
      Sheridan's debt to Congreve's Double Dealer is reserved
      for a later discussion.

5   P[OLLARD], A.W., ed. "Bibliographical Note." In Sheridan's
      Plays. Library of English Classics. London:
      Macmillan, pp. v-viii.
          Sketches the record of Sheridan first editions and
      assigns the highest textual authority to the "Moore
      Edition" of 1821 (i.e., the Murray edition), despite its
      inclusion of The Camp, "the authorship of which is now
      universally assigned to Thomas Tickell" (p. vii), and
      despite evidences of careless proofreading. The first
      edition of The School for Scandal, that published by J.
      Ewling in Dublin, presumably in 1778, was no doubt
      published with the consent of the manager of Dublin
      Theatre, who had bought a manuscript copy of the play
      from Sheridan's sister, Mrs. LeFanu.

6   RAE, W. FRASER. "Sheridan's Brother." Temple Bar 119
      (March): 396-415.
          Begins a biographical account of Charles Francis
      Sheridan with the observation that "The elder brother of
      Richard Brinsley Sheridan possessed many natural gifts
      and much acquired knowledge; he wrote an interesting
      history and several pamphlets; he was a fluent speaker
      in the Irish Parliament, and, during many years, he
      was Secretary of War in the Irish Government. Yet he
      is now remembered because he was the brother of a
      greater man than himself" (p. 396).

7   STREET, G. S.   "Sheridan and Mr. Shaw."   Blackwood's
    Edinburgh Magazine 167 (June): 832-36.
        Argues that Sheridan's continuing popularity properly
    belongs to Congreve.   Congreve's characters have
    breeding; Sheridan's have not.   Congreve, who surpasses
    Sheridan in intellect, reveals in his comedies a truer
    understanding of human nature than Sheridan does, a more
    genuine comic substance.   When Sheridan touches subjects
    not quite superficial his plays become heavy.   Congreve's
    keep their gaiety.   Sheridan enjoys permanence only
    because he was born a generation after Congreve and
    inherited traditions of sensitive decency, traditions
    less skeptical and severe than Congreve's.   Despite his
    superficial wit and intellectual coarseness, however,
    Sheridan deserves to survive.   He is thin and farcical
    and lacks ideas, but he is an effective craftsman, a
    distinctive stylist, and a friend to the players.   By
    contrast, Shaw (in such a play as You Never Can Tell)
    sacrifices everything to an overabundance of ideas.   His
    obsession with philosophy produces two bad effects: "The
    first is that one seems to be listening to a lecture,
    a witty lecture but not a play.   The second is that it
    causes Mr. Shaw to use his actors worse than dogs" (p.
    834), for they must sacrifice consistency of tone to
    ideas.   Again, Congreve demonstrates the superior gift.
    His "ideas come naturally from the play of his characters,
    and out of the fulness of his experience" (p. 834).

8   WEDMORE, FREDERICK.   "Notes on Players and Old Plays."
    Nineteenth Century 48 (August): 249-55.
        Reviews the theatrical season just past by recalling
    revivals of The Rivals, The School for Scandal and She
    Stoops to Conquer.   Sheridan receives credit for the
    higher art.   He evinces technical perfection.   In The
    School for Scandal, for example, "a rare and fascinating
    perfection is bestowed upon the familiar and the old;
    and in place of absolute novelty of conception there is
    the charm of the heightened touch."   The dialogue,
    "ordered, tended, pruned into all-pervasive vigour,
    stands, and must stand to remote days, with the things
    that last" (p. 250).   She Stoops to Conquer, while a
    product of "gentle genius" (p. 249), reflects "the
    rougher achievements of spontaneous but farcical humour"
    (p. 250).

1901

1   OLIPHANT, MARGARET.   Sheridan.   English Men of Letters

1901

Series. New York: Harper & Brothers, 207 pp.
Reprints 1883.7.

2 SELLIER, WALTER. Kotzebue in England. Ein Beitrag zur
Geschichte der englischen Bühne und der Beziehungen der
deutschen Litteratur zur englischen. Leipzig: Oswald
Schmidt, 96 pp.
Discusses (1) the discovery in England of Kotzebue's
work, (2) the adaptation in English of eighteen of his
plays (from The Stranger in 1798 to The Poachers and The
Roebuck in 1824), (3) the grounds of his popularity in
England, and (4) the aftereffects of this popularity
both as to theatrical history and the study of German
classics in England. Discussion of The Stranger gives
general attention to the changes made in shaping the
original play (Menschenhass und Reue) for representation
in England, and discussion of Pizarro centers mainly upon
the political timeliness of Sheridan's version. Some
notice is given, too, to the early printed issues in
English of Pizarro.

1902

1 BANG, W. "Zu Sheridan's Rivals." Englische Studien 31
(1902): 350-52.
Proposes renderings in German of several troubling
passages in The Rivals. The phrase "gentlemen of the
professions" in act 1, scene 1 should be rendered not
"die herren gelehrten" (as is sometimes done) but "die
herren vom handwerk" since "professions" in this context
indicates not men of learning but guildsmen. In the same
speech of the coachman's the term "college," in the phrase
"tho' all the college should appear with their own
heads," implies not a university but a college of
physicians and should be rendered so. When, in act 2,
scene 1 Julia is termed by Acres the "bell and spirit of
the company," she is understood to be "the pipe and
balladmonger of a circle," and the translation should
reflect this concept.

2 CREEVY, THOMAS. The Creevey Papers. London: Macmillan,
passim.
Contains scattered references to Sheridan as he figures
in Creevey's correspondence between the years 1803 and
1816. The fullest references relate to Sheridan's
conduct during the second Regency Crisis (1811) and to
his deathbed suffering. In both cases he is treated
with admiration and affection. His death is said to be

hastened by his fear of arrest and prison, a fear
haunting him after his loss of parliamentary immunities.

3   DUFFERIN AND AVA, marquess of. Introduction to <u>Sheridan's</u>
    <u>Plays Now Printed As He Wrote Them</u>, edited by W. Fraser
    Rae. London: David Nutt, pp. vii-xii.
        Speculates briefly as to the continuing popularity of
    Sheridan's comedies and finds probable causes (1) in the
    way the plays adapt themselves to various casts and
    styles of acting and (2) in the way archaic manners and
    customs (e.g., the use of swords, powder, bagwigs, and
    paniers) now lend themselves to a pleasing theatrical
    artificiality. As regards the present edition of
    Sheridan's plays, it justifies itself as a resource
    against which to study Sheridan's many revisals of his
    work, a touchstone of his obsession with making the good
    better and best.

4   HALL, ARTHUR D., ed. <u>Selections from Comedies and Speeches</u>;
    <u>also Verses to the Memory of Garrick and Anecdotes and</u>
    <u>Witty Sayings</u> [by Sheridan]. Street and Smith Little
    Classics. New York: Street and Smith, 184 pp.
        Rejoices, in the introduction, over Sheridan's
    brilliance in repartee and writing and admires the care
    and precision of his work but chooses to "draw a veil"
    over the "irregularities" (p. xiii) of his private life.
    Provides (under such captions as "Mrs. Malaprop's
    Opinions," "Bob Acres' Valor," "The Art of Puffing," "A
    Reply to Burke") brief passages from selected works and
    sayings.

5   JEFFERSON, JOSEPH. Introduction to <u>The Rivals</u>, by Sheridan.
    New York: The Century Company, pp. i-xvi.
        Reprints portion of 1889.4 relating to <u>The Rivals</u>.

6   OLIPHANT, MARGARET. <u>Sheridan</u>. English Men of Letters Series.
    London: Macmillan, 207 pp.
        Reprints 1883.7.

7   RAE, W. FRASER, ed. "Prefatory Notes." In <u>Sheridan's Plays</u>
    <u>Now Printed As He Wrote Them</u>. And His <u>Mother's</u>
    <u>Unpublished Comedy, "A Journey to Bath</u>." London:
    David Nutt, 1: xiii-xxxx.
        Explains that this edition prints from manuscripts then
    at Frampton Court, Dorset, the texts of <u>St. Patrick's Day</u>,
    <u>The Duenna</u>, <u>The School for Scandal</u>, and <u>The Critic</u>. <u>The</u>
    <u>Rivals</u>, for which no manuscript exists at Frampton Court,
    appears in the text of the first edition of 1775,
    "Sheridan's own acting version of his comedy" (p. xiv).

1902

Prefatory comment on The Rivals notes respects in which
John Murray's text of 1821, presumably edited by John
Wilkie, differs from the first edition of 1775. Newspaper
excerpts here also record contemporary responses to The
Rivals. Comment on St. Patrick's Day notes that "The
version taken from Sheridan's manuscript differs in a
few unimportant particulars from that published in Murray's
edition and succeeding ones" (p. xxxv). The manuscript of
The Duenna is described as being incomplete and filled out
here "from current versions" (p. xxxv). The manuscript
of The School for Scandal "differs in many respects from
that which is generally known" (p. xxxvii), and the
manuscript of The Critic contains several additions to the
"current version," but "they are unimportant" (p. xxxviii).
Variant readings do not appear. The volume also contains
the text of Frances Sheridan's A Journey to Bath. (See
1902.8, 9.)

8   RHODES, CROMPTON. "An 'Authentic' Version of Sheridan."
     Times Literary Supplement, 4 July, p. 198.
        Responds to Fraser Rae's edition of Sheridan's plays (as
     printed for the first time from the original manuscripts)
     by agreeing that "the public should be enabled to judge
     of Sheridan's work exactly as it was when it first left
     his hands." Of "little or no importance," however, are
     the alterations and excisions noted by Rae as made by the
     editors of the 1821 edition of Sheridan's plays. Conven-
     tions of staging make such changes necessary, and--given
     the current naturalistic methods of acting--changes
     nowadays are much more extensive than they were in
     Sheridan's own time. In fact, these methods are imposing
     an obsolescence on Sheridan; and, while his plays may
     continue to be read, they are not likely to be acted much
     longer. The press clippings by which Rae offers to
     compensate for the missing manuscript version of The
     Rivals, clippings intended to characterize the first
     version of the play, actually achieve very little, for "the
     dramatic criticism of 1775 was very poor stuff, contenting
     itself with vague generalities and a few dogmas." It
     would be interesting, however, to see certain materials
     not provided by Rae: the press notices on Sheridan's
     wittiest play, The Critic. Do the newspapers answer
     Sheridan's attack upon them?

9   THOMPSON, FRANCIS. "Sheridan Un-Wilkied." Academy and
     Literature 63 (23 August): 192-93.
        Reviews Fraser Rae's edition of Sheridan's plays (see
     1902.7), giving the texts credit for restoring passages
     deleted by Wilkie, who prepared the Murray edition of

1821, but even the Rae edition "cannot be called altogether a good one" (p. 192). The type is not uniform and is too small; the prefatory notes allow factual errors; "so important a date as that of the original publication of The Rivals is left unrecorded" (p. 192). The commentary does not show "a very fine literary sense" (p. 192). Omission of punctuation in the tests (following the practice of the manuscripts) reflects "a whimsical pedantry" (p. 192). Sheridan, however, is due the praise given him in the Rae edition, for his personality was such as to "bring a touch of romance into the most prosaic of epochs" (p. 192).

<u>1903</u>

1 ARMES, W. D. "The Source of Sheridan's <u>Rivals</u>." <u>Transactions and Proceedings of the American Philological Association</u> 34 (1903): cv-cvii.

Insists, despite denials from some critics, that Humphry Clinker is the source of The Rivals. As to plot, "Substitute Beverly for Wilson, Languish for Melford, and aunt for uncle, and this is the plot of The Rivals" (p. cv). As to characters, "Change maiden to widow, and this describes Mrs. Malaprop" (p. cv). Sir Anthony recalls Matthew Bramble; Jack Absolute recalls young Wilson; Sir Lucius O'Trigger recalls Sir Ulic Mackilligut. Julia and Faulkland are amplifications of the supposed Jery Melford-Miss Willis relationship. In the novel, too, Sheridan finds inspiration for the duelling episode in King's Mead Fields. "The plot, then, most of the important characters, and the principal incidents in The Rivals, were developed by Sheridan from suggestions in Humphry Clinker." Humphry Clinker is the raw one, but in The Rivals "we have the refined metal stamped with the hall-mark of Sheridan's brilliant wit" (p. cvii).

2 ELIZABETH, LADY HOLLAND. The Journals of Elizabeth Lady Holland (1791-1811), edited by the earl of Ilchester. 2 vols. London: Longmans, Green, passim.

Includes (among scattered references to Sheridan) an assessment of his character as follows: "About him my reason and impulse always are at variance; reflection convinces me he ought to be despised for his private life and doubted for his political, but whenever I see him, if but for five minutes, a sort of cheerful frankness and pleasant wittiness puts to flight all ye reasonable prejudices that I entertain against him" (1: 255). Other comment touches upon Sheridan's qualifications as a

1903

speaker (2: 96), his relationship with the Prince of
Wales (1: 221-22; 2: 283-84), his admirable conduct in
behalf of the royal family after an attempt on the king's
life at Drury Lane in 1800 (2: 81).

3   GREEN, EMANUEL. Thomas Linley, Richard Brinsley Sheridan, and
Thomas Mathews: Their Connection with Bath. Bath: At the
Herald Office, 81 pp.
    Purposes to correct misconceptions and to provide
accurate information about the careers in Bath of the
Linleys, the Sheridans, and Thomas Mathews. As it touches
these careers, Richard Sheridan's conduct gathers little
credit, even though his best plays were the story of his
Bath years. His marriage to Elizabeth Linley, for example,
broke up the "prosperous Bath home" of the Linleys, and
"largely tended through disappointment and a constant
lasting regret to break up the life if not the heart" (p.
14) of Thomas Linley. His elopement with Elizabeth issued
from a selfish petulance which had seen him systematically
isolate her from the affections of other admirers and
render her wholly dependent upon him. The duels with
Mathews arose from provocations whereby Sheridan made
Mathews odious first to Miss Linley and then to the whole
town, and biographers who derogate from the character of
Mathews in the matter of Miss Linley derive their
information from biased sources, such as Sheridan himself
or his sister Mrs. Henry LeFanu. Contemporary record
indicates that Mathews acquitted himself honorably in the
eyes of Bath society. In fact, Sheridan's ultimate
distaste for Bath was aggravated by his inability to
vilify Mathews there.

1904

1   BEAVER, ALFRED. "The Beautiful Sheridans." Longman's
Magazine 45 (November): 70-79.
    Credits Sheridan with establishing a brilliant line,
then celebrates (through numerous anecdotes) the beauty,
wit, and accomplishment of Tom Sheridan and his children,
especially the three daughters Helen Selina (Mrs.
Blackwood, later Lady Dufferin, who died Lady Gifford),
Caroline Elizabeth Sarah (who became the Hon. Mrs. Norton
and afterward Lady Stirling Maxwell), and Georgiana (wife
of Lord Seymour, twelfth duke of Somerset).

2   GREEN, EMANUEL. Richard Brinsley Sheridan and Thomas Linley,
Their Residences at Bath, with a Notice of the Sheridan
Grotto. Bath: Herald Office, 32 pp.

Fixes the residential address of the Sheridans in Bath
at No. 9 New King Street, quarters shared with the owner,
William Bowers. In establishing this address it is
necessary to understand that New King Street was
originally part of Kingsmead Street (the street in which
Thomas Moore places the Sheridans in Bath) and that the
surviving rate books, from which the exact address can
be computed, make no distinction between Kingsmead Street
and New King Street, names which appear interchangeably
in contemporary advertisements and notices. Contemporary
documentation also indicates that the grotto celebrated
in Sheridan's love poems was not in Spring Gardens (as
Moore supposes) but in the North Parade field and that
the Linleys lived at what is today No. 1 Orchard Street.

3   MATTHEWS, BRANDER, ed. "Richard Brinsley Sheridan. A
    Biographical Sketch." In Sheridan's Comedies: The Rivals
    and The School for Scandal. New York: Thomas Y. Crowell,
    pp. xi-lv.
        Reprints 1885.1 with minor revisions based upon Fraser
    Rae's recently published biography of the playwright.
    (Rae had himself adopted from the issue of 1885 Matthews's
    explanation of the financial arrangements by which
    Sheridan got control of Drury Lane Theatre.)

4   SHERIDAN, WILFRED. "Some Account of the Sheridan Family."
    Ancestor, no. 9 (April): 1-5.
        Traces the Sheridan line from its beginnings (with
    Oscar O'Sheridan in 1014) through the generation of the
    playwright's grandchildren (late in the nineteenth
    century). Family portraits accompany the sketch and
    continue into the article following it. They include
    pictures of the playwright, his grandfather, his parents,
    his wife Elizabeth, and his son Tom.

5   STRONG, ARTHUR S. "Warren Hastings's Own Account of His
    Impeachment: A Hitherto Unpublished Document." Harper's
    Monthly Magazine 110 (December): 89-95.
        Prints a letter written by Hastings on 17 July 1788
    to his secretary, Thompson, who had remained in India
    during the trial of Hastings to collect from the natives
    petitions on Hastings's behalf. The letter "is preserved
    at Nottell Priory among the papers of Lord St. Oswald,
    by whose permission it is printed here" (pp. 89-90). In
    it Hastings describes Sheridan's performance at the trial
    as consisting of "impudent assertions of facts which were
    not in proof; dull, dry & fallacious applications of the
    Evidence, which he magnified, and suppressed, as either
    served his purpose; of some Wit, but much more buffoonery;

of gross Invective, & foul Language throughout; many
flights of fine Imagination; much Bombast, & even
unintelligible Declamation; and Patches of highly wrought
Oratory, evidently got by heart, & of perfect Composition
had it borne any just Relation to the subject" (p. 90).
Of special annoyance to Hastings was Sheridan's practice
of moving his audience first to passion then to laughter.

1905

1 GOSSE, EDMUND, ed. Introduction to The Critic, by Sheridan.
   London: William Heinemann, pp. v-x.
   Surmises that the immediate occasion of The Critic was
   a run of failed tragedies at Drury Lane, including
   Alexander Dow's Zingis and Sethona and Richard Cumberland's
   The Battle of Hastings. In general, however, Sheridan
   "determined to write a sort of renovated Rehearsal, in
   which people should still see the ridiculous side of
   overstrained tragical language, but in which they should
   not be puzzled by allusions which were intelligible only
   to an older generation" (p. vii). He succeeded handsomely,
   especially in his caricature of Richard Cumberland as
   Sir Fretful Plagiary. "There is perhaps no other example
   of the absolute destruction of a reputation by ridicule
   so complete as that of Cumberland's by the picture of
   Sir Fretful Plagiary" (p. ix).

2 _____. Introduction to The Rivals, by Sheridan. Favourite
   Classics. London: William Heinemann, pp. v-xiv.
   Introduces The Rivals by noticing the autobiographical
   features of its action, by recounting the details of its
   disappointing reception and subsequent great success, and
   by describing its comic spirit. It "presents us with the
   results of no close anatomy of human character, and is
   illuminated by no subtle flashes of analysis or intuition.
   Its object, frankly, is to entertain, and the unbroken
   merriment of more than a century proves that it attained
   what it aimed at" (p. viii).

3 NETTLETON, GEORGE HENRY. "The Books of Lydia Languish's
   Circulating Library." Journal of English and Germanic
   Philology 5 (October): 492-500.
   Authenticates all the titles in Lydia Languish's library
   and describes (by means of contemporary book notices and
   reviews) so many of them as have never previously been
   located, or were located incorrectly by previous
   commentators, or have not enjoyed sufficient elucidation
   from commentary. Nettleton incorporates these materials

in the introduction to his edition of Sheridan's major dramas (see 1906.3). A contemporary reviewer of Mrs. Chapone's Letters (1773) takes occasion to observe that most sentimental novels inflame the passions of youth, excite expectations of adventure, and aggravate absurd conduct. Lydia is a "concrete presentation" of that reviewer's "abstract truths" (p. 500).

1906

1 KNIGHT, JOSEPH, ed. Introduction to The Dramatic Works of Richard Brinsley Sheridan. London: Oxford University Press, pp. vii-xxi.
   Observes that Sheridan's popularity ranks second only to that of Shakespeare and that his greatness as a statesman is now unfairly obscured by the haphazard record of his speeches. Provides a biographical sketch based upon genealogy and offers sympathetic accounts of the plays, noticing that "Idle as Sheridan represented himself and was, he was not sparing of the limae labor et mora--counselled by Horace--and the polish assigned to characters and expression is the work of a thorough artist" (pp. xvi-xvii).

2 L[IVINGSTON], L. S. "First Edition of 'The School for Scandal.'" Nation 83 (30 August): 179-80.
   Examines two early printed texts of The School for Scandal (the undated "Ewling" edition and a Dublin edition of 1780) and concludes from collations that the Ewling is probably the earliest printed text (as it had widely been thought to be) but that the text of 1780, a carelessly printed one probably taken from the same source as the Ewling, is the first dated text. Comparison of this text with the American edition of Hugh Gaine (1786) and the Thomas Moore edition of 1821 (i.e., the John Murray edition) reveals, furthermore, that in declaring in his biography of Sheridan that the Dublin edition is "perfectly correct," Moore refers to an edition published later in Dublin than the Ewling and the 1780.

3 NETTLETON, GEORGE HENRY, ed. Introduction to The Major Dramas of Richard Brinsley Sheridan. The Rivals, The School for Scandal, The Critic. Athenaeum Press Series. Boston: Ginn, pp. vii-cxvii.
   Provides extensive introductory comment (110 pages) upon Sheridan's life, his relation to Elizabethan, Restoration, and sentimental dramatists, his comedy as

1906

compared to Goldsmith's, the supposed sources of his
major plays, and matters of special interest to each of
these plays, e.g., "Eighteenth-Century Bath," "The Books
of Lydia Languish's Circulating Library," "The Composition
of The School for Scandal," "Sheridan's 'Jupiter,' A
Forerunner of The Critic," "Personal Caricature in The
Critic," "The Element of Actual History in The Critic."
While suffering reversals of fortune in his later life,
Sheridan the man owes no apologies to history for his
character. It is firmer than those of most public men
in his day. Among Elizabethan playwrights his kinship
to Ben Jonson is the closest. Among Restoration
playwrights it is closest to Congreve and Etherege. In
comparison to Goldsmith he perhaps sacrifices naturalness
to brilliancy, but in mastery of stage effect he "clearly
excels Goldsmith, and indeed is not unworthy of
comparison with Shakespeare" (p. xlix). Not at all the
plagiarist detractors mark him to be, his sources are his
observations of life. Contemporary Bath, for example,
supplied him amply with caricatures for The Rivals. He
did not need to borrow characters from other writers or
to rifle his own life for situations. Furthermore, the
slow evolution of The School for Scandal, a documented
record, demonstrates the independent care with which he
crafted his art.

4   OLIPHANT, MARGARET. Sheridan. English Men of Letters
     Series. London: Macmillan, 207 pp.
          Reprints 1883.7.

5   RANGER. "The Choice of Books: Richard Brinsley Sheridan."
     Bookman (London), 30 (September): 210-12.
          Recommends Sheridan to new readers on the strength of
     his place among great Irish playwrights, his brilliant
     comic wit (as distinguished from the "humor" of Goldsmith),
     his distinction as the beneficiary of a fortunate family
     lineage, his exciting and romantic youth, and his
     achievements as playwright and statesman.

*6   SHAW, GEORGE BERNARD. "The Second Dating of Sheridan." In
     Dramatic Opinions and Essays. London: Brentano's,
     2: 28-36.
          Reprints 1896.17.

1907

1   HOWE, WILL DAVID, ed. Introduction to The Rivals and The
     School for Scandal, by Sheridan. New York: Macmillan,

pp. i-xxxiii.

Concludes a general biographical sketch by remarking that Sheridan was a typical product of the eighteenth century: "Graceful and charming in society, witty and amiable in conversation, versatile in achievement . . . generous to a fault, and . . . possessed of a rashness and improvidence in money matters that worked his ruin" (p. xviii). Sheridan can claim no such profound originals as Shakespeare's Sir John Falstaff, but "for real fun . . . we know nothing better than a few hours with Sheridan" (p. xxii). "His excellence is his wit, his play of fancy, his ability to create types, and his appeal to the interest of his audience by an untiring array of surprising scenes" (p. xxii).

2   MATTHEWS, BRANDER, ed. Introduction to The Rivals, by Sheridan. New York: T. Y. Crowell, pp. ix-xxxi.

Reprints the introduction, text and apparatus of 1885.1 (that part pertaining to The Rivals). The body of the book contains eighteen illustrations by M. Power O'Malley based upon lines from the play.

1908

1   ANON. "Sale of Sheridan Letters." Times (London), 17 July, p. 13.

Announces the sale, through Messrs. Robinson, Fisher, and Co., of "engravings, prints, miniatures and autograph letters 'the property of a gentleman,' among which were some interesting letters of R. B. Sheridan." The ones mentioned here are addressed to the duchess of Devonshire.

2   PHELPS, WILLIAM LYON, AND NETTLETON, GEORGE HENRY. Preface and Introduction to The Critic; or A Tragedy Rehearsed, by Sheridan. New Haven, Conn.: Arthur Amory Gammell, pp. v-xii.

Prints the text acted by the Yale Dramatic Association on 23-24 April 1902 and in its revival of The Critic in 1908. The preface places the play among works of "distinct historical or literary value" (p. v), as prescribed for its productions by the founding principles of the Association. The introduction recognizes The Critic as "the supreme instance in English drama of the triumph of sheer wit over the ephemeral nature of burlesque" (p. x). Its permanence appears in how far the characterization of a Sir Fretful Plagiary transcends the mere caricature of jealous and sensitive Richard Cumberland. In The Critic, Sheridan takes a stand for

1908

"sanity in the drama" (p. ix), a stand applicable to all
ages.

1909

1   BROUGHTON, JOHN CAM HOBHOUSE, baron. Recollections of a
    Long Life, edited by Lady Dorchester. London: John
    Murray, 1: 347.
        Offers, in a brief entry for 13 July 1816, a firsthand
    account of Sheridan's funeral. Although attended by
    every kind of dignitary, "The Burial Service was
    ill-performed by Dr. Fynes, Prebendary of the Cathedral,
    and no one seemed much affected as the coffin was lowered
    into the grave, except Mr. Charles Sheridan and Mr.
    Linley." But, generally speaking, "public funerals are
    not affecting."

2   DEVONSHIRE, GEORGIANA, duchess of. "Georgiana, Duchess of
    Devonshire's Diary." In Sheridan, by Walter Sichel.
    London: Constable, 2: 399-426.
        Collects notes relating to the First Regency Crisis
    (1788-89) written during that time for the information
    of the duchess' mother. Sheridan figures prominently in
    his role as adviser to the prince, and it is remarked of
    him that should the regency succeed he might, if he wished
    it, become chancellor of the exchequer. In a preface
    added by the duchess in 1802, obviously by way of
    preparing the notes for publication, she remarks that
    Sheridan's conduct "not only gave convincing evidence
    of his talents but at the same time evinc'd the danger
    of his character." She continues: "I do not mean to
    accuse him of any duplicity; in fact He has stood the
    test of even poverty and I feel convinc'd of the honor
    of his political sentiments--but he cannot resist playing
    a sly game; he cannot resist the pleasure of acting
    alone, and this, added to his natural want of judgment
    and dislike of consultation frequently has made him
    commit his friends and himself" (p. 400).

3   OLIPHANT, MARGARET. Sheridan. English Men of Letters Series.
    London: Macmillan, 207 pp.
        Reprints 1883.7.

4   SICHEL, WALTER. "Bibliography of Sheridan's Works Published
    and Unpublished." In Sheridan. London: Constable,
    2: 445-59.
        See 1909.5. Brings up to date and corrects confusions
    in the British Museum Bibliography of Sheridan's works

1909

compiled by John P. Anderson for Lloyd Sanders's <u>Life of Sheridan</u> (1890.1). While the Anderson bibliography is a valuable foundation for any complete catalog of Sheridan's works, it fails in some cases to make distinctions between skits based upon Sheridan's plays and the plays themselves. Since its appearance, furthermore, new issues of the plays have come into print.

5   ____. <u>Sheridan, from New and Original Material; Including a Manuscript Diary by Georgiana, Duches of Devonshire.</u> 2 vols. London: Constable.

    Attempts a comprehensive account of Sheridan's life, drawing heavily upon sources not utilized by earlier biographers: e.g., the Holland House manuscripts, the Devonshire House papers, the manuscript correspondence of Betsy Sheridan, the autograph letters of the duchess of Devonshire and her sister Lady Bessborough. Representing Sheridan's life in two divisions, literary and political, the book first develops a "Sheridan anthology" (p. ix), basing literary analysis and comment upon early printed editions. Sheridan's political career is then set in social contexts, the events seen against his dealings with other men and women of prominence and in settings, when apposite, of political intrigue. An "Overture" precedes the whole wherein Sheridan's character is seen within its environment: "The base of Sheridan's nature is good, but by virtue of his sentimentality he often came to be romantic where he should have been experienced; sensuous, even sensual, where he ought to have been loving; dependent on the outward where he should have been self-poised" (1: 4). His "bent was an actor's, and his knowledge of the public (one essential of statesmanship) was unerring" (1: 23). He "at once expressed and contradicted the paradoxes of his age, its ornateness yet oddity, its shabbiness and splendour, its love both of the formal and the flamboyant, its dead levels ranged below heights of aspiration, its passion for criticism, yet creativeness of modern ideas" (1: 124). The appendix to the first volume prints two poems sometimes attributed to Sheridan: "An Ode to Scandal" and "The General Fast." Appendixes to the second volume include "Mrs. Sheridan's Letters from Harrow to Alicia LeFanu," "The Prince of Wales's Answer (Written by Sheridan) to . . . Mr. Pitt," "Georgiana, Duchess of Devonshire's Diary," "Letters from Sheridan to the Duchess of Devonshire and Her Sister, Lady Bessborough," and "Bibliography of Sheridan's Works Published and Unpublished." Reviewed in <u>Living Age</u> 264 (8 January 1910): 76-82; <u>Current Literature</u> 48 (February

1909

1910): 199–201; <u>New York Times</u> , 12 February 1910,
pp. 73–74; <u>Nation</u> 90 (26 May 1910): 531–34; by James W.
Tupper in the <u>Dial</u> 48 (16 June): 424–25; also in 1910.7.

6   SPENCER, A. E. F., trans. <u>The School for Scandal Act IV,
      Scene 1</u>. Gaisford Prize for Greek Verse. Oxford, 15 pp.
          Prints a text recited in the Sheldonian Theatre on
      23 June 1909.

<u>1910</u>

1   ADAMS, JOSEPH QUINCY, JR., ed. Introduction to <u>The Rivals</u>,
      by Sheridan. Riverside Literature Series. Boston:
      Houghton Mifflin, pp. iv–xxvi.
          Surveys Sheridan's literary and political careers,
      drawing information from the biographies of Rae (1896.15)
      and Sichel (1909.5). Discusses the play as reflecting
      several categories of comedy—comedy of intrigue, comedy
      of humours, comedy of wit, comedy of society—but, while
      admiring this complexity, faults the action for being
      "too evident" (p. xvi) in its machinery and too
      artificial in its language. Examines the sources of the
      action and the history of the text.

2   _____. "The Original Performance of <u>The Rivals</u>." <u>Nation</u>
      90 (April): 374–75.
          Offers to correct an error prevalent in many
      biographies of and comments upon Sheridan (e.g., works by
      Sichel [1909.5], Fitzgerald [1886.3], Sanders [1890.2],
      Matthews [1885.1], Sigmond [1848.1], Aitken [1897.1]) that
      <u>The Rivals</u> was withdrawn after the second night of
      representation (i.e., after 18 January 1775) rather than
      after the first (17 January). In <u>The Major Dramas of
      Sheridan</u> (1906.3), G. K. Nettleton traces the mistake
      to an ambiguous comment in the <u>Town and Country Magazine</u>
      for January 1775. A more likely source is a playbill
      actually announcing the second performance for
      18 January, a bill no doubt printed for Covent Garden
      Theatre in advance of the decision to withdraw the play.
      Contemporary newspaper comment upholds the view that the
      play was withdrawn after the performance of 17 January.

3   _____. "The Text of Sheridan's <u>The Rivals</u>." <u>Modern
      Language Notes</u> 25 (June): 171–73.
          Observes that while W. Fraser Rae, in his edition of
      Sheridan's plays (1902), allows the impression that he
      prints <u>The Rivals</u> from a manuscript version, there is no
      known manuscript of this play. What Rae in fact has

done is to reproduce a modern reprint of the play, one
based, after the Murray edition of 1821, upon the third
edition corrected (1776); into this he has inserted
passages taken from the first edition (ones omitted from
the third edition corrected) and has introduced
corrections here and there from the first edition.
Containing a large accumulation of errors, the Rae text
has no scholarly value and is unworthy the distinction
given it by G. K. Nettleton in making it a basic text
for his The Major Dramas of Sheridan (1906). In point
of fact, "the only complete and authoritative text of
The Rivals is the first edition; this has never been
reprinted" (p. 173). It was published by John Wilkie
in London in 1775.

4   ANON. "The MS of the 'School for Scandal.'" Times (London),
    26 May, p. 8.
        Announces the sale at Sotheby's on 17 June of the
    Chetwynd manuscript of The School for Scandal, an
    autograph in 137 quarto pages presented by the author
    to William Chetwynd, the official examiner of plays,
    and slightly damaged in 1834, when, as the property of
    Sir George Chetwynd, it narrowly escaped destruction
    in a fire at the book bindery. "The MS exhibits many
    minor differences from the printed version."

5   ANON. "Sale of Valuable Books and MSS." Times (London),
    18 June, p. 12.
        Includes mention of the sale at Sotheby's on 17 June
    of the Chetwynd MS of The School for Scandal for 75 pounds.
    (See 1910.4.)

6   BENJAMIN, SAUL LEWIS. "Sheridan." Bookman (London),
    37 (March): 257-66.
        Pronounces it a "sad day for literature" when Sheridan
    "abandoned the study for the senate" (p. 262), for he
    displayed the genius of a true dramatist. In their
    durability, his plays demonstrate that "a great comedy
    must contain inimitable character-drawing, great and
    fanciful humour, a touch of malice, and kindly satire
    on society, and that it must have its foundation fixed
    firmly on a broad aspect of life" (pp. 260, 262). While
    history may lament the want of continuity in Sheridan's
    life, it is fruitless to assume that he kept a wealth of
    plays unwritten in him. A man knows "when he has spent
    his gold" (p. 265). It is only proper to rejoice that
    Sheridan enriched the theater so generously as he did.
    Walter Sichel's newly published biography of Sheridan,
    while certainly ample in its means, will not prove a

1910

definitive work because Sichel buries his presentation
under mounds of erudition: "he is the slave and not the
master of his erudition" (p. 257). (See 1910.7.)

7   MELVILLE, LEWIS. "Sheridan." Bookman (London), 37 (March):
    257-66.
        See 1910.6. (Lewis Melville is the pseudonym of Saul
    Lewis Benjamin.)

                            1911

1   ANON. "Letters of Sheridan." Times (London), 14 December,
    p. 11.
        Lists several Sheridan items sold at Sotheby's on
    13 December. They include, from the W. S. Sichel
    collection, Sheridan's "Letter Journal" to the duchess
    of Devonshire, a letter from Sheridan to Lady Bessborough,
    written from the House of Commons and admiring a speech
    of Pitt's, and a copy of the first edition of The Rivals.
    These items brought 107, 27, and 16 pounds respectively.

2   BENSLY, EDWARD. "R. B. Sheridan and Bishop Hall." Notes
    and Queries 122, 11th ser., 3 (11 February): 104.
        Notes a resemblance between a passage in The Rivals
    (I, ii) and the opening lines of book 6 of Joseph Hall's
    Virgidemiae, an edition of which had appeared (edited by
    William Thompson) in 1753. In The Rivals, Lady Slattern
    Lounger is said to make marginal notes with her finger-
    nails, and in Hall's Virgidemiae "Labeo reserues a long
    nayle for the nonce / To wound my margent through ten
    leaues at once."

3   BESSER, RHEINHOLD. "R. B. Sheridan." Die neueren Sprachen
    19 (December): 462-75.
        Declares Sheridan worthy of high praise in his ability
    to give distinctiveness to received dramatic practices;
    then draws upon the biographies by Fraser Rae (1896.15)
    and Walter Sichel (1909.5) (after mentioning the ones
    by Watkins [1817.4], Earle [1859.1], Moore [1825.9],
    Oliphant [1883.7], Fitzgerald [1886.3], and Sanders
    [1890.2]) to sketch the playwright's ancestry and early
    life.

4   BLACK, CLEMENTINA. The Linleys of Bath. London: Martin
    Secker, 339 pp.
        Devotes substantial space to the courtship and marriage
    of Sheridan and Elizabeth Linley. During the courtship
    (especially during the Waltham Abbey period) "Sheridan,
    fundamentally kind and affectionate, was nevertheless

inconsiderate and neglectful; even when he was deeply
in love he could not be trusted to write with decent
regularity; and although in matters of real importance
he was magnanimous and devoted, he could never control a
rather petty jealousy upon trifling occasions" (p. 75).
For Elizabeth, the married years "must have been years
of the experience of Sisyphus, so greatly did the task
to be achieved always exceed the achievement." Sheridan
"was a circus-rider attempting to stand on three horses
at once" (p. 127). "When we consider the frittered life
of Sheridan, the saddest reflection is not that the
opportunity of being great in politics never came to him,
but that in pursuing that opportunity he threw away a
greater one" (p. 128). The book nowhere mentions Lord
Edward Fitzgerald.

1912

1 BESSER, RHEINHOLD. "R. B. Sheridan." Die neueren Sprachen
19 (January): 524-41.
   Draws upon the biographies of Sheridan by Fraser Rae
and Walter Sichel (in continuation of 1911.3) to recount
the major events of Sheridan's adult life--the elopement
with Elizabeth Linley, the duels with Mathews, the
theatrical and parliamentary careers, the ruinous
friendship with the Prince of Wales, etc. An assessment
of Sheridan's character as quoted from Sichel concludes
the sketch.

*2 GREEN, EMANUEL. Sheridan and Mathews at Bath. A Criticism
of the Story as Told in the Several Sheridan Biographies.
London: Harrison & Sons, 56 pp.
   Cited in 1971.9, item 5632.

*3 MILNE, JAMES MATHEWSON. Molière and Sheridan. Glasgow:
Findley, 90 pp.
   Appears in NUC as a thesis (Rennes). Also listed
1971.9, item 5633.

4 SADLE [I] R, MICHAEL T[HOMAS] H[ARVEY]. The Political Career
of Richard Brinsley Sheridan. Followed by Some Hitherto
Unpublished Letters of Mrs. Sheridan. The Stanhope Essay
for 1912. Oxford: Blackwell, 87 pp.
   Suggests "why a career, which opened with such
brilliance and promise, closed dismally in obscurity and
failure" (p. 3). In political principle, Sheridan was
idealistic, radical, and incorruptible. He upheld
freedom of the press; he urged Catholic emancipation in

1912

Ireland; he sought abolition of slavery; he favored
parliamentary reform and all humanitarian causes. "Being
a thorough sentimentalist, much of his attitude was
dictated by a vague philosophical hatred of oppression
and a love of change for its own sake" (p. 30). His
eventual failure in politics takes root in personal and
circumstantial causes: he was not suited by nature to the
political life; he never learned or practiced the rules of
the political game. His attachment to the prince, based
upon vague conceptions of a patriot king, was
misconceived and ultimately ruinous. It allowed
his colleagues to mistrust him and to foster jealousy of
him. Furthermore, after the death of his first wife,
he lost direction in his personal life. He gave way
to drink; he nurtured vanity. Honorable though he was,
he lacked the means of inspiring confidence; and,
given his lack of birth and his general poverty, he
gradually lost all means to scotch his ruin.

5   _____. "Sheridan as He Appears in Contemporary Caricature
and Satire." In The Political Career of Richard Brinsley
Sheridan. Oxford: Blackwell, pp. 64-70.
     Sees Sheridan's special vulnerability to cartoon attack
as deriving from five causes: (1) his poverty, (2) his
theatrical past, (3) his reputation for improvidence and
overindulgence in drink, (4) his political idealism, and
(5) his allegiance to a party rarely in power. The
dominant caricature of Sheridan, with heavy jowls and
flaming nose, originates with Gillray, who tarred him
with every kind of political offense. The most frequent
attacks, from Gillray and others, came during the French
Revolution and the Napoleonic Wars. They generally
charge Sheridan with bartering his country for private
gain. That no extant cartoon represents him as being
loose with women suggests that in this offense at least
he was thought to be restrained.

6   _____. "Sheridan's Change of Attitude During the War with
France." In The Political Career of Richard Brinsley
Sheridan. Oxford: Blackwell, pp. 71-73.
     Sees Sheridan's apparent inconsistencies in his attitude
to Bonaparte--seeing the emperor first as a harbinger
of peace then as a tyrant--as partly accounted for by
"Sheridan's incautious rhetoric" (p. 72) and partly by
his sentimental devotion to liberty. When liberty, as
represented by Bonaparte, began taking the form of
ambitious aggression, Sheridan recoiled against French
pretensions. He seemed unable to realize that the Reign
of Terror had also been tyrannical. "Being himself a

tangle of conflicting emotions, it was inevitable that
his actions should sometimes share the incongruity"
(p. 73).

7   _____. "Some Unpublished Letters of Mrs. Sheridan to Mrs.
Canning." In The Political Career of Richard Brinsley
Sheridan. Oxford: Blackwell, pp. 71-85.
    Prints letters (mostly portions of letters) from the
years 1787, 1789, and 1791. Those from 1787 and 1789
relate to Sheridan's gallantries with Lady Duncannon (and
with a governess) at Crewe Hall, the outrageous conduct
nearly resulting in the Sheridans' separation and in Mrs.
Sheridan's indiscretions with the duke of Clarence. A
final letter, written from Mrs. Sheridan's deathbed,
pleads with Mrs. Canning to raise the infant Mary Sheridan
as her own and asks Sheridan to accede to this arrangement.

1913

1   ANON. "The Art Sale Season in London." Times (London),
        17 November, p. 12.
        Announces for 10 December the sale at Sotheby's of a
    manuscript of The School for Scandal, the property of "a
    well-known American amateur."

2   ANON. "'Original Manuscript.' Sheridan and the Censors."
        Times (London), 10 December, p. 13.
        Raises the question "is it justifiable to describe an
    author's fair copy of his play or novel or poem as the
    original manuscript" and decides in the negative. The
    Chetwynd manuscript of The School for Scandal, then, is
    not properly called the "original" manuscript. It is
    a fair copy prepared for the censors.

3   ARMSTRONG, CECIL FERARD. "Richard Brinsley Sheridan.
        1751-1816." In Shakespeare to Shaw: Studies in the Life's
        Work of Six Dramatists of the English Stage. London:
        Mills and Boon, pp. 147-67.
        Surveys Sheridan's life and career observing that his
    two best plays, The Rivals and The School for Scandal,
    distinguish themselves for being highly unified: the
    earlier one centering upon the action of the duel, i.e.,
    the conclusion toward which it builds systematically, the
    later one centering upon the fall of the screen in act 4,
    an action prepared in the earlier scenes by metaphor.
    The other plays distinguish themselves by general
    attributes. The Duenna, for example, achieves great
    charm; The Critic speaks to timeless theatrical offenses.

1913

But while Sheridan's finished works thus distinguish
themselves, his fame "seems to depend almost as much upon
what he might have done as upon what he did. His
finished works . . . are only forerunners" (p. 166).

4   BALSTON, T., ed.   Introduction to The Rivals, by Sheridan.
     Oxford: Clarendon Press, pp. v-xi.
          Identifies The Rivals as a comedy of manners (1) because
     it is "unphilosophical," propounding "no views of human
     life or destiny," (2) because it touches but lightly "on
     the surface of human character," treating its persons as
     puppets, (3) because its characters are "like masks, each
     with one fixed distortion of human features," and (4)
     because "Its essence, on the positive side, is to be witty
     and ingenious and plausible" (p. vii).   In writing The
     Rivals, Sheridan is no more to be charged with plagiarism
     than is any other artist sensitive to the traditions of
     his art. Nor is he to be thought any more nor less
     autobiographical.

5   JALOUX, E.   "L'Ecole de la Medisance."   Le Gaulois, 11 April,
     p. 1.
          Anticipates a new adaptation of The School for Scandal
     scheduled for production at the Odéon Theatre in Paris
     by sketching Sheridan's life and commenting on his play.
     Adapted to French usage, the play loses a bit of its
     piquancy. It is not the great repository of human nature
     one finds in a play by Molière. But its comment upon
     manners and social follies has pertinence for the Paris
     of today, just as it spoke to English society in
     Georgian times.

*6   SHAW, GEORGE BERNARD.   "The Second Dating of Sheridan."   In
     Dramatic Opinion and Essays.   New York: Brentano's,
     2: 28-36.
          Reprints 1896.17.

7   SHERIDAN, WILFRED.   "A Clerk's Copy."   Times (London),
     10 December, p. 13.
          Insists that the Chetwynd manuscript of The School for
     Scandal, announced for sale at Sotheby's (see 1913.1), is
     not, as it is advertised, the "original" manuscript of the
     play but is in fact "a clerk's copy and innocent of
     Sheridan's handwriting."

8   _____.   "A Sheridan Manuscript."   Times (London), 28 November,
     p. 10.
          Declares, in a letter to the editor, that the "original
     manuscript of The School for Scandal" continues in the
     possession of the Sheridan family at Frampton Court,

Dorchester, and is not, therefore, for sale at Sotheby's as announced earlier in the Times (see 1913.1). An editorial response, however, identifies the sale item as being the Chetwynd manuscript, a copy of the play presented by Sheridan to William Chetwynd, then examiner of plays.

9   STEUBER, FRITZ. Sheridans "Rivals." Entstehungsgeschichte und Beiträge zu einer deutschen Theatergeschichte des Stückes. Borna-Leipzig: Robert Noske, 99 pp.
     Describes the introduction and reception of The Rivals in London, then provides a history of the play on the eighteenth-century German stage, a history beginning as early as 10 November 1775 with a performance in Hamburg of Die Nebenbuhler, the first "prize-translation" play to be presented in that city, and including translations by Engelbrecht, also performed in Hamburg, and F. C. Hiemer, performed in Stuttgart and Würtemberg. The Engelbrecht and Hiemer translations are discussed in relation to the English text.

10   TUPPER, JAMES W. "News for Bibliophiles." Nation 97 (25 September): 284.
     Describes the action of a farcical allegory entitled "The School for Scandal" and currently housed in the Harvard College Library. Published in 1779, the piece features the dramatis personae of Sheridan's play with actors drawn from the contemporary political scene. Charles, for example, is played by King George III, Joseph by the earl of Bute, Moses by Lord North. The play ridicules the political mismanagement in England of the American War for Independence.

1914

1   BAYLEY, A. R. "A Note on Sheridan." Notes and Queries, 11th ser. 10 (23 July): 61-63.
     Describes pictures, clippings, and letters inserted into a copy of Moore's Memoirs of the Life of Sheridan (1825.9) by William Linley, the youngest child of Thomas Linley and the brother of Sheridan's first wife Elizabeth. Included are twenty-two portraits, woodcuts, and mezzotints picturing individuals mentioned in Moore's text (e.g., Mrs. Sheridan, Lord Byron, Samuel Whitbread, Edmund Burke) and, at the end, a collection of notes relating to the contents of the Memoirs. Chief among these is a copy of a letter--here printed and commented on--sent by Linley to Moore on 7 November 1825. It

1914

expresses admiration for Moore's work, gives thanks for
the treatment in it of the Linley family, and makes
observations on the life of Sheridan as treated in the
book and as recalled by Linley himself.

2 _____. "A Note on Sheridan." Notes and Queries, 11th ser. 10
(1 August): 81-83.
Continues comment upon William Linley's letter of
7 November 1825 to Thomas Moore (see 1914.1) and prints
yet another of the documents inserted by Linley in his
copy of Moore's Memoirs of the Life of Sheridan: "A
Sermon on the Abuse of Riches." Comment on this sermon
(a work of Sheridan's mentioned only in a footnote of
Moore's book) identifies the "Rev. Mr. O'B___ (afterwards
Bishop of _____)" of Moore's footnote as being the
Reverend Mr. O'Beirne, bishop of Meath. He had
delivered the sermon for Sheridan. Chief among the
remaining insertions (and also printed here) is a copy
of verses addressed by Sheridan to Lord Forbes, presumably
George John, Viscount Forbes. They begin "While you sit
yawning in the Kirk."

3 HOLL, KARL. "Sheridan's 'Verses to the Memory of Garrick'
and Schiller's 'Prolog zum Wallenstein.'" Modern
Language Review 9 (April): 246.
Notes that Sheridan's monody and Schiller's prologue
resemble one another in lamenting the transience of the
actor's art and in admonishing the audience to preserve
in its memory the actor's fame.

4 MONAHAN, MICHAEL. "Richard Brinsley Sheridan." In Nova
Hibernia; Irish Poets and Dramatists of Today and
Yesterday. New York: Kennerly, pp. 267-74.
Sees Sheridan as prostituting his rare gifts to the
delusion that a playwright cannot truly be a man of
society. As a player's son he enjoyed admiration; as
an Irishman, he was cruelly sensitive to any kind of
depreciation. Acceding to the lures of an arrogant
and tyrannical society, he denied his genius for the
honor of associating with Beau Brummel and the Prince
of Wales. Much like his countryman Congreve, "he gave
to society and the bottle what was meant for mankind"
(p. 268).

5 NETTLETON, GEORGE HENRY. "Richard Brinsley Sheridan." In
English Drama of the Restoration and Eighteenth Century
(1642-1780). New York: Macmillan, pp. 291-313.
Remarks, after surveying Sheridan's career as a
dramatist, that "Sheridan's powers developed early. A

dramatic artist, not a deep interpreter of life, he
brilliantly touched the surface without sounding the
depths. There are more things in heaven and earth than
are dreamt of in his philosophy. . . . Unable to follow
Shakespeare through the depths of the 'comedié humaine,'
Sheridan wisely chose, under the leadership of the comic
dramatists of the Restoration, to pursue the easier path
of the comedy of manners. . . . He is at once the heir
to the best traditions of Restoration comedy and the
most notable English dramatist of the eighteenth
century" (pp. 312-13).

6   ROUTH, HAROLD V. "The Georgian Drama." In The Period of
    the French Revolution. The Cambridge History of English
    Literature. Cambridge: Cambridge University Press,
    pp. 284-314.
        Includes Sheridan within a broad historical survey of
    Georgian drama and singles out for special emphasis his
    mastery of stagecraft--the management of incident and
    the pacing of action--and his sense of societal
    over-cultivation. He "perceived that the intellectually
    unemployed turn social intercourse into a competitive
    struggle" (p. 298). Despite this perception, however, he
    did not achieve true greatness in comedy. Even The School
    for Scandal "lacks inspiration" (p. 300). As one of many
    mirrors of "metropolitan wit and gentility," it confronts
    none of the "puzzles and anomalies of human nature, out
    of which the greatest comedies are made" (p. 300). And
    with The Critic, Sheridan showed that he "had nothing
    fresh to say concerning life" (p. 300).

1915

1   BERNBAUM, ERNEST. "Sheridan and the Final Triumph of
    Sentimental Comedy: 1773-1780." In The Drama of
    Sensibility: A Sketch of the History of English
    Sentimental Comedy and Domestic Tragedy 1696-1780.
    Harvard Studies in English, vol. 3. Boston: Ginn,
    pp. 247-67.
        Gives Sheridan his place among those who tried in the
    1770s to scotch the tide of sentimental comedy but
    notices that Sheridan was not himself a committed enemy
    of the form. As playwright he colored his plays with
    sentimentality, and as theater manager he was as much
    responsible as anyone else for holding open the
    floodgates of sentimentality. When he left the comic
    field in 1779, no one stood by to sustain the spirit of
    true comedy. The sentimental muse then reigned until well

1915

past the middle of the nineteenth century.

2   CABELL, JAMES BRANCH. "Irresistible Ogle." Lippincott's
    Monthly Magazine 96 (October): 101-8.
        Builds a fictional narrative around Sheridan's proposal
    of marriage to Esther Jane Ogle. Having followed her
    into Scotland, Sheridan discovers her at two in the
    morning dressed as a man and rifling his belongings in
    search of a valuable diamond, the Honor of Eiran. It
    is the property of Sheridan's cousin, the earl of Eiran,
    and is supposed at this time to be in Sheridan's own
    possession. Esther belongs, she explains, to the league
    of Philanthropic Larcenists, an organization given to
    stealing from the rich to help the poor, and she hints
    that she will marry Sheridan (having already rejected
    eleven proposals from him) if he will steal in behalf of
    the Larcenists a property worth 10,000 pounds. He agrees
    to do so and contrives a stratagem in which Esther Jane is
    herself the property so highly valued. She accepts his
    twelfth proposal.

3   CHASE, F. E., ed. Introduction to The School for Scandal,
    by Sheridan. Boston: Walter H. Baker, pp. 3-6.
        Reviews the American stage history of the play, dating
    the first performance at 26 May 1781 in Jamaica, and
    citing other performances, those within the United States,
    in 1784 (Baltimore), 1785 (New York), 1787 (Philadelphia)
    and 1792 (Boston). The play is "undoubtedly superficial
    in character and full of faults from a critical
    standpoint. . . . Its plot by itself is of the slightest
    interest, the progress of its dramatic story involves no
    searching or ingenious development of character and no
    single member of its cast, save perhaps Sir Peter
    Teazle, makes any legitimate claim upon one's sympathy
    or affection." It survives "by dint of sheer skill in
    the management of its materials . . . a triumph of
    unscrupulous dramaturgy" (p. 3).

1916

1   ANON. "Richard Brinsley Sheridan." Times Literary
    Supplement, 13 July, p. 331.
        Honors the centenary of Sheridan's death by insisting
    that while, in the sense that he outlived his closest
    political colleagues, he died ten years too late, his
    death is not tragic but ironic. Ironically, fate has
    allowed to accumulate around his memory many dismal
    accounts of his drunkenness and improvidence. What

dominated his character, however, was pride, the desire
to play the hero, and out of this one attribute his
strengths and weaknesses spring. His plays "come nearer
to perfection within their own form and limits than any
others in the English drama." "To be brilliantly witty
without ever being merely smart; to be thoroughly
'artificial' and theatrical, yet true not only to the
manners of the time, but to so much of the quality of
human nature as the type of play will bear; to reveal
character through dialogue over which the connoisseur
can gloat; to combine wit and humour, and to invent a
comedy which was neither lewd nor mawkish--that was
Sheridan's achievement." Sheridan's character might be
harshly judged, but no age, however judgmental, has been
willing to forego his comedy.

2   ANON. "Shakespeare and Sheridan." Times (London), 26 June,
      p. 11.
         Announces that the Stratford-on-Avon summer season will
      honor the centenary of Sheridan's death by performing
      (among other plays) The Rivals and The School for Scandal.

3   ANON. "Sheridan Centenary Plays." Times (London),
      29 August, p. 9.
         Declares that four performances of each of The Rivals
      and The School for Scandal will appear at the Royal
      Victoria Hall to commemorate the centenary of Sheridan's
      death. The first performance, on 23 September, will also
      commemorate the 100th anniversary of the foundation stone
      of the "Old Vic."

4   ANON. "A Sheridan Gift to Harrow." Times (London),
      10 January, p. 11.
         Announces that Wilfred Sheridan "has presented to the
      library of Harrow School his 'grangerized' copy of
      Fraser Rae's biography of Sheridan (1896.15), extended
      to six volumes quarto. They contain hundreds of prints,
      portraits, and reviews, as well as many autograph letters,
      old play-bills, and a pass for the 75th day of the trial
      of Warren Hastings."

5   GOWER, GRANVILLE LEVESON, LORD, FIRST EARL GRANVILLE.
      Private Correspondence 1781 to 1821, edited by Castalia
      Countess Granville. 2 vols. London: John Murray.
         Includes letters written to Lord Granville by Lady
      Bessborough describing Sheridan's unwelcome attentions
      to her and his bizarre conduct to her between the years
      1798 and 1809. The letters also touch upon Sheridan's
      character (e.g., his "duplicity and inordinate vanity"

1916

[1, 427]) and certain of his political views (e.g., his
fears in 1803 of a coalition between Fox and Pitt [1:
436). For discussion of these letters (as regards the
Sheridan-Lady Bessborough relationship) see Hewlett
(1919.1).

6   HIRTH, FRIEDRICH. "Sheridan." Schaubühne, pp. 104-10.
       Gives an account of Sheridan's theatrical and political
    careers and avers that the current decline in England's
    political, cultural, and artistic respectability will not
    end until a playwright of Sheridan's range, perception,
    candor, and vitality emerges upon the scene. Such a
    one is not currently in sight.

7   SAINTSBURY, GEORGE EDWARD BATEMAN. "The Garden of Minor
    Verse and the Later Drama--Anstey to Sheridan." In The
    Peace of the Augustans: a Survey of Eighteenth Century
    Literature as a Place of Rest and Refreshment. London:
    G. Bell, pp. 275-85.
       Denigrates Sheridan's political career and all his
    theatrical pieces except The Rivals, The School for
    Scandal, and The Critic, but finds in these plays more
    than enough to justify the playwright's fame. The School
    for Scandal succeeds as imitative art but captures too
    the authentic spirit of the age. The Rivals is alone of
    a type, its spirit caught only by Sir William Gilbert.
    The Critic, a masterpiece of pure farce-burlesque,
    betters all its precursors. When one considers that
    these three plays, each representing a distinct class
    of comedy, were written before the playwright's
    twenty-ninth year, one has to admire the achievement.

1917

1   BROTHER LEO. "Richard Brinsley Sheridan (1751-1816)."
    Catholic World 104 (February): 593-605.
       Organizes Sheridan's life after the parts of a play--a
    prologue (the Bath days and the elopement), a first act
    (the career as dramatist), a second act (the career as
    orator and M.P.), a third act (the years as "Old Sherry,"
    the man about town), and an epilogue (the gorgeous
    funeral). Through it all, Sheridan is himself an actor.
    Consequently, his life carries as much interest as his
    writing. To both he brought "a keen observation, a
    disquieting power of analysis and a sense of incongruity
    which made his comments on manners pointed and palpable,
    and his men and women actual and convincing" (p. 600).
    In the distinction between the dramatic and the theatrical,

112

his work is almost wholly theatrical: it carries
conviction to an audience (as dramatic work does), but
it does not supply thought recollected in tranquillity.
It is "thrilling rather than emotional, laugh-provoking
rather than profoundly humorous, clever rather than
great" (p. 601). Consequently, Sheridan, for all his
excellence, is a second rate dramatist. But he is a
dramatist whose wit will never cloy because it is more
than wit of words. It stands on perceptions of basic
truth.

2   FRIEDELL, EGON. "Die Lästerschule." Schaübuhne, pp. 225-29.
    Sees The School for Scandal as being totally representa-
    tive of its time. Based upon an ancient biblical conflict
    (the good and bad brother), it accommodates tested themes
    to current applications, reflecting the complexities and
    contradictions of a revolutionary era. Colored by every
    kind of wit and word play--parody, burlesque, raillery,
    insult, pathos--it embraces such oppositions as sentiment
    and cynicism, sophistication and naiveté, hypocrisy and
    candor. It catches the light of the time and refracts it
    brilliantly through the prism of Sheridan's genius.

3   STOKES, HUGH. The Devonshire House Circle. London: H.
    Jenkins, 346 pp.
    Attributes Sheridan's success with the duchess of
    Devonshire and her circle to his quick and amiable wit
    and to his kinship in spirit with the duchess: "They were
    both impetuous, uncertain, and not wholly to be relied
    upon, ready to seek distraction in practical jokes and
    horseplay, inclined towards sentimentalism, and very
    restless and ever seeking for incessant distraction from
    the dull round of everyday life" (p. 130).

4   WEBSTER, HANSON HART., ed. Introduction to The School for
    Scandal, by Sheridan. Riverside College Classics.
    Boston: Houghton Mifflin, pp. v-liii.
    Provides a biography, a history of sentimental comedy
    (contrasting it with romantic comedy, classical tragedy,
    and comedy of manners), an account of Sheridan's reaction
    against sentimentalism (first in The Rivals and then, less
    tentatively, in The School for Scandal), a brief study of
    the evolution of The School for Scandal (seeing it to
    originate with the "Ode to Scandal"), a discussion of
    early printed texts of the play (nominating J. Ewling's
    Dublin edition, 1779 or 1780, as the first imprint), and
    finally a collection of critical comments, including
    comments by Lamb, Hazlitt, Taine, and Sichel.

1917

5   WILLIAMS, STANLEY THOMAS. Richard Cumberland: His Life and
    Dramatic Works. New Haven: Yale, pp. 131-50.
        Recounts the Sheridan-Cumberland relationship, especi-
    ally as to the production in 1778, under Sheridan's
    management at Drury Lane, of Cumberland's tragedy The
    Battle of Hastings. Other experiences lying behind the
    caricature in The Critic of Cumberland as Sir Fretful
    Plagiary also come into consideration.

1919

1   HEWLETT, MAURICE HENRY. "Sheridan as Maniac." Fortnightly
    Review 111 (May): 723-31.
        Finds, in the correspondence of Lady Bessborough to
    her lover Lord Granville Gower (published in 1916.5),
    evidence to support the view that Sheridan, in his
    conduct to Lady Bessborough between 1798 (when her
    affair with Lord Granville had become a notoriety) and
    1816 (within three days of the playwright's death), was
    "either a very bad rogue or a madman" (p. 731). His
    conduct, as reported in her letters, included long
    visits to her every evening, a series of obscene letters
    sent by him over various signatures (some addressed to
    the Lady herself, others to her daughter--then a child--
    and yet others to her sister the duchess of Devonshire),
    a lurid scene in 1807 in which he professed passionate
    love for her in the company of his wife Hecca, a threat
    at the end of his life to visit her after his death (this
    last reported to Lord Broughton, the correspondence with
    Granville Gower having ended with his marriage in 1809).
    Not one of Sheridan's biographers has "pointed out the
    extent of his moral aberration" (p. 731).

2   POLAND, HARRY B. "Sheridaniana." Times Literary Supplement,
    22 May, p. 279.
        Declares himself the owner of a copy of Sheridaniana
    (1826.9) and asks for assistance in identifying the
    author of this now-rare book.

3   _____. "Sheridaniana." Times Literary Supplement, 26 June,
    p. 349.
        Acknowledges agreement with Mr. N. W. Hill, who, in
    response to Poland's own query of 22 May (see 1919.2),
    had nominated the dramatist Frederick Reynolds as the
    author of Sheridaniana. An anecdote within Sheridaniana
    suggests that a copy of Sheridan's celebrated speech in
    the House of Commons against Warren Hastings might indeed
    be in existence. Sheridan hinted in conversation that

he had a copy of the speech but would never release it
for publication because, since delivering it, he had
shaken hands with Hastings and drunk wine with him.

1920

1   BEERS, HENRY AUGUSTIN. "Sheridan." In Connecticut Wits
    and Other Essays. New Haven: Yale University Press,
    pp. 159-78.
        Bases a sweeping appreciation of Sheridan's comedies
    on the conviction that they fail to "touch the springs
    of universal comedy" (p. 161) but draw their freshness
    instead from cleverness and artistic cunning. Sheridan's
    quality "was not genius, but talent, yet talent raised
    to a very high power" (p. 161). He is properly called
    the English Beaumarchais, and just as Beaumarchais took
    Molière for a model, Sheridan took Congreve. He and
    Congreve sin alike in making all their characters witty.
    But Sheridan excels Congreve as a master of plot; and
    Sheridan's comedies, unlike Congreve's, always play.
    Perhaps Congreve's characterization cuts deeper; perhaps
    his dialogue achieves a more "epigrammatic solidity"
    (p. 177). "But on the whole, 'The Rivals' and 'The
    School for Scandal' are better plays than Congreve ever
    wrote" (p. 178).

2   HEWLETT, MAURICE HENRY. "Sheridan as Maniac." In In a
    Green Shade: a Country Commentary. London: G. Bell and
    Sons, pp. 105-18.
        Reprints 1919.1.

3   PHELPS, WILLIAM LYON, ed. Introduction to The Rivals, by
    Sheridan. Living Literature Series. New York: Gregg.
        Establishes the importance of the play by declaring
    it one of the three best plays between Shakespeare and
    Wilde, the other two being She Stoops to Conquer and
    The School for Scandal. The "darkest blot" on Sheridan's
    character is that he abandoned playwriting for politics.
    "Compared with this direct sin against his talents, his
    later debts and various lapses are mere peccadilloes"
    (p. vi). The play is to be admired for the unity of
    its construction and the speed of its action. While
    the Julia-Faulkland plot can now be omitted, it forms
    an "almost necessary" (p. xiii) foil to the main action.

4   RUFFIN, JOHN DEMOSTHENES N. Forms of Oratorical Expression
    and Their Delivery; Or, Logic and Eloquence Illustrated.
    London: Simpkin, Marshall, Hamilton, Kent, pp. 158-63.

1920

Credits Sheridan with possessing "the best trained
voice of all his contemporaries" because "he was a great
playwright and Shakespearean actor" (p. 158). Assessments
of Sheridan's oratorical skill, as derived from a variety
of sources (e.g., Thomas Moore, Lord Holland, Fraser Rae),
support the general impression that Sheridan was "like
the Greek Master AEschines, in that he had a splendidly
cultivated voice, tones diversified and gestures graceful,
and that he excelled in Dialogismus, Descriptio and
Asteismus. He was master of all the forms of oratorical
expression, and he had the art of well rounding a sentence
or period. He held that vivid conception induces belief"
(p. 160). Extracts from the Begum Speech illustrate these
and other attributes of his skill.

5   V., T. J. "Sheridan." Athenaeum, no. 4689 (12 March): 348.
Remarks of The Rivals (recently revived by the Old Vic
Company) that "The text is feminist, it was at its first
performance, perhaps, as didactic as Shaw; it is an
anti-duelling play, it advocates slightly better education
for women, it is a 'revolt of youth' play; and, despite
these sins against utterly-utter aestheticism, it has
escaped the corruption of time." As to dramaturgical
traditions, "The art of playwriting from Shakespeare to
Molière, and from Molière to Sheridan, is the art of
making a certain number not of wholly empty 'types' nor
yet of absolutely 'solid' individuals; but of, as it
were, half-hollow, half-transparent, reservoirs into
which the actor can pour his interpretation." Consequently,
one production of The Rivals is apt to be markedly
different from another. If the play is to be kept "in
scale," however, Sheridan's indications of the ages of
his characters should be scrupulously observed.

1921

1   R[AE], F[RASER]. "Sheridan, Richard Brinsley (1751-1816)."
In Dictionary of National Biography. Oxford: Oxford
University Press, 18: 78-85.
Chronicles Sheridan's life with an intention of freeing
it from misrepresentation. "As a dramatist Sheridan
carried the comedy of manners in this country to its
highest pitch, and his popularity as a writer for the
stage is exceeded by that of Shakespeare alone. As an
orator he impressed the House of Commons more deeply
than almost any predecessor, and as a politician in a
venal age he preserved his independence and purity"
(p. 84). From his seventh year to the end of his life
calumny attached itself to his name, but he made no

practice of answering it. Many of the favorite traditions relating to him--e.g., that his mother represented him to his schoolmaster as being an "impenetrable dunce" and that an arrest for debt was laid upon his dead body--have no basis in fact.

1922

1 H., J. R. "'Extempore Lines' by Sheridan." Notes and Queries, 12th ser. 11 (30 December): 531-32.
    Asks if anything is known about certain "Extempore Lines" quoted here as they are printed in the biographical introduction of a collection of Sheridan's plays published in Paris in 1822. The "Lines" begin "I gave my love a budding rose / My infant passion to disclose." The four volumes of the collection were published by Malépeyré, Rue Git-le-Coeur, No. 4, Paris, and each carries the half title The British Prose Writers, with Biographical and Critical Prefaces by J. W. Lake, Esq. The poem appears in a letter sent to Lake by "one of Sheridan's dearest and truest friends." No other identification is given. In his biographical sketch Lake attributes The Camp to Sheridan, and he prints it in the collection, even though received editions of Sheridan's works, such as that of Stainforth (1874.6), exclude it (and make no reference to the "Extempore Lines"). It would therefore be useful to know something of the history of Lake's collection.

2 THALER, ALWIN. Shakspere to Sheridan: A Book About the Theatre of Yesterday and To-Day. Cambridge, Mass.: Harvard University Press, passim.
    Makes many brief references to Sheridan in discussing the problems of theatrical management in England during the seventeenth and eighteenth centuries.

1923

1 ABBOTT, L AWRENCE F. "The Rivals." Outlook 134 (30 May): 75-77.
    Applauds the Equity Players, a federation of actors, for producing The Rivals despite the prevailing indifference in New York of a highly commercialized and neglectful press. While too little noticed by newspaper commentators, the production attracted respectable audiences to its short run and succeeded admirably in catching the spirit of the play. More than a mere

1923

attack upon affectation, pomposity, and false sentiment,
the play is a "plea for the intellectual liberation of
woman" (p. 76). In truth, Sheridan precedes Jane Austen
in being a champion of female intelligence.

2   ANON. "Dickens and Sheridan." Living Age 316 (24 March):
733-34.
     Reprints 1923.3.

3   ANON. "Dickens' Debt to Sheridan." Times (London),
2 February, p. 8.
     Lists several instances of phrasing in which Dickens's
ear seems to recall Sheridan's language: e.g., Fag, in
The Rivals, says "But I was sly, Sir--devilish sly" and
Major Bagstock in Dickens's Dombey and Son says "Sly,
Sir, Sly, Sir--dev-il-ish sly." Mrs. Micawber, in David
Copperfield, adapts some of Mrs. Malaprop's language, and
Mr. Feeder, in Dombey and Son, actually quotes as his own
the opening lines of a song from The Duenna ("Had I a
heart for falsehood framed"). Such parallels are probably
unconscious on Dickens's part; but, by this unconscious
process, Dickens borrowed more from Sheridan than from any
other author.

4   ANON. "Mr. Shaw's Tribute to Sheridan." Times (London),
27 October, p. 12.
     Reports the event in which Shaw first unveiled a tablet
at 9 New King Street, Bath, where Sheridan had lived with
his father in 1771 and 1772, and then, having unveiled
the tablet, gave a tribute to Sheridan in the Pump Room.
Emphasized in this tribute was the point that Sheridan,
whose plays are the crown of manners comedy, was not alone
among writers in that mode who gave up the craft at an
early age. Congreve and Vanbrugh had done the same, and
the reason was, probably, that they did not find their
lives fulfilled by play making. The plays of Sheridan,
while highly entertaining, are not profound. They could
not command from him the interest he held for politics.
But, with the possible exception of Goldsmith, he remains
the greatest dramatist of the eighteenth century.

5   ANON. "News in Brief." Times (London), 5 September, p. 7.
     Announces that "Mr. George Bernard Shaw has promised
to visit Bath on October 27 to unveil a mural tablet in
memory of Richard Brinsley Sheridan."

6   ANON. ["Shaw and Sheridan"]. Times (London), 20 October,
p 4.
     Reports that "Mr. Bernard Shaw will unveil a tablet

commemorating the house in which Sheridan resided, on the opening day of the annual festival of the British Drama League at Bath next Friday."

7   ANON. "Sheridan and Shaw." New York Times, 25 November, sec. 2, p. 6.
     Complains that comments made by George Bernard Shaw after unveiling a tablet at the Sheridan house in Bath slighted Sheridan's real merits and faulted Sheridan to the extent that he failed to be Shaw, i.e., to the extent that he refused to construct his plays around modish social causes and to accompany his plays with long discursive prefaces.

8   ANON. "Sheridan's 'Duenna.' Performance in Paris." Times (London), 8 October, p. 11.
     Admires a production of The Duenna newly set to the music of Voldemar Bernardi, who, in period garb, conducted the opera from his harpsichord. The performance was staged at the Comedié des Champs Elysées in Paris.

9   ARCHER, WILLIAM. "Lecture VIII." In The Old Drama and the New: an Essay in Re-Evaluation. Boston: Small, Maynard and Co., pp. 203-27.
     Refuses to rank Sheridan below Wycherley and Congreve in literary merit but sees him as contributing little to the advancement of drama. While The Rivals and The School for Scandal may long hold the stage, they imitate life far less truly than many a more recent, and probably ephemeral, play.

*10 COTTERELL, TOM STURGE. Richard Brinsley Sheridan. Bath. Cited in 1962.9, p. 561.

*11 HOWES, C. Catalogue of Books Mainly of the 17th and 18th Centuries from the Library of Richard Brinsley Sheridan. Offered by C. Howes, St. Leonards-on-Sea, England. [Birmingham: F. Juckes, Ltd., 1923?], 36 pp.
     Listed in 1971.9, item 5523, where it is described as "456 items arranged alphabetically" in full bibliographical form with some annotations.

12 MONCKTON, N. "Dickens and Sheridan." Times (London), 8 February, p. 11.
     Reminds the author of "Dickens's Debt to Sheridan" (1923.3) that in Humphry Clinker (four years before The Rivals) Smollett had written the line "Ah! I have been sly--sly--damned sly," a line Dickens is supposed to have lifted, however unconsciously, from Sheridan. "If it is

1923

an indication that both Sheridan and Dickens had read
Smollett and were unconsciously quoting from him, what a
temptation is set before the dram-drinkers!"

1924

1 ANON. "Songs for 'The Duenna' in 'Beggars's Opera' Style."
   New York Times, 23 November, sec. 8, p. 7.
       Marks a revival of The Duenna in London by sketching
   the circumstances of its composition and by commenting
   briefly upon the two Thomas Linleys, father and son, who
   composed the music according to Sheridan's instructions.

1a ARMSTRONG, MARTIN. "'The Duenna' and 'The Pelican.'"
    Spectator 133 (1 November): 637-38.
        Finds the delight of The Duenna to stem from Sheridan's
    self-conscious manipulation of the Restoration comic
    convention, a convention in which he does not believe
    "though it is still a part of himself" (p. 637). The
    play, then, is a glass bowl in which his "wit and
    sentiment can conveniently disport themselves" (p. 637).
    It thrives upon an "unstable equilibrium between poetry
    and parody" (p. 637), a phenomenon whereby we laugh
    at one moment at the sparkle of the dialogue and feel
    at the next the very real poignancy of the music and
    lyrics.

2 BARBEAU, A. Sheridan. Paris: La Renaissance du Livre,
   170 pp.
       Provides a biographical survey and a descriptive
   commentary on the plays. Sheridan is acknowledged to be
   less rich, copious, and profound than many another
   playwright, but more ingenious, various, piquant, and
   elegant than most. Bibliographic notes precede the texts
   of the plays (translations of The School for Scandal and
   acts two and three of The Critic). And explanatory
   footnotes accompany the texts.

3 BARRINGTON, E. "The Wooing of Sir Peter Teazle." In The
   Gallants, Following According to Their Wont the Ladies,
   edited by Lily Moresley Adams Beck. Boston: Atlantic
   Monthly Press, pp. 246-308.
       Bases a short story on the supposed courtship of Sir
   Peter and Lady Teazle. They meet one another at a dinner
   party given by Sir Tivy Terrier at Hardacre Hall in Kent.
   A headnote characterizes Lady Teazle as "the country girl
   aspiring to be the lady of fashion," a conception given
   proper treatment by Marie Lohr in the Beerbohm Tree

production of <u>The School for Scandal</u> in 1909. Sir Peter
is, during the period of his wooing, "A middle-aged, and
lonely, and overcredulous human being."

4 ESDAILE, ARUNDELL. "Bibliographica." In <u>The Year's Work in
   English Studies, vol. 4 (1923)</u>. London: Oxford University
   Press, p. 258.
      Reports that "The British Museum has . . . found a
   copy of the very rare Sheridan piece, <u>St. Patrick's Day</u>
   (no place, but certainly Dublin), 1788; also <u>The Camp</u>,
   1795, attributed to Sheridan on the title-page, but
   known to be mostly by Richard Tickell."

5 WILLIAMS, IOLO A. "Richard Brinsley Sheridan." In <u>Seven
   XVIIIth Century Bibliographies</u>. London: Dulau, pp. 210-39.
      Arranges, with descriptive bibliographic details, the
   first editions of Sheridan's works in the order of their
   publication. Five of the seven bibliographies in the
   collection are preceded by introductory essays. For
   Sheridan and Goldsmith, however, no such treatment is
   given. So much has been written, "and well written,"
   about them "that it appeared that short essays from my
   pen would be needless and presumptuous" (p. 11). Several
   items known not to be Sheridan's (e.g., a 1776 edition of
   Israel Pottinger's <u>The Duenna</u>) are included to protect
   from confusion collectors who might see them in
   catalogues.

                              1925

1 ANON. "Barry V. Jackson's Design for <u>The Rivals</u>, Act I,
   Scene 1." <u>Theatre Arts Monthly</u> 9 (April): 253.
      Pictures the set in black-and-white and describes the
   colors: "The general tone is gray, warmed by a soft yellow
   light. The sky at the left is a pale blue green, against
   which the warm sepia of the half-timbering, the veridian
   of the rain barrel, and the magenta hangings on the clothes
   line stand out in brilliant contrast. Balancing this
   violent color on the right is a table, with its pewter
   mugs, a bench, and a bright coach advertisement above
   it." The production is designed for the Birmingham
   Repertory Theatre.

2 BENNETT, RODNEY. "'The Duenna' (1776-1924)." <u>Bookman</u>
   (London), 67 (March): 328-29.
      Takes issue with Byron's famous assessment of <u>The
   Duenna</u> ("far before that St. Giles's lampoon, the 'Beggar's
   Opera') by remarking that Gay's flair for light verse is

brighter than Sheridan's and that Gay's characters are
the truer to life. Sheridan's people, while excellent
stage types, have not a full air of reality, and his
broad humor in this play is better than his wit. Yet he
"tells a good and complicated story with dexterity and
resource. He is never at a loss for action or incident.
His touches of broad comedy are amusing. And above all
he has the gift of stage dialogue" (p. 328). For its
part, Linley's music, "while not remarkable for wit or
vivacity, is uniformly musicianly, graceful and well
built" (p. 328). In reviving The Duenna in 1924, Nigel
Playfair fails of complete success because he does not
subordinate the low comic business to the more intricate
and attractive love intrigues. Consequently, the
continuity of the play is destroyed.

3   KRUTCH, J[OSEPH] W[OOD]. "Creative Production." Nation
     120 (27 May): 607-8.
          Observes, with reference to a performance at the
     Neighborhood Playhouse, that the success of The Critic
     depends more on the performers than the playwright. The
     opening act manages to make several timeless thrusts at
     "puffing." But the burlesque itself is, "so far as mere
     lines are concerned" (p. 608), as dull as its subject.
     It is basically a scenario written by Sheridan for a
     select group of players, and his concept of it died with
     him. The actors at the Neighborhood Playhouse have
     succeeded because they know that bad acting does not
     itself constitute burlesque. They know that "a good
     burlesque must have style, its badness must be of a
     self-consistent, harmonious sort," and they have achieved
     this style by affecting in their performances a hilarious
     "combination of contempt, egotism, and boredom" (p. 607).

4   NICOLL, ALLARDYCE. British Drama: An Historical Survey from
     the Beginnings to the Present Time. New York: Thomas Y.
     Crowell, pp. 293-95.
          Lists Sheridan's dramatic works and comments on The
     Rivals ("the very atmosphere of Congreve modified by
     exaggerated humours of the Jonsonian type" [p. 294]) and
     The School for Scandal, with which "we reach the
     culmination of the anti-sentimental movement" (p. 295).
     It is, in efect, "the last word of the Augustan writers,
     for sentimentalism is, in its own way, the forerunner of
     romance" (p. 295).

5   PLAYFAIR, NIGEL, ed. Introduction to The Duenna. A Comic
     Opera in Three Acts, by Sheridan. London: Constable.
     pp. ix-xix.

Prints, without editorial apparatus, the London edition
of 1794. The introduction argues that The Duenna has
faded in reputation through the years only "because it
has been neglected in the theatre" (p. xi). Contrary to
received critical view, the work does not form a new
departure. In story and characterization it is highly
conventional. "The whole affair is saved by good spirits,
lively, if not very deep jests, and the beauty of
[Sheridan's] lyric verse" (p. xiv). These properties
are best revealed through the "point" and "go" of
theatrical production, and they affirm the kinship held
by The Duenna with the previous operettas of O'Hara and
Bickerstaffe, pieces slighted in the study but by no
means lacking in obvious theatrical vitality. Twelve
production sketches by George Sheringham (prepared for
Nigel Playfair's 1924 revival of the piece adorn the
text.

6   RHODES, R. CROMPTON. "The Early Editions of Sheridan. I.
     The Duenna." Times Literary Supplement, 17 September,
     p. 599.
          Demonstrates that The Duenna, as printed in The Dramatic
     Works of R. B. Sheridan, Esq. (London: Printed for A.
     Millar, W. Law, and R. Cater, ca. 1797) is a reprinting
     (with the names of the characters returned to their
     original form) of The Governess, a piratical text using
     Sheridan's songs with fabricated dialogue and with newly
     named characters (e.g., Don Lorenzo for Don Ferdinand,
     Enoch for Isaac Mendoza). It was produced on 31 January
     1777 at the Theatre Royal, Crow Street, Dublin. The
     standard bibliography of Sheridan (see 1924.5) does not
     indicate that this spurious text is parading as the
     authentic one. The earliest edition of the authentic text
     known to Rhodes is the Oxberry one of 1820.

7   _____. "The Early Editions of Sheridan. II. The School for
     Scandal." Times Literary Supplement, 24 September, p. 617.
          Puts forth the Dublin edition of 1799 as the editio
     princeps of the genuine text of The School for Scandal.
     It thus replaces the Ewling text (1779?)--probably a
     pirated text--as the received editio princeps and the
     Oxford text of 1906 (based upon the John Murray edition
     of 1823) as the standard modern text. Authority for the
     Dublin edition of 1799 is provided by Thomas Moore, whose
     copy of it, newly discovered in the library of the Royal
     Irish Academy of Dublin, bears his note: "The MS. copy
     given by S. to Mrs. Crewe was evidently revised by
     himself, and agrees with this printed copy, except in
     the few trifling instances marked in the margin." Moore's

1925

marginal emendations then collate the printed text with
the Crewe MS.

8   ROBERTS, W. "Sheridan's School for Scandal." Times Literary
    Supplement, 15 October, p. 675.
        Adds a 1786 issue of The School for Scandal to the list
    of known "surreptitious Dublin editions" of the play. It
    appears in a volume of plays acted at the Smock-Alley
    Theatre and carries the general imprint "Printed for the
    Booksellers, MDCC, LXXXVI."

9   SERGEANT, PHILIP W. "Young Ireland: An Unappreciated
    Jester." In Liars and Fakers. London: Hutchinson,
    pp. 239-93.
        Recounts the career in forgery of William Henry Ireland,
    whose play Vortigern and Rowena, said to be a lost play
    by Shakespeare, was produced by Sheridan at Drury Lane on
    2 April 1796. The first two acts proceeded uneventfully;
    but, by the third act, the audience perceived the fraud,
    and the whole collapsed in merriment in the fifth act when
    Kemble, in the role of Vortigern, began burlesquing his
    lines. Sheridan is said to have scolded him for this
    misconduct. Of the forgery itself, Sheridan is said to
    have found the ideas "bold" but "crude and undigested,"
    the product of Shakespeare's very young years. But "Who
    can possibly look at the papers and not believe them
    ancient" (p. 257)?

1926

1   AGATE, JAMES. "'The Rivals' By Richard Brinsley Sheridan:
    Lyric Theatre, Hammersmith." In The Contemporary Theatre,
    1925. London: Chapman and Hall; Reprint ed., New York:
    Benjamin Blom, 1969, pp. 211-14.
        Sees Nigel Playfair's new production of The Rivals as
    proving once again that "when a man of genius sets out
    to tell a story it really matters very little what sort
    of story he has to tell" (p. 211). All roles in this
    production are acted ably but none more ably than that
    of Faulkland as played by Claude Rains. "He delivered
    the outpourings of rodomantade as they were Almanzor's
    purple torrents, and with every magnificence of voice
    and gesture. The modesty of nature being overstepped by
    just that degree which secures the very nicety of
    burlesque, the performance made the best of both
    worlds--the tragic and comic" (p. 213).

2   ANON. "The Duenna." Theatre Arts Monthly 10 (September):

645.
Pictures a stage setting for Alexander Dean's production
of The Duenna at the North Shore Theatre Guild in Chicago.
A "wide arch at the back is ingeniously planned so that
it can either be divided into two smaller arches or
entirely removed. The performance of this rarely seen
play of Sheridan's is in this way expedited and the many
scenic shifts are conveniently handled."

3   ATKINSON, J. BROOKS. "Sheridan--Whom the Gods Loved."
     North American Review 223 (December-February 1926-1927):
     645-55.
        Appreciates Sheridan's extraordinary wit and talent.
     He "touched life in many places; simultaneously he wrote
     plays, managed a theatre, debated in Parliament,
     trafficked with statesmen and agreeable fellows most of
     the night, enlivened the ballroom. But over the mundane
     affairs of life he had no vistage [sic] of control"
     (p. 652). The untimely death of his first wife might
     well be thought the cause of his final ruin, but in fact
     the seeds of his own destruction lay planted from the
     outset in his character. "Upon Richard Brinsley Sheridan
     the gods let themselves go with a jaunty, ironic flourish"
     (p. 645). He adorned everything he touched. "Yet where
     the world touched him it did not adorn" (p. 655).

4   BLACK, CLEMENTINA. The Linleys of Bath. London: Martin
     Secker, 316 pp.
        Reprints 1911.4. Reviewed in Times Literary Supplement
     25 November, p. 840.

5   COLINE, MARTIN. "Sheridan or Luttrell?" Times (London),
     3 August, p. 15.
        Suggests that lines addressed to Lady Erskine (see
     1926.10) should be attributed to Sheridan and not to
     Luttrell (contrary to the suggestion of the Reverend E. V.
     R. Powys in the Times for 16 July, p. 15). It is true,
     however, that these lines are sometimes given also to M.G.
     Lewis. (A writer to the Times for 6 August, p. 14,
     attributes the lines to Lewis.)

6   HAMILTON, CLAYTON M. "Introduction." In Sheridan's Plays.
     New York: Macmillan.
        Remarks Sheridan's distinction of having provided
     two thirds of the most memorable plays written between
     Shakespeare and Pinero (Goldsmith having provided the
     other third), then sketches the playwright's life, giving
     emphasis to his lucky background and parentage (an Irish
     son of gifted parents), his desire for recognition as

1926

a gentleman, and his extraordinary theatrical skill,
especially in fitting roles to available actors.

7   H[ORSNELL], H[ORACE]. "Period Farce." Outlook, 58
     (18 December): 609.
          Comments on a performance of The Critic at the East
     London College Theatre under the supervision of Allardyce
     Nicoll. "The first act, which sets out the situation and
     prepares for the rehearsal of Mr. Puff's bombastic
     tragedy, is an acting test of great severity. Once the
     burlesque is under way, and the satire has generalised
     itself, makeup and mannerism are almost enough to do the
     trick and make laughter inevitable." The play is said
     to be "strong meat for elocutionary sucklings."

8   LUGG, ALBERT S. "A Disputed Stanza." Times (London),
     11 August, p. 8.
          Finds in "Jeux d'Esprit" collected by Henry L. Leigh
     (Chatto and Windus, 1877) the lines addressed to Lady
     Erskine (see 1926.10) attributed not to Luttrell or Lewis
     (see 1926.5) but to Sheridan.

9   MATTHEWS, BRANDER. "Old Playwrights and Modern Playbooks."
     Literary Digest International Book Review 4 (June): 428-29.
          Comments, in reviewing Nigel Playfair's issue of The
     Duenna, that "There is no more local color in the Spain
     of Sheridan and Beaumarchais than there is in the Bohemia
     and the Illyria of Shakespeare's, and nobody is a penny
     the worse" (p. 428). The Duenna is properly considered
     the "best comic opera in our language" between The Beggar's
     Opera and the operas of Gilbert and Sullivan.

10   NICHOLSON, I. G. "Sheridan and Lady Erskine." Times
     (London), 22 July, p. 10.
          Quotes from Stainforth's edition of Sheridan's works
     an impromptu verse inspired by the annoyance felt by
     Lady Erskine when her husband observed that "a wife was
     only a tin cannister tied to one's tail." The verse
     wittily smooths out the annoyance by declaring that,
     after all, "A Cannister's polished and useful and bright,"
     unless tied to the tail of a lazy dog.

11   PANTER, GEORGE W. "Early Editions of Sheridan." Times
     Literary Supplement, 15 April, p. 283.
          Corroborates R. C. Rhodes's convictions that the Dublin
     edition of 1799 is the editio princeps of the original
     School for Scandal by quoting an inscription found in his
     own copy of the issue: "The gift of Richard Brinsley
     Sheridan to my grandfather, Gustavus Hume Rochford, M. P.,

when on a visit to Rochford, Co. Westmeath- Letitia C. R.
Brooke." In making such presentations, Sheridan was likely
to choose what he knew to be the best available edition of
the work. In another matter, it is puzzling that Mr.
Rhodes should raise questions about the earliest edition
of The Duenna. It is well known by bibliographers that
the earliest edition of the authentic text is 1794. (See
1926.13.)

12 RHODES, R. CROMPTON. "Sheridan Apocrypha." Times Literary
    Supplement, 26 August, p. 564.
        Challenges the likelihood that Sheridan was the author
    of "The General Fast: a Lyric Ode." Having assumed
    management of the Theatre Royal Drury Lane on 21 September
    1776, Sheridan would not likely have found the time or
    inclination to ridicule the fast ordered by George III
    (for 28 November 1776) on behalf of the rebel American
    colonists. The tone of the poem is not at all
    Sheridanesque; nor would the attack in it on the earl of
    Sandwich be in character for Sheridan in 1776. In
    declaring itself as being "by the Author of the Duenna,"
    the ode probably points not to Sheridan but to the author
    of a political satire published before July 1776, one
    parodying Sheridan's songs and bearing the title "The
    Duenna."

13 _____. "Sheridan Bibliography." Times Literary Supplement,
    17 June, p. 414.
        Issues a call for information about unrecorded editions
    of Sheridan's works before 1837. "No editions other than
    those of London and Dublin have yet in general been
    recorded, but there must have been others, as those which
    Oliver and Boyd, of Edinburgh, issued in paper wrappers
    1810-1816." With reference to George W. Panter's
    "admirable and informative" letter of 15 April (1926.11),
    the 1794 edition of The Duenna (having now been examined
    and collated by Rhodes) does not settle the question of
    the earliest issue of the authentic text.

14 ROMNEY, GEORGE. "Portrait of Sheridan." International Studio
    84 (May): 60.
        Admires George Romney's full-length portrait of Sheridan
    (reproduced here) as a "superb" example of Romney's
    portrait art.

15 SAINTSBURY, GEORGE. Introduction to The Linley's of Bath, by
    Clementina Black. London: Martin Secker, pp. v-x.
        Admires Black's book for treating Sheridan, whose
    life gives importance to the lives of the Linleys,

1926

substantially but not overextensively. "There is quite
enough of Sheridan but not in the least too much, and
both his merits and his faults, typical Irishman that
he was in both ways, are treated fairly but not dwelt on
excessively" (p. vii). The most interesting parts of the
book are quite properly the interchange of letters
between Elizabeth and Mary Linley and Charles Ward.

16   WATSON, ERNEST BRADLEE. Sheridan to Robertson: A Study of
      the Nineteenth-Century London Stage. Cambridge, Mass.:
      Harvard University Press, passim.
             Touches Sheridan only briefly, mentioning (in various
      contexts) his purchase of the "dormant patent" in 1793,
      a document subsequently shown to be worthless, his
      construction of the new theater in 1794, his reaction
      (generally one of indifference) to Robert William
      Ellerton's burlettas (ca. 1809), his relationship with
      J. P. Kemble (one of mutual trust and admiration) after
      the opening of the new theater.

17   WILLIAMS, IOLO A., ed. Introduction to The Plays of Richard
      Brinsley Sheridan. New York: Lincoln MacVeagh, Dial
      Press, pp. 7-19.
             Surveys Sheridan's literary career, showing him the son
      of literary parents, and reviewing his poems, especially
      the juvenile ones, as well as his plays and theatrical
      collaborations. Admires the character contrasts in The
      Rivals, the "book" and lyrics of The Duenna, the
      "penetrating study of human character" (p. 16) provided
      by The School for Scandal, but acknowledges a troubling
      lack of dramatic symmetry in The Critic.

*18   WRAY, EDITH ARMSTRONG. "English Drama from Sheridan to
      Byron, 1780-1815." Ph.D. dissertation. University of
      Wisconsin.
             Listed in The Comprehensive Dissertation Index 1861-1972
      (Ann Arbor, Mich.: Xerox University Microfilms, 1973),
      30: 505.

                                  1927

1   DOBELL, P. J. "Sheridan and the 'Ode to Scandal'"   Times
      Literary Supplement, 28 April, p. 299.
             Recalls that critics in 1819 hesitated to ascribe "An
      Ode to the Genius of Scandal" to Sheridan and feels that
      R. C. Rhodes's new edition of the poem (see 1927.7)
      amplifies the doubt. One known copy of the Kearsley
      quarto of the poem (1781) carries the contemporary

                                  128

inscription "By Mr. Tierney." George Tierney, a young
man then at Cambridge (whence, according to the preface
of the quarto, the poem emanates), is likelier to have
written it than Sheridan. Like Sheridan, he was active
in political life; and perhaps he wrote the ode after
noticing the recent success of The School for Scandal.
"The variations in metre can easily be explained as the
attempt of a young man trying his hand; but this explanation can hardly be applied to Sheridan, who was an
experienced writer by this time."

2 _____. "Sheridan and the 'Ode to Scandal.'" Times
Literary Supplement, 26 May, p. 375.
Insists that long-standing uncertainties about the
authorship of "An Ode to the Genius of Scandal" (e.g.,
misgivings expressed by a reviewer in 1819, an inscription
attributing the poem to George Tierney, the "unexplained
preface to the quarto of 1781") are enough to discredit
the ascription to Sheridan. Moreover, the Calcutta
Gazette for 22 July 1819 quotes the Bath Herald of
"Saturday last" in observing that the poem had first
appeared in the Bath Herald on 18 June 1803 and "was
there announced as an early poetic flight of that
eloquent, witty, sarcastic orator and most acute financier,
the Right Hon. G. Tierney, M. P."

3 G[ABRIEL], G[ILBERT] W. "The School for Scandal is 150 Years
Old." Mentor 15 (May): 8-11.
Surveys Sheridan's career, giving special emphasis to
The School for Scandal, a play which marries "two
very separate and independent plots" (p. 9). The lord
chamberlain was reluctant to license it, thinking it "a
naughty and demoralizing play" (p. 8). The London
audiences immediately adored it. It did not save
Sheridan from his imprudences and improvidences, but it
lives today as a vengeance on his detractors.

4 HERRING, ROBERT, ed. Introduction to The School for Scandal,
by Sheridan. London: Macmillan, pp. vii-xv.
Touches upon life in the eighteenth century and upon
the history of late eighteenth-century drama. Criticism
of the play holds that it "remains the best English
satirical comedy" (p. xi), even while lacking "a certain
universality" to be found in Molière. It unifies its
disparate structure by pursuing the theme "Never believe
what is said" (p. xiii), and its deficiencies in action
and characterization are concealed by Sheridan's flair
for dialogue.

1927

5   HINTON, PERCIVAL F. "Sheridan and the 'Ode to Scandal.'"
     Times Literary Supplement, 12 May, 336.
          Rejects P. J. Dobell's argument (1927.1) that "An Ode
     to the Genius of Scandal" is the work of George Tierney,
     not of Sheridan. In his edition of the poem, R. C.
     Rhodes suggests 1772 as the date of composition. At
     that time George Tierney was eleven years old. The
     metrical irregularities of the poem need not be
     explained. They are characteristic of the genre.
     Moreover, anonymous contemporary inscriptions (such as
     the one nominating George Tierney as the author) cannot
     alone determine attribution. It is best to leave the
     issue of authorship where Mr. Rhodes leaves it--as an
     open question.

6   NICOLL, ALLARDYCE. A History of Late Eighteenth Century
     Drama, 1750-1800. Cambridge: Cambridge University Press,
     pp. 160-62 and passim.
          Sees Sheridan recalling Restoration models (as Goldsmith
     had recalled Elizabethan ones). Apart from A Trip to
     Scarborough, a "fairly poor effort to make Vanbrugh's
     The Relapse fit for the audience of the time" (p. 160),
     Sheridan wrote two comedies of manners, one of them, The
     Rivals, a "thing of shreds and patches" (p. 160), the
     other, The School for Scandal, a work so authentic to
     Restoration comic models as to evince even their failings:
     an overintricate plot and an unrelentingly sparkling
     dialogue. But, of course, it differs in moral tone from
     the Restoration comedies it recalls. A section on
     "Burlesque" (pp. 214-17) comments on The Critic; a
     section on "Opera, Comic Opera and Kindred Forms" (pp.
     195-208) includes comment on The Duenna (p. 205).

7   RHODES, R. CROMPTON, ed. Introduction to An Ode To Scandal,
     Together with a Portrait. By Richard Brinsley Sheridan.
     Oxford: Blackwell, pp. 1-17, 25-34.
          Explains that the present text reprints the "Ode" as
     first printed (without mention of authorship) by G.
     Kearsley in 1781. This version of the poem augments the
     printed version of 1819 (published by W. Wright) attributed
     on the title page to Sheridan. The attribution is not at
     all certain, but arguments to support it reside in "(1)
     the posthumous ascription; (2) Sheridan's interest in the
     theme; (3) the poetical machinery of the form [which
     recalls Sheridan's poem "A Portrait"]; (4) its semi-
     dramatic quality; (5) the presumption of early unknown
     works; (6) the invalidity of objections previously offered
     against it [chiefly by Lloyd Sanders in his life of
     Sheridan (1890.2]" (p. 33). Perhaps it is not Sheridan's,

but "until every play and every poem accepted as Sheridan's has been printed in the most authentic text that can be attained" (p. 34), the proper study of Sheridan, "the most neglected of our great writers" (p. 1), cannot be undertaken. Reviewed in Times Literary Supplement, 14 April, p. 263.

8   _____. "Sheridan: A Study in Theatrical Bibliography." London Mercury 15 (February): 381-90.
Provides a bibliographical supplement to the introduction of Iolo A. Williams's The Plays of Richard Brinsley Sheridan (1926.17). Three texts are examined "according to bibliography as it appears from the aspect of theatrical history" (p. 383). The first of these, The Rivals, is properly enough printed (as Williams prints it) from the first edition of 1775, even though several passages included in Williams's edition were probably intended (judging from a later edition of 1775) to be deleted from the first edition. Williams also prints the best edition of The Duenna, that of 1794, the first correct and authorized edition of the play, all earlier ones deriving from corrupt sources. And Williams is the first to print the best text of The School for Scandal, the text collated by Thomas Moore from the Dublin edition of 1799 (the LeFanu MS) and the Crewe MS. This text, recently found by R. C. Rhodes with the assistance of W. J. Lawrence, disposes of the authority of other Dublin texts. It is "the one reliable text" (p. 390).

9   SEDGWICK, W. G. "Two Medieval Parallels to 'The Critic.'" Times Literary Supplement, 26 May, p. 375.
Recognizes forms of a Sheridanesque jeu d'esprit in two medieval sources. The passage "And Whiskerandos quits this bustling scene / For all eter--- / ---nity, he would have added" (wherein the Beefeater completes the dead Whiskerandos' speech [The Critic, III, i]) finds precedent in the De Bello Trojano of Joseph of Exeter (ca. 1190) and, "slightly earlier," in Y sengrimus. The three passages "seem independent of each other."

10   SHIPP, HORACE. "The Plays of Richard Brinsley Sheridan." Bookman (London), 72 (June): 202.
Complains that Iolo A. Williams, in editing the text of Sheridan, provides too little indication of ways in which his edition differs from earlier ones. Considered against Sheridan's own worth, however, the edition furnishes a welcome addition to the bookshelves, "an exact text based on scholarly research and a succinct introduction to the life and literature of the author."

1927

11   SMEDLEY, CONSTANCE. "An Undiscovered Heroine." <u>Bookman</u>
      (London), 72 (July): 210-12.
           Recognizes <u>The Rivals</u> as "an eulogy on woman" (p. 210)
      and posits Julia Melville as the heroine of the play.
      It is she who speaks the epilogue exalting the redemptive
      influence of women and she who dramatizes this redemptive
      force. Lydia is a selfish trickster, and Mrs. Malaprop
      is "an awful example of what Lydia will become" (p. 210).
      Julia, however, is "absolutely sincere in her relations
      with the other characters, including her lover: she is
      even honest with herself" (p. 210). Gentle and sensible,
      she is "a radiant and genuine heroine," and the only real
      problem she poses for the play is that few actresses are
      "sufficiently radiant, bouyant, wise-hearted, witty--and
      sincere" to play her as the playwright intended.

                              <u>1928</u>

1   ANON., ed. "<u>St. Patrick's Day; or, The Scheming Lieutenant</u>."
      <u>Golden Book Magazine</u> 7 (March): 351-60.
           Reprints the play without editorial or critical
      comment.

2   ATKINSON, J. BROOKS. "Sheridan--Whom the God's Loved." In
      <u>Essays of Today (1926-1927)</u>. Edited by Odel Shepard and
      Robert Hillyer. New York: Century, pp. 363-76.
           Reprints 1926.3.

3   CHAPMAN, R. W. "<u>Ye</u> for <u>The</u>." <u>Times Literary Supplement</u>,
      26 April, p. 314.
           Responds to a query raised by M. J. Ryan (1928.16) as
      to the use of the contraction "ye" for "the" during the
      late 1770s. Was this convention in general use at the
      time of the Sheridan manuscripts? It was. "Jane Austen
      often, and as late as 1814, writes 'ye.' There is no
      reason to suspect her of archaism." (On the grounds that
      the "ye" contraction was not widely used at the time of
      the Sheridan manuscripts, M. J. Ryan had questioned
      a textual reading proposed by R. C. Rhodes in emendation
      of the Oxford edition of <u>The School for Scandal</u>.)

4   _____. "'Ye' for 'The.'" <u>Times Literary Supplement</u>,
      24 May, p. 396.
           Answers M. J. Ryan once more (cf. 1928.3) in the matter
      of "ye" and "the." The Jane Austen manuscripts show
      frequent uses of "ye," as sentences quoted from 1813 and
      1814 indicate. It was a convention still practiced, then,
      decades after the <u>School for Scandal</u> manuscripts were

written.

5   ELTON, OLIVER. "Sheridan." In A Survey of English
    Literature, 1730-1780. London: Edward Arnold,
    1: 297-308.
        Surveys Sheridan's literary career, admiring it most
    for the treasure trove of language it unlocks. All his
    works, of whatever form, distinguish themselves by the
    brilliance of language, and, while his magnificent stage
    dialogue might have fathered bad practices upon
    subsequent playwrights, it is never lacking in his own
    plays. Of course, his flair for language accounts for
    his success as an orator, but his speeches (as they come
    down to us) lack the "weight of intellect behind them"
    (p. 308). As a master of prose, Sheridan "is to be
    judged by his dramas, where he is safe" (p. 308).

6   GABRIEL, MIRIAM, AND MUESCHKE, PAUL. "Two Contemporary
    Sources of Sheridan's The Rivals." Publications of the
    Modern Language Association of America 43 (March): 237-50.
        Argues of The Rivals that "neither the plot as a whole,
    nor the dramatic personae is original. The outline of
    the main plot of The Rivals Sherdian derived from
    Garrick's Miss in her Teens (1747) and the motivation of
    the subplot from Colman's The Deuce Is in Him (1763)"
    (p. 238). With the exception of Julia and Faulkland, all
    the characters in The Rivals find close parallels in
    Garrick's play. In both plays, furthermore, four rivals
    vie for the affection of an heiress; an ensign is the
    favored suitor; the hero must explain his false identity
    in the presence of both father and sweetheart; duel
    scenes heighten the farce. While critics have nominated
    several sources for Julia and Faulkland, only Colman's
    The Deuce Is in Him (hitherto unnoticed) will really
    serve. Colman anticipates the motive of Faulkland's
    malady, a "concept of self disassociated from all personal
    attributes," a "Metaphysical confusion which enmeshes the
    lover's sense of values" (p. 246). In readjusting the
    importance of certain characters and scenes, Sheridan
    asserts independence from his sources, but his debts are
    clear. They show him turning to two playwright-managers,
    men who knew what worked in the theater and who "were also
    in a position to reject or stage the offerings of a young
    dramatist struggling for recognition" (p. 250).

7   HINTON, PERCIVAL F. "A Sheridan Pamphlet." Times Literary
    Supplement, 28 June, p. 486.
        Prints bibliographic details of a pamphlet entitled
    "Authentic Copy of a letter from Mr. Pitt to His Royal

1928

Highness the Prince of Wales Containing the Restrictions
on the Intended Regency with His Royal Highness's Answer"
(printed for James Ridgway, 1788). The prince's answer,
long thought the work of Burke, was found by Walter Sichel
among the Sheridan papers and was printed by him in his
Sheridan (1909.5). The pamphlet corrects Sichel's
assumptions that the work was therefore "unpublished."
Students of Sheridan might also take note of Sheridan's
dealings with the Friends of the Liberty of the Press,
dealings noticed only slightly by Sichel. A pamphlet
reporting a meeting of the Friends on 19 January 1793
mentions three short speeches made by Sheridan and
announces that "Mr. Sheridan takes the Chair that day
four weeks." No report of the meeting chaired by
Sheridan is known.

8   JEBB, E. M., ed. Introduction to Sheridan's School for
     Scandal. Oxford: Clarendon Press, pp. 2-7.
         Sketches Sheridan's life and work in the general
     context of contemporary dramatic history, a period in
     which "The art of the actor . . . had outstripped that
     of the dramatist" (p. 4).

9   LAWRENCE, W. J. "The Text of 'The School for Scandal.'"
     Times Literary Supplement, 5 April, p. 257.
         Identifies, in response to a question raised by M. J.
     Ryan (1928.17), the text of The School for Scandal
     probably acted in the London theaters of Sheridan's time.
     The Widener Memorial Library at Harvard houses in its
     theatrical section "a neatly written octavo notebook
     containing a prompt copy of the play, made for use at
     Covent Garden circa 1810." An inscription on the flyleaf
     identifies the copy as a transcript from the Drury Lane
     promptbook.

10   RENDALL, VERNON. "The Long and Round 'S.'" Times Literary
     Supplement, 26 April, p. 314.
         Quotes a footnote from Leigh Hunt's Autobiography
     indicating that John Bell was the first English printer
     to confine the letter s to its round shape. The
     article, which supplies no dates for Bell, responds to
     M. J. Ryan's observations (1928.16) on the round s as
     a key to the dates of early Sheridan editions.

11   RHODES, R. CROMPTON, ed. Preface to The Plays and Poems of
     Richard Brinsley Sheridan. Oxford: Blackwell, 1: ix-xiv.
         Describes the extraordinary difficulty of editing
     Sheridan, since each of the plays, without exception,
     "was printed in at least two texts, with greater or lesser

differences" (p. ix), then explains the outlay of the
present edition (as to critical and bibliographic
apparatus) and pays tributes to precursors, especially
Thomas Moore and Walter Sichel, whose biographical work
has proved invaluable. (For the details of Rhodes's
editorial practice, see above, "The Sheridan Texts.")

12   _____. "Some Aspects of Sheridan Bibliography." <u>Library</u>,
    4th ser. 9 (December): 233-61.

    Examines into the financial protections available to
British dramatic authors in the latter part of the
eighteenth century: (1) "stage-right, or the right to
sanction or refuse performance," and (2) "copyright, the
right to sanction or refuse publication" (p. 236). Since
stage-right did not cover printed plays, theater managers
tried to keep good plays out of print, and since English
copyright did not apply in Ireland, Irish printers could
print copyrighted books and manuscripts with impunity.
Copyright and stage-right were enforcible in England; so
English piracies and illegitimate performances were at
least subject to control. But in Ireland piracy was
extensive, and stage-right did not apply there to plays
carrying Irish imprints. Because playwrights usually
sold their stage- and copyrights to the theater managers,
they concerned themselves little in the piratical
adventures of their plays. Consequently, legal reforms
were slow in coming. Had Sheridan enjoyed modern
protections, he and his heirs would have received at
least 2,000,000 pounds for <u>The School for Scandal</u> before
its copyright expired in 1856. The scrupulous care with
which (under the old systems of protection) Sheridan
guarded his promptbooks, may indicate, however, that the
text of <u>The School for Scandal</u> published by John
Cumberland in 1826, following the Drury Lane promptbook,
is the most reliable text, far more reliable, certainly,
than the John Murray text of 1821. The article concludes
with a select bibliographical summary of "Early Editions
of Sheridan's Plays and Poems."

13   _____. "The Text of 'The School for Scandal.'" <u>Times</u>
    <u>Literary Supplement</u>, 26 April, pp. 313-14.

    Assumes responsibility for the Iolo A. Williams text
of <u>The School for Scandal</u> and offers to explain, in
response to M. J. Ryan (1928.17), the discrepancies
between it and the Moore-Crewe text declared to be its
canon. The discrepancies occur because (1) the Crewe MS
and LeFanu MS (the basis of the Dublin edition of 1799)
contain several of the same inadvertent omissions; (2)
Moore's collation, not intended for publication, ignores

1928

obvious misprints and sustains the omissions occurring
in both the Crewe and LeFanu manuscripts; (3) "Accordingly
it was necessary to make a number of corrections and to
restore the few sentences which occur in the London
edition of 1823, the first authorized publication of the
authentic text (as opposed to the spurious copies)"
(p. 313). Furthermore, the text supplied to William
reflects "consideration" (p. 414) of yet other printed
versions of the play. An apparatus criticus in Rhodes's
own forthcoming edition of Sheridan's plays and poems will
clarify details.

14   _____. "The Text of 'The School for Scandal.'" Times
Literary Supplement, 24 May, p. 396.
Declares the belief that "the editio princeps of The
School for Scandal--the spurious text--is the Dublin
edition of 1780," not the Ewling edition, which M. J.
Ryan unjustly accuses him (1928.19) of confusing with the
Dublin edition of 1780. In the matter of the round s
(cf. 1928.10; 1928.15; 1928.16), the turn to it by John
Bell about 1789 was not adopted immediately by other
printers (as a variety of Sheridan editions indicates).
In the matter of the "ye" contraction (cf. 1928.3;
1928.4; 1928.15), Sheridan's copyist, Hopkins, was
accustomed to seeing it in the handwriting of David
Garrick. It could explain certain readings in the
Sheridan manuscripts.

15   RYAN, M. J. "The Long 'S" and 'Ye.'" Times Literary
Supplement, 17 May, p. 379.
Supplies further information--in response to Vernon
Rendall (1928.10)--about John Bell's abandonment of the
long s in English printing. The practice was made
fashionable with Bell's printing of The British Theatre
(ca. 1795). On the question of "ye," R. W. Chapman's
comment on Jane Austen's use of it (1928.3, 4) generalizes
too broadly on the matter. Manuscript pages by Burns,
Campbell, Crabbe, Cowper, Sheridan, and Jane Austen
herself show marked preference to "the," and the
appearance of "ye" in the usage of one writer does not
reduce the likelihood that the practice would be unusual
to Sheridan and his copyists.

16   _____. "The School for Scandal and the Round 'S.'"
Times Literary Supplement, 19 April, p. 290.
Observes that the round s seems to have entered
printing practices in the 1790s and that it was not at
all in evidence in 1777 at the beginnings and middles
of words. The "Ewling" edition of The School for Scandal,

which makes slight and erratic use of the long s, thus
clearly dates to a period much later than 1777. A
concluding bit of "mild paleography" questions the
currency of "ye" as a contraction for "the" at the time
of the Sheridan manuscripts. On the basis of this
practice, R. C. Rhodes had offered an emendation for the
Oxford text of The School for Scandal. (See 1928.10.)

17 _____. "The Text of 'The School for Scandal'--I." Times
Literary Supplement, 22 March, p. 212.
Challenges the view held by R. C. Rhodes and Iolo A.
Williams (see 1927.8) that Thomas Moore's collation of
the Crewe MS of The School for Scandal with the Dublin
edition of 1799 (a collation discovered in 1925 in the
Royal Irish Academy) provides the approved text of the
play. Itself a "slipshod and incorrect" text, the Dublin
edition of 1799 cannot logically be thought the first
printing of the manuscript given by Sheridan to his
sister and sold by her to the manager of the Dublin
Theatre in 1778 (the LeFanu MS). Nor can the Crewe MS,
which dates to August 1777, represent Sheridan's final
thinking on the play, since nineteen years later, as
Sheridan indicated to James Ridgway the bookseller, he
was still not ready to surrender it to the printers.
Many textual confusions yet need to be resolved, but
one thing clear is that Williams has not followed the
Moore-Crewe collation.

18 _____. "The Text of 'The School for Scandal'--II." Times
Literary Supplement, 29 March, p. 240.
Appends to his article of 22 March (1928.17) a
collation showing aspects in which Iolo A. Williams's
text of The School for Scandal, as published in his
edition of Sheridan's plays (see 1926.17) differs from
the supposed "approved" text, the Dublin edition of
1799 as emended by Thomas Moore in conformity with the
Crewe MS.

19 _____. "The Text of 'The School for Scandal.'" Times
Literary Supplement, 10 May, p. 358.
Responds in turn to R. C. Rhodes's response (1928.13)
to Ryan's own first article on the text of The School for
Scandal (1928.17). The Rhodes answer "pleaded confession
and avoidance." It confesses that Moore's revised text
cannot stand alone as the canon, that it requires
editorial adjustments. Furthermore, the answer avoids
comment on several very telling discrepancies between
the Williams and Moore texts. Rhodes is probably right,
however, in "setting up the Moore-Crewe text as the best

1928

extant--subject, as he now admits, to careful editing."
Among texts considered by Rhodes, however, the Dublin
edition of 1780 seems to have eluded him. He makes no
distinction between it and the Ewling edition.

20   _____. "The Text of 'The School for Scandal.'" Times
Literary Supplement, 7 June, p. 430.
        Justifies the inference (see 1928.19) that R. C. Rhodes
has confused the Ewling edition of The School for Scandal
with the Dublin edition of 1780 and that the separate
Dublin edition of 1780 has eluded him. In the Times
Literary Supplement for 26 April 1928 (1923.13, p. 314)
Rhodes had spoken of the "Ewling or 1780" text of the
play. In earlier discussions--The London Mercury for
January 1927 (1927.8, p. 390) and his edition (1927.7) of
An Ode to Scandal (p. 1)--he had demonstrated that the
Ewling edition was printed from the 1781 edition but much
later than 1781. Since he speaks of the "Ewling or 1780"
texts as being one-and-the-same, and since he discredits
the 1780 imprint of the Ewling edition, it is necessary
to infer that the Dublin edition of 1780--as an edition
separate from the Ewling--has eluded him. His failure
to mention the matter before having it called to his
attention confirms the inference. He is likely wrong,
furthermore, in explaining the origins of the 1781
editions of the play, which are based upon a manuscript
or a promptbook and are not the "vamped" versions he
sees them to be.

21   THOMPSON, L.F. Kotzebue, A Survey of His Progress in France, and
England, Preceded by a Consideration of the Attitude to Him in
Germany. Paris: Librairie Ancienne Honre Champion, 175pp.
        Comments in chapter 2 ("Kotzebue in England") on the
literary and/or theatrical history in England of each of
the thirty-seven plays translated from Kotzebue's German
into English. Sheridan's adaptation of The Stranger
(from Benjamin Thompson's translation) is credited with
making Kotzebue famous. Pizarro, while profiting from
Sheridan's improvements in certain features of
characterization and dialogue, suffers from the
disunifying effect of "two feeble and superfluous scenes"
(p. 67) added by Sheridan at the end. In general,
Kotzebue "freed the English dramatists from the moral
incubus and helped them to a more realistic representation
of life." He "shewed the incompatability of the moral,
sentimental and the realistic, or naturalistic type of
play . . . and so prepared the way for the development of
the latter" (p. 92).

1929

1 ANON. "First Editions." Times (London), 14 March, p. 13.
    Reports the sale at Sotheby's of a first edition of
    The Rivals for 400 pounds.

2 ANON. "Memorabilia." Notes and Queries 156 (9 February): 92.
    Announces the acquisition by Gabriel Wells, an American
    dealer in manuscripts and rare books, of the "original
    autograph MS of Sheridan's 'The School for Scandal.'"
    This manuscript, Sheridan's first draft of the play,
    "was arranged, collated, annotated, and bound in 1864
    by Sheridan's grandson." Written on 191 quarto pages,
    it is "inlaid to royal quarto size, and bound, with the
    printed text of Thomas Moore's 1821 edition of the play
    interleaved." It is "full of autograph corrections,
    elisions, interpolations, stage directions, and variants
    of dialogue." Brought to America by "a confidential
    representative of its former owner, a descendant of the
    author," it was privately sold. (Cf. 1929.3.)

3 ANON. "Rare Sheridan MS of Play Sold Here." New York Times,
    4 February, p. 14.
    Announces that Gabriel Wells, a "bibliophile and dealer
    in rare books at 145 West Fifty-seventh Street," has
    purchased from A. T. Brinsley Sheridan, of Frampton Court,
    Dorset, the "original autograph manuscript of 'The School
    for Scandal.'" It "is written on 191 quarto pages, inlaid
    to royal quarto size, and bound, together with the
    printed text of Thomas Moore's edition of the play (1821),
    interleaved in opposite juxtaposition to the manuscript."

4 BATESON, F. W. "The Text of Sheridan." Times Literary
    Supplement, 28 November, p. 998.
    Calls attention to two texts of The Rivals apparently
    unnoticed by Sheridan's recent editors I. A. Williams and
    R. C. Rhodes: (1) the Larpent MS, soon to be published
    by R. L. Purdy, and (2) an abbreviated version of the
    play printed in Mrs. Inchbald's The British Theatre (1808)
    and in similar theatrical collections published in 1814,
    1818, and 1823. Mrs. Inchbald's edition indicates that
    the play was "printed under the authority of the managers
    from the prompt book." The text is "characterized by
    three peculiarities: (1) the 'cuts' are short and do not
    interfere with the progression of the action; (2) the
    effect of a number of the omissions and alterations is
    to restore the text of an earlier form of the play;
    (3) the changes are often trivial and gratuitous." Since
    these peculiarities also characterize an earlier version

1929

of The Rivals, one known to be Sheridan's own, the text
printed by Mrs. Inchbald might well represent Sheridan's
final version of The Rivals and "should in future take the
place of the edition of 1776 as the textus receptus."
While there is no external evidence supporting this
attribution, Sheridan might have indicated in a letter
to the translator A. Chateauneuf (extant in ambiguous
French) that he revised The Rivals three times: i.e.,
for the performance of 28 January 1775, for the edition
of 1776, and for the prompt copy printed by Mrs.
Inchbald, probably made for the 1790 revival of the play.

5   ____. "The Text of Sheridan II--'The School for Scandal.'"
Times Literary Supplement, 5 December, p. 1029.
Nominates the John Murray edition of 1821 as the extant
version of The School for Scandal likely to represent
"Sheridan's final revision of that play." This text,
which possibly came to Murray from James Ridgway, who
owned the copyright of the play, probably reflects
revisions made quite late by Sheridan who could never
satisfy his own taste in the play (as he is reported to
have told Ridgway). The other top contender, the Crewe
MS, while said by Thomas Moore to be the last revised by
Sheridan, was rejected by Murray in favor of a manuscript
not known to Moore, i.e., the "better" Ridgway text on
which Sheridan worked until his death (hence the distaste
for Murray's edition expressed in Moore's biography of
Sheridan). Incidentally, the Crewe MS collated by Moore
with the Dublin edition of 1799 need not be the same early
copy given to Mrs. Crewe together with the poem "A
Portrait" soon after The School for Scandal opened (as
R. C. Rhodes supposes). Both the manuscript referred to
by Moore and the corrections on it "belong to Sheridan's
later years."

6   DRURY, CHARLES. "The Linleys of Norton." In A Sheaf of
Essays by a Sheffield Antiquary. Sheffield: J. W.
Northend, pp. 126-29.
Establishes the ancestry of the Linleys in the village
of Norton and sketches the lineage of the family through
Sheridan's granddaughters, the daughters of Thomas
Sheridan, who married into aristocratic families. Helen
was married first to Price, Lord Dufferin and Claneboye,
and later to the earl of Gifford; Caroline was married
first to G. C. Norton, the brother of Lord Grantley, and
later to Sir William Stirling-Maxwell, Bart.; Jane
Georgiana was married to Edward Adolphus, duke of Somerset.

6a   FRYE, PROSSER HALL. "Sheridan." In Visions and Chimeras.

Boston: Marshall Jones Company, pp. 3-19.

Classifies Sheridan among those "rare amphibians who live partly in literature, partly in politics" (p. 4) but denies him the seriousness given to others of the class. In everything, he lived for flair and effect, and he "combined in his own person the double rôle of Joseph and Charles Surface. He had all the former's sophistry of protestation devoid of profound sincerity of conviction,and all the latter's mischievousness of impulse devoid of the intentional malice" (p. 9). While "Sheridan's is the very best of anything like genuine comedy that we have" (p. 10), his comedies rarely rise above mere fun. Even his parliamentary oratory is waggish and might best be called "the comedy of parliamentarianism" (p. 18). Because he represents "the irruption of genius into a province usually reserved for other occupants" (p. 19), history has faulted him for inconsistency and lack of "officialism," but such attributes were always foreign to his character.

7 HERRING, ROBERT, ed. Introduction to The Rivals, by Sheridan. London: Macmillan, pp. ix-xxiii.

Reviews Sheridan's career and suggests that his gifts were more "constructive" than "creative," in that antecedents can be found to most of the characters and situations in his plays. The Rivals recalls several earlier literary works--e.g., Steele's Tender Husband, Smollett's Humphry Clinker, Fielding's Joseph Andrews--but it holds independent interest for its construction (which uses servants as a kind of comic chorus), its characterization (which draws admirably upon balanced contrasts), and its language (which, though not so polished as that in The School for Scandal, is fresh and vigorous). Historically, the play holds interest for hastening the demise of sentimental comedy and for reflecting the social life of Bath in the 1770s.

8 MacCARTHY, DESMOND. "An Old Comedy Very Much Revived." New Statesman 34 (14 December): 329-30.

Admires a revival of The School for Scandal at the Kingway Theatre in London because the production is "high-spirited and unaffected" (p. 329). All the roles are effectively cast, especially that of Lady Teazle as played by Angela Baddeley, who sees her character as "a provincial beauty whose high spirits and mischievous love of flippancy" (p. 329) enable her to shine in high society. The production succeeds, too, because the actors are not overartificialized by their eighteenth-century costumes and because the production

1929

respects the identity of the play as "a cross between
the old, artificial, heartless, husband-baiting comedy
of the Restoration and the sentimental, virtue-admiring
comedy Tom Jones made popular" (p. 330).

9   PLAYFAIR, NIGEL. "Faulkland on the Stage." Times Literary
Supplement, 10 January, p. 28.
       Takes issue, on the testimony of experience, with the
sentiment expressed by a reviewer of Sheridan's Plays
and Poems (see 1928.11) that Faulkland in The Rivals
cannot be found funny. Claude Rains, in a recent revival
of the play, had distinguished himself as the "outstanding
feature of the performance" and had drawn from the
audience "such laughter as honestly I have seldom heard
in a theatre." (In a brief note of response the reviewer,
who missed the performance, wonders if the fun raised
by Rains's Faulkland was "of the kind intended by
Sheridan.")

10 RHODES, R. C[ROMPTON]. "'The School for Scandal.'" Times
Literary Supplement, 26 December, p. 1097.
       Rejects F. W. Bateson's argument (1929.5) that John
Murray's edition of 1821 provides the best basic text
of The School for Scandal. "The case for the Murray
text is untenable--it is careless, and it retains
readings which demonstrably had been altered before
August, 1777." A document in the British Museum
(Egerton MS 1975 f. 21) indicates that when Sheridan
was negotiating a collected edition of his plays in
1809 he intended the text of The School for Scandal to
be taken from the promptbook of Drury Lane Theatre.
This text, as printed in Cumberland's British Theatre
in 1826 (and entirely ignored by Bateson) is the source
of Rhodes's own edition of the play. As to Bateson's
comments on the Crewe MS, it is highly unlikely (as a
biographical reality) that Sheridan sent a second copy
of the play to Mrs. Crewe after an interval of nineteen
years.

11 _____. "Sheridan Bibliography." Times Literary Supplement,
10 January, p. 28.
       Recalls that Sheridan authorized publication of only
two of his speeches but that others (e.g., a speech to
the Whig Club in 1788 on the centenary of the landing
of William of Orange and some of the speeches given on
St. Patrick's Day) actually saw print. Information about
these and other printed speeches (and about unpublished
letters) is invited.

12 _____. "The Text of Sheridan." Times Literary Supplement,
    19 December, pp. 1081-82.
    Insists that "there is no 'textual confusion' as to
    The Rivals." The third edition corrected (John Wilkie,
    1776), which contains Sheridan's corrections and bears
    his name, is the textus receptus of the play. It was
    followed by the fourth, fifth, and sixth editions
    published before 1798 by George and Thomas Wilkie.
    Despite F. W. Bateson's propositions to the contrary
    (1924.4), the abbreviated text published by Mrs. Inchbald
    in 1808 is "absolutely devoid of authority" (p. 1081).
    No evidence, external or internal, can support its claims;
    the cuts show no extraordinary subtlety of understanding;
    nor is it likely that Sheridan, who intended eventually
    to publish his plays with prefaces, turned his final
    work on The Rivals over to Mrs. Inchbald. More probably
    she printed a promptbook copy provided her by J. P.
    Kemble, then manager of Covent Garden, "who supplied Mrs.
    Inchbald with so many of her texts" (p. 1082).

13 THORNDIKE, ASHLEY H. English Comedy. New York: Macmillan,
    pp. 429-36.
    Acknowledges the excellence in their own sphere of The
    Duenna, The Critic, and A Trip to Scarborough, but sees
    Sheridan's contributions to comedy to lie in The Rivals
    and The School for Scandal. The former combines the
    spirit of Farquhar with the wit of Congreve; the latter
    translates conventional Restoration plots and characters
    into graceful, unoffending amiable comedy, comedy piquant
    without grossness. Sheridan's "powers as a dramatist
    are displayed in design, in dialogue, in a most effective
    representation of comic characters" (p. 436). He "had
    no rivals and few followers" (p. 436). In fact, since
    no one could emulate him, it is more logical to say that
    he killed the comedy of manners than that his successes
    revived it.

14 WHITE, NEWPORT B. "The Text of Sheridan." Times Literary
    Supplement, 5 December, p. 1032.
    Suggests that Sheridan's letter to A. Chateauneuf
    (quoted by F. W. Bateson in 1929.4) indicates a period
    of three years spent in correcting The Rivals. The
    phrase "trois années" is not likely to indicate "three
    different times," as Bateson would surmise.

1930

1 BATESON, F. W. "The School for Scandal." Times Literary

1930

Supplement, 23 January, p. 60.
Concedes to R. C. Rhodes (1929.10) the conviction that
John Cumberland's edition of The School for Scandal is
"accurate and authoritative" but insists that of the
eight principal versions of The School for Scandal, only
Murray's and the Crewe MS need to be taken seriously.
Since Murray's text has more original readings than
Cumberland's, it is probably a later draft. Readings
"confined to the Murray text are both more striking and
more certainly genuine" than those confined to the
Cumberland; and few readings of merit in the Cumberland
are not also incorporated into the Murray. Rhodes would
thus have done better to use the Murray text for his
edition of Sheridan's plays (see 1928.11) than the
Cumberland one.

2   _____. "The Text of Sheridan." Times Literary Supplement,
9 January, p. 28.
Defends his view (see 1929.4) that Mrs. Inchbald's
edition of The Rivals--published in 1808 from a revision
of about 1790--"embodies the last, and therefore the
most authoritative, revision of The Rivals in which
Sheridan can actually be implicated." R. C. Rhodes (see
1929.12) dates the revision at 1800 and identifies J. P.
Kemble as the reviser, but he offers no convincing
support. As "the only cut text of the play which we
possess," this revision suggests itself as the version
actually acted in the stock repertory, and the cuts
taken (short ones showing sensitivity to style and
continuity) suggest authorial concerns. It is not likely
that Mrs. Inchbald and several later editors would trouble
themselves with a revision lacking Sheridan's own
authority; and if, as Rhodes complains, the revision
wants literary excellence, it at least reflects the
textual development of The Rivals, which "was not
primarily from a bad to a good play, but from a long to
a short one."

3   DOLMAN, JOHN, JR. "A Laugh Analysis of The School for
Scandal." Quarterly Journal of Speech 16 (November):
432-45.
Tabulates act by act the laughter provoked by each of
five performances of The School for Scandal. When
analyzed according to sources of laughter (e.g., laughs
dependent on timing, laughs dependent on "following
through," laughs dependent on contrast), this tabulation
instructs directors in how best to excite and sustain
laughs at apposite moments in the play. The performances
analyzed gave rise to as many as 154 bursts of laughter

during the course of a single performance, bursts
audible to the prompter backstage and marked by him in
his script.

4   EDINGER, GASTON. Sheridan; ou, L'Insoucieux. Les Grandes
     Vies aventureuses. Paris: Berger-Levrault, 230 pp.
        Divides an account of Sheridan's life into four parts
     (1) from his birth through his marriage, (2) from The
     Rivals through The Critic, (3) from his election as M.P.
     to the death of his first wife, (4) from her death to his
     own. More and more he acquiesces in human frailty,
     especially a tendency to procrastinate, losing all with
     the loss of his wife: "La vie n'avait plus d'attraits
     pour Sheridan. En perdant Eliza il avait tout perdu"
     (p. 169). An "Epilogue" compares Sheridan's career to
     that of Disraeli and posits the earlier statesman as a
     model for the latter: "Sans Sheridan, Disraeli, peut-être,
     fut resté Disraeli et n'eût jamais été l'immortel
     Beaconsfield" (p. 227). (See 1930.10.)

5   GUTHRIE, TYRONE. Introduction to Complete Plays, by Sheridan.
     Collins Pocket Classics. London: Collins, pp. 11-16.
        Argues that the elegance of Sheridan's comedies limits
     them to a vogue now démodé and not really favored by
     theater audiences since the Treaty of Versailles. Until
     this vogue returns, performances of Sheridan's comedies
     will be few. If it never returns, The School for Scandal
     will likely be the only one of his comedies to hold the
     stage. The others show little authentic humanity, and
     "Sheridan succeeds in proportion as his characters are
     allowed to arouse our interest and our sympathy" (p. 16).
     He "treated the theatre as a toy, half affectionately,
     half with contempt. The result is one near masterpiece,
     a small group of immature talented trifles; a legend as
     romantic as that of Keats or Chatterton, and a reputation
     which will wax and wane with the changing values which
     fashion accords to the comparatively trivial manifestations
     known as Elegance" (p. 16).

6   MacMILLAN, DOUGALD. "Sheridan's Share in The Stranger."
     Modern Language Notes 45 (February): 85-86.
        Compares The Stranger with Kotzebue's Menschenhass und
     Reue and discovers three points of difference: "(1) the
     names of some of the characters are changed, not merely
     translated; (2) two vaudeville scenes have been added to
     the English version; (3) the English play is considerably
     shorter than the original" (p. 85). The vaudeville
     scenes add musical interludes not related to the action;
     the cuts remove excessive philosophizing and

1930

sentimentalizing. Through his small involvement in The
Stranger, "Sheridan has merely done what any producer is
likely to do to any play that comes under his direction"
(p. 86).

7   PURDY, RICHARD L. "The Text of Sheridan." Times Literary
Supplement, 2 January, p. 12.
    Corrects F. W. Bateson's view that "the version of The
Rivals frequently printed in theatrical collections of
the nineteenth century and completely ignored by scholars"
is "a third revision." The forthcoming edition of the
Larpent manuscript of The Rivals (1935.3) will demonstrate
that the version in question is not such a revision.

8   RHODES, R. CROMPTON, ed. Introduction to The School for
Scandal, by Sheridan. Oxford: Blackwell, pp. v-xxiii.
    Describes the social milieu of the comedy and emphasizes
the importance of costume to the dramatic effect. By
way of suggesting the style of early productions, the
introduction also describes gestures and dialects
appropriate to selected characters and situations. Hints
for these details derive from the stage directions
printed in the edition of The School for Scandal issued
by Thomas Hailes Lacy, undated, in 1856. These directions
presumably reflect the practices of the very earliest
performances.

9   _____. "The Text of The Rivals." Times Literary Supplement,
16 January, p. 44.
    Rejects F. W. Bateson's answers (see 1930.2) to earlier
objections (see 1929.4) touching the text of The Rivals.
As to the issue of length, evidence demonstrates that
"Sheridan, in twice revising his comedy, recognized no
necessity for any appreciable abbreviation." Bateson
errs, too, in interpreting the internal features of Mrs.
Inchbald's text, the text he thinks to be authoritative:
(1) he calls commonplace revisions "subtleties of style";
(2) he labels "pointless" revisions showing obvious
topical point; (3) he misunderstands the whole theatrical
practice of textual cutting. The literary worth of the
Inchbald text has no part in the issue, Bateson's arguments
to the contrary notwithstanding.

10 SHERIDAN. Sheridan; ou, L'Insoucieux. Les Grandes Vies
aventureuses. Paris: Berger-Levrault, 230 pp.
    "Sheridan" is the pseudonym of Gaston Edinger. See 1930.4.

11 SKINNER, RICHARD DANA. "The Play and Screen." Commonweal
11 (26 March): 590.

Takes the occasion of a theatrical review to remark of
Sheridan that "his mind was too thin to be able to pass
down through the centuries as anything more than a relic
of style sprinkled with a forced type of wit and a good
deal of broad humor." In Shakespeare's comedies "there
are always passages which are of the life breath of
poetry," the "solid substance of a great mind at play
among the foibles of humanity." But "Sheridan's works
can boast no such mental substance nor poetic endowment.
They are comedies of manners." For all its plot
involvements, for example, The Rivals follows "a
perfectly intelligible pattern with adroit ease."

12 THOMSON, C. LINKLATER. "Jane Austen's Reading." Times
    Literary Supplement, 27 March, p. 274.
        Sees Jane Austen's description of Laura and Sophia
    (in "Love and Friendship') "faintly alternately on the
    sofa" as a borrowing, perhaps unconscious, of Sheridan's
    "They faint alternately in each other's arms" in The
    Critic (III, i).

13 W., E. VR. "The Rivals." The Catholic World 131 (May):
    213-14.
        Admires a revival of The Rivals featuring Mrs. Fiske
    as Mrs. Malaprop. "The good lines still hold good.
    So does the business. As Sheridan took the best from
    his predecessors and his successors took the best from
    him, the result is not always original but it is sound
    comic psychology" (p. 213).

1931

1 BUTLER, E[LIZA] M. Sheridan: A Ghost Story. London:
   Constable, 312 pp.
        Seeks to locate Sheridan's character first by surveying
   all the major biographical accounts, then by sifting the
   traditions attaching to his life. None of these sources,
   however, yields up the secret so well as certain of
   Sheridan's letters and other personal writings (early and
   late) which reveal him troubled by apprehensions of
   death and driven by this fear away from the introspection
   and solitude required for creative work. His life, then,
   is a process of self-destruction prompted by an
   "unaccountable dejection of spirits without a cause" (p.
   300). He "endured for a time; but, restive and highly
   strung, he shied away finally from the labor and torment
   of creation into the 'grand deception' of public life"
   (p. 304). Until his wife's death in 1792, his life had

1931

been an "urbane evasion of responsibility" (p. 305).
Thereafter, he "became a hunted fugitive, fleeing not
only from others but also from himself; bolting away
from memories; decamping before pain; sheering off
from unhappiness and absconding from remorse" (pp.
305-6). Reviewed by F. T. Wood in Englische Studien 66
(1931): 133-34; in Times Literary Supplement, 16 April,
p. 303; in Spectator 146 (23 May): 830; by E. Sutton in
Week End Review 4 (4 July): 24; in Oxford Magazine,
11 June, p. 844; in Bookman (London), 80 (April): 33; by
A. P. Nicholson in Saturday Review 151 (21 March): 423-24.

2   GRAY, CHARLES HAROLD. Theatrical Criticism in London to
    1795. New York: Columbia University Press; reprinted,
    New York: B. Blom, 1964, pp. 191-249.
        Discusses the range and character of critical journal-
    ism during a decade especially interesting for being "the
    period of Richard Brinsley Sheridan's best dramatic
    work" (p. 192). During this decade the profession of
    the theatrical critic went far toward establishing
    itself. Newspapers in great numbers published regular
    critical articles about theater, plays, and acting.

3   NETTLETON, G[EORGE] H. Sheridan et la comédie de moeurs.
    Paris: C. Lavrut, 15 pp.
        Remarks the popularity of Sheridan as being second only
    to that of Shakespeare in terms of continuous stage
    presentation. Sheridan's comic spirit, however, gives
    lively reflections of the surface of life; Shakespeare's
    illuminates life in all its depth. Sheridan's world is
    that of the beau monde; Shakespeare takes all the world
    for his stage. Among antecedent English playwrights,
    Ben Jonson provides, with his humors comedy, a more
    direct ancestor to Sheridan than Shakespeare does.
    Congreve's ancestry is closer yet, for in The School for
    Scandal the Restoration comedy of manners is raised to
    its highest development, its wit and brilliance preserved,
    its indecencies expunged. Sheridan's comedy retains the
    spirit of Congreve while improving upon his plots. It
    combines character, dialogue, and intrigue in a
    consummate way. Sensing himself incapable of following
    Shakespeare's path into the depths of the human comedy,
    Sheridan chose wisely the course of the comedy of
    manners. In doing so he brought fresh gaiety to English
    comedy, and he should no more be faulted for his choice
    than Beaumarchais should be faulted for not being Molière.

4   SAWYER, NEWELL W. The Comedy of Manners from Sheridan to
    Maugham. Philadelphia: University of Pennsylvania Press,

275 pp.

Traces the history of comedy of manners from "its
brilliant exemplification" (p. 238) in The School for
Scandal to the beginning of World War I. Only
sporadic instances of it occur between Sheridan and
Robertson, and Robertson, who revived the type, gave it
a decidedly middle-class character. With Wilde, Jones,
Pinero, and Carton it returned to its original convention
of treating the manners of the upper class "without
deprecation and without moral implication" (p. 238). The
decline of the type was evident as early as 1778, when
critics of The School for Scandal attacked the play on
moral grounds. The success of the play throughout the
nineteenth century attests the power of its wit and
brilliance, but it continued "the last of a dramatic
dynasty, not the precursor of a new" (p. 19).

1932

1 ANON. "Sheridan Papers: Duke of Bedford's Gift to British
       Museum." Times (London), 16 May, p. 13.
       Describes a gift to the British Museum of letters and
   papers concerning the Sheridan family. "In addition to
   new documents bearing on the history of Drury Lane and
   Richard Brinsley Sheridan's relations with that theatre,
   there are three sets of correspondence dealing with the
   affairs of the children of his son, Thomas Sheridan."

2 F., R. "The Sheridan Papers." British Museum Quarterly,
       7 (September): 38-39.
       Describes a collection of papers presented to the
   British Museum by the duke of Bedford. Originally part of
   the Frampton court collection and property of Brinsley
   Sheridan, grandson of the dramatist, they fall into two
   groups: papers relating to the managment of Drury Lane
   Theatre under Tom Sheridan's administration, and papers
   relating to the lives of three of Tom's own children,
   Helen, Caroline, and Frank. The theatrical papers consist
   largely of "legal documents, correspondence with the
   Trustees, contracts with actors, and other business
   documents" (p. 38). The family papers include
   correspondence relating to an action for crim. con.
   brought by Caroline's husband against Lord Melbourne and
   a series of letters written by Helen relating to her
   marriage to the earl of Gifford in 1862 when he was on
   his deathbed. The papers are numbered Add. MSS.
   42767-42771. (See 1932.1.)

1932

3   FIJN van DRATT, P. "Sheridan's <u>Rivals</u> and Ben Jonson's
     <u>Every Man in His Humour</u>." <u>Neophilologus</u> 18 (October):
     44-50.
          Argues that "Sheridan's comedy was suggested to him by
     Jonson's <u>Every man</u> [<u>sic</u>], and Bob Acres is not the reputed
     author's original creation, but a compound of Jonson's
     Stephen, Bobadil, Cob, Matthew and Brainworm. . . . In
     other words, <u>The Rivals</u>, one of the best, if not the very
     best of 18th century English comedies, is not an original
     play at all, but the handiwork of the plagiarist. But
     if plagiarism is conceded, it must be acknowledged as
     plagiarism of the very highest order, amounting almost to
     the originality of genius" (p. 46).

                              <u>1933</u>

1   ANON. "Embassy." <u>Times</u> (London), 3 May, p. 12.
          Advertises <u>The Rivals</u> at the Embassy Theatre with Lady
     Tree as Mrs. Malaprop.

2   ANON. "Embassy Theatre: 'The Rivals' by Richard Brinsley
     Sheridan." <u>Times</u> (London), 2 May, p. 12.
          Admires a revival of <u>The Rivals</u> and recommends the play
     for its unity of form, its elegance of language, and its
     appositeness of point. If not so severe as Congreve, it
     succeeds in the manner of Jane Austen in ridiculing the
     extravagances of sensibility.

3   ANON. "An Old-Time English Bank." <u>New York Times</u>,
     9 December, p. 14.
          Reminisces over the "good old days of banking" and
     imagines the headaches of Thomas Hammersley, the London
     banker who dared to lend money to Sheridan and the Drury
     Lane management. Hammersley's memoranda, recently come
     to light, trace a history of resolve to recover Sheridan's
     debts, but there is no record of success.

4   ANON. "Sheridan and Old Drury." <u>Times</u> (London), 25 November,
     p. 13.
          Documents the financial fact that Sheridan's bankers,
     in assessing the debts of Drury Lane Theatre to them in
     1807, credited themselves with 560 pounds for not using
     the silver tickets attaching to the stock certificates
     they held. That is, they claimed this sum as "a
     compensation for having forborne the use of the silver
     tickets attached to the shares." Such forebearance no
     doubt excited Sheridan's sense of comedy.

                              150

5   DARLINGTON, W. A. Sheridan. Great Lives Series, no. 15.
      London: Duckworth, 144 pp.
        Recounts Sheridan's life with an aim to stating
      "nothing as fact that comes from any tainted source"
      (p. 141). Draws principally, then, from Moore, from
      writings of the Sheridan family, from private correspon-
      dence, and from "disinterested comment by outsiders"
      (p. 141). Acknowledges as inevitable a perfunctory
      treatment of Sheridan's life after the death of his first
      wife, in that these years brought Sheridan "neither
      material progress nor spiritual growth" (p. 142). In
      reviewing the work of earlier biographers Darlington
      deplores the moralistic bias of Mrs. Oliphant, the
      carelessness of Percy Fitzgerald, and the panegyric of
      Fraser Rae. He declares an effort to be objective while
      yet being sympathetic. Reviewed in Times Literary
      Supplement, 12 October, p. 687.

6   DIGEON, A[URELIEN]. "Un Nouveau Sheridan." Revue anglo-
      américaine 11 (October): 142-47.
        Comments upon Crompton Rhodes's edition of Sheridan's
      plays and poems (1928) and upon Rhodes's biography of
      Sheridan. The edition is admirable in every feature of
      text and apparatus. It allows the hope that methodical
      scholarship has disclosed a new Sheridan. But the
      biography, Harlequin Sheridan, the Man and the Legends
      (1933.6), does not fulfill the promise of its title.
      While Rhodes attempts to treat his subject objectively,
      he does not solve the mystery enveloping Sheridan's
      character. Later biographers will find Rhodes helpful,
      but they will yet have to unravel the complexity that is
      Sheridan.

7   PARSONS, COLEMAN O. "Smollett's Influence on Sheridan's The
      Rivals." Notes and Queries 164 (21 January): 39-41.
        Suggests that a scene in Ferdinand Count Fathom
      anticipates a scene in The Rivals and that Lydia Melford
      in Humphry Clinker foreshadows Lydia Languish in The
      Rivals. In the first of these parallels a letter "is
      purveyed to a vain stepmother or aunt, at whose
      interference the lover chafes; it contains sharp invective
      against the meddler and hints at means of tricking her
      vigilance. The reading of each is followed by an
      outburst--one of rage, the other of boisterous,
      self-confident mirth" (p. 40). In the second, both
      Lydias read romances; both have duels fought over them;
      both have suitors who quail with cowardice; both "are
      addressed by lovers of rank and fortune under assumed
      names and in rather humble characters" (p. 41).

1933

8   RHODES, R. CROMPTON. Harlequin Sheridan, the Man and the
     Legends. Oxford: Blackwell, 322 pp.
         Purposes to show Sheridan "in the round, as he appeared
     to his own generation, not only from his letters and
     plays and speeches, but surrounded by squibs and lampoons,
     newspaper-paragraphs and election-results, accusations
     and exculpations, libels and lies" (p. vii). New source
     materials assist accounts of Elizabeth Sheridan's
     relationship with Lord Edward Fitzgerald and Richard's
     with Pamela Seymour. New sources also enable an objective
     presentation of Sheridan's relations with the Prince of
     Wales, an association here held to be entirely honorable.
     Heretofore-obscure portions of the subject's life--events,
     for example, of the year 1806--also receive special
     attention and elucidation from new sources. Since in
     The Critic Sheridan had so narrowed the focus of his
     satire as to concern himself with theatrical life
     rather than life itself, it is possible to assume that
     by 1779 his theatrical career had lost much of its
     appeal to him. His parliamentary career, then, represents
     growth, not atrophy. But in it, as in the earlier phases
     of his life, he could not escape identity as a player's
     son. Always someone stood by to cry Harlequin. Reviewed
     in Times Literary Supplement, 12 October, p. 687; by W. J.
     Lawrence in Spectator, no. 5498 (10 November): 673-74;
     by R. Scargill in Bookman (London), 85 (November): 124;
     in English Review 57 (December): 678; by F. T. Wood in
     Englische Studien 69 (1934): 269-71; by J. M. Purcell in
     Philological Quarterly 13 (July): 318-19; also in 1933.6.

1934

1   ANON. "A Noted Painting Brought to America." New York Times,
     24 March, p. 3.
         Pictures "The portrait of Richard Brinsley Sheridan,
     playwright, by Sir Joshua Reynolds, formerly in the
     collection of Lord Willoughby De Broke, which has been
     purchased by the Atlanta Art Association and Hugh [sic]
     Museum of Art from the Newhouse Galleries."

2   ANON. "Sheridan Portrait Unveiled." New York Times, 27 May,
     sec. 4, p. 6.
         Describes the portrait of Sheridan recently acquired by
     the High Museum in Atlanta (see 1934.1). "The portrait,
     which is 26 by 22 inches in size and an excellent example
     of Reynolds's art, was presented to the High Art Museum
     by the Atlanta Chapter of the Friends of Art."

3   BROWN, JOHN MASON. "Richard Brinsley Sheridan to Noel
    Coward." In Letters from Greenroom Ghosts. New York:
    Viking Press, pp. 117-68.
        Imagines Sheridan writing from his crypt in Westminster
    Abbey a letter to Noel Coward counseling Coward, a kindred
    spirit, to discipline his multifarious gifts and devote
    himself to building lasting quality into his works,
    especially the serious works and the comedies in which
    Coward celebrates his own brand of facile sophistication,
    works, that is, requiring the interplay of wit and
    feeling. Sheridan confesses that his own theatrical
    career had been an embarrassment to him. He had wanted
    during life to be remembered as a statesman, but time
    in the grave has taught him to value his place in the
    Poets' Corner.

4   BRYANT, DONALD C. "Edmund Burke's Opinions of Orators of
    His Day." Quarterly Journal of Speech 20 (April): 241-54.
        Devotes three paragraphs to Sheridan (pp. 250-51),
    noting Burke's great admiration for the Westminster-Hall
    speech against Hastings but noting too Burke's distaste
    for Sheridan's tendency (observed after the rupture of
    their friendship) to give "long speeches without good
    materials" (p. 251).

5   HARMSWORTH, GEOFFREY. "Sheridan at Harrow: a Request for
    New Clothes." Times (London), 15 February, p. 10.
        Prints, within a letter to the editor, a letter
    recently presented to Harrow School in which young
    Sheridan, while a student there, had applied to his
    uncle, Richard Chamberlaine, for new clothes. He needed
    them in order to appear properly dressed for his
    academic station (having recently risen to the fifth form)
    and in order to show out properly while shooting for the
    silver arrow. The letter is endorsed "Answered and
    ordered cloaths on June 24th, 1766."

6   LEGOUIS, PIERRE. "Buckingham et Sheridan: ce que le
    Critique doit à la Répétition." Revue anglo-américaine
    11 (June): 423-34.
        Compares and contrasts The Critic and The Rehearsal,
    acknowledging respects in which Sheridan's originality
    asserts itself--e.g., Puff's urbanity versus Bayes's
    boorishness, the comic complexity of Dangle and Sneer
    versus the directness of Smith and Johnson--but insisting
    that his actors exit while praying is of a piece with
    When parallels do not appear in subjects and situations,
    they appear in comic processes. Puff's instructions
    that his actors exit while praying is of a piece with

1934

Bayes's requiring his dead soldiers to rise and walk off
in full view of the audience. Bayes's concellation of
conflicts "at Pallas's command" anticipates the fiat by
which Puff's beefeater resolves the dagger-and-poignard
scene in The Critic. Because of the currency of heroic
drama in 1671, The Rehearsal offers the richer parodic
interest. Sheridan can boast the higher spirit, but he
offers less intellectual substance than his predecessor.

7   NETTLETON, GEORGE H. "The First Edition of The School for
Scandal." Times Literary Supplement, 11 October, p. 695.
Affirms the view, with M. J. Ryan (1928.19, 20) and
R. C. Rhodes (1928.14), that the earliest known edition
of the spurious text of The School for Scandal is the
Dublin edition of 1780. This affirmation denies the
priority of the J. Ewling (Dublin) edition, an undated
one long held to be the first. The Dublin edition of
1780, furthermore, is demonstrably the source of the
Dublin edition of 1781, a text assumed by Rhodes (and
shown by Nettleton) to be a "Second Edition."

8   RYAN, M. J. "The First Edition of The School for Scandal and
Pranceriana." Times Literary Supplement, 25 October,
p. 735.
Responds to George H. Nettleton's article of 11 October
(1934.7) by listing yet other typographical peculiarities
of the 1780 Dublin edition of The School for Scandal. An
advertisement in this edition (for Pranceriana Poetica)
does not, as Nettleton had hoped, reveal the publisher of
Sheridan's play, for the Pranceriana series itself carries
no publisher's name. But it might be possible to
determine who printed it (and consequently who printed
the 1780 Dublin edition of The School for Scandal) by
"comparing the ornaments, type and setting with other
Dublin books of the period, the printers of which are
stated or known."

*9 VAN DER HOEF, GEORGE T. "Sheridaniana. Comment."
University of Chicago Literary and Critical Quarterly
2 (March): 8.
Cited in MHRA annual bibliography, 15: 171, item 2899.

10 WELLDON, J. E. C. "Sheridan's School days." Times (London),
17 February, p. 8.
Declares it an anomaly that Sheridan should have been
an unhappy and unpromising school lad when, at the end of
his life, admirers such as Lord Byron should rank his
literary achievements above the best of their types.
"So striking are not infrequently the reversals which

time effects in the judgments which are passed upon the
young."

1   COLUM, PEDRAIC. "Revaluing Sheridan." Commonweal 22
    (5 July): 261-63.
        See Sheridan as being first and foremost an opportunist,
    "one who can instantly mobilize all his forces to deal
    with the occasion" (p. 262), one who is "not integrated
    around any aim or passion." Such a one "is able to deal
    less and less with opportunities" and is apt more and
    more to find them, as Sheridan did, in the convivial
    party at which wit and personality are quickened by wine.
    Of the plays written at the height of Sheridan's powers,
    The Rivals is the best because it is a true Irish comedy,
    a broad comedy of humors fortified by brilliant verbalism.
    The School for Scandal, loose in structure and thin in
    content, is an English comedy written by an Irishman.
    It prevails because of the screen scene, a masterpiece
    of invention, and because it is the first modern
    drawing-room comedy. Because of its holiday spirit, The
    Critic is more closely related to The Rivals than to The
    School for Scandal.

2   NETTLETON, GEORGE H. "The School for Scandal: an Early
    Edition." Times Literary Supplement, 28 March, p. 200.
        Asserts the claim of Robert Bell's Philadelphia issue
    of The School for Scandal (1782) as being the first
    American edition of the play and as having priority of
    publication over Thomas Cadell's London edition of 1783.
    In fact, the "tell-tale phraseology" of Cadell's title
    page seems to have come directly from the Bell issue.

3   _____. "The School for Scandal: First Edition of the
    Authentic Text." Times Literary Supplement, 21 December,
    p. 876.
        Claims for Hugh Gaine's New York edition of The School
    for Scandal (1786) importance as an "early presentation
    in actual print of a virtually authentic text of Sheridan's
    play." Rejecting Robert Bell's piratical text of 1782,
    Gaine followed a manuscript supplied him by John Henry,
    joint manager with Lewis Hallam of the "Old American
    Company" and acquaintance, before coming to America, of
    the Sheridans in London. The manuscript is said on
    Gaine's title page to be a gift to Henry of the author
    of the play.

1935

4   PURDY, RICHARD A., ed. Introduction to The Rivals, A Comedy.
     As it was first Acted at the Theatre-Royal in Covent--
     Garden. Written by Richard Brinsley Sheridan, Esq.
     Edited from the Larpent MS. Oxford: Clarendon, pp. xi-lii.
        Notes that in preparing the first edition of The
     Rivals (1775) Sheridan revised the Larpent MS (the
     version licensed by the lord chamberlain for performance
     on 11 January 1775) in such a way as to show scrupulous
     response to first-night criticism: He removed all
     offensiveness from the character of Sir Lucius; he
     shortened the length of the play; he amplified the role
     of Jack Absolute. In addition, he reduced the goatishness
     of Sir Anthony, refined upon Mrs. Malaprop's malapropisms,
     and tightened the form of the play. Comparison also
     demonstrates, however, that the first edition of 1775
     makes copious additions to the Larpent MS. It spins out
     dialogue, adds ornamentation, and amplifies generously
     the roles of Julia and Faulkland. It is clearly not,
     then, the version successfully performed on 28 January
     1775; nor is the third edition corrected of 1777 (dated
     1776), although this later revision (the last one actually
     done by Sheridan for publication) shows refinements in
     the direction of the Larpent version. The acting version
     will probably never be known. In addition to textual
     matters, the introduction discusses the early productions
     of The Rivals and the historical background of the
     Larpent MS. Reviewed in Times Literary Supplement,
     28 March, p. 199; in Theatre Arts 19 (August): 648; in
     Notes and Queries 168 (4 May): 323-24; by F. W. Bateson
     in Review of English Studies 12 (July 1936): 359-62; by
     Harold Child in Modern Language Review 31 (January 1936):
     87-88; by H. Marcus in Deutsche Literaturzeitung (Berlin)
     57 (1936): 622-25; by H. S. in Modern Language Notes
     52 (July 1937): 77-78.

5   VEEN, HARM REIJNDERD SIENTJO van der. "Richard Brinsley
     Sheridan." In Jewish Characters in Eighteenth Century
     Fiction and Drama. Groningen: J. B. Wolters, pp. 160-78.
        Studies Sheridan's Jewish characters in relation to the
     stage conventions for such characters in eighteenth-
     century drama and finds Isaac Mendoza, of The Duenna, a
     good deal closer to the convention than Moses, of The
     School for Scandal. Like most stage Jews, Mendoza is
     (1) wealthy but (2) cowardly, (3) complacent as regards
     his appearance, and (4) satisfied as to his own cunning.
     Sheridan's source for him is probably Sancho of Dryden's
     Love Triumphant (1693). Moses, whose character probably
     derives from Little Transfer of Foote's The Minor (1760),
     is much less offensive than Isaac Mendoza, but he is

associated with a distasteful trade, usury, and is not wholly sympathetic. As an enlightened man, Sheridan no doubt felt good will for the Jews, but he never expressed regret for drawing Jewish characters the way he did.

6   WHEELER, ROGER, ed. "The Rivals." In Famous Plays in
    Miniature. Boston: Walter H. Baker, pp. 101-35.
       Reduces the text to thirty minutes of playing time,
    purposing in the abridgment to "retain all the essentials
    of the original plot, the principal characters, and
    the best lines of dialogue" (p. 5).

1936

1   ADAMS, RANDOLPH G. "Trailing Richard Brinsley Sheridan."
    Colophon, n.s. 1 (1936): 612.
       Prints a document found among the papers of Thomas
    Townshend, Viscount Sydney (1733-1800). Dated 6
    December 1788, it traces Sheridan's movements from
    3:00 p.m. to 1:00 a.m., following him on visits to Mr.
    Wedgewood, Mrs. Fitzherbert, Mr. Beckett, Brooks's Club,
    Mr. Fox, the duke of Devonshire, Mr. Fox again (for
    dinner), where he remained until 1:30, staying well past
    the departures of the duke of Portland and Lord
    Loughborough. The document seems to be the report of a
    private detective.

2   ANON. "Bond of Frederick, Duke of York signed, in 1792,
    Cognovit signed by R. B. Sheridan and others, 1797, and
    another legal document, 1798." British Museum Quarterly
    11 (October): 40.
       Describes, in the form given here, three manuscripts
    given to the Museum by Mr. E. W. F. Johnson.

3   BATESON, F. W. "The School for Scandal." Times Literary
    Supplement, 4 January, p. 15.
       Rejects G. H. Nettleton's contention (1935.3) that the
    New York edition of The School for Scandal (1786) was the
    first edition of the "genuine" text. "It contains far
    too many errors, omissions, pointless changes and
    obvious actors' gags to be descended, however distantly,
    from any manuscript of Sheridan's." Probably "it was
    compiled from memory by a dishonest prompter." A passage
    from act 4 illustrates the case.

4   BAUMANN, ARTHUR ANTHONY. "An Irish Triumvirate." In
    Personalities: a Selection from the Writings of A. A.
    Baumann. London: Macmillan, pp. 167-75.

1936

> Recognizes Goldsmith, Burke, and Sheridan as members
> of a vanishing breed, that of Irishmen prominent in the
> national life of Britain. "It is one of the gravest
> charges against modern democracy that it has smothered
> with the blanket of its dull and sour disputations, the
> grace and gaiety of the Irish spirit."

5   HAMMOND, J. L. "Gladstone on Sheridan." Times Literary
     Supplement, 4 July, p. 564.
        Summarizes the contents of an article in the Nineteenth
     Century (1896.10) in which Gladstone blamed the Whigs for
     denying Sheridan a Cabinet post in 1806. "Gladstone
     refused to admit that Sheridan's habits were a sufficient
     obstacle to his admission to the Cabinet." Gladstone's
     sympathy for Sheridan was influenced by Sheridan's
     humanitarian and reformist policies but chiefly by his
     opposition to the Irish Union.

6   JOHNSON, PHILIP, AND AGG, HOWARD. The New School for Scandal:
     an Impertinence in Three Acts. Year Book Press Series of
     Plays. London: H. F. W. Deane, 70 pp.
        Modernizes the language and setting of the play,
     applying its situations to the antics of a jaded leisure
     class in the 1930s. The action opens and closes in a
     cocktail lounge. The characters affect the manner of
     bored sophisticates, often drawling the word "darling"
     at one another. Few of Sheridan's jokes and yet fewer
     of his words survive the "impertinence."

1937

1   ANON. "Sheridan's Stables at Harrow." Times (London),
     8 October, p. 11.
        Describes the manner in which buildings known as
     Sheridan's stables (outbuildings related to a residence
     called "The Grove" at which Sheridan and Elizabeth Linley
     had lived in 1778) were preserved in the design of form
     rooms recently built at Harrow. An inscription reading
     "These form rooms embody the walls of Sheridan's stables"
     marks the fact.

2   DARLINGTON, W. A. "Richard Brinsley Sheridan." In From Anne
     to Victoria: Essays by Various Hands, edited by Bonamy
     Dobrée. New York: Scribners, pp. 379-91.
        Bases a sketch of Sheridan on the conviction that the
     greatness available to him through his talents was not
     sufficient to assuage his great desire for social
     acceptance. Hence he sought the society of privileged

men who laughed at his wit and enjoyed his company but
never fully admitted him to their inmost circles; and
when, in later life, he grew "increasingly irrational and
eccentric in his private behavior" (p. 391), they
contributed to the calumny which for so long colored his
reputation. "Not until Sheridan had been dead eighty
years, in fact, did it occur to anybody that he was not
a person who needed to be apologized for and explained
away," that his theatrical successes were not mere
accidents, and that "his failure to reach the highest
positions as a politican was due as much to his virtues
as to his shortcomings" (p. 381).

3   NEUMARK, PETER. "Sheridan's 'Critic.'" <u>Cambridge Review</u>
    58 (12 February): 253.
        Examines <u>The Critic</u> in the light of Sheridan's managerial
    ineptness and concludes that "Sheridan's exposure of the
    state of the theatre of his time is entirely superficial.
    Only effects are dramatised, for a consideraton of causes
    would soon have induced a direct attack on the laws
    governing theatrical performances, not to mention the
    whole system of private backing which has always obtained"
    in England. "<u>The Critic</u> does not contain a really
    penetrating attack on social types of the time, such as
    the screen-scene in <u>The School for Scandal.</u> But it is
    very well written, extremely funny to read, and provided
    that one resists the temptations of facile mannerisms on
    the one hand, and cheap farce on the other, it plays as
    a brilliantly realistic attack on the theatrical society
    of its time."

4   OLIVER, ROBERT T. "A Re-Evaluation of the Oratory of Burke,
    Fox, Sheridan and Pitt." Ph.D. dissertation, University
    of Wisconsin.
        Provides an account of the late eighteenth-century
    political milieu, then studies the four orators in such
    a way as "First, to bring into focus the oral stylistic
    qualities of these men: Their platform presence--
    appearance, mannerisms, poise or lack of it, gestures, and
    the like; and the quality, force, pitch and range of
    their voices. Second, to offer an estimate as to what
    are their greatest speeches. Third, to summarize the
    attitudes which have developed toward their style in the
    history of oratorical criticism. And fourth to make an
    independent analysis of their styles, for comparison with
    the traditional views" (pp. 99-100). Subsequent
    analysis examines the relative persuasiveness of the four
    speakers. About Sheridan it is generally concluded "that
    his oratory during the French Revolution and the later war

1937

between England and France was of fully as high a merit as that of his great antagonist Pitt" (p. 550). (Cf. 1946.8.)

5   SNIDER, ROSE. "Richard Brinsley Sheridan." In Satire in the Comedies of Congreve, Sheridan, Wilde, and Coward. University of Maine Studies, 2d ser., no. 42. Orono, Maine: University of Maine, pp. 41-73.
    Argues that as a satirist "Sheridan lavishly utilized an entire play for satirizing one quality or institution or person. Thus, The Rivals is almost entirely given over to an exposé of hypocritical sentimentality; The School for Scandal is a thorough-going criticism of malicious scandal-mongering and of sentimentality; and The Critic is a final belittling of not only the so-called 'genteel comedy' but also true comedy with a moral purpose" (p. 42). As agents of satire in the plays, Lydia Languish satirizes "romantic sentimentality"; Julia satirizes "moral sentimentality"; Faulkland satirizes false delicacy; Joseph Surface satirizes "sentimental hypocrisy"; Mrs. Malaprop satirizes female pretensions to education; Lady Sneerwell satirizes malicious gossip (as do Mrs. Candour and Lady Teazle); Snake satirizes the "social sycophant"; Bob Acres satirizes the affected rustic and is an instrument of satire against duelling. Sir Peter Teazle provides an amusing study in the old bachelor bemused by his changed estate. Reviewed by K. Wittig in Englische Studien 73 (1939): 281-83.

6   THOMSON, HECTOR. Sheridan, "The Rivals," Act III, Scene I, Translated in the Style of Menander. Oxford: Basil Blackwell.
    Prints the prize-winning entry of the Gaisford Prize for Greek Verse, a text presented in recitation at the Sheldonian Theatre, June 1937.

1938

1   ANON. "Buxton Drama Festivals." Times (London), 31 August, p. 8.
    Complains that a production of The Rivals performed in Buxton by the Old Vic Company calls attention to the unevenness of the play because the roles are in virtually every case miscast. The "applause at curtain fall seemed merely polite."

2   ANON. Catalogue the 19th. The School for Scandal: a Manuscript. London: Offered by George Bates, 24 pp.
    Announces for sale (at 500 pounds) "A manuscript of

major importance, being the earliest and most authentic
text" of The School for Scandal "as first acted at Drury
Lane on May 8th 1777." In "fine and perfect state," it is
"From the Frampton Court sale of Sheridan Material" and
contains "NUMEROUS CORRECTIONS BY THE AUTHOR." An
accompanying discussion asserts (1) that the pirated
editions of the play printed in Dublin before 1799 follow
the Drury Lane prompt text, (2) that the Dublin edition
of 1799 follows a Covent Garden prompt text of 1798, (3)
that the Crewe MS collated by Thomas Moore with the
Dublin edition of 1799 probably dates to the 1790s, not
to 1777 as is widely thought, (4) that Moore's collation
does not, then, restore the text of the play as it was
performed in 1777 but after 1798, (5) that there is no
evidence proving that the Dublin edition of 1799 is
based upon the LeFanu MS of 1778, (6) that the manuscript
here announced for sale accords more closely with the
pre-1799 pirated text (i.e., the "Drury Lane Text") than
with the Dublin edition of 1799 and with the later
editions (those of 1821 and 1823) based upon this Dublin
edition, (7) that references in this manuscript to the
Annuity Bills date it no earlier than 20 April 1777, (8)
that the mansucript predates the piracy of the Drury Lane
text (through evidence relating to the song "Here's to the
maiden"), (9) that the manuscript must therefore be "the
nearest to the original, and may conceivably be actually
the one spoken on the night of May 8th" (p. 24).

3   DUKES, ASHLEY. "The Scene in Europe." Theatre Arts Monthly
     22 (March): 181-86.
        Acknowledges that several Irishmen have held the English
     stage since the reign of Charles II, then comments on
     revivals in London of Candida and The School for Scandal.
     The latter play, under the direction of John Gielgud,
     suffers in this production from too marked a departure from
     tradition. Gielgud's "new stylization" robs the play of
     its dignity (a dignity "as essential to this comedy as a
     sense of humor is to Hamlet"). The new staging, obviously
     designed "to bring painted canvas into harmony with
     artificial movement " fails, too, because "neither party
     of the union goes the whole way. The movement is not
     formalized in any revealing fashion; the decor is just
     assertive enough to be noticeable" (p. 185).

4   STALLMANN, HEINZ. Malapropismen in englischen Drama von den
     Anfangen bis 1800. Inaugural Dissertation, Berlin, 1937.
     Bottrop I.W.: Postberg, 113 pp.
        Examines the malapropism in ninety-five English plays
     (beginning with the York Cycle of 1340/50 and ending with

1938

The School for Scandal of 1777). Considered collectively
the practice falls into several formal categories: shifts
in prefix (e.g., reprehend-comprehend), shifts in suffix
(e.g., misanthropy-misanthrope), shifts in sound value
(e.g., superfluical-superficial), inversions (e.g.,
successor-ancestor), misdirected phrases (e.g., parts of
speech for talents of speech). Fifteen such categories
prevail, and Sheridan applies virtually all of them.

1939

1 ANON. "£215 for a Sheridan First Edition." Times (London)
10 May, p. 11.
Announces the sale at Sotheby's of a copy of the Dublin
Edition of The School for Scandal (1780) from the
collection of the late Sir R. Leicester Harmsworth.

2 FOSS, KENELM. Here Lies Richard Brinsley Sheridan. London:
M. Secker, 390 pp.
Organizes the life of Sheridan after broad categories
of experience, achievement, and states of being (e.g.,
"An Elopement and Two Duels," "The Playwright," "The
Theatre-Manager," "The Politician," "The Orator," "The
Widower"). While a "failure as a man, a lover, husband,
father, theatre-manager, and politician" (p. 379),
Sheridan is in spite of himself an immortal. To follow
him from boyhood is to see him "lightly cast aside a great
career as dramatist, and through inertia miss a second
splendid chance as manager of Drury Lane. Until he
entered Parliament he never worked if he could help it,
but once M. P. he toiled unceasingly" (p. 275). Even so,
his "greatest parliamentary triumph," the prosecution of
Warren Hastings, "was founded on a lie," and from that
point forward "his path runs straight downhill" (p. 221),
the fall assisted by faithless friends, chiefly Fox,
Grenville, and the prince regent. "Restless, capricious,
trivial, he gave himself no time to think" (p. 135).
Constructive thought, however, was needless to his art,
which thrived on his gift for extempore invention. He
was not a great man, but his many blemishes "could not
stop him being a great artist" (p. 136). Reviewed in
Times Literary Supplement, 1 July, p. 392; by John Anderson
in Saturday Review 22 (August 31, 1940): 10; by Henry Ten
Eyck Perry in Yale Review 30 (1941): 619-21.

3 LOCKITT, C. H., ed. The School for Scandal and The Critic.
Heritage of Literature Series. London: Longmans,
Green, 212 pp.

Provides school texts (based on the Murray edition of 1821) accompanied by comprehensive apparatus: a biographical sketch, a comment upon the stage in the eighteenth century, critical comments on the two plays, summaries of their plots, explanatory endnotes, and appendixes touching general problems of dramaturgy, features of Sheridan's style, and representative opinion about the theater and society of Sheridan's time. Study questions about the two plays also appear. The view governing this apparatus is that Sheridan's plays rise above those of his contemporaries because of their superior dialogue and sense of stage effect.

4 NETTLETON, GEORGE H, AND CASE, ARTHUR E. British Dramatists from Dryden to Sheridan. Boston: Houghton Mifflin, pp. 715-17, 949-57.
   Locates Sheridan in English dramatic history by emphasizing the antisentimental caste of his comedies (pp. 715-17). Also provides detailed textual notes (pp. 949-57) for The Rivals, The School for Scandal, and The Critic, the three comedies printed in this anthology.

5 TOBIN, JAMES E. "Richard Brinsley Sheridan." In Eighteenth Century English Literature and Its Cultural Background. A Bibliography. New York: Fordham University Press, p. 155.
   Lists thirty-six items, including texts, biographies, and criticism.

1940

1 ARNAVON, JACQUES. "Une 'École de la Médisance' au Theatre des Mathurins." Études Anglaises 4 (January): 43-48.
   Admires Claude Spaak's adaptation of The School for Scandal as a brilliant comedy performed with style and taste but complains that it is not authentically Sheridan. In a time when Racine is venerated everywhere, the French should for their part be faithful to the literary patrimony of their friends across the channel. No more should they dare to tamper with and violate a Sheridan text than they should a Shakespearean one.

2 ASHTON, JOHN W. "Introduction to The Critic." In Types of English Drama. New York: Macmillan, pp. 533-80.
   Remarks, in a general introduction to the play, that Sherdian does much more than ridicule sentimental drama in The Critic, "He is concerned with states of mind rather than merely with theatrical fashions" (p. 533).

1940

As a playwright, he "brings to a fitting close an era of
drama at whose beginning stands Congreve" (p. 535).

3   BATESON, F. W. "Notes on the Text of Two Sheridan Plays."
    Review of English Studies 16 (July): 312-17.
        Proposes two conclusions about the text of The Camp:
    (1) the printed version (1795) is "wholly unreliable,"
    as collation with the Larpent text in the Henry E.
    Huntington Library indicates, and (2) the music in The
    Camp draws five of its nine songs from a comic opera
    called The Royal Merchant by Thomas Hull, a fact
    suggesting that Hull and not Tickell or Burgoyne (the
    names mentioned by Moore and Rhodes respectively)
    collaborated with Sheridan in composing the piece. A
    second Sheridan text, that of The Critic, promotes the
    conclusion "that Sheridan was capable of drawing a
    distinction between the acting and the reading versions
    of his plays" (p. 317), for the "authorized" text of 1781
    (the one sanctioned for publication by Sheridan himself)
    differs markedly in places from three acting versions:
    The Larpent manuscript (1779), a promptbook now at
    Harvard (prepared in 1782), and the edition in Cumberland's
    British Theatre (1826).

4   DIXON, CAMPBELL. "Sheridan." In English Wits, edited by
    Leonard Russell. London: Hutchinson, pp. 171-96.
        Characterizes Sheridan as a man of genius who was "very,
    very human" (p. 196). "His failure to gain the highest
    rewards was not due to lack of principles, or his vanity
    and indiscretions, or even his proud and obstinate
    adherence to his Prince, damaging though this was." He
    suffered only the presumption of aspiring to offices
    "desired by noblemen and great landowners with gold for
    the party funds and boroughs in their pockets" (p. 192).
    Victorian moralists see in his life the lesson that
    "Dissipation Never Pays," but no other writer, before or
    since, "has achieved the very highest rank as a dramatist,
    a wit and an orator, and at the same time played so
    conspicuous a part in public life" (p. 195).

5   GLASGOW, ALICE. Sheridan of Drury Lane: A Biography. New
    York: Stokes, 310 pp.
        Renders Sheridan's life in the form of a play, with
    prologue, setting, curtain, and epilogue framing the body
    of the narrative. Key episodes, such as the elopement
    with Elizabeth Linley, the Begum speeches, the Regency
    Crisis of 1788, the death watch beside his father,
    receive fictionalized heightening. Expository asides
    establish the character of the age and touch upon

contemporary events outside Sheridan's own ambience, e.g.,
"Priestly was investigating oxygen, and an energetic
Scotsman named James Watt was entertaining some fantastic
and impractical notions about steam" (p. 121). In a
variegated, self-indulged, and revolutionary time,
Sheridan stood, despite the reverses and calumnies
afflicting him, a model of rectitude and dogged
humanitarian purpose. Reviewed by Dougald MacMillan in
Philological Quarterly 20 (1941): 178; by E. V. R. Wyatt
in Commonweal 32 (October): 532; by Henry Ten Eyck Perry
in Yale Review 30 (1941): 619-21.

6   TAYLOR, GARLAND F. "Richard Brinsley Sheridan's The Duenna."
     Ph.D. dissertation, Yale University.
          See 1969.9.

7   VACHELL, HORACE ANNESLEY. Great Chameleon: A Biographical
     Romance. London: Hutchinson, 287 pp.
          Shapes Sheridan's life upon the premise that "The
     tyrannies of the flesh undermined his philosophy of
     success" (p. 287). His fight at Harrow with a lout who
     chided his ancestry, his duels with Mathews, his collapse
     into Burke's arms at the end of the great Westminster
     Hall speech, all these gestures give form to his conviction
     that he was equal to any difficulty, that he could rely
     wholly on himself and rebel as he chose against every
     form of restraint. At last he was broken by poverty and
     neglect, but "his determination to shine in whatever
     company he found himself remained to the last ineradicable"
     (p. 287). Reviewed in Times Literary Supplement, 16 March,
     p. viii.

1941

1   ANON. "Sheridan's 'Duenna' as an Opera." Times (London),
     9 January, p. 6.
          Notes that "Serge Prokofieff, the Russion composer, is
     writing an opera based on Sheridan's comedy The Duenna.
     He is preparing his own libretto, and in his own words
     is taking some liberties with Sheridan's work, altering
     certain of the scenes and introducing new characters."

*2   GELFAND, M. "Sheridan and the Moscow Art Theatre." Theatre
     (U.S.S.R.), 3 (1941): 115-23.
          Listed in MHRA, 22: 138, item 2388.

3   TURNER, KENNETH WESTON, adapter. The Rivals, Arranged and
     Adapted by Kenneth Weston Turner. Chicago: Dramatic

Publishing, 128 pp.
Adapts the play to production by young, nonprofessional performers by reframing it in three acts, simplifying the stage directions, providing copious production notes—on characterization, costuming, and staging—and enlivening the text (by adding lines from the Larpent MS to those of the basic text, which is the "British Theatre" edition of 1825).

1942

1 ANON. "The Rivals." Catholic World 154 (March): 728-29.
Observes of Sheridan that "There was never any genius more brilliantly dishonest" (p. 728). In his comedies "epigrams and oddities are the substitute for humor and character." His "creations are mostly one dimensional"; and, while "the tradition has been to play the parts to the hilt in that dimension," Eva Le Gallienne's Theatre Guild production tones down the idiosyncracies. Bobby Clark's performance as Bob Acres is "the pith of the production" (p. 729).

2 ANON. "The Rivals." Senior Scholastic 49 (23 February): 24.
Reviews Eva Le Gallienne's revival of the play for the Theatre Guild at the Shubert Theatre in New York. Bobby Clark's Acres receives special commendation. The rest is summary.

3 ANON. "Visit by Mrs. Malaprop." Newsweek 19 (26 January): 65-66.
Responds favorably to The Rivals as produced by the Theatre Guild under Eva Le Gallienne's directon. It is "still too witty and engaging to be pensioned off as a literary museum piece." Among the more daring aspects of the production is that it plays "a satiric comedy as farce" (p. 66).

4 BOOMSLITER, PAUL C. "The Parliamentary Speaking of Richard Brinsley Sheridan: A Study in War-Time Minority." Ph.D. dissertation, University of Wisconsin.
Acknowledges that Sheridan was "little of a political philosopher, little of a political leader, and in consequence responsible for few innovations" (p. 640) but sees his parliamentary efforts as generally effective, especially in that they served a wartime minority. In behalf of his principles, he helped to sustain a considerable amount of freedom in England during the war with France; and, as an especially gifted debater

(however slight a politician and theorist he was), he
held the majority at constant alert in defense of its
policies. Had circumstance dealt differently with him--had
conditions of peace permitted him to pursue his own
political programs and had private wealth minimized his
reputation for improvidence--he might have emerged a
much greater political figure than he was. But even so,
"Sheridan did much with a difficult situation, with
the uninviting possibilities of an essentially negative
argument, with poor political support, as can reasonably
be expected, and did it with no inconsiderable ingenuity,
humour, and deftness" (p. 647).

5   BURNHAM, DAVID. "The Rivals." Commonweal 35 (30 January):
    369.
         Labels The Rivals "a farcical burlesque of the
    sentimental theatre of Kelly and Cumberland." It is
    "three-quarters farce and only one-quarter comedy; the
    humor is more often slapstick than wit." In staging it
    for the Theatre Guild, Eva Le Gallienne has "suffered the
    same divided approach as its author"; and the production,
    though an able enough vehicle for the comic imagination of
    Bobby Clark (in the role of Acres), suffers shortcomings
    principally Sheridan's own.

6   GIBBS, WOLCOTT. "Romp." New Yorker 17 (24 January): 32.
         Judges a Theatre Guild production of The Rivals to be
    (except for the non-Sheridanesque antics of Bobby Clark as
    Acres) "merely a handsome and rather uncertain revival of
    a work that has little interest except as a typical
    specimen of its period." Since humor "is about the most
    perishable of all literary commodities," The Rivals is
    chiefly interesting for its "traceable influence" on
    current humorists. The rhythm of Sheridan's phrases and
    the alliterative flair of his epithets foreshadow the
    comic language of Coward and Berhman and Maxwell Anderson
    and Saroyan.

7   GILDER, ROSAMOND. "Time and The Rivals: Broadway in Review."
    Theatre Arts 26 (March): 149-56.
         Notices, in a review of a Theatre Guild production of
    The Rivals, that "The Rivals has within it rivalries
    other than those among the whimsical young men and women
    of the plot." In Acres and Mrs. Malaprop, it has "not
    one but two stellar roles that vie with each other for
    the focus of interest" (p. 154). When Mrs. Fiske played
    Mrs. Malaprop, it mattered little who played Acres; but
    when Joseph Jefferson and Bobby Clark played Acres, the
    play was theirs. Acres offers the true comedian "every

1942

opportunity for comic invention" (p. 154). Eva Le
Gallienne has directed this production "for speed and
high spirits rather than for style and high comedy"
(p. 154).

8   KRUTCH, JOSEPH WOOD. "Drama." Nation 154 (24 January): 101.
Admires a Theatre Guild production of The Rivals,
directed by Eva Le Gallienne, for returning the play to
its spirit of "refreshing irreverence" and "hokum." It
is a play no longer current in its choice of satiric
targets (romantic sentimentalism), but it is yet strong
in its "skilful use of farcical situations" and in the
"flashes of wit which still corruscate."

9   LOEWENBERG, ALFRED. "The Songs in 'The Critic.'" Times
Literary Supplement, 28 March, p. 168.
Announces discovery of the earliest issue of the songs
of The Critic, the pieces performed by the foreign visitors
in act 1, scene 2 of the play. Published by Longman and
Broderip late in 1779, the issue contains two numbers, a
French trio and an Italian duet. The composer is indicated
as being Signor Giordani (either Tommaso Giordani of
Naples or his brother Guiseppe, probably the former, who
had settled in Britain as early as 1762). The lyrics,
possibly because they are trifling, do not appear in the
1781 issue of the play, but they are nevertheless the
first part of The Critic to be published.

10   YOUNG, STARK. "The Guild Presents The Rivals." New
Republic 106 (26 January): 116.
Endorses a view of The Rivals held by the critic who,
in an issue of The Town and Country Magazine for 1796,
complained that the characters are largely stereotyped,
that the language is often barbarous, that Julia and
Faulkland are sentimental excrescences, but that some
scenes are "lively, spirited, and entertaining." The
current Theatre Guild production of the play evinces
these strengths and weaknesses, and adds its own
misjudgments by introducing new songs and interludes and
by adding new puns for Mrs. Malaprop to speak. "Making
Mrs. Malaprop say at a crucial moment that men are all
conceivers is not very funny, is broadish (whereas
Sheridan is not); and is only piling up an effect of
ignorance in Mrs. Malaprop. It should be distinctly
pointed out that many of her blunders are not from
ignorance but from a sort of pompous aphasia."

1943

1 HEWITT, BARNARD. "The Rivals and An Enemy of the People."
   High School Thespian 14 (February): 8-9.
   Cites The Rivals among the "Great Plays of All Times"
   (p.8) and attributes its durability to its farcical plot
   and (especially) its characters, all of which are
   "excellent acting parts" (p.8). (The subsequent
   discussion of Ibsen's An Enemy of the People does not
   bear upon The Rivals.)

2 NETTLETON, GEORGE H. "Robinson Crusoe: Sheridan's Drury
   Lane Pantomime--I." Times Literary Supplement
   25 December, p. 624.
   Summarizes Thomas Becket's scenario of Robinson Crusoe,
   a pamphlet published in 1781 under the title "A short
   Account of the Situations and Incidents in the pantomime
   of Robinson Crusoe at the Theatre Royal, Drury Lane, 1781."
   The first twelve scenes, accompanied in the scenario by
   passages from Defoe's text, follow the original quite
   closely. The second and third parts are dismissed very
   briefly by Becket and must be pieced together from
   contemporary reviews. Departing markedly from Defoe's
   narrative, they turn the action toward a fanciful
   harlequinade. (The London Chronicle for 27-30 January
   1781 provides an account.) The first act demonstrates,
   however, "the inherent dramatic appeal and perennial
   popularity" of Defoe's story.

3 ROSENFELD, SYBIL. "Some Notes on the Players in Oxford,
   1661-1713." Review of English Studies 19 (October):
   366-75.
   Takes note of an item in the Oxford Journal for
   21 September 1799 announcing that Thornton's Company
   had given "readings" at the Racket Court in Oxford of
   The Rivals and The Stranger and that Robinson Crusoe and
   Pizarro would be presented on the following Monday.
   These presentations broke a silence which had prevailed
   in Oxford since 1713, the date of the last known visit
   of the London players before the Licensing Act of 1737
   forbade acting within the university or within five miles
   of the city itself.

4 SLIKER, HAROLD G., adapter. Sheridan's The Rivals. Evanston,
   Ill.: Row, Peterson and Company.
   Reduces the play to six scenes, enabling presentation
   in about one hour.

1944

1   ANON. "Arts Theatre: 'A Trip to Scarborough' by Richard
     Brinsley Sheridan." Times (London), 27 May, p. 6.
       Observes of A Trip to Scarborough that "it has a
     shapeliness to which the original [The Relapse] does not
     pretend" and that it displays in all of Sheridan's
     alterations "the flavour of a mature wit." A company
     at the Arts Theatre plays it skillfully, keeping the
     two strains of comedy represented by its two plots in
     "delicate balance."

2   BOAS, F. S. "Sheridan's 'Robinson Crusoe' at Oxford."
     Times Literary Supplement, 29 January, p. 60.
       Provides a footnote to Nettleton's articles on
     Robinson Crusoe (1943.2; 1944.6) by recalling a notice
     in the Oxford Journal for 21 September 1799 announcing
     that Thornton's company from Windsor Theatre would give
     on the following Monday performances of Robinson Crusoe
     and Pizarro. "This is an additional proof of the
     popularity of the Defoe-Sheridan pantomime, and that its
     vogue was not confined to Drury Lane."

3   HARDING, HAROLD F. "The Listener on Eloquence, 1750-1800."
     In Studies in Speech and Drama in Honor of Alexander M.
     Drummond, edited by Donald C. Bryant et al. Ithaca,
     N.Y.: Cornell University Press, pp. 341-53.
       Suggests, "on a somewhat limited scale" (p. 341), what
     audiences in the House of Commons thought about the
     speaking done there between 1750 and 1800. About
     Sheridan, Samuel Rogers remarked the wrapt attention
     given his Begum speech. Nathaniel Wraxall, commenting
     on that same speech, admired the display of memory,
     judgment, passion, pity, humanity, and factual detail.
     Charles Butler, a Roman Catholic barrister, admired
     Sheridan's "happy vein of ridicule" (p. 345). These
     kinds of comments, together with similar ones made about
     Burke, Fox, and Pitt, justify the conclusion that
     audiences expected good speeches to move their feelings
     and hold their attention, to provide entertainment
     (through ideas or language), to observe standards of
     good taste, to display artistic flair.

4   LOEWENBERG, ALFRED. "An Uncollected Poem of Sheridan."
     Notes and Queries 186 (January): 3-4.
       Argues that a poem attributed by Walter Sichel to
     Elizabeth Linley (an answer to Thomas Percy's ballad "O
     Nancy, wilt thou go with me?") was written by Sheridan
     himself. It is attributed to him in "The Posthumous

Vocal Works of Mr. Linley, and Mr. T. Linley," a collection
edited by the widow of Thomas Linley, Sr., assisted by
her son William, and published in 1800. The poem begins
"O Henry, didst thou know the heart . . ." and consists
of four stanzas each having eight lines.

5   MOORE, JOHN R. "Sheridan's 'Little Bronze Pliny.'" Modern
    Language Notes 59 (March): 164-65.
        Recalls that before 1799 texts of The School for Scandal
    printed the phrase "little bronze Pliny" in Crabtree's
    circumstantial account of the supposed duels (V, ii)
    rather than "little bronze Shakespeare," as afterward
    appearing. The emendation, obviously an appeal to the
    familiar, actually levels Sheridan's original jest. For
    Pliny, against whose statue the pistol ball glanced
    before wounding the postman carrying a double letter
    from Northamptonshire, was a celebrated letter writer
    of classical antiquity, one admired, especially in the
    earlier eighteenth century, "as a model of epistolary
    elegance" (p. 164).

6   NETTLETON, GEORGE H. "Robinson Crusoe: Sheridan's Drury
    Lane Pantomime--II." Times Literary Supplement,
    1 January, p. 12.
        Considers evidence pointing to Sheridan's possible
    authorship of Robinson Crusoe: his earlier involvement
    in theatrical pageantry (through the concluding scenes
    of The Critic and through his production of the pantomime
    Harlequin Fortunatus by Woodward), his association with
    Robinson Crusoe as mentioned often in "newspapers, monthly
    reviews, and magazines, theatrical dictionaries, playlists,
    diaries, and memoirs." Against such evidence it is proper
    to recognize Sheridan "not as 'the only begetter' of the
    pantomime, but rather as one who had 'a main hand' in its
    success."

7   _____. "Sheridan's Robinson Crusoe.'" Times Literary
    Supplement, 15 April, p. 192.
        Adds to an instance supplied by F. S. Boas (1944.2) yet
    another provincial production of Robinson Crusoe, this
    one produced on the rural circuit by Tate Wilkinson,
    patentee of the theaters in York and Hull, and recounted
    in his book The Wandering Patentee; or, A History of the
    Yorkshire Theatres, from 1770 to the Present Time (1795).

8   ROSENFELD, SYBIL. "Robinson Crusoe." Times Literary
    Supplement, 4 March, p. 120.
        Recalls, as a footnote to Nettleton's surmises about
    Robinson Crusoe (1944.6), that a performance of the

1944

piece was given at the earl of Barrymore's private theater
at Wargrave on 21 September 1790. Anthony Pasquin, in
his life of Barrymore, lists the cast of the performance,
and the London Chronicle for 21-23 September takes notice
of the production. It was probably staged by Carlo
Delpini, who managed dumb shows and pantomimes for the
earl.

9   WOODRUFF-MONTAGUE, EDNA, adapter. All's Well That
     Ends--Better: A Condensation of Richard Brinsley Sheridan's
     Famous Comedy "The Rivals." Np: Privately printed.
        Purposes to "create a demand for condensations of
     standard, early period plays" by reducing The Rivals from
     five acts to three, eliminating the characters of Sir
     Lucius, Faulkland, Julia, and Bob Acres, "putting forth
     the love motif only," and providing for presentation
     within one hour--or within forty-five minutes, should
     the role of Fag also be cut.

                              1945

1   BROOKS, CLEANTH, AND HEILMAN, ROBERT B.   "Notes on The
     School for Scandal." In Understanding Drama.   New York:
     H. Holt, pp. 243-55.
        Argues that The School for Scandal bases most of its
     characterization and conflict on sentimental and
     melodramatic elements. (That is, it praises virtue
     rather than ridiculing vice; it resolves issues through
     discovery of the fact rather than through dramatic
     confrontation; it extols the basic good nature of
     mankind; it places feeling over thought.) What saves it
     from mere melodrama and sentimentality are the irony
     and wit complicating its textures, but "Sheridan comes
     very close to stating outright that he does not believe
     in intelligence" (p. 254).

2   DAGHLIAN, PHILIP B.   "Sheridan's Minority Waiters." Modern
     Language Quarterly 6 (December): 421-22.
        Suggests that Fag's reference to "seven minority
     waiters, and thirteen billiard markers" in The Rivals
     (II, i) alludes to the case widely discussed in the
     autumn of 1774 of Robert Mackreth, a former billiard--
     marker and waiter at White's Club, who was then a new
     member of Parliament for Castle Rising, the family borough
     of the Walpoles. George Walpole, earl of Orford and
     nephew of Horace Walpole, had given Mackreth the seat in
     payment for gambling debts, a gesture felt by Horace to
     discredit the name of the Walpoles.

4   HOUGHTON, NORRIS. "Notes on the London Season." Theatre
     Arts 29 (November): 614-17.
          Announces forthcoming London revivals of The Critic
     (by the Old Vic Company), The School for Scandal (by
     John Gielgud's Haymarket Theatre repertory company), and
     The Rivals (by the H. M. Tennent Company), giving
     Sheridan excellent representation in "England's first
     theatre season in six years to open without fear or
     actuality of buzz bombs or blitz" (p. 614).

4   MACQUEEN-POPE, W[ALTER] J. Theatre Royal Drury Lane. London:
     W. H. Allen, pp. 189-98, 210-27.
          Describes (pp. 189-98) the opening campaign of
     Sheridan's management of Drury Lane: the inauspicious
     beginning but the ultimate great success with The School
     for Scandal. Then recounts (pp. 210-27) the trials of
     rebuilding the theater in 1794, some memorable events in
     the new theater (e.g., the "Vortigern and Rowena"
     fiasco [1796], the box-office bonanza of The Stranger and
     Pizarro [1798-99], the faddish popularity of Master Betty
     [1804]), the fire and consequent end of Sheridan's
     managerial tenure (1809).

5   NETTLETON, GEORGE H. "Sheridan's Robinson Crusoe." Times
     Literary Supplement, 23 June, p. 300.
          Examines the scenario of the Newcastle-Upon-Tyne
     version of Sheridan's pantomime (a copy of which resides
     in the library of the University of Michigan) and
     concludes that the recovery of this version "affords
     unusual chances to restudy the original London scenario,
     to establish the common bases of agreement and the
     salient differences in content and method, and to confirm
     the persistent popularity of Sheridan's Drury Lane
     pantomime on the provincial as well as on the London
     stage."

6.   _____. "Sheridan's Robinson Crusoe." Times Literary
     Supplement, 30 June, p. 312.
          Concludes the note begun on 23 June by describing
     "outstanding aspects" and "typical examples" of the
     Harlequinade of Robinson Crusoe as presented "in vivid
     and colorful detail" by the Newcastle-Upon-Tyne scenario.
     The London scenario dismisses the Harlequinade in a
     single sentence. The Newcastle edition, however, devotes
     "thirteen full pages" to it and thus asserts a "novel
     interest and unique importance."

1946

1 ANON. "Arts Theatre. 'The Scheming Lieutenant' by R. B.
   Sheridan." <u>Times</u> (London), 5 September, p. 8.
      Remarks, in criticizing a performance of the play, that
   the director makes the curious mistake of valuing the
   text too much. Lines written by Sheridan in the
   "plenitude of wit" need not be uttered with studied
   preparation. There is ample wit to survive a bracing
   pace, and the present production has "everything but the
   one essential--pace."

2 ANON. "The Critic." <u>Catholic World</u> 163 (July): 358-59.
      Considers the Old Vic production of <u>The Critic</u> to be a
   "masterpiece of satire" (p. 359). British productions
   of Sheridan are generally better than American ones
   because they "present him simply but with both relish
   and style" (p. 359).

3 ANON. "On with Olivier." <u>Newsweek</u> 27 (3 June): 83.
      Admires the performance of Laurence Olivier as Puff
   in the Old Vic Company production of <u>The Critic</u>. The
   play itself, although eighteenth-century comedy, "could
   be latter-day comment on critics, playwrights, and
   assorted theater lovers."

4 DAVIES, H[ENRY] S[YKES]. "Old Sherry on Draught Again."
   <u>Theatre Today</u> 1 (March): 29-33.
      Attributes Sheridan's success in the theater to the
   heritage given him by a theatrical family and to methods
   in acting practiced and promoted by David Garrick.
   Thanks to Garrick, Sheridan found actors around him
   "who could give the old materials the full benefit of
   a modern rendering" (p. 31). Consequently, his best
   plays were "created for him by the theatre, rather than
   for the theatre by him" (p. 31). His work disappoints
   literary critics, however, because it is wholly lacking
   in "some sincerely felt central attitude, moral,
   social or political, which integrates the old materials
   into a new shape and puts them to the service of some
   living purpose" (p. 31). In morals as in politics,
   however, Sheridan's only principle "was to make money and
   a name for himself" (p. 31). His thoroughgoing personal
   hypocrisy could give rise to no truly great comedy. His
   plays "represent our older dramatic tradition at its
   weakest, thinnest, and most barrenly theatrical." They
   "do little or nothing to increase the reputation of the
   classics with modern audiences" (p. 32), and it is no
   credit to the London theaters of 1946 that three Sheridan

plays (The Rivals, The Critic, and The School for Scandal) are running concurrently.

5   GIBBS, WOLCOTT. "Mainly Mr. Olivier." New Yorker 22 (1 June): 51-52.
        Attributes merriment in an Old Vic production of The Critic to brilliantly stylized acting, especially on the part of Laurence Olivier, who, in the role of Puff, sustains two levels of comedy: One plays the joke on "what Sheridan intended to satirize," the other on "the now observable quaintness" (p. 51) of Sheridan's wit and manner.

6   KERNODLE, GEORGE R. "Excruciatingly Funny Or, The 47 Keys of Comedy." Theatre Arts 30 (December): 719-22.
        Lists "repetition," among other reliable "comic controls," as a "powerful technique" of comedy: "One lover in pain may be made slightly comic but a second lover or a servant following exactly the same pattern will be extremely comic, as in Sheridan's The Critic" (p. 721).

7   KRUTCH, JOSEPH WOOD. "Drama." Nation 162 (8 June): 700.
        Reviews a production of The Critic staged by the Old Vic Company as an afterpiece to Oedipus the King. The audience makes easy accommodation with the two plays because one of them (the Oedipus) is "timeless" and the other is "timely." The attacks made by The Critic against theatrical idling, the influence of theatrical critics, the techniques of playwriting, the conventions of puffing have as much point today as they did in the mid-1770s. Perhaps Oedipus "purges the soul," but The Critic "tickles both the mind and the ribs."

8   OLIVER, ROBERT T[ARBELL]. Four Who Spoke Out: Burke, Fox, Sheridan and Pitt. Syracuse, N.Y.: Syracuse University Press, 196 pp.
        Places four prominent political figures--Burke, Fox, Sheridan, and Pitt--in loose relationship with one another as to political attitudes and parliamentary achievements. For his part, Sheridan "verged on radicalism" (p. 165). He often advocated his principles so violently as to render himself ineffective to his own causes. As a speaker he favored "an intermingling of humor and ridicule with argument, until it is almost impossible to tell where logic leaves off and sophistry begins." In fact, the mixing of sense and nonsense "stands as a symbol of Sheridan's parliamentary career. He was a jester who could be terribly in earnest at

1946

times" (p. 150). Yet "he entered politics not for what
he could get, but for what he could give" (p. 165),
supporting especially such causes as "anti-militarism,
freedom of the press, abolition of slavery, home rule
for Ireland, parliamentary reform, reform of penal laws,
free trade," and "even the excesses of the French
Revolution" (p. 165). Reviewed by Warner F. Woodring in
American Historical Review, 53 (October 1947): 157.

9   SAINTSBURY, GEORGE EDWARD BATEMAN. "The Garden of Minor
Verse and the Later Drama--Anstey to Sheridan." In
The Peace of the Augustans: A Survey of Eighteenth-Century
Literature as a Place of Rest and Refreshment. World's
Classics Series. London: Oxford University Press.
pp. 275-85.
Reprints 1916.7.

10   STOKES, LESLIE. "The Revivals." Theatre Arts 30 (January):
22-24.
Mentions a revival of The Rivals in London featuring
Edith Evans as Mrs. Malaprop. "It is a pity that Sheridan
did not write a part worthy of our first comedienne, but
it does not make matters any better for Miss Evans to
dress herself up magnificently for the part which does
not exist, and then to speak the stale malapropisms as
though they were the sharp wit of the brilliant creature
she appears to be" (p. 23). Also mentions The Critic
as revived by the Old Vic Company with Laurence Olivier as
Puff.

1947

1   COVE, JOSEPH WALTER. Sheridan: His Life and Theatre.
London: Dent, 280 pp.
Recounts Sheridan's life on the basis of his "three
careers," remarking that the second and third of them
(those of theater manager and member of Paliament) were
extensions of the first (that of playwright), in that
the first gave rise to the second and the second
provided means for the third. To pedestrian minds, it
might seem better that Sheridan had died at the end of
his first career, before subjecting himself to the
contempt of political enemies and censorious moralists;
but the character of his later life need not be attributed
to mere vanity and self-indulgence. In assuming public
life, he "could show no passport but his own natural
gifts" (p. 263). Lacking the advantages of wealth, he
yet maintained high political principles. His reputation

for improvidence originated with those who did not know
need, and his imprudences with wine and women were
amplified in the reports of those "not only who had no
mind to them, but also (and even more zealously) by
those whose inclination ran that way but was baulked by
want of courage or opportunity" (p. 255). Despite the
trials and disappointments of his life, "it is most likely
that he would have lived it the same way, for in the main
it had given him what he wanted" (p. 263). "To the end
there was something of the archangel ruined about him"
(p. 227). Reviewed in Times Literary Supplement,
20 September, 1947, p. 476; by Thomas Quinn Curtiss in
New York Times Book Review, 19 December, p. 4; by Walter
Prichard Eaton in New York Herald Tribune Book Review,
14 November, p. 3; by Frederick T. Wood in English
Studies 29 (1948): 89-90; in Theatre Arts 33 (1949): 95;
also in 1948.7.

2   GIBBS, LEWIS. Sheridan: His Life and Theatre. London:
Dent, 280 pp.
    See 1947.1. "Lewis Gibbs" is the pseudonym of Joseph
Walter Cove.

3   PURDY, RICHARD LITTLE. "A Gift of Sheridan Manuscripts in
Honor of Professor Nettleton." Yale University Library
Gazette 22 (1947): 42-43.
    Describes documents given to the Yale University
Library by friends and former students of G. H. Nettleton
in his honor. They include (1) the Chetwynd manuscript
of The School for Scandal, (2) the notebook for Sheridan's
unwritten comedy Affectation, (3) a manuscript copy of
The Caravan, an interlude translated from a French opera
and altered here in Sheridan's hand, (4) nine pages of
witty rules drawn up by Sheridan for a fishing expedition
taken in 1800 (or thereabouts), and (5) a copy of the
Songs, Duets, Trios, Etc. in The Duenna printed in London
in 1775. To these items are added three gifts of
Nettleton's own: Sheridan's algebra book from Harrow and
two letters written by Sheridan to his second wife.
These items had come to Nettleton from the Sheridan
family through Mrs. Clare Sheridan.

4   REID, LOREN D. "Sheridan's Speech on Mrs. Fitzherbert."
Quarterly Journal of Speech 33 (February): 15-22.
    Demonstrates that Sheridan's famous speech in defense
of Mrs. Fitzherbert is a "straddle speech wherein the
orator, flouting the moral principles of public discourse,
attempts to draw opposite conclusions within the same
speech" (p. 15). To accomplish this feat, Sheridan first

1947

created good will for the Prince of Wales, whose secret
marriage to Mrs. Fitzherbert, a Roman Catholic, stood in
violation of both the Acts of Settlement of 1689
(disallowing British sovereigns to marry Roman Catholics)
and the Marriage Act of 1772 (forbidding royal children
under the age of twenty-five from marrying without the
king's consent). Second, Sheridan spoke in behalf of Mrs.
Fitzherbert, asserting her good character without once
mentioning her name. Bypassing all logic, he appealed to
the "gallant instincts and gentlemanly conduct" (p. 21)
of his audience and persuaded them to ignore the statutes
in question.

5   VINCENT, HOWARD P. "An Attempted Piracy of The Duenna."
    Modern Language Notes 62 (April): 268-70.
        Describes the issue in a Chancery suit in which
    Sheridan sought to "reserve to himself his right" (p. 269)
    to the music of The Duenna. When one Robert Falkener of
    Peterborough Court published and sold portions of this
    music, Sheridan and the music publishers to whom he sold
    the copyright, Charles and Samuel Thompson, sued to have
    the piracy stopped. Falkener argued in his defense that
    the music was as much as forty years old when he printed
    it; but Sheridan seems to have succeeded in his
    injunction for all copies of the Falkener printing
    have disappeared.

6   WITTOP, FREDDY. "Two Costume Designs for The School for
    Scandal." Theatre Arts 31 (February): 19.
        Pictures two costume sketches drawn by Wittop for The
    School for Scandal. The stylized drawings depict Richard
    Waring as Charles Surface and Eva Le Gallienne as Lady
    Sneerwell in a production to be staged by the American
    Repertory Theatre.

                            1948

1   ANON. "Canterbury Week: 'The Critic'" Times (London),
    5 August, p. 7.
        Pronounces The Critic a perfect play of
    celebration--one well-suited to "Canterbury Week"--because
    "The display of wit, elegance, and absurdity leaves so much
    scope for individual quirks of fancy."

2   BRUMBAUGH, THOMAS B. "An Unpublished Letter of Richard
    Brinsley Sheridan." Emory University Quarterly
    4 (March): 55-57.
        Prints a letter written from Randalls on Thursday,

6 April 1809 (?) to Dr. Jack Graham inviting him to
visit and playfully chiding him first for being long out
of circulation and second for framing an overly complex
scheme for re-building Drury Lane Theatre. Dr. Jack
Graham is identified as being proprietor of "a successful
mud bath establishment named the Temple of Hygeia" (p. 56).

3   COVE, JOSEPH WALTER. "Sheridan Against Warren Hastings."
    Quarterly Journal of Speech 34 (December): 464-68.
        Recounts the circumstances surrounding and giving rise
    to Sheridan's great speeches against Hastings: Sheridan's
    access to excellent training in elocution, the background
    of the charges against Hastings, the exciting opening of
    the impeachment trial, the histrionic vigor of Sheridan's
    speeches (especially the one in Westminster Hall), the
    anticlimactic conclusion of the impeachment trial, and
    the ultimate vindication of Hastings. (See 1949.6; see
    also 1948.4.)

4   GIBBS, LEWIS. "Sheridan Against Warren Hastings." Quarterly
    Journal of Speech 34 (December): 464-68.
        See 1948.3. "Lewis Gibbs" is the pseudonym for Joseph
    Walter Cove.

5   JAMES, HENRY. "The School for Scandal at Boston." In The
    Scenic Art. Notes on Acting and the Drama: 1872-1901.
    Edited by Allan Wade. New Brunswick: Rutgers University
    Press, pp. 13-21.
        Reprints 1874.4.

6   McKILLOP, ALAN DUGALD. "Later Comedy." In English
    Literature from Dryden to Burns. New York: Appleton-
    Century-Crofts, pp. 306-7.
        Credits Sheridan with achieving the "Cibberian ideal,
    not hitherto fully realized on the stage, of polite virtue
    and triumphant wit reconciled with the reformation of
    manners" (p. 307).

7   MASON, FRANCIS, JR. "Great Borrower." Saturday Review
    31 (25 September): 15.
        Asks why Sheridan abandoned the theater for Parliament
    and answers the question--on the basis of Joseph Walter
    Cove's biography of the playwright (1947.1)--by seeing
    Sheridan as an actor seeking an inexhaustible variety
    of roles. "He was an actor who liked best to write for
    himself, a playwright who was his own hero."

8   SHERBURN, GEORGE. "Sheridan." In A Literary History of
    England , edited by Albert C. Baugh. New York:

1948

Appleton-Century-Crofts, pp. 1044-48.
Sees Sheridan's fame as resting upon The Rivals, The School for Scandal, and The Critic, and sees the last of these to be of a largely topical interest, favoring "impersonation and mimicry" over "verbal dexterity" (p. 1045). The Rivals succeeds principally for the "lightness, crispness, and elegance of point" in its dialogue (p. 1047). The School for Scandal succeeds both for its dialogue and for "the perfect manipulation of the intrigue leading inevitably to the thrilling resolution in the famous screen scene" (p. 1047).

1949

1   ANON. "New Theatre. 'The School for Scandal' by Richard Brinsley Sheridan." Times (London), 21 January, p. 7.
    Recognizes at least two ways to play The School for Scandal: (1) through the director's own eyes, emphasizing the comic situations over the historical past, and (2) through the eyes of a theatrical historian, reflecting the play as it might have been to audiences of its own time. In the new Old Vic production, Laurence Olivier has taken the latter of these courses and has produced a play elegant in both its visual and aural dimensions. As a whole it is "all very entertaining."

2   COPELAND, LEWIS, ed. "At the Trial of Warren Hastings." In World's Great Speeches. Garden City, N.Y.: Garden City Publishing, pp. 165-68.
    Prints the peroration (the last ten paragraphs) of Sheridan's Westminster Hall speech against Hastings (13 June 1788). A brief headnote (recognizing Sheridan as "conqueror of two worlds") introduces the piece.

3   HUNT, LEIGH. "The Rivals." In Leigh Hunt's Dramatic Criticism, edited by Lawrence Huston Houtchens and Carolyn Washburn Houtchens. New York: Columbia University Press, pp. 248-50.
    Reprints 1830.4.

4   LANDRÉ, LOUIS. Introduction to L'École de la médisance, translated by M. Huchon. Paris: Aubier-Flammarion.
    Places The School for Scandal in the contexts of Sheridan's era, his life, his other works, his political career, his character, and his comic traditions. Also examines the play as to composition, plot, characters, and spirit, observing, for example, that the plot achieves a general unity despite the variety of scenes,

1949

that the characters, all colored by Sheridan's own
personality, usually reflect his amused irony and piquancy
of observation, that his spirit is ample and supple
enough to adapt itself to different types of scenes, that
the play endures because it displays today the same youth
and vigor it had shown at its creation. Provides notes
on the translation, explanatory notes, and bibliographic
notes. Prints English and French texts facing one
another.

5   MILLER, TATLOCK, ed. The Old Vic Theatre Company. A Tour
     of Australia and New Zealand. London: British Council,
     60 pp.
        Includes photographs of an Old Vic production of The
     School for Scandal (pp. 14-29). A brief comment by Alan
     Dent (pp. 27-38) emphasizes the basic conventionality of
     the play but remarks the distinctive genius by which
     Sheridan so endows his characters with vitality as to
     cause the complications to "spring directly from their
     dispositions" (p. 28). It is a play, however, which
     "teaches no lesson and points no moral unless it be Sir
     Peter's that true wit is nearly allied to good nature"
     (p. 28). Expectation awaits the performances in this
     production of Vivien Leigh as Lady Teazle and Laurence
     Olivier as Sir Peter. The Old Vic tour of Australia
     will unveil the production.

6   NETTLETON, GEORGE H. "A Comment on Sheridan against Warren
     Hastings." Quarterly Journal of Speech 35 (February):
     71-72.
        Responds, by invitation of the editors, to an account
     of Sheridan's career in political oratory prepared by
     Joseph Walter Cove (Lewis Gibbs) for an earlier number
     of the Quarterly Journal of Speech (see 1948.3, 4).
     While Gibbs performs outstanding service in behalf of
     Sheridan's gifts, his comments relate more to history
     than to critical interpretation. He "is at his best as
     the annalist of Sheridan's fame as an orator rather than
     as critical analyst of his speeches" (p. 71). Gibb's
     tendency is to supply too little illustrative detail and
     to obscure Sheridan's "quick wit, readiness of retort,
     and brilliant powers of observation" (p. 172) by
     insisting upon the care with which he prepared his
     speeches. In general, however, Gibbs displays "fully
     informed and sound judgment" (p. 71).

7   NICOLL, ALLARDYCE. "Growth of Bourgeois Comedy." In World
     Drama from Aeschylus to Anouilh. London: Harrap,
     pp. 371-97.

1949

Touches briefly on Sheridan's apparent intent as a
comic playwright: "he was an opportunist and himself a
theatrical manager, with the consequence that,
fundamentally opposed though he was to sentimentalism,
he permitted a faint flavour of that style to colour
scenes penned mainly for their laughter, and, moreover,
soon abandoned the effort to emulate Etherege and
Congreve" (p. 394). His larger debt was to Vanbrugh
and Farquhar.

8   OLIVIER, LAURENCE. Introduction to The School for Scandal,
by Sheridan. London: Folio Society, pp. 5-11.
Provides a souvenir edition based upon the Crompton
Rhodes text and adorned with costume and set designs
prepared by Cecil Beaton for the Old Vic Company. The
introduction discusses problems posed by the play to
both actor and producer. For the actor, "Sheridan's
cunning and deceptive appearance of formal realism can
usually be understood only after much acting experience,
or, in rare instances, by an instinctive gift for the
style" (p. 6). Producers of Sheridan must rely upon
hints of the author's intention, not wholly upon their
own invention. They must apply Sheridan's spirit to
the demands of their own theater. This spirit calls in
The School for Scandal for the Pollock's Theatre convention of painted backcloths and sparse props. Sheridan's
own casualness in handling time lapses and durations
enables the modern producer to satisfy modern expectations
in lighting and costume without compromising the
Sheridanesque spirit.

9   SINKO, GRZEGORZ. Sheridan and Kotzebue: A Comparative
Essay. Wroclaw Society of Science and Letters, ser. A,
no. 27, Wroclaw: Sklad Glowmy W. Domu Ksiazki, 32 pp.
Compares and contrasts the characters and careers of
the two playwrights, noting especially their impeccable
sense of theater. Other discussion examines The
Stranger and Pizarro in relation to their German
sources, listing significant changes made by Sheridan.
It also examines the reception of the two plays in
England and the political controversies excited by the
latter of them. Consideration of Sheridan's possible
influence upon Kotzebue points up reminiscences of The
School for Scandal in Die Verläumder (1796), an attack
on scandal-mongering, and Die Verwandtschaften (1798), a
charity-test play. Other Sheridanesque influences
"cannot be quite firmly established" (p. 27).

10 TREWIN, J. C., ed. Preface to The Critic, or A Tragedy

Rehearsed, by Sheridan. The Falcon Plays. London:
Falcon Educatonal Books, pp. 5-16.
    Declares that "Parody is the only theme" of The Critic
(p. 6) and that "the core" of the play is found in
Puff's observation that it is "always the way at the
theatre: give these fellows a good thing, and they never
know when to have done with it" (p. 13). That is, the
play attacks the unending abuse of theatrical conventions.
Furthermore, it is properly seen as a sustained "domestic
joke" exposing what is ridiculous about every branch of
the theatrical family. Reference is made to
twentieth-century revivals of the play, most notably
to Laurence Olivier's performances as Puff in 1945.

11 WILLIAMS, GEORGE WOODS. "The Stage History of Sheridan's
    Less Known Plays." Master's thesis, George Washington
    University.
        Studies the extent to which Sheridan "modified his
    creative offerings to meet the changes in dramatic taste
    which occurred in the last quarter of the eighteenth
    century" (pp. 1-2). Such works of his as St. Patrick's
    Day, A Trip to Scarborough, The Camp, and Robinson
    Crusoe show him according by degrees to the popular demands
    for sentimentality and spectacle.

                        1950

1   ANON. "Irma Is a Lady." Life 29 (14 August): 65-66.
        Comments briefly upon Marie Wilson, an actress well
    known for radio performances as "My Friend Irma," in
    the role of Lady Teazle at the Circle Theatre in
    Hollywood. "Only rarely does the shrill giggle of My
    Friend Irma break into the speeches of Lady Teazle"
    (p. 65). Pictures show a bit of stage business in which
    full-figured Marie Wilson bends with studied care to
    retrieve her fan from the floor.

2   ANON. "New Zealand Gift to Theatre." Times (London),
    21 March, p. 10.
        Reports the gift to Drury Lane Theatre of a lock of
    Sheridan's hair. "The presentation was made in the room
    in which he wrote The School for Scandal."

3   NETTLETON, GEORGE H. "Sheridan's Introduction to the
    American Stage." Publications of the Modern Language
    Association of America 65 (March): 163-82.
        Sets out the emergence of Sheridan's plays upon the
    American theatrical scene, discussing first the

1950

performances given in Jamaica by Lewis Hallam's American
Company between 1779 and 1785, then the performances given
in continental America by the British Military Thespians
under Sir Henry Clinton between 1778 and 1783. Other
segments of the account discuss "Sheridan on the Post-War
Stage (1784-86)" and "Sheridan's Initial Impress on
American Comedy (1787)," a comment upon The School for
Scandal, and Royall Tyler's The Contrast. While Clinton's
Thespians actually introduced Sheridan to the continental
stage, it is the American Company, extending its wartime
Jamaican productions of him onto the postwar professional
stage, who decisively established him in the history of
American theater.

4   WILLIAMS, GEORGE W. "A New Source of Evidence for
Sheridan's Authorship of The Camp and The Wonders of
Derbyshire." Studies in Philology 47 (October): 619-28.
     Draws evidence from the Drury Lane account books to
suggest that two afterpeices, The Camp and The Wonders
of Derbyshire, are works of Sheridan's own hand. Except
for instances involving Sheridan himself, the account
books are "scrupulously regular" (p. 624). The accounts
relating to these two afterpieces, however, do not show
regular treatment. Sixth-night net receipts, the standard
benefit payments to authors, are not recorded. Instead,
the books show two open payments to Sheridan himself.
They also show a payment of 35 pounds to the set designer,
De Loutherbourg, covering expenses for his trip to
Coxheath and Derbyshire, presumably to sketch sets for the
two afterpieces. Since Sheridan had not yet written
afterpieces for the theater, he chose not to identify
himself openly with these two pieces. He chose quietly
to pay himself and De Loutherbourg for services rendered.

1951

1   ANON. "Sheridan." Times (London), 30 October, p. 5.
     Marks the bicentenary of Sheridan's birth by citing his
literary achievements and admiring their excellence,
especially that of The School for Scandal. "The Rivals is
full of delightful inventions of farcical character and
plot, The Critic is a glorious hybrid of literary pamphlet
and burlesque, The Duenna is an ingenious operetta with
lyrics that still seem charmingly written; but The School
for Scandal is much more than any of these, for its
characters are real people and its story is one that
continues to be at once witty and moving." Sheridan has
won lasting success in the most difficult of literary

forms, the drama; and, quite properly, when Sir Laurence
Olivier remembers him today by placing a wreath on his
grave, it will be the young Mr. Sheridan whose memory is
evoked, not the drunken grotesque of Gillray's cartoons.

2   ANON. "200th Anniversary of Sheridan's Birth." Times
      (London), 31 October, p. 8.
        Describes a ceremony in which wreaths were placed on
      Sheridan's grave in Westminster Abbey, a wreath to
      represent the city of Bath, another to represent the
      Sheridan family, and a third to represent the stage.
      In paying the tribute of the stage, Sir Laurence Olivier
      remarked that Sheridan "was a man who created an
      atmosphere of gallantry, gesture, charm, and marvellous
      whimsicality, a man who presented the best qualities of
      his time, and a man of glamour." It was announced that
      the family were undertaking to have the inscription on
      Sheridan's tombstome recut, it having been worn to
      virtual illegibility by the feet of visitors to the Abbey.

3   ATKINS, JOHN WILLIAM HEY. "Critical Cross-Currents:
      Fielding, Sheridan, Cowper, Shaftesbury, Hume, Burke,
      Kames, Reynolds, and Beattie." In English Literary
      Criticism: 17th and 18th Centuries. New York: Barnes &
      Noble, pp. 314-55.
        Cites The Critic among "diverse contributions" made by
      literary artists themselves to the history of criticism.
      Inspired by Buckingham's Rehearsal, Sheridan's play
      ridicules sentimental comedy but reserves its best thrusts
      for "the absurd methods of contemporary playwrights and
      critics" (p. 318): e.g., "the naïve and obvious methods
      of conveying information to the audience, the use of
      double plots frankly unrelated, the thrusting of
      incongruous love-passages into stately historical scenes,
      and the clearing-up of complications and disguises with
      unconvincing crudity" (p. 318). These and other such
      judgments are "kept alive by unfailing wit and humour"
      (p. 318).

4   DARLINGTON, W. A. Sheridan, 1751-1816. Bibliographical
      Series of Supplements to British Book News. London:
      Longmans, for the British Council and National Book
      League, 29 pp.
        Organizes a sketch of Sheridan's life and career upon
      the assumption that "he had only one deep ambition, and
      this had nothing to do specifically either with politics
      or the theatre. His determination was from the first
      to be an important figure in the little Great World of
      London society" (p. 6). This determination presided

over his management of Drury Lane Theatre and over the
conduct of his political career. Consequently, both
enterprises came to disappointment. His fame rests
almost wholly upon the work he valued least, his career
as playwright, and in this success he holds in common
with Shakespeare one characteristic: his plays were
"written only to be acted and not at all to be read"
(p. 19). They also trace their longevity to their
"essential decency" (p. 23). A select bibliography of
texts and studies follows the sketch. Reviewed (briefly)
in Times Literary Supplement, 11 January 1952, p. 30.

5   FAWCETT, L'ESTRANGE. "Bicentenaries in 1951." Times
    (London), 6 February, p. 7.
        Suggests, in a letter to the editor, that the
    bicentenary of Sheridan's birth be "celebrated in
    connexion with the Festival of Britain or otherwise."
    Similar recognition is suggested for William Sheraton.
    An appropriate exhibition or stage production of the
    works of these two men would draw their achievements
    to the attention of foreign visitors.

6   LANDSTONE, CHARLES, "Enigma of Sheridan." Times (London),
    5 November, p. 5.
        Suggests that Sheridan stopped writing plays at so
    early an age because the theater he inherited from
    Garrick "was a theatre in which the author was subsidiary
    to the actor, who bowdlerized the classics or adapted
    foreign works, altered and tailor-made to suit his
    personality." Not until Shaw did the British theater
    again become a playwright's theater, and since 1940 it
    has been again an actor's theater.

7   NYHAN, D. "Forgotten Author." New York Times, 25 November,
    sec. 2, p. 3.
        Complains, in a letter from Cork, Ireland, that the
    works of Sheridan, "the Irish patriot and dramatist,"
    are too much neglected. Now that the bicentennial of
    his birth has come, there should certainly be revivals
    of his major plays.

8   PURDOM, C. B. "Enigma of Sheridan." Times (London),
    15 November, p. 5.
        Agrees with an earlier correspondent (1951.6) that
    Sheridan stopped writing plays because of the nature
    of his theater. The "huge barns of theatres gave no
    opportunity for drama, only for theatrical displays."
    Until actor-managers were prepared to make the
    distinction between drama and mere theatricality, good

playwriting could not flourish, and even now this important distinction is too often obscured.

9   SHUTTLEWORTH, BERTRAM. "Early Editions of The School for
     Scandal." Theatre Notebook 6 (Fall): 4-7.
        Recognizes the bicentenary of Sheridan's birth by
     listing and giving descriptive details of the editions
     of The School for Scandal (all of them pirated) printed
     up to 1782. "To the work of Rhodes and Nettleton, at
     present available only in scattered form, two substantial
     additions are made, and a number of details are corrected"
     (p. 5). Two Dublin editions, one of 1781, the other of
     1782, are indicated as "hitherto unrecorded" (p. 6).

10   TROUBRIDGE, ST. VINCENT. "Enigma of Sheridan." Times
     (London), 8 November, p. 7.
        Argues, in response to an earlier correspondent (see
     1951.6), that Sheridan quit writing plays not because
     he served an actor's theater but because, after taking
     over full management of Drury Lane in 1778, he needed
     more money. It was "not an artistic but an economic
     phenomenon." Not before the advent of the royalty
     system, about 1860, could playwrights expect major
     income from their plays.

11   VAN LENNEP, WILLIAM. "The Chetwynd Manuscript of The
     School for Scandal." Theatre Notebook 6 (Fall): 10-12.
        Announces acquisition by the Yale University Library
     of the licenser's copy of The School for Scandal, a copy
     thought lost or destroyed. After leaving the possession
     of Sir George Chetwynd, grandson of William Chetwynd,
     the licenser of plays under George III, it had passed
     through various hands, including those of Augustus Daly,
     the New York producer and theater owner, before arriving
     at Yale. Comparison of the Chetwynd manuscript with an
     earlier one (the Frampton Court) and a later (the Crewe)
     reveals a closer similarity to the latter. "Yet numerous
     lines in the Frampton Court draft that are absent or
     changed in the Crewe manuscript appear in the Chetwynd
     manuscript unaltered. On the other hand, a few lines
     in the Frampton Court draft are present in the Crewe
     manuscript but not in the Chetwynd manuscript--evidence
     that Sheridan restored them after the first performance"
     (p. 11), the performance represented exactly by the
     Chetwynd manuscript.

12   WHITE, ERIC WALTER. The Rise of English Opera. New York:
     Philosophical Library, pp. 72-73.
        Illustrates, by quoting from one of his letters to his

1951

father-in-law, Thomas Linley, Sheridan's role in shaping the music for The Duenna.

1952

1   ANON. "£420 Paid for Sheridan Letters." Times (London) 16 July, p. 9.
    Announces the sale at Sotheby's of 110 autographed letters addressed by Sheridan between 1795 and 1799 to John Grubbe, a partner of his in the management of Drury Lane Theatre. "In many of them Sheridan appeals for money; others relate to his engagement of actors, and references are made to Mrs. Siddons, Harriet Mellon, Mrs. Jordan, and others."

2   CLINTON-BADDELEY, V. C. "Richard Brinsley Sheridan." In The Burlesque Tradition in the English Theatre after 1660. London: Methuen, pp. 71-79.
    Credits Sheridan with bringing to perfection the rich tradition of theatrical burlesque he had inherited from Buckingham, Fielding, Duffett, and Carey. His own most striking contribution to this tradition was the Shakespearean burlesque, i.e., the pseudo-Shakespearean blank-verse line intended less to parody specific offenses than to expose a whole vogue of feeble Shakespearean imitations. The Critic also marks a beginning of the burlesque patriotic joke, a joke given further popularity by Gilbert and Sullivan. "The Critic not only attacked all the follies of the contemporary stage at once, but revived and preserved within the compass of the work almost the whole canon of the burlesque tradition (p. 72).

3   KRONENBERGER, LOUIS. "Sheridan." In The Thread of Laughter: Chapters on English Stage Comedy from Jonson to Maugham. New York: Alfred A. Knopf, pp. 191-202.
    Places Sheridan in the lineage not of Goldsmith, his near contemporary, but of Congreve, who held advantages over him of both a larger talent and an era better suited to good comedy. Sheridan's theatrical brilliance cannot be faulted, but his address to the world can be. Since, as a satirist, he attacked only what was safe and bowed before conventional morality, his plays lack thematic substance and artistic integrity. In truth The Rivals is "not only a relative failure, but a relative bore" (p. 194), and The School for Scandal, for all its surface glitter, is less brilliant in its wit than in its capacity to seem more wicked than it is.

188

It "is concerned with the imputation of sinning; of sin
itself there is absolutely nothing" (p. 196). Reviewed
by Edmund Wilson in New York Herald Tribune Book Review,
2 November, p. 6; by Joseph Carroll in Theatre Arts 36
(November): 9-10; by Howard Mumford Jones in Saturday
Review 35 (18 October): 24; by J. W. Krutch in New York
Times Book Review, 28 September, p. 26; by Francis
Fergusson in Yale Review 42 (December): 289-90.

4   NICOLL, ALLARDYCE. A History of English Drama, 1660-1900.
    Cambridge: Cambridge University Press, 2: 160-62 and
    passim.
        Reprints 1927.6.

5   SARDI, JOSÉ NUCETE. "The Rivals--Spanish Style." Américas
    4 (May): 37-38.
        Recounts the author's own experience of completing a
    translation of The Rivals begun by the Venezuelan writer
    Andrés Bello, a contemporary of Sheridan's who possibly
    knew him through the Venezuelan patriot Miranda, a
    resident in London at the turn of the eighteenth century.
    Although Bello shortened the play, Hispanicized its
    setting and names, and reduced the number of its characters
    from twelve to eight (combining several roles), he
    preserved its basic aim of pointing out "the ridiculous
    aspects that appear in mankind everywhere: the character
    who talks and talks, thinking he always speaks well;
    the duel; deceptions arising from false appearances,
    and the resulting comic situation; the false concept of
    honor" (p. 37). The principles governing the beginning
    of the translation are extended into the completion of
    it.

6   SHAW, GEORGE BERNARD. "The Second Dating of Sheridan." In
    Plays and Players: Essays on the Theatre, selected by
    A. C. Ward. World's Classic Series. London: Oxford
    University Press, pp. 95-104.
        Reprints 1896.17.

1953

1   ANON. "King's Theatre, Hammersmith. 'The School for
    Scandal' by Richard Brinsley Sheridan." Times (London),
    25 August, p. 2.
        Admires the capacity of the players in a revival of
    The School for Scandal to discover in the language of
    the play clues to the humanity of the characters they
    must interpret. Donald Wolfit, as Sir Peter, discovers

these clues just after the screen falls in act 4.
Dorothy Green, as Lady Sneerwell, discovers them in her
account of the slander she has suffered. Rosalind
Iden, as Lady Teazle, discovers them in the lines she
must speak after her "supposed perfidy" is discovered.
If Ellen Pollock does not discover them in the lines
of Mrs. Candour, she is to be excused, for Mrs. Candour
resides basically within the realm not of humanity but
of "formal invention."

2   ANON. "Mr. Wolfit as Overreach." *Times* (London), 3 August,
    p. 11.
        Announces a season at the King's Theatre, Hammersmith,
    which will open on 24 August with The School for Scandal.
    Later in the season, Mr. Donald Wolfit, the manager of
    the company, will play Sir Giles Overreach in Massinger's
    A New Way to Pay Old Debts.

3   ANON. "Pitlochry Festival." *Times* (London), 11 May, p. 3.
        Reports "a large audience for the gala performance of
    Sheridan's The Rivals, which opened the coronation season
    of Scotland's 'Festival Theatre in the Hills' at Pitlochry
    last night."

4   BOAS, FREDERICK SAMUEL. "Richard Brinsley Sheridan." In
    An Introduction to Eighteenth-Century Drama, 1700-1780.
    Oxford: Clarendon Press, pp. 345-57.
        Describes, against a background of basic biographical
    details, the career of Sheridan as a playwright,
    crediting him with bringing "to a victorious close
    Goldsmith's campaign against sentimental comedy" (p. 345).
    His own most important contribution lies in his
    dialogue, the high quality of which was not to be
    equalled until Shaw, Yeats, Synge, and O'Casey (themselves
    all Irishmen) began writing a century and more later.

5   BROWN, JOHN MASON. "The Man Who Wrote 'The Rivals.'"
    Saturday Review 36 (10 January): 25, 28-29.
        Sees Sheridan's life as a success story with an unhappy
    ending. "After a glittering beginning it became grubby"
    (p. 25). The fame of Sheridan rests upon The Rivals
    and The School for Scandal, plays which restored light
    to a tradition of comedy palled since Congreve. Of the
    two, The Rivals is clearly the more innocent. When
    Sheridan wrote it "he wrote as a happy man and his
    happiness is present in almost every line" (p. 29).
    This contagious happiness accounts for the longevity of
    the play, for through it the play transcends its
    limitations as a period piece.

6   DIXON, CAMPBELL. "Sheridan." In English Wits, edited by
     Leonard Russell. London: Hutchinson, pp. 171-96.
        Reprints 1940.4.

7   DOWNER, ALAN S., ed. Introduction to The Rivals, by Sheridan.
     New York: Appleton-Century-Crofts, pp. v-x.
        Comments on the play in relation to Pope's famous
     definition of "wit": "what oft was thought, but ne'er
     so well expressed." In this respect, The Rivals is
     seen to draw upon standard comic materials--structural
     conventions of Restoration comedy, satirization of
     manners, humor characterization, the old comic method
     of castigans ridendo, "pedagogy by laughter and ridicule"
     (p. ix). In it Sheridan makes us laugh at our own
     dreams, the better to bear the failure of them, and to
     laugh at our own follies, the better to sympathize with
     the follies of others.

8   HEWES, HENRY. "Dick Sheridan's 'Scandals'" Saturday
     Review 36 (11 July): 34-35.
        Laments the failure of two revivals of The School for
     Scandal, one under the direction of Albert Marre at the
     Westport Country Playhouse, the other under the direction
     of Terese Hayden at the Theatre de Lys. The latter of
     them (a traditional period staging) stifles comedy with
     "sobriety and slowness" (p. 35). The former (with a
     1912 setting) succumbs to its own eccentricities.
     Since The School for Scandal reflects the social
     attitudes of colonial America, it rings true to Americans.
     It needs no artificial modernizing.

9   LANDFIELD, JEROME B. "Man of Action." Saturday Review
     36 (21 February): 25.
        Identifies, in a letter of response to John Mason
     Brown's "The Man Who Wrote 'The Rivals'" (1953.5), the
     "most outstanding single action" of Sheridan's
     parliamentary career as being his decisive conduct in
     putting down the naval mutinies of 1797. Despite such
     decisive political and ethical action, there is no
     certain evidence that Sheridan valued his political
     career more highly than he did his literary one (as
     Brown seems to declare).

10 LYNCH, JAMES J. Box, Pit, and Gallery: Stage and Society
     in Johnson's London. Berkeley: University of California
     Press, pp. 176-80 and passim.
        Demonstrates that Sheridan is "the exceptional
     dramatist among that large group of writers who had
     other connections with the theater. He shared with

1953

them the propensity for farcical situation and
caricature; but he went beyond them in providing the
stage with 'literary' drama. Equally skillful in
creating effective stage business, he surpassed them
in that he was able, by gaining a detachment impossible
in sentimental comedy, to open out his plays on larger
horizons" (p. 179).

11   SHUTTLEWORTH, BERTRAM. "The First London Edition of The
       School for Scandal." Theatre Notebook 8 (Fall): 23.
            Adds to the list of early editions of The School for
       Scandal a heretofore unrecorded one of 1781. Printed
       for John Bew in Pater-Noster-Row, it supplants the
       issue identified by R. C. Rhodes as being the first
       edition published in London, that printed for Cadell
       in 1783. The rarity of the Bew edition suggests that
       it, like the Cadell one, was suppressed.

12   SMITH, DANE FARNSWORTH. "The Critic, Its Sources, and
       Its Satire." In The Critics in the Audience of the
       London Theatres from Buckingham to Sheridan: A Study of
       Neoclassicism in the Playhouse, 1671-1779. University
       of New Mexico Publications in Language and Literature,
       no. 12. Albuquerque: University of New Mexico Press,
       pp. 115-43.
            Acknowledges the importance of The Critic as an attack
       on sentimentality but sees it as being equally important
       as an assault on theatrical critics, its first act
       showing the critic in his own home, the last two showing
       the critic-author suffering castigation at the hands of
       two ruthless critics. Sheridan's source for these
       actions was almost certainly George Colman's New Brooms,
       a prelude commissioned by Sheridan for the opening of
       his own management at Drury Lane on 21 September 1776.
       It presents a gathering of critics at the home of a
       fellow critic, and offers burlesque comment on such
       topics as foreign entertainers, the craft of acting, and
       the influence of critics upon theatrical art, topics
       certainly suggestive to Sheridan as he wrote The Critic.
       It also presents (suggestive of the character of
       Sheridan's Puff) a critic who writes "under different
       headings for several newspapers" (p. 127), and it brings
       onto the scene critics who are also authors (again to
       suggest Puff). The six dramatic sketches forming the
       basis of The Critic--(1) the Dangles at home, (2) the
       introduction of Sneer, (3) the roasting of Sir Fretful,
       (4) the reception of the foreign entertainers, (5) the
       account of Puff's journalism, (6) the abuse of Puff at
       the theatre--show, when considered as topics, Sheridan's

debt to Colman; and, when analyzed as action, they amount
to a comprehensive attack upon theatrical criticism and
its abuses. Reviewed by John Harrington Smith in
<u>Philological Quarterly</u> 33 (1954): 255-56; by George
Winchester Stone, Jr. in <u>Modern Language Notes</u> 69 (1955):
375-76; by St. Vincent Troubridge in <u>Theatre Notebook</u> 8
(1955): 67-68; by Jean Dulck in <u>Études Anglaises</u> 8 (1956):
346; by Vivian de Sola Pinto in <u>Modern Language Review</u>
50 (1956): 107-8; by Cecil Price in <u>Review of English
Studies</u>, n.s. 6 (1955): 88-89; by Albert E. Johnson in
<u>Quarterly Journal of Speech</u> 41 (1955): 187-89.

1954

1   ANON. "Magpies in the Library." <u>Times</u> (London), 26 May,
    p. 7.
        Marvels at the "bibliomania" that could induce a
    collector--as was recently the case--to pay 2,000 pounds
    for "an early draft of <u>The School for Scandal</u>." As for
    Sheridan, it is pleasing to think "What a Regency night
    out he could have enjoyed had he found a four-figure
    bidder for his handwriting!"

2   ANON. "News in Brief." <u>Times</u> (London), 10 November, p. 3.
        Reports that "Plaques are to be affixed by London
    County Council to No. 10, Hertford Street, W., to
    commemorate the residence there of General John
    Burgoyne and Richard Brinsley Sheridan."

3   ANON. "Sheridan in the Sale Room." <u>Times</u> (London),
    26 May, p. 10.
        Lists the main items included in fifty lots of Sheridan
    materials, possessions of his great-great-granddaughter,
    Lady Wavertree, sold at Sotheby's on 25 May for a total
    of 5,271 pounds. For the forty-six page manuscript of
    "Sir Peter Teazle," a fragment preliminary to <u>The School
    for Scandal</u>, Michael Papantonio of New York paid 2,000
    pounds. Other material included "the manuscript prompt
    copy" of <u>The Critic</u>, a Dublin edition of <u>The School for
    Scandal</u> (1780), a first edition of Moore's <u>Life</u> of
    Sheridan (1825.9), and the manuscript draft of Sheridan's
    unfinished opera <u>The Foresters</u>. The purchasers' names
    are given.

4   ANON. "Westminster Theatre. 'The Duenna' by Richard
    Brinsley Sheridan. Music by Julian Slade." <u>Times</u>
    (London), 29 July, p. 10.
        Approves the practice of refashioning minor classics

1954

to suit modern taste and applauds a revival of The
Duenna which features new music by Mr. Julian Slade,
"a young composer clever enough to depart from Linley's
period without straying too far outside comic opera
tradition."

5   BROWN, JOHN MASON, AND van DOREN, CARL, eds. Introduction
     to The Rivals and The School for Scandal: Two Comedies
     by Richard Brinsley Sheridan. London: Printed at the
     Curwen Press for the Heritage Press of New York, pp. 7-13.
        Recognizes the diversity of Sheridan's career but sees
     his fame as resting wholly upon The Rivals and The School
     for Scandal. While highly derivative in its comic
     materials, The Rivals succeeds for being unalloyed fun.
     Sheridan wrote it "as a happy man and his happiness is
     present in almost every line" (p. 12). By contrast, The
     School for Scandal succeeds for being subtle and
     sophisticated. While ethically somewhat bland, "its
     scandalmongers are devasting in their malice; its
     characters are brilliantly drawn; its observation of
     society is witty and merciless" (p. 11).

6   GUTHRIE, TYRONE. Introduction to Sheridan's Complete Plays.
     Collins Classics, no. 624. London: Collins, pp. 11-16.
        Reprints 1930.5.

7   PETERSON, HOUSTON, ed. "Richard Brinsley Sheridan Brings
     the Hastings Trial to a Climax." In A Treasury of the
     World's Great Speeches." New York: Simon and Schuster,
     pp. 180-84.
        Prints "the peroration on the fourth day" (13 June
     1788) of Sheridan's Westminster Hall speech against
     Hastings. "This speech, just because it was so carefully
     contrived, so loudly publicized in advance, lacked the
     spontaneity and power of his six-hour speech on the same
     subject before the House of Commons in the previous year"
     (p. 184). A brief biographical and historical headnote
     precedes the excerpt; a short commentary (including the
     judgment quoted here) follows it.

1955

1   MATLAW, MYRON. "English Versions of Die Spanier in Peru."
     Modern Language Quarterly 16 (March): 63-67.
        Describes thirteen English versions of Kotzebue's Die
     Spanier in Peru, oder: Rolla's Tod (1795), classifying
     them according to three general types: "theatrical
     adaptations, blank-verse renditions, and literal

translations" (p. 63). "The ultimate explanation for
the many adaptations and translations unquestionably
lies in the phenomenal popularity of Sheridan's Pizarro"
(p. 67). In fact, most of them (especially those in the
first two classifications) are based on his work.

2   MUDRICK, MARVIN. "Restoration Comedy and Later." In
    English Stage Comedy. English Institute Essays, 1954.
    Edited by W. K. Wimsatt. New York: Columbia University
    Press, pp. 98-125.
        Blames Sheridan's defects upon his audience and upon
    his own lack of talent. His audience, "bottle-fed on
    sermons and sentimental comedy, refused to recognize
    entire continents of vitality" (p. 115). His two major
    plays "are miscellanies of stagey, actable situations
    incorporating sentimental and stock-comic types" (p. 115).
    His characters are too often not involved in the actions
    they perform, and Sheridan himself, "after one has
    deplored his audience and the sentimental tradition
    it venerates and imposes," is "a second-rate and
    second-hand playwright" (p. 120). Neither he nor his
    contemporaries compares favorably to the best playwrights
    of the Restoration.

3   NOVAK, J. Z., trans. Skola Pomluv [The School for Scandal].
    Prague: Orbis, 175 pp.
        Translates into Czeckoslovakian the text of the
    Everyman Library (1911). Includes a commentary ("R. B.
    Sheridan and The School for Scandal") by Frank Tetauer.

4   SHAW, GEORGE BERNARD. "The Second Dating of Sheridan." In
    Plays and Players: Essays on the Theatre, selected by
    A. C. Ward. World's Classics Series. London: Oxford
    University Press, pp. 95-104.
        Reprints 1896.17.

1956

1   ANON. "Plaque to Commemorate Sheridan's Elopement." Times
    (London), 6 February, p. 10.
        Announces the unveiling at #11, Royal Crescent, in Bath,
    of a plaque bearing the inscription "Thomas Linley lived
    here and from this house his daughter Elizabeth eloped
    with Richard Brinsley Sheridan on the evening of 18th
    March, 1772."

2   ANON. "Saville Theatre. 'The Rivals' by Richard Brinsley
    Sheridan." Times (London), 24 February, p. 7.

1956

Praises "An altogether delightful revival making the
cheerful old comedy as good as new."

3   COVE, JOSEPH WALTER, ed.   Introduction to Sheridan's Plays.
    Everyman's Library, no. 95.   London: J. M. Dent & Sons,
    pp. v-xiv.
        Sketches Sheridan's life, noticing the peculiar force
    by which his personality makes virtually as strong an
    impression upon history as his work does. A general
    assessment of his comedy recognizes in it a distinctive
    blending of the artificial, the sentimental, and the
    ludicrous, ingredients promoting a genial spirit, a
    sense of the natural goodness as well as the habitual
    depravity of human nature. Paragraphs on the several
    plays (the collection excludes A Trip to Scarborough)
    recall in each case details of reception and early stage
    history. (See 1956.4.)

4   GIBBS, LEWIS.   Introduction to Sheridan's Plays. Everyman's
    Library, no. 95.   London: J. M. Dent & Sons, pp. v-xiv.
        See 1956.3. "Lewis Gibbs" is the pseudonym of Joseph
    Walter Cove.

5   HUNT, LEIGH.   "The Late Mr. Sheridan." In Leigh Hunt's
    Literary Criticism, edited by Lawrence Huston Houtchens
    and Carolyn Washburn Houtchens. With an Essay of
    Evaluation by Clarence DeWitt Thorpe. New York: Columbia
    University Press, pp. 103-15.
        Reprints 1816.15.

6   OLFSON, LEWY, adapter.   "The Rivals." Plays 15 (March):
    87-95.
        Adapts the play for radio presentation by cutting many
    lines, adding transitional language, and excising the
    Julia-Faulkland plot.

7   PRICE, J. B.   "Richard Brinsley Sheridan (1751-1816)."
    Contemporary Review 190 (September): 159-63.
        Applauds the "pervading wholesomeness in the writings
    of R. B. Sheridan" (p. 159). Sheridan exemplifies the
    unselfconscious artist. He "was a healthy, hearty
    Irishman, so genuine that he need not ask whether he
    was genuine or no, so sincere as quite to forget his
    own sincerity, so truly pious that he could be happy
    in the best world that God chose to create, so humane
    that he loved even the foibles of his kind" (p. 159).
    He is original, "not in the sense that he thinks and
    says what nobody ever thought and said before, and what
    nobody can ever think and say again, but because he is

always delightfully fresh, because he sets before us
the world as it honestly appeared to him, and not a
world as it seemed proper to certain people that it
ought to appear" (p. 161).

8   RAMONDT, MARIE. "Between Laughter and Humour in the
    Eighteenth Century." Neophilologus 40 (1956): 128-39.
        Mentions The School for Scandal (p. 139) as a
    manifestation of Fieldingesque comedy of affectation.

9   SCHILLER, ANDREW. "The School for Scandal: The Restoration
    Unrestored." Publications of the Modern Language
    Association of America 71 (September): 694-704.
        Demonstrates that the "fabric" of The School for
    Scandal "is woven from characters, situations and devices
    which are either in direct continuity from the
    Restoration or are throwbacks to it" but that "Sheridan's
    play manages not to say a single one of the most
    significant things which the Restoration comedy of
    manners was designed to express" (p. 698). If separated
    into four motifs--"(1) The scandal plot; (2) The
    cuckolding-revenge plot; (3) The Town-country antithesis;
    (4) The two brothers ('male Cinderella')" (p. 698)--the
    play is clearly seen to be traditional. But examination
    of these motifs in relation to their antecedents reveals
    that Sheridan managed "to turn the comedy of manners
    into a vehicle for Addisonian didacticism" (p. 704). His
    play "did indeed restore to some extent the wit, bustle
    and brilliance of the high tide of English comedy." But
    it also "satisfied in every particular the moral as well
    as the esthetic sensibilities of the dominant group who
    sat in judgment upon it" (p. 704).

10 TODD, WILLIAM B. "Sheridan's The Critic." Book Collector
    5 (1956): 172-73.
        Provides a list of points by which the earlier issues
    of the 1781 edition of The Critic may be distinguished
    from the later ones, the five later "editions" of the
    play actually showing themselves to be "reimpressions
    of the type set for the first" (p. 172). Another list
    of points assists in distinguishing a fake second
    edition from the first two impressions of the authorized
    first edition. Heretofore this insidious facsimile has
    not been recognized as a pirated text.

1957

1   ANON. "A. D. C. Theatre, Cambridge, 'School for Scandal.'"

1957

Times (London), 14 June, p. 3.
Deplores a mannered revival of The School for Scandal,
in Cambridge, in which the setting is changed to
mid-nineteenth-century New Orleans and the actors
affect American accents. "When an apologetic prologue
has been spoken to the strumming of a banjo and Mrs.
Sneerwell's guests have tried out their American accents
on her sunny patio the joke has more or less run its
course."

2   GREGOR, JOSEPH. "Die Lästerschule." In Der Schauspielführer.
Stuttgart: Hiersemann, 6: 115-17.
Offers, in German, a scene-by-scene summary of The
School for Scandal. A brief headnote describes the play
as "eine der köstlichsten Komodien des ausgehenden
englischen Rokoko" (p. 115).

3   JAMES, HENRY. "The School for Scandal at Boston." In The
Scenic Art: Notes on Acting and the Drama, 1872-1901,
edited by Allan Wade. New York: Hill and Wang, pp. 13-21.
Reprints 1874.4.

4   KRONENBERGER, LOUIS. "The Best of Sheridan." Theatre Arts
41 (February): 29-30, 89-90.
Prints those portions of the introduction to Richard
Brinsley Sheridan, Six Plays (1957.5) treating of The
School for Scandal and The Critic. The School for Scandal
is a masterpiece of language, plotting, and pace, but is
"almost obstreperously fictional" (p. 30). It does not
unmask pretenses in such a way as to reveal human nature;
it rather allows its own characters to find out about one
another "in the nick of time" (p. 89). For all its grace
and sheen it is "simply a very brilliant stage piece,
superlative box-office comedy" (p. 89). For its part,
The Critic is "easily the best, which means also the most
playable, stage burlesque in the language" (p. 89).
Especially through its sideline commentary, it touches
what is eternal about stage production. "The School for
Scandal graces a distinguished tradition, but The
Critic stands alone" (p. 90).

5   _____. Introduction to Richard Brinsley Sheridan. Six
Plays. Mermaid Dramabook MD 5. New York: Hill and Wang,
pp. vii-xxi.
Surveys Sheridan's theatrical career, especially with
reference to the six plays printed (i.e., The Rivals, St.
Patrick's Day, The Duenna, A Trip to Scarborough, The
School for Scandal, and The Critic), after assessing his
talent generally: "a born feeling for situation and gift

for the spoken word," "an ample Irish inheritance of wit,"
"A sense of the great world," "a natural polish and
grace," "no striking intellectual development," "no
sudden deepening of perception or widening of scope."
He "put the theater ahead of life, the vivid effect
ahead of the revealing essence. His, accordingly, is a
view of human nature that is curiously undistinctive and
even shallow; his brilliance itself is only phrase deep"
(pp. vii-viii).

6   LANDFIELD, JEROME B. "Sheridan's Maiden Speech: Indictment
    by Anecdote." Quarterly Journal of Speech 43 (April):
    137-42.
        Examines the tradition that Sheridan's maiden speech
    in the House of Commons was unsuccessful, a tradition
    chiefly supported by the story that William Woodfall,
    the parliamentary reporter, told Sheridan after the
    speech that public speaking was not his line ("you had
    much better have stuck to your former pursuits"). In
    his biography of Sheridan (1825.9), Thomas Moore gives
    credit to this anecdote. The speech is not likely,
    however, to have been as bad as supposed. In that
    Sheridan was obliged in it to defend himself against
    charges of election fraud, he could not indulge high
    rhetorical flights. No doubt he also felt it best to
    show deference to the House, hoping to earn respect from
    colleagues who, because of his middling birth, were
    disposed to disfavor him. In purpose and circumstance
    the speech was properly subdued and therefore not highly
    celebrated. But it accomplished its aim because the
    charges giving rise to it were never substantiated by
    Sheridan's accuser, and Sheridan maintained his seat
    in Parliament.

7   MALONE, KEMP. "Meaningful Fictive Names in English
    Literature." Names 5 (1957): 1-13.
        Surveys "meaningful fictive names" in English
    literature from the seventh through the twentieth
    centuries using The School for Scandal as the
    eighteenth-century instance. In it the names of
    Rowley and Maria are the only ones not meaningful. All
    other characters mentioned or seen (from the prologue
    through the end of the play) have names somehow
    generically apposite: e.g., Lady Sneerwell, one good at
    sneering; Sir Peter Teazle, one equipped with verbal
    hooked prickles, recalling the prickly teazle plant;
    the Surfaces, people who "play a surface part that
    differs greatly from the reality beneath" (p. 10); the
    scandal group and all their victims (Backbite, Crabtree,

Candour, Gadabout, Flirt, Frizzle, Bowzie, Nicely, etc.),
representatives of a multitude of social peculiarities
and ills.

8   MATLAW, MYRON. "Adultery Analyzed: The History of The
    Stranger." Quarterly Journal of Speech 43 (February):
    22-28.
        Examines the century-long popularity of The Stranger
    and finds that its durability lay in its strong
    sentimentality, its appearance of being a problem play,
    the attraction it held for major actresses, its
    excellent construction (as sharpened by Sheridan), and
    its durable theme. "Mrs. Haller is the first in a
    line of famous modern women who have sinned for the
    edification of the public, and one of the few fictitious
    women who got away with it" (p. 28). What finally
    caused the play to pall were its pathetic language (as
    testified to by numerous burlesques) and the Stranger's
    own absurd Weltschmerz.

9   ____. "'This is Tragedy!!!'" The History of Pizarro."
    Quarterly Journal of Speech 43 (October): 288-94.
        Recounts details of the original great success of
    Pizzaro then traces the irrepressible vogue of the play
    through the nineteenth century. The original craze had
    capitalized on a new taste in England for German
    melodrama and on a nationalistic defiance of Napoleon's
    threats of invasion. Continuing success derived from
    the five strong roles offered by the play, from the
    powerful sentimental appeal made by it, from its
    celebration of the noble savage, and from its vast
    exciting spectacle. It finally failed because it added
    so few lasting artistic qualities to this spectacle--no
    timeless characters and themes--and because the bombast
    and fustian of its dialogue assailed the patience of
    theatregoers.

10 MOORE, JOHN ROBERT. "Lydia Languish's Library." Notes
    and Queries, n. s. 4 (February): 76.
        Raises the possibility that Sheridan included The Whole
    Duty of Man in Lydia Languish's library less because of
    a new edition of it published in 1773 (as G. H. Nettleton
    surmises--1906.3) than because of passages in two works
    of Defoe's still current in the 1770s: Religious Courtship
    and The Family Instructor. In the first of these a
    husband chides his wife for having "Chevy Chase" bound
    into her prayer book (cf. Lydia's hiding The Innocent
    Adultery inside The Whole Duty of Man). In the second
    a mother had destroyed her daughter's sentimental and

licentious books and replaced then with The Practice of
Piety and The Whole Duty of Man. Sheridan would logically
have been attracted to these episodes, particularly to
the semidramatic form in which Defoe presents them.

11 SHERBO, ARTHUR. English Sentimental Drama. East Lansing:
Michigan State University Press, pp. 84-85, 158-62.
Touches Sheridan in two respects. The first one
(pp. 84-85) confronts the enigma of the Julia-Faulkland
plot in The Rivals (Should it be read comically or
seriously?) and concludes that dramatic history provides
no sure answer. The second one mentions the popularity of
Sheridan's plays as suggesting a taste (between 1773-1780)
for non-sentimental plays and, in general, for variety in
theatrical fare.

12 SHERIDAN, CLARE [CONSUELO]. To the Four Winds. London:
Andre Deutsch, p. 304.
Includes brief reference to the sailing mishap in 1935
which resulted in the loss at sea of the original
manuscripts of The Critic, The Duenna, St. Patrick's Day,
and Pizarro. The accident occurred in the Mediterranean
while the author's son, Richard Brinsley Sheridan, was
sailing alone on his yacht the Clapotis from Algiers to
England. He managed to swim ashore, but the manuscripts
sank with the boat.

13 WEBSTER, MARGARET. "A Look at the London Season: The
Rivals," Theatre Arts 41 (May): 25-26.
Admires a production of The Rivals at the Saville
Theatre in 1956, noticing especially the performances
of John Clements, as Sir Anthony, who endowed his
character with "humanity and heart," and Paul Doneman,
who, as Faulkland ("one of the most difficult parts ever
written"), achieved a "beautiful mixture of satire and
comprehension" (p. 26). "You don't laugh if you don't
care," and, in the case of this production, "audiences
did both" (p. 26).

1958

1   ANON. "Notes and News." Bodleian Library Record 6
(February): 393.
Announces acquisition of some 200 Sheridan items
through the gift of M. Bertram Shuttleworth, who "has
been collecting Sheridan for many years and has built
up the finest collection of the dramatist's work in
private hands in the country." Included in the gift

are a first edition (Dublin, 1780) of <u>The School for Scandal</u>, music for the songs in the plays, and some separate speeches from the plays, e.g., Rolla's defiance of the invaders in <u>Pizarro</u>, which was printed in Dublin and London in 1803 (during the Napoleonic threat) under the title "Sheridan's Address to the People."

2   HOPPER, VINCENT F. AND LAHEY, GERALD B., eds. Introduction to <u>The Rivals</u>, by Sheridan. Great Neck, N.Y.: Barrons Educational Series, pp. 9-44.

Sketches Sheridan's life and career, characterizing his plays as continuations of Goldsmith's crusade to stem the tide of sentimentality in English drama. Provides notes on staging, especially admonishing contemporary producers to keep in mind the dominant features of eighteenth-century production: "The elegant everyday dress, the <u>a vista</u> scene change (which probably groaned and creaked enormously) the lighted auditorium and above all the artificial quality of the painted wings and flats" (p. 44).

3.   _____. Introduction to <u>The School for Scandal</u>, by Sheridan. Great Neck, N.Y.: Barron's Educational Series, pp. 9-38.

Analyzes the play by examining three components: (1) the activities of the scandal club, (2) the domestic conflicts of the Teazles, and (3) the fortunes of the Surface brothers. Despite shows of antisentimentality, the play is clearly sentimental in tone and attitude, exalting charity and benevolence in the characters of Sir Oliver, Maria, Charles, and Sir Peter and Lady Teazle. The comments on biography and staging duplicate those in the Barron Educational Series issue of <u>The Rivals</u> (1958.2).

4   LANDFIELD, JEROME BLANCHARD. "The Speeches of Richard Brinsley Sheridan against Warren Hastings." <u>Dissertation Abstracts International</u> 19 (December): 1474-75 (Missouri).

Describes a study in which Sheridan's speeches against Warren Hastings (especially those of 1787 and 1788) are closely examined as to concept, presentation, and response. The speeches give evidence of having extensive literary and rhetorical range. "Sheridan has suffered in comparison with Pitt, Burke, and Fox because his public stature suffered more from imperfections of character. As a statesman, he is probably not in the same class, yet for sheer talent in speaking, he is. The powers of communication exhibited by these four men distinguish them as the foremost speakers of their time, and Sheridan seems rightly to belong to this exclusive group" (p. 1475).

5   PRICE, CECIL. "Hymen and Hirco: A Vision." Times Literary
     Supplement, 11 July, p. 396.
        Nominates Sheridan as the author of a satiric poem,
     "Hymen and Hirco," which appeared in the Bath Chronicle
     for 9 May 1771, obviously attacking the conduct of a
     fifty-nine-year-old Wiltshire squire, Walter Long, who
     was rumored to have broken his engagement with Elizabeth
     Linley, the future Mrs. Sheridan, because she refused
     to sleep with him before marriage. The evidence derives
     from a letter written to Sheridan by Lewis Ker, once
     his tutor and still his literary adviser, acknowledging
     receipt of a satiric poem by Sheridan ("your piece of
     the Chronicle") just one week after the poem appeared.
     Since eventually Walter Long settled 3,000 pounds on
     Elizabeth--the money assumed by Moore to have furnished her
     dowry of 1,000 pounds--Sheridan perhaps thought it best not
     to acknowledge authorship of the poem, seeing himself,
     through his marriage, as the beneficiary of Long's
     conciliatory gift.

6   WOEHL, ARTHUR L. "Richard Brinsley Sheridan,
     Parliamentarian." In The Rhetorical Idiom: Essays in
     Rhetoric Oratory, Language, and Drama. Presented to
     Herbert August Wichelns, with a Reprinting of His
     "Literary Criticism of Oratory [1925]," edited by Donald
     Cross Bryant. Ithaca, N.Y.: Cornell University Press,
     pp. 221-49.
        Surveys Sheridan's career in Parliament, emphasizing
     the more famous moments: e.g., the maiden speech, the
     repartee comparing Pitt to Jonson's angry boy (1783),
     Sheridan's continuing philosophical and oratorical
     opposition to Pitt, his intercession in behalf of the
     Prince and Mrs. Fitzherbert, the speeches against Hastings,
     the ultimate rift with Burke, the efforts at parliamentary
     reform, his decisive response to the naval mutinies of
     1799. Byron's tribute ("Whatever Sheridan has done or
     chosen to do has been, par excellence, always the best
     of its kind") closes the essay.

1959

1   ANON. "Cameo View on Sheridan. Spirited School for Scandal."
     Times (London), 29 July, p. 11.
        Observes that Sheridan's type of comedy depends for
     comic effect upon "unity of spectacle" but that what was
     sacrificed of such unity in a recent television production

1959

of The School for Scandal was compensated for by a
technique of presenting the main characters in "vivid
cameos" rather than in "group portrait." In general,
then, the production, directed by Hal Burton, was
successful.

2   ANON. "Prokofiev Opera from Sheridan." Times (London),
16 March, p. 3.
Reports (dateline Moscow, 14 March) that "The opera
Betrothal in a Convent, by Mr. Sergei Prokofiev, has had
its premiere in the opera studio of the Moscow
Conservatoire, the Soviet news agency Tass reported.
The opera is based on a play by Sheridan."

3   ANON. "R. A. D. A. Students Act in Switzerland." Times
(London), 8 December, p. 4.
Notes that performances of The School for Scandal given
in Geneva by the Royal Academy of Dramatic Art mark the
play's first appearances in Switzerland in the original
language. Before this production, it had been represented
in Geneva by "A French adaptation by René Louis Piachaud."

4   ANON. "Tragedy of Getting What One Wants." Times (London),
2 March, p. 12.
Describes a double bill at Eton College in which The
Critic is combined with Marlowe's Doctor Faustus. At the
end of The Critic Puff discovers that his own play must
make way for Doctor Faustus, which is to be rehearsed by
the company of players who have just performed it. This
is a clever device, but, in general, the staging of The
Critic moved too slowly for effectiveness.

5   PRICE, CECIL. "The Text of the First Performance of The
Duenna." Bibliographical Society of America Papers 53
(3d quarter): 268-70.
Argues that the edition of 1794--said by Crompton
Rhodes to be the version of The Duenna first acted--is
not in fact the first acted version. Critical notices
in the Morning Chronicle and the Morning Post for 22
November 1775 mention several witticisms thought offensive
to taste, and the 1794 issue contains only one of the
witticisms mentioned. Several others of them do appear
in Fraser Rae's edition of the play (1902), suggesting
that his version is closer to the original than the
issue of 1794. The omissions from the 1794 text indicate
Sheridan's usual practice of removing from later
performances passages offensive to first-night critics.

1960

1   ANON. "No Reason to Neglect Sheridan." Times (London),
    14 April, p. 15.
        Suggests that recent British revivals have favored
    Restoration playwrights over Sheridan because he makes
    his moral points too plainly. Yet the sheer entertainment
    value of such a play as The School for Scandal justifies
    its continuing place in the repertory. Such values
    override the play's moral overdirectness.

2   DE SELINCOURT, AUBREY. "Sheridan." In Six Great Playwrights:
    Sophocles, Shakespeare, Molière, Sheridan, Ibsen, and Shaw.
    London: Hamish Hamilton, pp. 105-31.
        Identifies Sheridan not as a great playwright but as
    a "blameless" one, one good of his kind. His reputation
    rests upon "two slight comedies and one amusing skit"
    (p. 105). The first of these, The Rivals, is "a bubble--a
    nothing" (p. 117). It lacks roots in reality and lives
    on its irrepressible gaiety. It is "cut flowers" (p. 119)
    made of "laughter which is wholly devoid of irony and
    leaves no sting" (p. 118). The second of them, The
    School for Scandal, does not, like the greatest comedies,
    "illuminate the heart" with laughter, but it does
    "present a picture of a certain aspect of society with
    unsurpassed brilliance and precision" (p. 122). It
    provokes more "inward laughter" (p. 123) than The Rivals
    does and is better plotted. The third of them, The
    Critic, is as high-spirited as The Rivals, and reads
    like a glorified charade" (p. 126). It is Sheridan's
    last notable effort.

3   GALE, CEDRIC, ed. Preface to The Rehearsal, as Performed at
    the Theatre Royal, Drury Lane to Which Is Added a Key, or
    Critical View of the Authors and Their Writings Exposed
    in This Play, by S. Briscoe, 1704; and Richard Brinsley
    Sheridan, The Critic, or A Tragedy Rehearsed, A Dramatic
    Piece in Three Acts as Performed at the Theatre Royal in
    Drury Lane. Great Neck, N.Y.: Barron's Educational
    Series, pp. 5-20.
        Places the two plays in historical contexts and draws
    contrasts between them. The Critic "differs from The
    Rehearsal in manner and spirit." It is "Broader than
    The Rehearsal and more diffuse." Its satire is "scattered
    and soft," and it "has an air of geniality and a delight
    in foolishness that lessens its sting" (p. 16). Although
    most of its satire is general, it aims at a few specific
    targets: John James Hamilton, Hugh Kelly, John Philip
    Kemble, and especially Richard Cumberland, whose

1960

character is authentically burlesqued in Sir Fretful
Plagiary.

4   JOHNSON, MAURICE. "Charles Surface and Shaw's Heroines."
     Shaw Review 3 (May): 27-28.
          Suggests that Shaw's liberated heroines should be seen
     as Sheridan's Charles Surface rendered as women. The
     suggestion rests on a theatrical review of 1896 in which
     Shaw observes that "If you want to bring 'The School for
     Scandal' up to date you must make Charles a woman, and
     Joseph a perfectly sincere moralist" (see 1896.17).
     Like Charles, such characters as Candida and Anne
     Whitefield are "philandering, extravagant, and endearing"
     (p. 27). If such characters are to be persuasive, they
     must be played attractively, for through them Shaw
     demonstrates that the double standard of sexual conduct
     allowed by Sheridan is not applicable to his own view of
     morality.

5   LeFANU, WILLIAM, ed. Betsy Sheridan's Journal: Letters
     from Sheridan's Sister, 1784-1786 and 1788-1790. London:
     Eyre and Spottiswoode; New Brunswick: Rutgers University
     Press, 223 pp.
          Prints seventy-one letters written by one of Sheridan's
     sisters (Elizabeth) to the other (Alicia) during the
     former's stays in London between 1784-1786 and 1788-1790.
     The earlier stay, during which she kept house for her
     father, concerns itself chiefly with him--his lectures
     and writing and his quarrels with Richard. The later
     stay, during which she lived with Richard and Eliza,
     enters the life of Sheridan's own household during
     significant political moments--chiefly the first Regency
     Crisis--and elucidates many of Sheridan's political and
     social relationshps, including his liaisons with Lady
     Duncannon. The whole opens insights into his private
     and public ambiences, but particularly the private ones.
     Reviewed by Mary Motley in Twentieth Century 158 (October):
     371-73; in Times (London), 18 August, p. 11; in Times
     Literary Supplement, 26 August, p. 543; by Sir Charles
     Petrie in Illustrated London News 237 (3 September): 386;
     by Colin Haycraft in Spectator 205 (7 October): 533; by
     Margaret Lane in New Statesman 60 (8 October): 539; by
     DeLancey Ferguson in New York Herald Tribune Book Review,
     26 February 1961, p. 34; by Jean Dulck in Études
     Anglaises 14 (1961): 248-49; by William Plomer in
     Listener 64 (1961): 389.

6   MARSHOVA, NATAL'IA MATVEENA. Richard Brinsli Sheridan, 1751-
     1816. Mockba: Iskussto, 122 pp.

206

Carries in Stratman's <u>Restoration and Eighteenth-Century Theatre Research</u> (1971.9, item 5749) the annotation "A short but documented biography in Russian."

7   MATLAW, MYRON. "<u>Menschenhass und Reue</u> in English." <u>Symposium</u> 14 (Summer): 129-34.

Gives a chronological account of the English renderings of Kotzebue's play, citing versions by George Papendick (1793), Schink (1797), Benjamin Thompson (1798), and (in New York) William Dunlop (1798), who also translated Kotzebue's own unsuccessful sequel in 1800. In preparing an acting version (<u>The Stranger</u>) for Drury Lane, Sheridan adapted the literal translation by Benjamin Thompson. He "abridged or omitted those scenes and speeches which were repetitious, those which were superfluous and detrimental to the development of the plot, and those which were excessively sentimental" (p. 131). He added a few "musical and pastoral interludes" (p. 131) which amplified the appeal of a play already popular for its controversial theme.

8   O'CONNELL, RICHARD B. "Gorostiza's <u>Contigo, pan y cebolla</u> and Sheridan's <u>The Rivals</u>." <u>Hispania</u> 43 (September): 384-87.

Argues that the Spanish play is clearly influenced by the English one, its author having spent a number of years (after 1833) in England and having achieved idiomatic mastery of the language. Both plays treat of a young girl whose suitor must disguise himself to accommodate her sentimental notions. Both plays ridicule the ill-effects of sentimental novels. The Spanish play is not, however, merely a slavish imitation of the English. "By shifting the emphasis from the winning of the girl to the process of her disillusionment with the view of life she had acquired from the novels she had read, Gorostiza goes beyond imitation and creates a new play" (p. 387).

9   SEN, SAILENDRA KUMAR. "Sheridan's Literary Debt: <u>The Rivals</u> and <u>Humphry Clinker</u>." <u>Modern Language Quarterly</u> 21 (December): 291-300.

Answers critics who charge Sheridan with plagiarism by observing that Sheridan's comedies are the last great English comedies of a classical stamp and that classical comedy depends for its effects upon generalized character types. Mrs. Malaprop, however, is not a typical character, and she can be shown to originate in Frances Sheridan's play <u>A Journey to Bath</u>. <u>The Rivals</u> also show debts to Smollett's <u>Humphry Clinker</u>, paralleling

1960

the novel in several distinct situations (e.g., an aunt
pretending to the suitor of a niece, a braggart suddenly
afflicted with cowardice, a challenge given and answered
without cause). Sheridan is to be charged only with
these debts, and they, especially those to Smollett, were
probably not deliberate. Ironically, they have the
general effect of interfering with the "ordered evolution
of the plot" (p. 300) of the play.

10 SHERWIN, OSCAR. Uncorking Old Sherry: The Life and Times of
    Richard Brinsley Sheridan. New York: Twayne Publishers,
    352 pp.
        Sets Sheridan's life against a backdrop of his age. It
    is an age of drinking, gambling, debt, money-worship,
    conversation, scandal, literature, color and costume,
    elopements, duels, intrigues, "a carnival of the animal
    man in which leading roles are played by Sheridan and
    his circle" (p. 38). Sheridan's literary career is
    "merely a stepping stone to political renown," for "The
    stage of the House of Commons appeals to a larger
    audience than that of Drury Lane" (p. 137) and "The
    House of Commons is the theatre of the country" (p. 11).
    In work and play, Sheridan is usually "brimming over with
    fun" (p. 297), and the best assessment of his life is
    that given by Lord Byron to Thomas Moore in 1818:
    "Without means, without connexion, without character
    (which might be false at first, and made him mad
    afterwards from desperation), he beat them all, in all
    her ever attempted. But alas° poor human nature"!
    (p. 338) Reviewed by Charles Poore in New York Times,
    17 November, p. 5; in Times Literary Supplement,
    24 February 1961, p. 118; in Times (London), 9 March 1961,
    p. 15; by Jerome Landfield in Quarterly Journal of Speech
    47 (October 1961): 317-18.

11 STYAN, J. L. "Tempo and Meaning." In The Elements of
    Drama. Cambridge: Cambridge University Press, pp. 141-62.
        Demonstrates that "precise and startling effects of
    tempo are easier in a play which moves at some distance
    from real life" (p. 154) by analyzing the quarrel
    between Sir Peter and Lady Teazle in act 3, scene 1 of
    The School for Scandal, where "Sheridan's object is to
    give us a magnified preposterous portrait of how quarrels
    may come and go in married life" (p. 155). The pace of
    the scene moves slowly through a series of reminiscences,
    accelerates through a series of shaded insults, builds
    in pace, pitch, and tone as tentative harmony gives place
    to disagreement. "It is the tempo that speaks to us.
    The image is made to expand by shrinking the time that

would naturally elapse in a real quarrel" (p. 157).

12   TRAINER, JAMES. "Tieck's Translation of The Rivals."
     Modern Language Quarterly 21 (September): 246-52.
        Suggests that students of Ludwig Tieck should give close
     attention to his translation of The Rivals, a work
     undertaken in 1850, the last of his translations from
     English, and never published. Going beyond mere
     substitution of German words for English ones, it offers
     to recreate "the mood and spirit of the play in a
     German environment" (p. 248). The rendering of
     malapropisms is not uniformly successful, but the
     character of Mrs. Malaprop seems to have influenced the
     language of the garrulous Barbe in Tieck's novel Der
     Aufruhr in den Cevennen, just as other features of The
     Rivals had influenced a comedy written by Tieck when he
     was only sixteen. The spirit of Sheridan was with him
     early and late.

1961

1   Anon. "Charm of Miss Fay Compton. A Brilliant Mrs.
     Malaprop." Times (London), 15 November, p. 19.
        Applauds a revival of The Rivals ("young Sheridan's
     apprentice play") at the Pembroke Theatre, Croydon, and
     especially admires, in addition to Miss Fay Compton's
     Mrs. Malaprop, the use of stage movement to compensate
     for the play's lack of genuine "dramatic evolution."

2   ANON. "A Distinguished Cast." Times (London), 8 December,
     p. 17.
        Announces the opening at the New Theatre, Oxford, of
     John Gielgud's Tennent production of The School for
     Scandal, featuring Sir Ralph Richardson as Sir Peter
     Teazle, Anna Massey as Lady Teazle, Margaret Rutherford
     as Mrs. Candour, and actors of comparable excellence in
     the other roles. The production will visit Liverpool,
     Newcastle, and Brighton before going to London.

3   ANON. "German Festival with a Strong British Flavour."
     Times (London), 21 June, p. 15.
        Gives a general survey of the Schwetzingen Festival,
     in which The School for Scandal is the "festival play"
     (see 1961.4). Other British offerings include Benjamin
     Britten's opera A Midsummer Night's Dream as performed
     by the English Opera Group.

4   ANON. "German View of Sheridan's Masterpiece." Times

1961

(London), 1 June, p. 6.

Agrees with those who say that The School for Scandal,
so often revived through the years, needs restudying and
finds in a new German production, performed at
Schwetzingen, some interesting new perspectives on the
play. This German adaptation combines the roles of Snake
and Moses, giving both to Snake, and subjects Charles to
severer deprivations than even Sheridan heaps upon him.
It robs him of all his friends except Jack Ford, who
substitutes for Sheridan's Careless, and a yet more daring
change gives the roles of both Charles and Joseph to the
same actor, a concept compatible with the view that the
two brothers represent two sides of the same character.

5   ANON. "Sheridan As Party Piece." Times (London),
      16 November, p. 14.
      Pronounces The School for Scandal an apt choice for
celebrating the golden jubilee of the Liverpool Repertory
Theatre because it lacks essential seriousness and enables
the players to play "to" the audience "in a manner in
keeping with the party spirit" of the occasion.

6   FISKE, ROGER. "A Score for 'The Duenna.'" Music and Letters
      42 (April): 132-41.
      Lists musical items constituting most of the orchestral
and vocal score of The Duenna. The contributions of Thomas
Linley, Jr. amount to more than a quarter of the whole.
These scores are collected in Egerton MS 2493 at the
British Museum. Other scores derive from published issues
of melodies accommodated to Sheridan's libretto from
popular and traditional songs. From such sources the
musicologist can reconstruct in authentic form the
orchestration of the original opera and can thus restore
a grievous loss. The vocal score survives in five
distinct editions of the opera published between 1775 and
1835, but the orchestral score and parts have heretofore
been out of reach.

7   JACKSON, J. R. de J. "The Importance of Witty Dialogue in
      The School for Scandal." Modern Language Notes 76
      (November): 601-7.
      Illustrates "ways in which Sheridan's dialogue has a
determining effect upon the dramatic action of The School
for Scandal" (p. 606). As the dialogue found in the early
draft manuscripts of The School for Scandal finds its way
into the finished play, four effects come to light: (1)
whole pieces of dialogue are transferred from one
character to another, suggesting that at least some of the
dialogue has no relevance to the plot; (2) inconsistencies

in characterization result from the practice of giving
dialogue originally written for one character to another
not really suited to it; (3) characters are modified
through the process of polishing the original language;
and (4) the practice of salvaging favorite aphorisms
controls the whole tone and emphasis of certain dramatic
scenes. "A preoccupation with witty sayings and brilliant
dialogue seems to account for both the unique virtues and
the special faults of The School for Scandal" (p. 607).

8   KNAPP, MARY E[TTA]. Prologues and Epilogues of the Eighteenth
     Century. New Haven: Yale University Press, passim.
        Includes consideration of Sheridan's prologues and
     epilogues--among hundreds of prologues and epilogues
     of the eighteenth century--in deducing the conventions
     of the genre.

9   LANDFIELD, JEROME. "The Triumph and Failure of Sheridan's
     Speeches against Hastings." Speech Monographs 28
     (August): 143-56.
        Offers five reasons why Sheridan's first two speeches
     against Hastings, "though they created an immediate
     sensation" (p. 143), failed to achieve lasting applause:
     (1) the issue of India was overshadowed by the profounder
     issues of the American and French revolutions; (2) the
     complex detail of Sheridan's arguments dulled and curtailed
     real interest in his speeches; (3) the style of the
     speeches, while immediately moving, did not achieve
     universal appeal; (4) the texts, being faultily reported,
     misrepresented Sheridan's words and sentiments; and (5)
     "the decline in admiration for Sheridan's character both
     contributed to and was caused by a dimmer view of the
     two speeches" (p. 154).

10   MOTLEY, MARY. Morning Glory. London: Longmans, Green,
     pp. 272-74.
        Describes the loss of valuable Sheridan manuscripts in
     a boating accident off the coast of Algiers in 1935 (cf.
     1957.12). Mary Motley, the comtesse de Reneville, is the
     daughter of Clare Sheridan and the sister of the young
     adventurer, Richard Brinsley Sheridan, whose sailing
     mishap lost the manuscripts.

11   n., g. "Kritische Ruckschau." Neues Forum 8 (December):
     454.
        Observes of The School for Scandal that it expresses
     its author's universal good will by refusing to vilify
     anyone. Even its worst character, Joseph Surface, redeems
     himself by an exhilarating wit.

1961

12   PRICE, CECIL. "The Columbia Manuscript of <u>The School for</u>
      <u>Scandal</u>." <u>Columbia Library Columns</u> 11, no. 1 (1961):
      25-29.
           Suggests that a manuscript now in the Columbia
      University Libraries might reflect refinements made by
      Sheridan himself <u>after</u> the preparation of the Georgetown
      Crewe MS of <u>The School for Scandal</u>. Although unfinished
      and copied in five separate hands, the Columbia MS
      probably dates to a period later than the Crewe MS.
      Watermarks on two pages of the manuscript place the sheets
      in the late eighteenth century. A third watermark
      belongs to the early nineteenth century. If the Crewe MS
      represents a date earlier than 1792 (as is likely in
      relation to the period of Sheridan's closest friendship
      with the Crewes), then it dates to a time earlier than
      Sheridan's declaration to James Ridgway, the publisher,
      that the play did not yet satisfy the playwright's own
      taste, a statement made after 1796. The Columbia MS,
      possibly the work of copyists in Sheridan's own prompter's
      department, might very well contain changes authorized
      by Sheridan well after the date of the Crewe MS.

13   REINERT, OTTO. "<u>The Rivals</u>. Comment." In <u>Drama: An</u>
      <u>Introductory Anthology</u>. Alternate Edition. Boston:
      Little, Brown, pp. 382-87.
           Roots the exuberant fun of <u>The Rivals</u> in its
      love-masquerading, its social and literary satire, and
      its variegated language. Although slight in structure
      and in moral substance, it is yet "intelligent and
      graceful farce, scintillating with fun and wit, and
      radiant with romantic joy" (p. 387), a play to be
      identified with Goldsmith's <u>She Stoops to Conquer</u> in
      many of its comic qualities, especially in the very motif
      itself of "stooping to conquer."

14   SHARP, WILLIAM L., ed. Introduction to <u>The School for</u>
      <u>Scandal</u>, by Sheridan. Chandler Editions in Drama. San
      Francisco: Chandler Publishing, pp. vii-xiii.
           Accedes to the view that Sheridan reveals little
      "mature or intelligent perception of the world" (p. vii),
      that he is sentimental and superficial, but
      acknowledges his absolute mastery of drama as a visual
      and verbal art form. "One enjoys Sheridan not because
      of what he says but because of the way he says it"
      (p. xiii).

1962

1   ANON. "Easy Elegance in Sheridan." <u>Times</u> (London),
    22 January, p. 5.
        Commends Hal Burton's adaptation of <u>The Rivals</u> for
television but acknowledges that several problems of
adaptation were not solved by Burton: in cutting the
text for performance in one hundred minutes, he so
reduced the "elaborations" of the action as to reveal
that nothing really lies behind them. And in cutting
the lines of Sir Anthony and Sir Lucius (who are valid
comic figures) while not cutting those of Mrs. Malaprop
(who is a "mechanical comic device"), he made large
sacrifices.

2   ANON. "Kensington Palace, May 30." <u>Times</u> (London),
    31 May, p. 14.
        Announces that the duchess of Kent, Princess Marina,
had attended a performance of <u>The School for Scandal</u> at
the Haymarket Theatre given in aid of the National
Benevolent Institution, of which the princess is a
patron.

3   BOR, MARGOT AND LAMOND CLELLAND. <u>Still the Lark. A</u>
    <u>Biography of Elizabeth Linley</u>. Lonond: Merlin Press,
    185 pp.
        Recounts the lives of the Linleys, centering the
narrative upon Elizabeth, who fell victim to the romantic
persuasions of Sheridan. Her fame and brilliance
reinforced his affection for her, especially when he
considered the benefits their marriage might bring to
his career as a writer. While his ambitions for social
status brought her career as a singer to a close, it is
to be assumed that the musicales given in their drawing
room on Orchard Street were in fact concerts subscribed
to by people of fashion. Money no doubt came into the
Sheridan household through them. Sheridan's absorption
in his career and his attention to ladies of fashion
contributed to Eliza's gradual addiction to gambling
and eventually to her indiscretion with Lord Edward
Fitzgerald, by whom she gave birth to her daughter Mary
on 30 March 1792, just three months before her own
death on 28 June. Sheridan's inordinate grief at the
loss of her (and at the loss of the infant Mary on
26 November) suggests that "he had come to realize
Eliza's worth too late"; but "His sorrow over Eliza was
short-lived" (p. 165), for a few months later he proposed
marriage to Pamela, ward to Madame de Genlis. Pamela,
however, eventually married Lord Edward Fitzgerald.

1962

Reviewed in Times Literary Supplement, 1 February 1963, p. 74.

4   BRUSTEIN, ROBERT. "At Work and Play with the APA." New Republic 146 (14 May): 37-38.
        Comments upon The School for Scandal as one of several plays recently staged by the Association of Producing Artists. Observing that the APA is perhaps "primarily qualified for works which do not demand much emotional depth" (p. 38), the reviewer admires this production of The School for Scandal, especially applauding the Screen Scene which "moved with such vigor, invention, style, and surprise that the entire producton was redeemed" (p. 38).

5   CAMDEN, CARROLL. "Songs and Chorusses in The Tempest." Philological Quarterly 41 (January): 114-22.
        Describes an undated leaflet, Songs and Chorusses in The Tempest, now in the collection of the Fondren Library, Rice University, and suggests that two of the eleven songs contained in it are the work of Sheridan (the other nine being Shakespeare's own songs or songs prepared for Garrick's operatic adaptation of the play in 1756). Since the songs appearing in the collection do not correspond entirely with those in Garrick's version, and since they do not correspond with those in John Philip Kemble's later musical version of the play (1789), they might well be the songs of Sheridan's "last" version of 1777, a successful revival staged in the first year of his theatrical management. Some bowdlerizations of the Shakespearean originals recall, furthermore, the bowdlerizations of Vanbrugh in A Trip to Scarborough. "Songs and Chorusses was probably prepared for free distribution in 1777" (p. 121).

6   DAVIES, ALAN. "Plays in Production: VII. The Rivals." The Use of English 14 (Winter): 91-94.
        Advances the theory that a good play needs no apology and declares that a production of The Rivals staged at a preparatory school for boys in Kenya was unsuccessful not because it lacked fluency, pace, and characterization but because the play had to be apologized for. Unlike earlier productions of Everyman, Macbeth, and Henry the Fifth, it impressed no lasting meaning on the audiences who saw it. "I shan't be able to justify Sheridan again; he needs an apology and, as we know, 'a good play needs no epilogue'" (p. 94).

7   DEELMAN, CHRISTIAN. "The Original Cast of The School for Scandal." Review of English Studies, n.s. 13 (1962):

214

257-66.

Demonstrates that Sheridan shaped the characters of
The School for Scandal to the personalities and abilities
of his cast. In three instances--the roles of Joseph and
Charles Surface and of Trip (as played by John Palmer,
William Smith, and Philip La Mash respectively)--he took
inspiration from the actual characters and personalities
of his actors, shaping the fiction to fit the fact. In
the remaining instances he provided roles best suited
to the tested skills of the cast. Only one role failed
to receive high critical praise, the role of Maria as
played by Priscilla Hopkins. It was originally designed
for Perdita Robinson, who had to decline it because of a
pregnancy.

8   DELPECH, JEANINE. "Sheridan, le Beaumarchais anglais." Les
     Nouvelles littéraires, no. 1811 (17 May): 3.
          Sketches the life and career of Sheridan after first
     noticing his resemblances to Beaumarchais in vitality,
     prodigality, and especially in his desire to shine in
     the great world, a world of wealth and fashion into
     which he was not born. Achieving celebrity at a younger
     age than Beaumarchais had done, Sheridan claims credit,
     through The School for Scandal, for displaying the last
     flash of brilliance which, at the end of the eighteenth
     century, was to precede a long night in English dramatic
     history.

9   DONALDSON, IAN. "New Papers of Henry Holland and R. B.
     Sheridan. (I) Holland's Drury Lane, 1794." Theatre
     Notebook 16 (Spring): 90-96.
          Finds, in a newly discovered correspondence between
     Sheridan and the architect Henry Holland (letters written
     between 1791-1805), evidence to conclude that responsibil-
     ity for the excessive cost of the new Drury Lane Theatre
     and even for the fire that destroyed it in 1809 lay
     principally with Sheridan himself. When problems in
     settling the patent delayed construction of the new house,
     Sheridan immediately encountered unexpected expenses; and
     when he insisted, once construction got underway, that
     time be made up and money saved, he aggravated new
     expenses and reduced both the safety and structural
     integrity of the building. So repeatedly did Holland
     remind him of these deficiencies that he could not really
     have been surprised when the theater burned less than
     fifteen years after it was completed.

10   _____. "New Papers of Henry Holland and R. B. Sheridan: (II)
     The Hyde Park Corner Operas and the Dormant Patent."

1962

Theatre Notebook 16 (Summer): 117-25.
Deduces from the newly found papers of Henry Holland, architect of Drury Lane Theatre, that Sheridan purchased the so-called "dormant" theatrical patent from the managers of Covent Garden Theatre not to establish legitimacy of the new Drury Lane Theatre, whose patent had been lost, but to secure the theatrical monopoly. An earlier plan to secure the monopoly had proposed that an auxiliary theater (or, as later proposed, an opera house) be built at Hyde Park Corner, that it be established on the dormant patent, and that the two patented theaters manage it jointly. But Sheridan apparently thought the purchase of the dormant patent to be the best plan for securing the interests of Drury Lane Theatre, and he made the purchase without telling the subscribers to the new theater precisely why he had done so. Subsequent theatrical history proves that his action in behalf of the monopoly was not a wise one.

11   DULCK, JEAN. Les Comédies de R. B. Sheridan: Étude
littéraire. Études anglaise, no. 12. Paris: Didier,
611 pp.
Opens with a detailed examination of the status of English comedy in 1775: the Elizabethan and Jacobean heritage, the influences of Ben jonson, of Moliere, of the Restoration playwrights, the destructive force of sentimentality, the variety of comic types. Proceeds to an examination of Sheridan's personality, noticing it to be a composite of many dispositions but dominated by a duality of serious and comic tempers. Next, separate chapters discuss each of the comedies in turn, providing comment on sources, circumstances of composition, first performances, and receptions. The Rivals is seen to synthesize Elizabethan, Restoration, and contemporary comic attributes, showing Sheridan to be neither an innovator nor a revolutionary but a remarkably supple and adaptable beginner. St. Patrick's Day blends the French tradition of Molière with the English tradition of Ben Jonson, adding to the repertoire of farce an element of importance (élément de valeur). The Duenna evinces Sheridan's fertility of invention, his maturing grasp of the whole dramatic metier, and his knowledge of public taste. A Trip to Scarborough shows his kinship of temperament with Vanbrugh and thus with the great continuum of English comedy. In The School for Scandal he rises to his full powers, clearly in control of the methods and problems of his art. And in The Critic he achieves the fulfillment of a genre and the culmination of a career the more distinctive for having explored so large a

variety of comic forms. General chapters study the
principles of form in his works, his characters (which,
more than life itself, reveal vitality), his depiction
of manners (which generates laughter out of the
complexities and contradictions of his life), his comic
(which always promotes a sense of liberation), and his
style. Appendixes (1) tabulate types and numbers of
plays performed in London between 1660 and 1800, (2)
list the plays performed at Drury Lane during Sheridan's
management, (3) chronicle the history of Drury Lane from
1663 to 1812, (4) provide French renderings of Sheridan's
characters' names, and (5) list nineteenth-century London
revivals of Sheridan's comedies. Reviewed by Louis
Lanoix in Les Langues Modernes 57 (1963): 220-22; by
Cecil Price in Études Anglaises 16 (1964); 392-94; by
Ian Donaldson in Review of English Studies, n.s. 16
(1965): 108-9.

12   HEWES, HENRY. "Surface Comparisons." Saturday Review
       45 (28 April): 38.
          Compares John Gielgud's British revival of The School
       for Scandal with Ellis Rabb's American one (through the
       Association of Producing Artists) and finds the American
       cast devoted too much to affecting the mannerisms of the
       period, to merely "finishing off a delivery," a problem
       not encountered by British actors, who can concentrate
       upon the "inception" of a sentiment or motive, taking
       for granted "style and verbal facility."

13   KNIGHT, G. WILSON. The Golden Labyrinth: a Study of British
       Drama. London: Phoenix House, pp. 183-88.
          Places Sheridan within "the golden age of our national
       comedy" (p. 188), an age in which comedy forewent "sex
       wit and literary finesse" (p. 188) in favor of human value,
       normality, and warmth. "It is sex friendly and sex warm,
       as the other was not" (p. 188). As gifted as Sheridan
       was in adopting tried theatrical themes and conventions
       to his purpose, he did not, even in The Rivals, have to
       resort to caricature. His way was simply to allow us
       to "watch the normal springing to life under comic
       emphasis" (p. 184).

14   LANDFIELD, JEROME. "Sheridan." In "After Goodrich: New
       Resources in British Public Address–A Symposium," edited
       by Donald C. Bryant. Quarterly Journal of Speech 48
       (February): 5-7.
          Assesses the continuing value of Chauncey A. Goodrich's
       treatment of Sheridan in his Select British Eloquence
       (1852.2), a work first published in 1852 and strongly

influential in rhetorical studies of the nineteenth
century. Among Goodrich's faults are (1) his tendency
to supplant evidence with anecdote, (2) his tendency to
indulge the moralistic bias current in his time, (3) his
failure to identify his sources, (4) his use of too few
sources. He remains reliable in his description of
Sheridan's characteristics as a speaker and in his
exposition of the literal argument of Sheridan's second
speech against Hastings, the speech printed in Select
British Eloquence. Goodrich's work is still valuable in
qualified ways.

15   MAROWITZ, CHARLES. "Rampant Promiscuity: Charles Marowitz
     Reviews The School for Scandal." Plays and Players
     9 (December): 49-50.
        Insists, after commenting on the Tennent production of
     The School for Scandal (especially as to differences
     between the New York and London casts), that Sheridan's
     comedies need not always be performed with rigid period
     conventions: "Stiff backs, arched eyebrows, limp wrists
     and prominent calves, curving sumptuously into elaborate
     buckled shoes that cling to feet which are permanently
     splayed out in elegant fifth position" (p. 50). Hardly
     the museum pieces they are invariably represented as
     being, they "deal with greed, jealousy, lechery,
     materialism and duplicity--all of which abound in our own
     society" (p. 50). It is appropriate, then, that their
     material be shaped to current ends.

16   OLIVER, EDITH. "The Theatre: Off Broadway," New Yorker
     38 (24 March): 122, 124.
        Reviews a revival of The School for Scandal staged by
     the Association of Producing Artists, admiring all
     performances and remarking apt interpretations of the
     roles of Lady Teazle (Rosemary Harris), "young, witty,
     and ingenuous," Sir Peter (Will Geer), "a scratchy
     masculinity," and Charles Surface (Clayton Corzatte),
     "whose wit is as pure as his heart" (p. 122). The play
     pleases by intruding warmth upon brittleness and by
     tempering satire with good humor and delight.

17   PEARSON, HESKETH. "Richard Brinsley Sheridan." In Lives of
     the Wits. London: Heinemann, pp. 70-123.
        Gives emphasis, in narrating the life of Sheridan, to
     the view that he "was the wittiest and most fascinating
     character of his age" (p. 70). Although given to
     improvidence and self-indulgence his motives were in
     general praiseworthy. He loved applause, but he did not
     curry favor with the mighty. He needed success with

women, but he continued to adore his wife. He wasted his
private substance, but he guarded the public wealth
scrupulously. At last he was buried in the Poets'
Corner next to Garrick, "and perhaps the worst thing
that can be said against him is that he would much
rather have been placed among the politicians" (p. 123).

18 PRICE, CECIL. "Sheridan's 'Doxology.'" Times Literary
     Supplement, 4 May, 309.
          Describes an item in the Library of Congress (a single
     leaf of paper) which is probably the authentic "doxology"
     mentioned in Moore's Memoirs of Sheridan (1825.9) as
     "written hastily in the handwriting of the respective
     parties" on a leaf of the newly completed School for
     Scandal. Moore's version reads "Finished at last. Thank
     God! / R. B. Sheridan / Amen! / W. Hopkins." The version
     in the Library of Congress reads "-----finis----- / Thank
     God! / R B S / Amen! / W. Hopkins." It is wholly in
     Sheridan's handwriting and "suggests a typical jest by
     Sheridan at his own and his colleague's expense."
     Despite the variant readings, the version in the Library
     of Congress is probably the one seen and recorded by
     Moore.

19 WALKER JOAN [SUTER]. Marriage of Harlequin: A Biographical
     Novel of the Important Years in the Life of Richard
     Brinsley Sheridan. Toronto: McClelland and Stewart;
     London: Jarrolds, 236 pp.
          Imagines the thoughts and passions motivating Sheridan's
     life from 1770, with the removal to Bath, to 1792 and the
     death of Eliza. The "Author's Note" indicates that "None
     of the characters in this book is fictitious. All of the
     events took place. The letters and poems are authentic,
     as is also some of the dialogue." Assessments of
     character, it continues, rest upon "extensive research
     into the lives of the Sheridans and Linleys,
     eighteenth-century papers and books."

                              1963

1 ANON. "Elegantly on the Harpsichord." Time 81 (February 1):
     65.
          Approves of the Tennent production of The School for
     Scandal but sees the play itself ("a kind of dramatic
     harpsichord") as having "surface vivacity rather than
     inner strength" and "elegance of style rather than
     profundity of substance." If "Thumped by realism's heavy
     hand, it would jangle and go mute."

1963

2   ANON. "Not a Seat for Sheridan." Times (London),
        11 January, p. 4.
            Reports from Toronto that the run of Sir John Gielgud's
        Tennent production of The School for Scandal is completely
        sold out there. Audiences who have come to see Gielgud,
        Sir Ralph Richardson, and other great names of the theater
        have gone away "with a new liking for Sheridan" himself.
        The performances and the elegant sets do him eminent
        justice.

3   ANON. "Pssst . . . Who Murdered Manners?" Life 54
        (22 February), 47-48.
            Discusses, among pictures of The School for Scandal in
        the Tennent production (directed by John Gielgud), the
        demise of manners comedy, tracing its end to changes in
        fashion, to the quick pace of modern living, to the
        decline of aristocracy, and to social and cultural
        mobility.

4   ANON. "Sheridan in Need of Style." Times (London),
        25 April, p. 16.
            Complains that a revival of The Rivals at the Lyric
        Theatre, Hammersmith, fails for lack of period style and
        for the absence of unified direction. Even actors who
        have succeeded elsewhere in their parts, notably Fay
        Compton as Mrs. Malaprop (see 1961.1), here seem to be
        adrift.

5   BARKER, JOHN W. "From Command, Sheridan's 'The School for
        Scandal.'" American Record Guide 29 (February):
        422-23, 486.
            Admires a recording of The School for Scandal based
        upon the Tennent production of the play, as directed by
        John Gielgud, and featuring the stage cast. Even to one
        who has not seen the stage production, the recording is
        a "virtuoso affair" (p. 422). The spatial effects of
        stereophonic sound serve it extremely well, especially
        in the Screen Scene.

6   BROWN, JOHN MASON. "Richard Brinsley Sheridan to Noel
        Coward." In Dramatis Personae: a Retrospective Show.
        New York: Viking Press, pp. 159-83.
        Reprints 1934.3.

7   BRUSTEIN, ROBERT. "The Anti-Establishmentarians." New
        Republic 148 (23 February): 29.
        Complains that the Tennent production of The School for
        Scandal, while "handsome" and "very competent," fails to
        "spark or crackle." The play itself is perhaps at fault,

for "only the auction and the screen scenes have any intrinsic dramatic interest." The acting is "establishment," never rising above the "known capabilities" of the actors--except in the case of Ralph Richardson as Sir Peter Teazle.

8   CIARDI, JOHN. "With Malice for All." Saturday Review
     46 (23 February): 52.
          Reviews the Command Records recording of The School for
     Scandal, John Gielgud directing (RS 13002 SD), and
     concludes it to be a "living monument" to the trivial and
     to the "theatre of elegance." As a dramatist Sheridan
     stands as far above his contemporaries as they (and he)
     stand below the great masters of English drama. "Perhaps
     the very slightness of the play is its strength, for
     certainly it is as elegantly empty today as it was when
     it first curtsied to the Georgian fops."

9   CLURMAN, HAROLD. "Theatre." Nation 196 (9 February):
     126-27.
          Acknowledges, of The School for Scandal in the Tennent
     production, a quality "more stylish than sharp, more
     outstanding for costumes and settings than for concentra-
     tion on the play's bite" (p. 126) but admires both
     production and play. "The writing is a constant
     delight--one is tempted to say Mozartian. We enjoy it as
     a kind of music for the mind. It has sprightly movement,
     euphony, grace and edge. The play is superbly constructed,
     with an unsurpassed knowledge of the stage. . . . Shining
     through its surface sheen is sovereign good humor and
     generosity of spirit" (p. 126).

10   DERRY, JOHN W[ESLEY]. The Regency Crisis and The Whigs.
     1788-9. Cambridge: Cambridge University Press, passim.
          Suggests, throughout a detailed running narrative (in
     which Sheridan is but one of many actors), Sheridan's
     role in the first Regency Crisis, characterizing it
     as primarily a conciliatory role, one devoted to
     mitigating rivalries for power among the Whigs, should
     the regency succeed.

11   [GEORGE IV.] The Correspondence of George, Prince of Wales.
     Edited by A[rthur] Aspinall. 8 vols. New York: Oxford
     University Press, 1963-1971, passim.
          Contains many references to Sheridan, including
     thirty-five letters written by him and twelve written to
     him over the period 1788 to 1811. The references and
     letters concern matters both of private friendship and
     public policy, mostly the latter.

1963

12 GILMAN, RICHARD. "Revival Time." Commonweal 77
    (15 February): 542-43.
        Reviews briefly the Tennent production of The School
    for Scandal directed by John Gielgud. Despite the high
    English polish, the evening is "somewhat flat and pallid."
    Ralph Richardson's rendering of Sir Peter Teazle, however
    brilliant, clashes with the more orthodox renderings of
    other roles. Gielgud brings little imagination to the
    part of Joseph Surface.

13 GOODRICH, CHAUNCEY ALLEN. "Richard Brinsley Sheridan." In
    Essays from Select British Eloquence, edited by Albert
    Craig Baird. Carbondale: Southern Illinois University
    Press, pp. 165-74.
        Reprints 1852.2.

14 HEWES, HENRY. "Lead, Kindly Knights." Saturday Review
    46 (9 February): 20.
        Sees John Gielgud's revival of The School for Scandal
    (the Tennent production) as attempting with "considerable
    success" to "bring out the gentler aspects of Sheridan's
    comedy, and to perform it in a style suggested by
    theatrical drawings of the late eighteenth century."

15 LANDRÉ-AUGIER, GERMAINE, trans. Introduction to The Critic,
    by Sheridan . Le Critique; ou Répétition d'une tragedie.
    Editions Montaigne, Collection Bilingue. Paris: Aubier.
        Surveys the career of Sheridan and discusses The Critic
    as to antecedents in genre and technique. Critical
    comment emphasizes Sheridan's management of his characters.
    Of two types (the personages of act 1 and the performers
    in Puff's tragedy) they serve his comprehensive satiric
    design, his ridicule of human vanities and of theatrical
    offenses. Mrs. Dangle serves as intermediary between the
    audience and these types of characters. The total comic
    effect of The Critic derives from Sheridan's dramaturgical
    sense, his knowledge of men, and a certain light cynicism
    (cynisme léger) redolent of Restoration comedy. He
    catches in his work the basic unchangeableness of the
    theaters of life and art.

16 McCARTEN, JOHN. "Unsteady Revival." New Yorker 38
    (2 February): 69.
        Complains that this revival of The School for Scandal
    (under the direction of Sir John Gielgud at the Majestic
    Theatre in New York) aims too much at archness and
    quaintness in stage manner and leaves too little to
    Sheridan's own mockery. "After all, Sheridan was a funny
    man, and if his verbal ingenuity has grown familiar over

the years, it seems to me that it is still the core of
the matter."

17   NUSSBAUM, R. D. "Poetry and Music in 'The Duenna.'"
      Westerly, June, pp. 58-63.
          Exemplifies from The Duenna the mutually limiting
      effects poetry and music have upon one another. In
      accommodating itself to music, poetry must avoid abstract
      philosophical concepts, minimize complex images, and in
      general avoid five-beat lines. For its part, music
      must adapt its measure to that of the poetic setting and
      must condition its moods--either in a literal or dramatic
      way--to the text it sets. The Duenna retains its appeal
      throughout the years because the music and poetry accede
      very comfortably to the limitations each imposes upon the
      other. "In writing The Duenna, both Sheridan and the
      Linleys were aware of their mutual roles, and neither
      tried to outshine the other" (p. 63).

18   OLFSON, LEWY, adapter. "The Rivals." Plays, the Drama
      Magazine for Young People 22 (March): 87-96.
          Reduces the play to a twenty-five minute sketch intended
      for high school or junior high school presentation. The
      Julia-Faulkland plot is removed, as are the roles of
      Acres and Sir Lucius. The recognition scene between
      Jack and Lydia (and the action preparing for it) provide
      the main comic action, and the language is pruned and
      simplified throughout.

19   PRICE, CECIL. "Another Crewe MS. of The School for Scandal?"
      Bibliographical Society of America Papers 57 (1st
      quarter): 79-81.
          Hypothesizes, after collating G. H. Nettleton's text of
      The School for Scandal (based on the Crewe MS at
      Georgetown University) with Thomas Moore's corrected
      version of the Dublin edition of 1799, that Moore used a
      source differing at times from the "accepted Crewe MS"
      (p. 80), a source used also by the copyist of a manuscript
      now housed at Yale, one duplicating readings applied by
      Moore but at variance with Nettleton. Readings thought
      by Nettleton to result from Moore's inattentiveness might
      result instead from his reference to this second Crewe MS,
      the manuscript not available to Nettleton but known to
      Moore and to the copyist of the Yale MS.

20   PRYCE-JONES, ALAN. "The School for Scandal." Theatre Arts
      47 (March): 57-58.
          Reviews a New York revival of The School for Scandal
      staged by the Tennent Production Company and directed by

1963

John Gielgud. A bit excessive in its "period graces,"
the production yet shines brilliantly and elucidates the
comedy of an overworked "school piece" whose "wit has
passed into that cold twilight of tradition where merit
is taken for granted" (p. 57).

21   SKINNER, QUENTIN. "Sheridan and Whitbread at Drury Lane,
      1809-1815, I." Theatre Notebook 17 (Winter): 40-46.
      Draws upon the Whitbread papers to reassess Samuel
Whitbread's role in the reconstruction of Drury Lane
Theatre after the fire of 1809 and in managing the theater
thereafter. These huge tasks involved problems not
acknowledged by Sheridan's biographers: (1) renters of
the earlier theater, having seized its remaining assets
(the insurance), had first to be placated; (2) powerful
lobbying for a rival theater then had to be overcome in
Parliament; (3) the quite impossible task of turning a
profit at the new theater had to be faced; and (4) the
"Fickle, malicious, selfish, vain" conduct of Sheridan
had constantly to be endured. Very probably the suicide
of Whitbread in 1815 was aggravated by these torments and
by the added one that creditors were threatening him with
legal action even though he had spent much of his
private wealth in reducing the deficits constantly
accumulated against the new theater.

22   _____. "Sheridan and Whitbread at Drury Lane, 1809-1815, II."
      Theatre Notebook 17 (Spring): 74-79.
      Answers the attitude held by Sheridan himself and by
his biographers that Samuel Whitbread was a scoundrel
and was (as chairman of the Drury Lane Committee after
the fire of 1809) the machinator of Sheridan's sad
decline. The charges made against him by Sheridan were
that he refused for selfish reasons to allow Sheridan a
seat on the Drury Lane Committee, that he cheated Sheridan
of proper compensation for his share in the Drury Lane
patent, and that he cost Sheridan his seat in Parliament
by refusing to advance him a small part of this
compensation (2,000 pounds) to support his election
campaign. In truth, however, the 24,000 pounds paid
Sheridan for his share in the patent was more than fair
(the renters of the old house having offered only 11,000
pounds for it); because of heavy building expenses, the
money he sought for his election was not available through
the committee at the time he needed it; and his seat on
the committee was denied not by Whitbread but by his
own reputation for improvidence. Subscribers to the new
theater insisted that he not take part. These factors and
many others justify Whitbread's conduct to Sheridan in

times crucial to the lives of both men.

23 TAUBMAN, HOWARD. "Sheridan Comedy Given in New York."
    New York Times, 26 January, p. 5.
        Sees The School for Scandal as a play requiring rare
    and special resources. "You will not get its full bounty
    of laughter unless it is played in the high style required
    by flowing gowns, powdered wigs and knee breeches. The
    lines must be delivered with lightness and accuracy even
    as the minuet of the action is carried out with the
    elegance of fashionable society at an 18th century
    festivity." Not even English actors can always achieve
    these effects, but the present company, in the Tennent
    production under the direction of John Gielgud, succeeds
    admirably.

24 WERKMEISTER, LUCYLE. The London Daily Press, 1772-1792.
    Lincoln: University of Nebraska Press, passim.
        Provides, in many scattered references, a record of
    Sheridan's vigorous involvement in the daily press of
    London during the earlier years of his political career.
    At few times during these years was he without a newspaper
    to serve at his bidding and further the interests of his
    party.

1964

1   ANON. "Musical Based on Sheridan." Times (London),
    17 March, p. 13.
        Condemns a musical comedy based on The Rivals as
    illustrating that popularizations of the classics can
    succeed "only when the new material supports the spirit
    of the original, or when the new work completely supplants
    the old." In this "artless" off-Broadway musical, called
    All in Love, neither desideratum is achieved. Instead,
    the parts of the production go their separate ways and
    destroy one another's effects.

2   BRADBROOK, FRANK W. "Lydia Languish, Lydia Bennet, and Dr.
    Fordyce's Sermons." Notes and Queries, n.s. 11 (November):
    421-23.
        Adds to the observation made by E. E. Phare (1964.8)
    the suggestion that the lending library in The Rivals
    came to Jane Austen's mind when, in Pride and Prejudice,
    she "made Mr. Collins refuse a novel from the circulating
    library" (p. 421). Furthermore, Lydia Bennet, of Pride
    and Prejudice, reflects in her own conduct the bad
    influence of novels. Like Sheridan's Lydia Languish,

1964

she personifies a "feminine vanity" (p. 422) aggravated
by popular novelists.

3   BRYANT, WILLIAM CULLEN. "The Character of Sheridan." In
    Prose Writings of William Cullen Bryant, edited by
    Parke Godwin. New York: Russell and Russell,
    2: 365-69.
        Reprints photographically 1884.3.

4   DRUMMOND, MARY M. "Sheridan, Richard Brinsley." In The
    History of Parliament. The House of Commons, 1754-1790.
    London: Her Majesty's Stationery Office, 3: 431-34.
        Sets out the main events of Sheridan's earlier political
    career, i.e., from his election to Parliament in 1780 to
    his rupture with Burke in 1790, but lists all his
    political offices and distinctions, both early and late.

5   ENKVIST, NILS ERIK. British and American Literary Letters
    in Scandinavian Public Collections. Acta Academiae
    Aboensis, Humaniora, vol. 27, no. 3. Abo: Abo Akademi,
    pp. 102-4.
        Transcribes two letters written by Sheridan. The first
    (dated "May 27 [1792]") seeks clemency for "Mary
    Haydocks," a poor girl condemned at "Shefford" for
    "House-stealing." The second, addressed to "Mr. James"
    and dated "Wednesday, Oct. 7," applies for a time
    convenient to meet with James "respecting what remains
    unsettled with Sir W. Geary," whose estate in Surrey
    Sheridan had purchased. Note: In The Letters of Richard
    Brinsley Sheridan (see 1966.11), Cecil Price prints the
    first of these letters as no. 178 1: 254), giving the
    name of the subject as "Mary Haydock," a poor girl
    condemned at "Stafford" for "horse-stealing." Price
    prints the second of the two letters as no. 21 in his
    "Appendix of Further Letters" (3: 332); he assigns it
    to the year 1807 and assumes the recipient to be "Charles"
    James (although other London attorneys named "James"
    offer themselves as possibilities).

6   GRIEDER, THEODORE. "The German Drama in England, 1790-1800."
    Restoration and 18th Century Theatre Research 3, no. 2
    (November): 39-50.
        Mentions Pizarro in a consideration of why German drama
    rose to a "rage" of enthusiasm in the late 1790s and came
    under attack very soon thereafter. The reasons for its
    rise were (1) that it caught in England a transient taste
    for "piquant moral situations" in drama (p. 41), (2) that
    it answered a heightened demand for emotionalism in the
    theater, (3) that it pandered (when shaped to do so, as

in the case of Pizarro) to nationalistic, anti-French,
sentiments, and (4) that it lent itself to displays of
sensibility and benevolence. It quickly came under
attack because (1) the translations were of inferior
quality; (2) it represented the usurpation by a foreign
interest of the English stage; and (3) it was vulnerable
to imputations of social and political immorality.

7   HARRIS, LEON A.   "Richard Brinsley Sheridan." In The
    Fine Art of Political Wit: Being a Lively Guide to the
    Artistic Invective, Elegant Epithet, and Polished
    Impromptus as well as Gallant and Graceful Worldly Wit
    of Various British & American Politicans from the 18th
    Century Through our Own Days of Grace. A Handbook for
    Piercing the Epidermis of Opponents. New York: Dutton,
    pp. 21-40.
       Discusses and exemplifies, in a loose biographical
    framework, Sheridan's gifts for sharp repartee and
    crackling wit. Concludes that "the best-remembered words
    today are not Sheridan's long flights of invective [such
    as those taken in the speeches against Hastings], but his
    quips" (p. 23), the most celebrated of which are recalled
    here.

8   PHARE, E. E. "Lydia Languish, Lydia Bennet, and Dr.
    Fordyce's Sermons." Notes and Queries, n.s. 11 (May):
    182-83.
       Suggests that Lydia Bennet, of Jane Austen's Pride and
    Prejudice (1814), recalls Lydia Languish, of The Rivals,
    in that both are named Lydia; both are attracted to young
    military officers; both favor romantic elopement; and
    both show a distaste for Dr. James Fordyce's Sermons for
    Young Women. These sermons, in fact, participate in
    shaping the character of Jane Austen's Mr. Collins, who
    uses their sentiments in the wrong contexts and "produces
    an impression of stiff-necked self-importance that is all
    his own" (p. 183).

9   SPRAGUE, ARTHUR C. "In Defence of a Masterpiece: The School
    for Scandal Re-examined." In English Studies Today.
    Third Series: Lectures and Papers Read at the Fifth
    Conference of the International Association of Professors
    of English Held at Edinburgh and Glasgow August 1962,
    edited by G. I. Duthie. Edinburgh: Edinburgh University
    Press, pp. 125-35.
       Demonstrates that The School for Scandal is "a drama
    of extraordinary theatrical skill; an acting play and,
    what is not quite the same thing, a play for actors"
    (p. 128) by emphasizing respects in which the play

1964

opens a "fine spread of possibilities" (p. 133) in the
interpretation of parts, a spread at least partially
opened by the opportunity given actors to reconcile
opposites in the play: e.g., "Lady Teazle's rustic past
and high-flying, fashionable present; Joseph's sentiments
and rakishness; Sir Peter's tetchiness and ultimate
amiability" (p. 134).

<u>1965</u>

1 EVANS, IFOR. <u>A Short History of English Drama</u>. Riverside
   Studies in Literature. Boston: Houghton Mifflin,
   pp. 139-41.
      Makes mention of <u>The Rivals</u>, admiring especially its
   dialogue, <u>The School for Scandal</u>, admiring its
   characterization and plot, and <u>The Critic</u>, admiring the
   insights it provides into Sheridan's understanding of
   the stage. Sheridan's other dramatic works are listed
   within a brief biographical sketch.

2 GIELGUD, JOHN. "Commentary." In the <u>Production Folio</u> of
   the Caedmon Recording of <u>The School for Scandal</u>, pp. 3-4.
      Ranks <u>The School for Scandal</u> among "the most brilliant
   successes in our English theatrical literature" but
   considers it to lack "the poetic genius of Shakespeare,
   the nonsensical fantasy of Wilde, and the scholarly
   classical richness of Congreve" (p. 3), while yet
   reflecting exactly the manners and society of London in
   the late 1770s. In it "The dialogue is as sharp as a
   diamond, spontaneous, essentially English, with an added
   spice of true Irish wit--an extraordinary feat from an
   author still only in his twenties" (p. 4).

3 LIGHT, ENOCH, producer. <u>The School for Scandal</u>. Caedmon
   Records. Command Series RS 13002 (3 record set).
      Records the Tennent production of <u>The School for Scandal</u>
   as directed by John Gielgud and featuring Ralph Richardson
   as Sir Peter Teazle, John Gielgud as Joseph Surface,
   Geraldine McEwan as Lady Teazle, Gwen Ffrangcon-Davies as
   Mrs. Candour, Meriel Forbes as Lady Sneerwell, Laurence
   Naismith as Sir Oliver Surface, Malcolm Kean as Rowley,
   Richard Easton as Charles Surface, Pinkie Johnstone as
   Maria, and others.

4 MAHONEY, JOHN L. "Sheridan on Hastings: The Classical
   Oration and Eighteenth-Century Politics." <u>Burke
   Newsletter</u> 6 (1965): 414-22.
      Demonstrates that Sheridan's great Westminster Hall

speech against Hastings follows the form of a classical
oration. A solemn exordium pursues the classical aim of
establishing benevolence and securing attention and
docility. A narration establishes the conditions of the
case before proceeding to a proof. A proposition brings
complex but unified perspectives upon Hastings' guilt.
A confirmation proves the case by linking arguments
together in a chain of logical reasoning. And a
peroration disposes the audience to favorable feelings
toward the argument.

5   MARSHALL, P[ETER] J. The Impeachment of Warren Hastings.
    London: Oxford University Press, passim.
        Mentions Sheridan's involvement in the impeachment and
    sets out the issues argued in his speeches against
    Hastings.

6   NELSON, DAVID ARTHUR. "The Laughing Comedy of the
    Eighteenth Century." Dissertation Abstracts 26
    (December): 3347 (Cornell).
        Concludes, from a study of the comedies of Vanbrugh,
    Farquhar, Goldsmith, and Sheridan, that "The formal
    structure of the laughing comedy of the eighteenth century
    is basically optimistic, or melioristic," that, while
    similar to sentimental comedy in employing good nature,
    laughing comedy differs from sentimental comedy in
    applying "a number of characteristic devices to maintain
    aesthetic distance," that, in managing these devices,
    Goldsmith is an artistic heir of Farquhar while Sheridan
    shows debts to Vanbrugh, for Sheridan "adapted the
    Restoration comedy of manners to the requirements of
    eighteenth-century laughing comedy and thus . . . carried
    on the satiric tradition in English comedy."

7   OLIVER, ANTHONY, AND SAUNDERS, JOHN. "De Loutherbourg and
    Pizarro, 1799." Theatre Notebook 20 (Fall): 30-32.
        Presents stylistic and circumstantial evidence to
    support the belief that a newly discovered glass painting
    depicting Pizarro, act 5, scene 2 is the work of
    De Loutherbourg, the artist "equally responsible for
    designing the scene and recording it" (p. 32). In subject,
    technique, coloration, and background, the work is typical
    of De Loutherbourg, and it is "not unlikely" (p. 32) that
    John Philip Kemble, who in 1799 was in practical charge
    of Drury Lane, approached De Loutherbourg for scenic
    ideas for Pizarro, despite the artist's estrangement after
    1781 from Sheridan and from theatrical design.

8   PETERSON, HOUSTON, ed. "Richard Brinsley Sheridan Brings the

1965

Hastings Trial to a Climax." In <u>A Treasury of the World's Great Speeches</u>. Rev. and enl. ed. New York: Simon and Schuster, pp. 180-84.
Reprints 1954.7.

9   PHYTHIAN, B. A.   <u>The Rivals, The School for Scandal, The Critic</u>. Notes on English Literature. New York: Barnes & Noble, 91 pp.
Comments upon the characteristics of comedy as to the psychology of laughter, the sources of the comic, and the prevailing types of comic expression; then provides chapters upon "Sheridan and His Times" and upon the three major plays, emphasizing the varieties of comic contrast in <u>The Rivals</u>, the tonal and thematic ambivalences in <u>The School for Scandal</u>, and the inadequacies of <u>The Critic</u>, which is "a less satisfactory play than the other two because its success in performance depends too much on the actors and the directors . . . and not enough on solid literary merits" (pp. 85-86). Concludes with mention of some books about Sheridan and the age.

10   PRICE, CECIL.   "Noverre and Sheridan, 1776." <u>Theatre Research</u> 7 (Fall): 45-46
Pursues into Sheridan's early management of Drury Lane Theatre the arrangements opened by Garrick to engage the great ballet-master Jean-Georges Noverre, who had agreed to commit himself to Garrick for the season of 1776, the year in which the management changed hands. Two undated letters--one written by Sheridan, the other by his Harrow friend Charles Grenville--indicate (as does a notice in the <u>London Packet</u> of 17-19 July 1776) that the new management undertook to engage Noverre, but he chose instead to take a position as ballet-master at the Opera, preferring a permanent post in Paris to a temporary one in London.

11   TILLETT, JEFFREY, ed.   "St. Patrick's Day." In <u>Shakespeare, Sheridan, Shaw</u>. London: Heinemann Educational Books, pp. 49-82.
Prints "St. Patrick's Day" as one of three farces for acting, the other two being "The Comedy of Errors" and "Androcles and the Lion." A brief editorial preface emphasizes the single most important element of farcical action, speed (assisted by simple settings, clear speech, and ease of movement). A brief introduction to each play provides a biographical sketch and a comment, that for Sheridan's play emphasizing its similarity to "the Rivals": viz., "the various stratagems (especially change of identity and disguise) resorted to by a young soldier to

win the young lady of his choice" (p. 53).

12 UDEN, GRANT. "Sheridan, Richard Brinsley (1751-1816)." In
    They Looked Like This: An Assembly of Authentic Word-
    Portraits of Men and Women in English History and
    Literature over 1900 Years. Oxford: Basil Blackwell,
    pp. 238-39.
        Cites Captain R. H. Gronow's Reminiscences in describ-
    ing Sheridan's appearance on the hustings in Stafford,
    presumably in 1812: "In consequence of his continued
    excesses, he had lost much of the charm of outward
    appearance that had won him friends at an earlier period,
    and nothing remained of his once expressive face but the
    remarkable brilliancy of his eyes; his cheeks were
    bloated, his nose was a fiery red, and his general
    aspect bespoke the self-indulgence of the reckless man."

1966

1 ANON. "Politician Playwright Seen in His Correspondence."
    Times (London), 7 July, p. 16.
        Reviews Price's edition of Sheridan's letters (see
    1966.11), judging the letters not great but "continuously
    interesting, reliable, and invaluable." They reflect the
    fullness and variety of Sheridan's life and show him
    coming face to face with "reality." Whether writing to
    his loved ones or to his future sovereign, he is "always
    the man, real."

2 CLURMAN, HAROLD. "Theatre." Nation 203 (12 December): 651.
        Reviews a revival of The School for Scandal produced by
    the Association of Producing Artists (APA) under the
    direction of Ellis Rabb. Remarks of the play: "Its
    theme--the pleasures, absurdities and bloodshed of gossip
    in polite society--is ever fresh. Its writing sparkles
    with canny good humor, its spirit is wise, its construc-
    tion solid." In this production, Keene Curtis, as Sir
    Oliver, earns special admiration. Helen Hayes, as Mrs.
    Candour, performs her role "rather more like a provincial
    American housewife than a lady of 18th-century London high
    society--a society which was literally 'select' because
    it constituted a very confined circle immersed in a sea
    of filth."

3 DARLINGTON, WILLIAM AUBREY. Sheridan. London: Published for
    the British Council and the National Book League by
    Longmans, Green, 31 pp.
        Reprints 1951.4, expanding the select bibliography to

1966

include F. S. Boas's <u>Introduction to Eighteenth Century</u>
<u>Drama</u> (1953.4), Bor and Clelland's <u>Still the Lark</u> (1962.4),
Pearson's <u>Lives of the Wits</u> (1962.18), and Dulck's <u>Les</u>
<u>Comédies de Sheridan</u> (1962.12).

4   G[ILMAN], R[ICHARD]. "Two by APA." <u>Newsweek</u> 68 (5 December):
     96; 98.
          Sees a revival of <u>The School for Scandal</u> (staged by the
     Association of Producing Artists under the direction of
     Ellis Rabb) as suffering from "a cautious, uncolored,
     pedantic approach" (p. 98), hardly the approach for a
     "comedy about gossip and malice as ways of life" (p. 98).

5   HOGAN, CHARLES BEECHER. "The London Theatres, 1776-1800. A
     Brief Consideration." <u>Theatre Notebook</u> 21 (October):
     13-14.
          Quotes Sheridan's monody on Garrick to the effect that
     Garrick's death foreboded (even in the mind of Sheridan
     himself) the end of a golden age of theater. But, in
     truth, through such acting careers as those of Kemble and
     Mrs. Siddons and through such comedies as <u>The School for</u>
     <u>Scandal</u> and <u>The Critic</u>, a new golden age emerged. The
     period 1776-1800 is a rich one for the student of theater.
     Much has been done in studying it, but much remains to do.

6   HOLLOWAY, JOHN. "The Rivals." <u>Spectator</u> 217 (29 July):
     149-50.
          Insists, in an essay reviewing (tangentially) Sheridan's
     <u>Letters</u> (see 1966.11), that "in the end, Sheridan's
     baseless brilliance will simply not do" (p. 150). While
     Molière and the Restoration playwrights subjected the
     ethic of society "to fundamental challenge" (p. 149),
     Sheridan's plays "condemn what all condemn . . . and they
     leave thus unchallenged society's verdicts on life, because
     they leave unchallenged its sense of what life contains"
     (p. 149). His comedy is situational, and his wit lies in
     "how dialogue brings out situation" (p. 149). Devoting
     his life to "making Drury Lane pay," Sheridan left
     undisturbed the ethical conventions of his audience.
     Similarly, his service as member of Parliament brought
     nothing but shallow brilliance to politics.

7   LOFTIS, JOHN, ed. Introduction to <u>The School for Scandal</u>, by
     Sheridan. Crofts Classics. New York: Appleton-Century-
     Crofts, pp. v-xiv.
          Emphasizes that <u>The School for Scandal</u>, like <u>The Way of</u>
     <u>the World</u>, is "neoclassical in tidiness of construction,
     characterization, laughing and satirical approach to
     didactic objective, and aphoristic summaries of experience"

232

but that the two plays so differ from one another in
"social assumptions and moral evaluations" as to represent
separate dramatic traditions. While Congreve's play
measures conduct by "conversational ability and social
finesse," Sheridan's sees benevolence ("something very
like the New Testament conception of charity"), as being
"the decisive, normative quality" (p. viii). Like Sterne
and Goldsmith, Sheridan, for all that he is witty and
intelligent, explores the principal sentimental theme:
"the emotional responsivenss of some if not all men to
the distresses of others" (p. ix). The text is that
prepared by George H. Nettleton from the Crewe MS
(Georgetown University) for the anthology British
Dramatists from Dryden to Sheridan (see 1939.4).

8   LUTAUD, OLIVER. "Des acharniens d'Aristophane au critique
    de Sheridan." Les Langues Modernes 60 (July): 433-38.
        Recognizes in The Critic an alliance of the serious and
    burlesque through which comedy becomes the vehicle of
    earnest attack upon man's warring tendencies. Sheridan
    thus recalls a tradition as old as Aristophanes's The
    Acharniens, one which, through theatrical burlesque,
    represents history as a theater of worldlings and treats
    the ironies of tragedy in a comic mode. Sheridan's
    parody, like Aristophanes's, thus quite transcends the
    limits of mere parody.

9   MANDER, RAYMOND, AND MITCHENSON, JOE. "De Loutherbourg and
    Pizarro, 1799." Theatre Notebook 20 (Summer): 160.
        Suggests that a picture belonging to a gentleman in
    Australia (one identified as depicting a scene from act 5
    of Pizarro) possibly derives from the same "lost" original
    by De Loutherbourg that had furnished the source of the
    glass picture discussed in 1965.7. Pizarro excited much
    artistic interest. Portraits of Mrs. Jordan as Cora and
    J. P. Kemble as Rolla are well known. But there seems
    to be no portrait of William Barrymore as Pizarro. An
    engraving of 1804 depicts a scene from the play as staged
    at Covent Garden Theatre. It shows Kemble in his original
    part as Rolla.

10 NIEDERAUER, REVEREND GEORGE H. "Wit and Sentiment in
    Sheridan's Comedies of Manners." Dissertation Abstracts
    International 27 (November): 1379A (Southern California).
        Analyzes The Rivals and The School for Scandal in such
    a way as to show in them the interplay of Restoration and
    sentimental comic conventions. The Rivals combines these
    conventions awkwardly; it allows the Restoration-like
    deceptions of the main plot to clash with the "morbid

sentimentality" of the Julia-Faulkland subplot. The
School for Scandal skillfully blends Restoration and
sentimental devices in all elements of the comedy: in
plotting, characterization, and language. It tempers
Restoration wit with morality and enlivens sentimental
morality with wit. In it Sheridan brings to perfection
the character who combines a good heart with a clever
head, and in this concept of characterization he makes
his most lasting mark upon later theatrical comedy.

11   PRICE, CECIL. "The Larpent Manuscript of St. Patrick's
      Day." Huntington Library Quarterly 29, no. 2 (February):
      183-89.
          Demonstrates, by comparing the Larpent text with
      portions of the Fraser Rae text (1902) and with editions
      of St. Patrick's Day printed in Dublin (1788) and London
      (1831?), that the Larpent text is "trustworthy enough"
      (p. 184), that its earlier scenes "are closer to the
      Sheridan's original text than any version so far printed"
      (p. 185), and that it is "important in establishing a
      text for the conclusion of the farce" (p. 186). In
      general, "it shows most clearly Sheridan's personal touch.
      The later printed versions only blunt its subtler points"
      (p. 189).

12   _____, ed. Introduction to The Letters of Richard Brinsley
      Sheridan. Oxford: Clarendon Press, 1: xiii-xx.
          Sees the main value of the letters to be biographical.
      Since Sheridan wrote most of his letters hurriedly, they
      lack high elegance of language. Since most of them relate
      to the practical conduct of life, they offer no coherent
      philosophy. In them "He tantalizes us, but there is
      something so human in his foibles that he remains a
      curiously sympathetic character. Perhaps his gift of
      phrase-making catches our attention; or his rueful remarks
      about his own shortcomings endear him to us. Yet what
      holds us in the end is this intimate communing with a man
      of genius who knows his own faults only too well but can
      do nothing to change his nature" (p. xix). The letters
      "clearly reveal the nature of the man and are a necessary
      supplement to his actions, speeches, and plays" (p. xx).
      Reviewed in Times Literary Supplement, 24 November, p. 1066;
      by Constance Kyrle Fletcher in Theatre Notebook 21 (Spring
      1967): 138-40; by Allardyce Nicoll in Review of English
      Studies, n.s. 18 (August 1967): 344-46; by H. Trevor-Roper
      in The Listener 76 (1967): 136; in Philological Quarterly
      46 (1967): 366-67; by George M. Kahrl in Modern Philology
      65 (May 1968): 402-405; also in 1966.6 and 1966.13.

1966

13   PRITCHETT, V. S. "Anglo-Irish." New Statesman 72
      (12 August): 230.
           Renders Sheridan's character in terms of the Anglo-Irish
      disposition. "A Clever mind had not contaminated the
      heart. He told lies; he loved the excitement of secrecy;
      he was unscrupulous and not to be trusted, but one cannot
      say that he was false to his principles, that he was a
      hypocrite." The product of a proud Anglo-Irish tradition,
      Sheridan conquered the great world self-taught, self-raised,
      and self-supported. His newly published letters largely
      fail to project the vigor of this tradition.

14   RODWAY, ALLAN. "Goldsmith and Sheridan: Satirists of
      Sentiment." In Renaissance and Modern Essays Presented to
      Vivian de Sola Pinto in Celebration of His Seventieth
      Birthday, edited by G. R. Hibbard. London: Routledge and
      Kegan Paul, pp. 65-72.
           Notices that Sheridan "has a harder edge" (p. 68) than
      Goldsmith, that in Sheridan wit "is all important"
      (p. 69), while in Goldsmith situation dominates, that
      Goldsmith's characters merely serve the farcical fun while
      Sheridan's "take themselves seriously" (p. 70)--in that
      they need show no awareness of the audience--but that
      both playwrights, even while purporting to attack sentimen-
      tality, are at best ambivalent about it. "This ambiguity
      of attitude, present in all their comedies, though not to
      the same degree, may well go far to explain their holding
      the stage so much better than the more consistent work of
      Jonson and the Restoration dramatists" (p. 65).

15   STRONKS, JAMES R. "'The Rivals' as a Possible Source for
      'Walden.'" Thoreau Society Bulletin, no. 95 (Spring):
      5.
           Suggests that Thoreau's lines "A man is not a good man
      to me because he will . . . pull me out of a ditch if I
      should fall into one. I can find you a Newfoundland dog
      that will do as much" (from the "Economy" segment of
      Walden) derives from Lydia's comment in The Rivals that
      Julia is not obliged to Faulkland for saving her life:
      "Obligation!--why, a water spaniel would have done as
      much" (I, ii).

16   VEST, EUGENE B. The Rivals: The School for Scandal:
      Act-by-Act Analysis with Notes. New York: American
      R. D. M., 64 pp.
           Sketches outlines of Sheridan's life and theater, then
      offers running commentary on each of the two plays,
      concluding with general critical appraisals, lists of
      characters, study topics, and select bibliography.

1966

17   WOEHL, ARTHUR L. "Richard Brinsley Sheridan, Parliamentarian."
      In The Rhetorical Idiom: Essays in Rhetoric, Oratory,
      Language, and Drama. Presented to Herbert August Wichelns,
      with a Reprinting of His "Literary Criticism of Oratory"
      (1925), edited by Donald Cross Bryant. New York: Russell
      and Russell, pp. 221-49.
         Reprints photographically 1958.6.

1967

1   ANON. Notes on Sheridan's The School for Scandal. Study-Aid
     Series. London: Methuen, 29 pp.
        Provides notes intended to assist the reader in
     preparing for matriculation examinations. The sections
     include a "General Introduction" (chiefly biographical),
     a comment upon "Eighteenth-Century Comedy," a "Brief
     Sketch of the Plot," an act-by-act "Summary of the Play,"
     a character-by-character comment on "Characterization,"
     a set of "General Observations" (on such matters as plot,
     language, dramatic irony, sentimentality), and a list of
     "Revision Exercises" (i.e., questions of the sort often
     asked on matriculation examinations). The controlling
     premise throughout is that Sheridan's greatness "lies in
     the exhilaration and sparkle of his wit and in his
     unerring sense of theatre" (p. 19).

2   BROOKING, JACK. "From the Director's Notebook: The School
     for Scandal (Notes for the Production as Presented at
     the University of Kansas Theatre, February 8, 1967)." In
     The School for Scandal: Thomas Rowlandson's London.
     Lawrence: Kansas University Museum of Art, pp. 46-57.
        Provides a brief stage history of The School for
     Scandal, mentioning the original production and revivals
     in 1779, 1785, 1789, 1866, 1909, 1948, 1951, 1962, and
     1966. Analyzes the content and form of the play (i.e.,
     action, purpose, means, environment) by means of a
     Stanislavsky formula and records therefrom a "unity of
     action statement": "One attempts to intrigue (action) in
     order to assure one's personal success and happiness in
     eighteenth-century London (purpose) by means of scandal,
     making the right impression, plots and disguises (means)
     in a time of sentiment, embellishments, leisure and
     eccentricity (environment)!" (pp. 51-52). "Intrigue" is
     thus the main dynamic of the play. And, in all phases
     of production, the director must "strike a balance between
     external manners and fashion and the human being who dwells
     beneath the facade" (p. 51).

1967

3   BRUSTEIN, ROBERT. "Consensus Theatre." New Republic 165
    (7 January): 41-42.
        Complains, in reviewing a revival of The School for
    Scandal, that the Association of Producing Artists makes
    Sheridan's dialogue "indistinguishable from Broadway
    conversation" and makes itself, through its unoffending
    blandness, "a perfect candidate for official American
    consensus theatre" (p. 41). Such established actors as
    Helen Hayes (Mrs. Candour) hurt the production by playing
    to their admirers rather than probing their roles.

4   CONNELLY, JAMES L. "The Prospect Before Us: A Drama in
    Four Acts of High and Low Life." In The School for
    Scandal: Thomas Rowlandson's London. Lawrence: Kansas
    University Museum of Art, pp. 3-21.
        Remarks that Sheridan and Thomas Rowlandson both
    caricatured "the same social follies, pretensions, and
    vices" (p. 4) and that the theater is "the common focal
    point which most specifically unites" (p. 4) the two
    artists. The School for Scandal and Rowlandson's graphic
    renderings of London life are perfect complements. In
    short comments on the life of Rowlandson (pp. 4-7), the
    life of Sheridan (pp. 8-11), the London society
    (pp. 11-18), and the London Theater (pp. 18-21), Connelly
    supplies background for simultaneous presentations at
    the University of Kansas of a production of The School
    for Scandal and a showing of Rowlandson's drawings and
    prints. "Sheridan and Rowlandson working together
    constitute as incomparably witty and articulate a pair
    of guides to the London of their day as one could hope
    to find, but they are equally effective as guides to the
    broader territory known as human nature" (p. 21).

5   COOK, WILLIAM EWALD. "Sheridan's Comedy of Deception."
    Ph.D. dissertation, Harvard University.
        Attributes Sheridan's persistent popularity to his
    amiable characters, his complex wit, and his masterful
    stage effects but sees him, too, as having a moral
    depth not often attributed to him. It is a depth
    achieved by his insight into (and dramatic manipulation
    of) the deceptivenss of words, by falsenesses exposed
    in his plays through deceptive physical appearances, and
    by his assertation in drama of accessible stage ideals:
    the prudent, sensible, and compassionate woman, the
    generous, open, and generally imprudent man.

6   CREHAN, T., ed. Introduction to The School for Scandal, by
    Sheridan. London English Literature Series. London:
    University of London Press, pp. 9-46.

237

1966

Provides a detailed introductory comment analyzing the
dramatic flow of action and demonstrating that "Sheridan
makes all consistent and convincing in his play" (p. 23).
Complementing the comic rhythm of the play is a careful
symmetry of design. Verisimilitude is sustained
throughout by close fidelity to character. "High spirits
and humour are the leading motifs" of the comedy, not
morality (p. 41). "Laughter that reveals and exposes is
Sheridan's supreme purpose, skill in making contrivance
like reality his principal method" (p. 42). Reprints the
text of the first Crewe MS, including "A Portrait."
Includes a biographical sketch, suggestions for further
reading, and explanatory endnotes.

7   FISKIN, A. M. <u>The Rivals and The School for Scandal Notes</u>.
Lincoln, Nebraska: Cliff's Notes, 80 pp.
Provides information about Sheridan's life and
theatrical milieu, then, before summarizing and commenting
upon the two plays, describes the main features of
Sheridan's comic art: varied comic situations that never
"disintegrate into literal statement" (p. 14), characters
who follow a consistent comic bent, extraordinary richness
of wit. Review questions, essay topics, and a select
bibliography come at the end.

8   HASLOG, JOSEF. "Zur Reduktion des Sentimentalen in Sheridans
<u>The School for Scandal</u>." <u>Anglia</u> 85 (1967): 321-49.
Examines the means whereby Sheridan reduces the emotional
force of sentimentality (and thus rescues the comedy) in
<u>The School for Scandal</u>. While working within the
sentimental ethos, Sheridan favors an "exposure-mortifica-
tion" nexus over the "reunion-gratitude" nexus favored by
such playwrights as Cumberland. The "Trial of Hearts"
action in the play is managed so as to minimize sentimental
effects. Sheridan also reduces such stock features of
sentimental comedy as "repetition" and "prolongation." In
general, he controls aesthetic distance in such a way as
to defeat sentimental reaction, integrating benevolence,
generosity, and tenderness so closely into the action as
always to allow space for comic response.

9   JEFFARES, A NORMAN, ed. Introduction to <u>The Rivals</u>, by
Sheridan. Macmillan's English Classics, New Series.
London: Macmillan, pp. ix-xix.
Remarks the staples of Sheridan's life: his brilliant
youth, his misguided maturity, his improvident old age.
Notices the emergent need in the eighteenth century for
playwrights to respond to bourgeois tastes (hence the
growth of sentimentality), then comments on Sheridan and

Goldsmith as reactionaries against sentimentality.
Tougher minded than their contemporaries, "They delighted
in contrasts between appearance and reality, in the
exposure of fools and hypocrites, in the quick
give-and-take of dialogue, and in amusing, sharply dramatic
situations" (p. xiv). Sheridan's sense of farce "stemmed
from the traditions of Restoration wit," while Goldsmith's
harked back to Elizabethans (p. xv).

10 _____. Introduction to The School for Scandal, by Sheridan.
Macmillan's English Classic, New Series. London:
Macmillan, pp. ix-xix.
Provides a brief biographical sketch, an account of
English dramatic history in the eighteenth century, and
a brief critical comment on the play. In part, the play
is a satirical attack upon scandal journalism. Its main
dramatic business is to expose hypocrisy. "All is not
what it seems, or, indeed, what it is said to be"
(p. xviii). Characters, while basically types, are
differentiated by dialogue. In general, "The School for
Scandal revived the brilliance of Restoration comedy
without its coarseness or immorality" (p. xviii). The
text printed is a collation of the Crewe MS (Georgetown
University) and the Dublin edition of 1799. Sheridan's
poem "A Portrait" is reprinted from the John Murray
edition of 1821. Endmatter includes explanatory footnotes,
details of the history of the play, and extracts of
criticism dating from 1777 to 1933. Among them are
extracts from Hazlitt (1819.4), Lamb (1822.4), Moore
(1825.9), James (1874.4), and Darlington (1933.5).

11 KRUTCH, JOSEPH W. Introduction to Eighteenth-Century English
Drama. Bantam World Drama. New York: Bantam.
Sees Goldsmith's example as encouraging Sheridan "to
fly in the face of the sentimental tradition by basing
The Rivals on a farcical plot and aiming at nothing more
than laughter" (p. xvi). The School for Scandal, while
displaying "a wit more biting than that of either
Farquhar or Goldsmith" is, like their plays, "essentially
good-humored and simple enough to please almost any taste"
(p. xvii). While The Rivals is "a sort of hodgepodge as
near to burlesque as it is to comedy" (p. 269), The School
for Scandal "is a genuine comedy of manners, plotted with
great skill and always theatrically effective even though
it never probes very deeply and offers solutions rather
too easy to the moral problems it touches upon" (p. 348).
(Only The Rivals and The School for Scandal appear in this
collection.)

1967

12   LEWIS, THEOPHILUS, "Theatre." America 116 (7 January):
       25-26.
           Gives brief notice to a revival of The School for
       Scandal staged in New York by the Association of Producing
       Artists under the direction of Ellis Rabb. Remarks that
       The School for Scandal "is a playwright's rather than
       an actor's play." The actors must "compete with Sheridan's
       vivid characterization and firecracker lines," for "The
       audience quickly becomes too much involved in the
       embarrassing situations and brilliant conversation to
       notice an equally brilliant portrayal" (p. 26).

13   MACEY, SAMUEL LAWSON. "Theatrical Satire As a Reflection
       of Changing Tastes." Dissertation Abstracts 27 (March):
       3014A.
           Describes a doctoral study in which "theatrical satires"
       (i.e., "plays which ridicule their own medium") are shown
       to leave the stage as "a result of changing tastes during
       the bourgeois ascendancy." The genre comes to a close
       with Sheridan's The Critic, which is studied in the
       dissertation, as are works by Buckingham, Duffett, Gay,
       Carey, Fielding, Foote, Murphy, and Goldsmith.

14   MONTAGUE-SMITH, PATRICK W. "Sheridan's Maternal Ancestors,
       The Chamberlaines, of Kingsclere." Geneologists'
       Magazine 15 (March): 319-30.
           Observes that in his own time Sheridan's maternal
       ancestors, the Chamberlaines, were known to have
       Hampshire origins. A property in the parish of Kingsclere,
       Hants, was owned until his death in 1670 by John
       Chamberlaine, an uncle of Dr. Philip Chamberlaine, the
       father of Frances Sheridan. In writing the memoirs of
       Mrs. Sheridan, Alicia LeFanu has misled "many biographers"
       (p. 319) by declaring her grandmother to descend from Sir
       Oliver Chamberlaine, an "English baronet" of whom there
       is no record. Montague-Smith, the editor of Debrett,
       provides close notes on the authentic, i.e., the
       Kingsclere, branch of the family.

*15   Morozov, M. M. "Sheridan i ego epokha." Literaturnaya
        Rossiya 8 (17 February): 22-23.
            Listed in the MHRA annual bibliography for 1967:
        42: 292, item 5050.

16   PRICE, CECIL J. "The Completion of The School for Scandal."
       Times Literary Supplement, 28 December, p. 1265.
           Offers evidence that The School for Scandal "was
       completed rapidly, that some of the characters were
       based on people he [Sheridan] knew, and that he threw

in some important topical references." The "people he
knew" include Jacob Nathan Moses, on whom he based the
character of Moses in the play, and Benjamin Hopkins,
Chamberlain of the City of London, whose name was then
scandalously associated with an instance of lending
money to a sixteen-year-old nobleman. The "important
topical references" are those made in the play (III, i
and ii) to the Annuity Bill, a measure then pending
(April-May 1777) to bring fines and imprisonment against
"persons soliciting a minor to grant an annuity."

17   _____. "The Second Crewe MS. of 'The School for Scandal.'"
    <u>Bibliographical Society of America Papers</u> 61 (4th quarter):
    351-56.
      Compares the Hodgson MS of <u>The School for Scandal</u> with
the Georgetown MS and the Frampton MS, two texts in
which Sheridan's own hand appears, the latter of them
being his original draft of the play. Observes that the
two manuscripts originally owned by Mrs. Crewe--the
Georgetown and the Hodgson--"contain some readings that
are different one from the other but are both approved
by Sheridan" (p. 354). Concludes that both these
manuscripts "represent a fairly advanced stage in the
history of the text" (p. 354) but that the Hodgson is
the earlier, its text seeming closer to the Frampton MS
than does the text of the Georgetown MS and closer, too,
to a third early text, the Buckinghamshire MS at Yale.
While the Hodgson MS is in fact a second Crewe MS, it is
not the manuscript described in an earlier bibliographic
essay of Prices' (1963.19). There is apparently yet a
third Crewe MS in existence.

18   _____. "Sheridan-Linley Documents." <u>Theatre Notebook</u>
    21 (Summer): 165-67.
      Gives brief descriptive accounts of several documents
donated to the British Theatre Museum by the British
Records Association. "The best of them is a copy of the
marriage articles of Richard Brinsley Sheridan and
Elizabeth Ann Linley. There are also included two diaries
kept by Elizabeth's youngest brother, William, as well as
a number of legal papers for the Linley properties at
Bath" (p. 165). The marriage articles divide among
Thomas Linley, Elizabeth and Richard, and any children
born to the marriage the sum of 3,453 pounds (in three
percent reduced bank annuities) then held in trust for
Elizabeth: 1,200 pounds to the father, in compensation for
the loss of his daughter's services, 1,203 pounds to the
couple, and 1,050 pounds to be placed in trust for the
children. William Linley's diaries cover the last

1967

eighteen months of his life, "a round of visits to the
Garrick Club . . . and the theatres" (p. 166).

19 ROTHWELL, KENNETH S. "The School for Scandal: The Comic
Spirit in Sheridan and Rowlandson." In The School for
Scandal: Thomas Rowlandson's London. Lawrence: Kansas
University Museum of Art, pp. 23-45.
    Demonstrates that Sheridan's characters, while
conventional to all classic comedy and drawn from
autobiographical experience, are distinctive and timeless.
"What The School for Scandal reveals then is an
equilibrium between time and timelessness, between
invention and convention, between nature and art" (p. 34).
Sheridan's comic characters resemble the figures in
Thomas Rowlandson's famous watercolor of Vauxhall
Gardens; and, like Rowlandson, Sheridan recognized that
comedy impinges upon tragedy. Through such a realization
the two artists gave permanence to their art.

20 TUCKER, SUSIE I. "Notes on Sheridan's Vocabulary." Notes
and Queries, n.s. 14 (May): 189-90.
    Cites some "points of interest" in the "linguistic
pattern" of Sheridan's letters. They include (1)
noncewords, such as "suffocateful" (for "suffocating"),
(2) anomalies, such as "stretch-leg" (for "walking on"),
and (3) variants upon popular sayings, such as "we are all
in a Boat" (for "all in the same boat"). Other
unorthodox usage appears (1) in an abstract sense given
to the phrase "in lag," (2) in a revival of the
fifteenth-century verb "to blood-suck," and (3) in an
unusual application of the term "rusticated," an application originating, according to the O.E.D., in Frances
Sheridan's Sidney Bidulph (1761).

1968

1 BONAZZA, BLAZE ODELL, AND ROY, EMIL. "Introductory Comment"
to The School for Scandal. In Studies in Drama. 2d ed.
New York: Harper & Row, pp. 127-28.
    Characterizes The School for Scandal as "an admirable
blend of the satiric and the sentimental" (p. 127).
While having the outward form of a comedy of manners,
it lacks the cynicism and brittleness of the most
representative such pieces and determines the worth of
its characters not by their cleverness and wit, as a
comedy of manners might do, but by the spontaneity of
their good will. Even so, a large part of the appeal
of the play resides in its clever language, language

distinguished "by the skilful use of paradox, antithesis, parallelisms, and the choice of the precise words combined with a graceful economy of expression" (p. 127).

2   HOGAN, CHARLES BEECHER, ed. Introduction to The London Stage, 1776-1800. Pt. 5. The London Stage, 1660-1800: A Calendar of Plays, Entertainments & Afterpieces Together with Casts, Box-Receipts and Contemporary Comment. Carbondale: Southern Illinois University Press, 1: xix-ccxviii.
       Includes several of Sheridan's plays (The Critic, The Duenna, Pizarro, Robinson Crusoe, and The School for Scandal) in comprehensive considerations of broad theatrical matters: e.g., the introduction of new plays into the repertory (pp. cxl-cxliii) and the frequency of performance of stock plays as opposed to new ones (pp. clxxi-clxxiii). While not frequently mentioning Sheridan by name, the introduction, in touching upon virtually every facet of London theatrical life, discusses matters in which he was professional involved, and the body of the book (the calendar itself) includes among its records the performances of his plays in London between 1776 and 1800.

3   _____. The London Stage 1776-1800: A Critical Introduction. Carbondale: Southern Illinois University Press, 224 pp. Reprints 1968.2.

4   McGUINNESS, ARTHUR E., ed. Introduction to The Rivals, by Sheridan. San Francisco: Chandler Publishing, pp. vii-xiv.
       Introduces the play by sketching theatrical conditions in the 1770s and by placing it in the context of tested comic conventions: (1) conflicts between youth and age, wit and dullness, deceiver and deceived, (2) use of generic names, (3) action based upon youth in search of independence. Assesses the question of antisentimentalism in the play and finds Sheridan possibly challenging the sentimental doctrine in such quiet ways as that of having Julia deliver the second prologue. Appended to the text, which reprints the third edition of 1776, is a discussion of the malapropism taken from G. H. Nettleton's The Major Dramas of Richard Brinsley Sheridan (1906.3).

5   MOORE, THOMAS. Memoirs of the Life of the Right Honourable Richard Brinsley Sheridan. 5th ed. 2 vols. Grosse Pointe, Mich.: Scholarly Press.
       Reprints photographically 1827.2.

6   _____. Memoirs of the life of the Rt. Hon. Richard Brinsley Sheridan. 2 vols. New York: Greenwood Press, 1968.

1968

Reprints photographically 1858.1.

7 OLIPHANT, MARGARET (WILSON). Sheridan. English Men of
Letters Series. New York: AMS Press, 207 pp.
Reprints 1883.7.

8 PRICE, C[ECIL] J[OHN] L[AYTON], ed. Introduction to The
Rivals, by Sheridan. London: Oxford University Press,
pp. 7-12.
Emphasizes Sheridan's practice in composition of letting
his first-night audience stand as critics at a final
dress rehearsal. Attributes the perennial success of The
Rivals to such features as its irrepressible youthful
zest, its well-turned dialogue, its neat plot and brisk
movement, its riotous reversal scenes, in which reversals
issue from character, and its broad imaginative farce,
especially in the relationship between the father and son,
which is touched by "nice irony and a rich humor" (p. 11).
Although the play purports to be antisentimental it
reflects the "uneasy mixture of the satirical and the
sentimental" (p. 12) in Sheridan's own temperament. The
text derives from the "third edition corrected" (1776).
Footnotes and endnotes provide glossary and information.

9 SALLÉ, J.-C. "An Allusion to The Rivals in a Keats Letter."
Notes and Queries, n.s. 15 (September): 335-36.
Recognizes in a letter from Keats to John Hamilton
Reynolds (dated 17 April 1817) an echo of the scene in
The Rivals (III, i) in which Sir Anthony regales the
impassive Jack Absolute with Lydia's beauties: "Then,
Jack, her cheeks! her cheeks, Jack! so deeply blushing at
the insinuations of her tell-tale eyes!" Keats writes:
"But the sea, Jack, the sea--the little waterfall-then
the white cliff--then St. Catherine's Hill--" (Letters,
ed. Hyder Rollins, I, 131). When not referring to
Reynolds by his surname, Keats usually called him "John."

10 WALKER, FRED BYNUM. "A Rhetorical Study of the Parliamentary
Speaking of Richard Brinsley Sheridan on the Rights of
Ireland" Dissertation Abstracts International 29, no. 5
(November): 1614A-15A (George Peabody College).
Describes a study of the speeches given by Sheridan
between 1782 and 1809 on issues of Ireland. Sheridan
achieves persuasive force in these speeches through "an
astute application of the principles of rhetoric," through
"expressive language," through the "three Aristoelian
methods of proof: ethical, emotional and logical"
(p. 1615A). In his speeches on Ireland Sheridan "set a
pattern of logical thinking, careful reasoning, and

stirring appeals for fair treatment of a sister nation"
(p. 1615A).

1969

1   ANON. "Memoir of the Right Honourable Richard Brinsley
    Sheridan." In The Speeches of the Right Honourable Richard
    Brinsley Sheridan. With a Sketch of His Life. Edited by
    a Constitutional Friend. New York: Russell and Russell,
    I, i-xiv.
        Reprints photographically 1842.2.

2   ANON. "Note." In The School for Scandal, 1780. A Scolar
    Press Facsimile. Menston, Yorkshire: Scolar Press, 1
    unnumbered page.
        Notes the dates of the first performance (8 May 1777)
    and the first printed issue (1780) of The School for
    Scandal. Locates "Sheridan's manuscript" of the play in
    Georgetown University and announces that "The title-page,
    and a number of pages (in which Sheridan's corrections and
    added stage-directions are evident) are reproduced in the
    Appendix" of this facsimile volume.

3   DURANT, JACK D. "R. B. Sheridan's 'Verses to the Memory of
    Garrick': Poetic Reading as Formal Theatre." Southern
    Speech Journal 35 (Winter): 120-31.
        Suggests that the metric of Sheridan's "Verses to the
    Memory of Garrick" reflects (when studied alongside the
    signals for spoken expression given in the earliest
    printed texts of the poem) the concept of "Variety in
    uniformity" espoused in Thomas Sheridan's theories of
    prosody and in an unfinished treatise on prosody written
    by the playwright himself in his youth. The operation
    of deliberate prosodic effects heightens the poem's
    suitability for theatrical presentation.

4   KRONENBERGER, LOUIS. "The School for Scandal." In The
    Polished Surface: Essays in the Literature of Worldliness.
    New York: Knopf, pp. 73-84.
        Adapts (with minor formal revision) the commentary on
    The School for Scandal originally published in 1952.3.

5   LANDRÉ, LOUIS. "Introduction." In L'École de la médisance.
    Translated by M. Huchon. Paris: Aubier-Flammarion.
        Reprints 1949.4.

6   OLIVER, ROBERT TARBELL. Four Who Spoke Out: Burke, Fox,
    Sheridan, Pitt. Freeport, N.Y.: Books for Libraries

1969

Press, 196 pp.
Reprints photographically 1946.8.

7   PRICE, CECIL. "The First Prologue to The Rivals." Review
    of English Stuides, n.s. 20 (May): 192-95.
        Prints the prologue composed by Sheridan for the first
    performance (17 January 1775) of The Rivals. Until
    discovery of this manuscript in the Amelia Edwards
    Collection at Somerville College, Oxford, only the
    prologue for the revised version of the play (introduced
    on 28 January 1775) was available. The second differs
    from the first in two details relating to the
    reintroduction of the play (eleven nights after its
    withdrawal). "For the rest, Sheridan repeated twenty
    lines almost word for word, recast some, and gave a
    neater twist to others" (p. 195).

8   TAYLOR, GARLAND F. "Richard Brinsley Sheridan's The Duenna."
    Dissertation Abstracts International 30, no. 4 (October):
    1537A-38A (Yale).
        Describes a doctoral study (submitted at Yale in 1940)
    which traces the development of the text of The Duenna and
    documents many details of the background and history of
    the play: the sources of the songs, the first season of
    performance, contemporary reception, early revivals, a
    history of known piracies, an extensive bibliography of
    early editions. "Evidence is presented to show that in
    the eyes of some of his contemporaries The Duenna was the
    great turning point in Sheridan's fortunes" and that the
    piece was "less successful as an opera than as a comedy
    with interpolated songs" (p. 1537A).

1970

1   BARNES, CLIVE. "Theater: Canadians Impress in 'School for
    Scandal.'" New York Times, 11 June, p. 51.
        Admires a production of The School for Scandal at
    Stratford, Ontario, and admires the play and playwright
    as well: "This is such a good play, with all its plots
    and counterplots intermeshing like the parts of a watch,
    with Sheridan's timeless jokes as funny as ever, and with
    Sheridan's insight into his fellow beings as sharp as a
    surgeon's scalpel."

2   BLOCK, TUVIA. "The Antecedents of Sheridan's Faulkland."
    Philological Quarterly 49 (April): 266-68.
        Finds the source of Sheridan's Faulkland not in
    Colonel Tamper of Colman's The Deuce Is in Him (1763)--as
    Gabriel and Mueschke argue (1928.6)--but in Beverley of

Arthur Murphy's <u>All in the Wrong</u> (1761), who, in turn,
derives from Malvil in Fielding's <u>Love in Several Masques</u>
(1728). As early as 1728, then, the prototype of
Faulkland had emerged: the sentimental hero who
struggles with "uncontrollably prolonged unpleasurable
emotions, which are ultimately condoned because they
result from his extreme sensibility" (p. 268). This
Facet of the eighteenth-century man of feeling has
largely been ignored by commentators.

3   COVE, JOSEPH WALTER. <u>Sheridan: His Life and Theatre</u>. Port
    Washington, N.Y.: Kennikat Press, 280 pp.
        Reprints photographically 1947.1.

4   CRINKLEY, RICHMOND. "The 1970 Stratford Festival."
    <u>National Review</u> 22 (11 August): 851.
        Admires the ensemble playing in a production of <u>The
    School for Scandal</u> at the 1970 Stratford (Ontario)
    Festival. The play, heretofore consigned by Crinkley to
    classroom study, comes to life in this production because
    of the "argumentative give and take" and the "grotesques
    in which the plays of this period abounded."

5   DIXON, CAMPBELL. "Sheridan." In <u>English Wits</u>, edited by
    Leonard Russell. Port Washington, N.Y.: Kennikat Press,
    pp. 171-96.
        Reprints photographically 1940.4.

6   DONOHUE, JOSEPH W., JR. "Sheridan's <u>Pizarro</u>: Natural
    Religion and the Artifical Hero." In <u>Dramatic
    Character in the English Romantic Age</u>. Princeton:
    Princeton University Press, pp. 125-56.
        Reviews the immediate success of <u>Pizarro</u>, attributing
    it to "Pathos, spectacle, song, and the peculiar
    attractiveness of the Germanic" (p. 128); then, after
    an account of the reception of the play (especially as
    to contemporary response to its benevolistic ethic),
    examines Sheridan's rendering of Rolla in relation to
    "the traditional English hero of Marlowe, Chapman and
    Dryden" (p. 150), seeing Rolla as "an epitome of the
    Romantic man of feeling, a man whose heroism consists in
    the greatness and nobility of his beating heart's
    responses" (p. 150). Like Marlowe's Tamburlaine and
    Dryden's Almanzor, Rolla triumphs over all human
    antagonists. Unlike them, however, he is not a master
    of circumstance and accident. His vulnerability to
    accident, which destroys him despite his blameless
    character, marks him as a distinctly Romantic tragic
    hero, one who, discovering himself in an illogical

world, "can do no more than respond to it with the
passion that springs from his inherent sensibilities"
(p. 156).

7   KAUL, A. N. "A Note on Sheridan." In The Action of
    English Comedy: Studies in the Encounter of Abstraction
    and Experience from Shakespeare to Shaw. New Haven:
    Yale University Press, pp. 131-49.
        Holds that Sheridan "originates nothing of any
    importance, and he leads nowhere" (p. 131). During
    the middle of the eighteenth century, the best traditions
    of theatrical comedy are preempted by the novel. In
    recalling themes and traditions of sixteenth- and
    seventeenth-century theatrical comedy, Sheridan makes
    "daring suggestions against the sentimental formula"
    applied to the drama of his own day, but he does not
    support or mean these suggestions "in the least" (p. 136).
    In fact, though they add a liveliness to his plays, they
    really make the plays "more trifling and less relevant"
    than standard sentimental pieces are. In the Lydia-Absolute
    plot of The Rivals, Sheridan foreshadows Jane Austen, not
    because he imitates older comedies but because he "shares
    their critical purpose" (p. 143). Only in this case does
    he look ahead at all.

8   KERR, WALTER. "In 'Hedda Gabler,' Irene Proves Her Worth."
    New York Times, 21 June, sec 2, p. 23.
        Reviews the Stratford, Ontario, summer festival season
    (in which Irene Worth plays Hedda Gabler) and concludes
    that while Hedda Gabler provides the best all-round
    production, The School for Scandal, staged farcically by
    Michael Langham, is likely the most popular of the several
    plays performed "because Sheridan's screen scene is not
    only foolproof but probably genius-proof (all the helpful
    invention in the world can't hurt it) and because Mr.
    Langham has shrewdly accelerated the bumptious and broad
    stage business as the evening plunges on."

9   LEFF, LEONARD J. "The Disguise Motif in Sheridan's The
    School for Scandal." Educational Theatre Journal 22
    (December): 350-60.
        Argues that The School for Scandal "is unified through
    Sheridan's use of a series of disguise images beginning
    in Act I with Lady Sneerwell's veiled love of Charles
    Surface and concluding with Snake's plea in Act V that
    his one good deed remain hidden" (pp. 350-51). The play
    features two groups of characters, "Those who mask
    themselves and those who do not" (p. 351). The action,
    "a series of elaborate disguise motifs," systematically

"condemns and dismisses masquerade by presenting the unification of two characters [Charles and Maria] who stand for a world without masks" (p. 360).

10 LOEWENBERG, ALFRED. "Linley: The Duenna; or, the Double Elopement." In Annals of Opera, 1597-1940. New York: Rowman and Littlefield, pp. 348-49.
    Chronicles the stage history of The Duenna from its introduction in 1775 through a revival at the Lyric Theatre (Hammersmith) in 1931. Note: The Annals first appeared in 1943.

11 MACEY, SAMUEL L. "Sheridan: The Last of the Great Theatrical Satirists." Restoration and Eighteenth Century Theatre Research 9, no. 2 (1970): 35-45.
    Sees the history of eighteenth-century drama as a "tragic structure" in which Goldsmith and Sheridan provide the "glimmer of hope" preceding the final catastrophe. While speaking out themselves for true sentiment, they attacked the inferior taste reflected in the false sentiment of bourgeois values. Goldsmith's most vigorous attack is given in his "Essay on the Theatre," Sheridan's in The Critic. The Rivals and The School for Scandal, like The Good-Natured Man and She Stoops to Conquer, allow ambivalent attitudes toward sentimentality; but The Critic, in deriding the corrupting influence of popular taste, calls unequivocally for "Aristophanic laughter" (p. 35). Like Pope in Dunciad IV, Sheridan "stood aghast at that upsurge of middle-class manners and taste which the eighteenth century has since bequeathed to our brave new world" (p. 44).

12 MITCH, ALBERT EUGENE. "A Study of Three British Dramas Depicting the Conquest of Peru." Dissertation Abstracts International, 30 (April): 4595A-96A (Northwestern).
    Describes a dissertation examining (in a study of three plays treating of the Conquest of Peru) Sheridan's Pizarro as to "staging, costumes, settings, music, and acting styles" (p. 4595A). The study considers the 1799 premiere of Sheridan's play together with "performances recorded in Oxberry's 1824 edition of the script and Charles Kean's 1856 production which stressed historical authenticity" (4595A).

13 MUIR, KENNETH. "Decline and Renewal." In The Comedy of Manners. Hutchinson University Library. London: Hutchinson, pp. 154-65.
    Observes that Sheridan's comedies, for all their brilliance and theatricality, do not capture the spirit

1970

of the Restoration comedies of manners. Nor do the
comedies of his successors in the form--those of Wilde,
Shaw, and Maugham. "It appears that comedy of manners
requires equality between the sexes together with social
inequality. The gradual erosion of class, a manifest
good in itself, makes it increasingly difficult to write
the kind of comedy with which we have been concerned in
this book" (p. 165).

14   NOVICK, JULIUS. "Theatre." Nation 210 (16 February):
189-90.
Reviews (favorably) a production of The Rivals staged
in New Haven by the Yale Repertory Company under the
direction of Alvin Epstein. As to the play itself, "its
good nature and high spirits are genuine . . . and though
many of the characters are quite clearly modeled on those
of previous playwrights, a number of the main ones are
still amusing, even endearing" (p. 189). Admires Mrs.
Malaprop, as played by Elizabeth Parrish, "as an
overblown but still voluptuous beauty" (p. 190).

15   PARKS, STEPHEN. "The Osborn Collection: A Biennial Progress
Report." Yale University Library Gazette 44, no. 3
(January): 114-38.
Describes acquisitions in the Osborn Collection at Yale
for the period 1967-70, including "Two letters and a
document" signed by Sheridan, four letters addressed to
him, and "several items of Sheridaniana" (p. 126).
Remarks that the Sheridan holdings at Yale "were already
the largest gathering known" (p. 126).

16   WÜRZBACH, NATASCHA. "Sheridan--The Rivals." In Das englische
Drama: Vom Mittelalter bis zur Gegenwart, edited by
Dieter Mehl. Dusseldorf: A. Bagel, 2: 94-117.
Examines respects in which wit, dialogue, characterization, motivation, and comic resolution assist a marriage
of sentimental comedy and comedy of manners in The Rivals.
In attempting such a marriage the play confronts a major
conflict of the late eighteenth century and declares its
own major thematic question: how does the individual
accept moral responsibility while yet enjoying freedom of
character and conduct?

1971

1   AUBURN, MARK STUART. "The Comedies of Richard Brinsley
Sheridan and Theatrical Tradition, 1747-1780." Ph.D.
dissertation, University of Chicago.

Establishes the characteristics of the English
theatrical tradition between 1747-1780 (by examining
stock comedies, new comedies, and dramatic criticism of
the time), then demonstrates that Sheridan's dramatic
work--which purposed from the outset (for financial
reasons) to please the popular taste--stands well within
the tradition. That is, it draws upon clearly moral
material, presents characters whose faults are venal at
worst, and recommends benevolent good nature; it does
not restore the Restoration or undertake bold new
departures. Each play, however, shows Sheridan's
capacity to bring interest to the tradition. The Rivals,
for example, constructs a system of parallel scenes,
situations, and characters for the purpose of defining a
warm and compassionate view of love. The Duenna, while
never other than amiable in spirit, achieves comic
liveliness through intricate situational ironies, and A
Trip to Scarborough, while it lacks the psychological
depth of its source, The Relapse, yet achieves a tight
unity well suited to the popular playing pieces of
Sheridan's time. In adapting the fragments from which he
constructed The School for Scandal, Sheridan moved away
from a Restoration-like cynicism toward a benevolistic
Georgian spirit. The product is thoroughly Georgian,
but it reflects a moral depth not apparent in Sheridan's
earlier plays, a sense that evil finds means to persevere
even after the happy ending of the comedy.

2   BLACK, CLEMENTINA. The Linleys of Bath. Rev. ed.
    London: Miller, 300 pp.
        Reprints 1926.3 with a new introduction by the countess
    of Rosse, a descendant of the Linleys, and a genealogy of
    the Linley family compiled by Sir Anthony Wagner.

3   DONALDSON, IAN. "Drama from 1710 to 1780." In Dryden to
    Johnson. Sphere History of Literature in the English
    Language, vol. 4. Edited by Roger Lonsdale. London:
    Sphere Books, pp. 190-225.
        Finds the history of English Drama between 1710 and
    1780 to be more distinctive for its dramatic taste than
    its dramatic writing. Since audiences in this period
    tolerated the merging of dramatic kinds, it is hard to
    define rigid formal categories forplays, but the concepts
    of "sentimental" and "laughing" comedy provide
    serviceable, if tentative, distinctions, and the work of
    Sheridan can be considered in relation to them. Always a
    champion of "good nature," he became ever surer in his
    attacks upon false sentiment, and he remained from the
    beginning a proponent of laughter. Through his gifts

1971

for parody, farce, and comic timing, he was able, in The
School for Scandal, to bring laughing comedy to its
zenith. "Not until the time of Shaw and Wilde--two more
Irishmen--was such comedy to be seen again in the
English theatre" (p. 206).

4   MACEY, SAMUEL. "Theatrical Satire: A Protest from the Stage
Against Poor Taste in Theatrical Entertainment." In The
Varied Pattern. Studies in the 18th Century, edited by
Peter Hughes and David Williams. Publications of the
McMaster University Association for 18th Century Studies,
no. 1. Toronto: A. M. Hakkert, pp. 121-29.
        Discusses reflections of changing taste in the theater
as seen through theatrical satires from Buckingham's
Rehearsal to Sheridan's The Critic. These changes derive
from "the middle-class ascendance" (p. 128) and have the
effect of destroying theatrical satire as a genre.
"Today, not merely theatrical satire, but also such
traditional elements in the lanx satura as the ridicule of
priests, lawyers, and doctors seem to have been virtually
barred from the vehicles for mass media" (p. 128).

5   MITCHELL, L. G. Charles James Fox and the Distintegration of
the Whig Party, 1782-1794. Oxford Historical Monographs.
London: Oxford University Press, pp. 128-36 and passim.
        Treats of Fox's resistance to Sheridan's counsel in
the Regency Crisis of 1787-1788, i.e., his growing concern
that to accede to Sheridan's influence in the matter
would be to confirm the authority of Sheridan with the
Prince and to diminish his own. Other features of the
Fox-Sheridan relationship are touched upon throughout the
book.

6   MOORE, THOMAS. Memoirs of the Life of the Rt. Hon. Richard
Brinsley Sheridan. 2 vols. Freeport, N.Y.: Books for
Libraries Press.
        Reprints photographically 1825.10.

7   MURRAY, ISABEL. "'Great Expectations' and 'The Critic.'"
Notes and Queries, n.s. 18 (November): 414.
        Identifies the title of a club in Great Expectations,
"The Finches of the Grove" Club, as coming from a line
spoken by Tilburina in The Critic: "Nor William sweet,
nor marjoram--nor lark, / Linnet, nor all the finches of
the grove!" "Recognition of the source of the club's
name prepares the reader at once for the absurd,
self-dramatizing love affairs of its members."

8   PRICE, C[ECIL] J[OHN] L[AYTON], ed. Introduction to The

School for Scandal, by Sheridan. London: Oxford
University Press, pp. 9-13.
   Provides a biographical sketch of Sheridan and a
comment upon his play based generally on the observation
that the distinction between good and bad in it turns
upon "the degree of heartlessness" in the behavior of
the characters. "Sheridan wanted this to be clearly
recognized rather than strongly reproved. Good nature
could not cure all the ills of society, but real
generosity of spirit might enhance the life of an
extravagantly competitive, fashionable set" (p. 12).
By acknowledging Sir Peter's good nature, Lady Teazle
saves herself from Joseph's seduction and from the evil
influence of the scandal group. The text is that of the
first Crewe MS (Georgetown) collated with the second
Crewe MS, the Buckinghamshire MS, the lord chamberlain's
copy, and the copy owned by Robert H. Taylor of Princeton.
Apparatus includes a list of pertinent dates, a selected
list of readings, explanatory footnotes, and endnotes
explaining features of diction (the terms "sentiment"
and "sentimental") and certain topical references (cf.
1967.16). Sheridan's poem "A Portrait," following the
manuscript in the Harvard Theatre Collection, precedes
the text of the play.

9   STRATMAN, CARL J., C. S. V., SPENCER, DAVID G., AND DEVINE,
    MARY ELIZABETH, eds. "Sheridan, Richard." In
    Restoration and Eighteenth Century Theatre Research: A
    Bibliographical Guide, 1900-1968. Carbondale: Southern
    Illinois University Press, pp. 659-88.
       Lists 256 items (including some editions and
    translations of the plays) with brief annotations. This
    list augments the serial bibliographies published annually
    in Restoration and 18th Century Theatre Research between
    1961 and 1967. The subsequent annual bibliographies
    serve, then, as supplements to the Stratman list.

                          1972

1   ANON. "Campaign Starts to Save Sheridan Papers." Times
    (London), 28 March, p. 2.
       Restates the announcement of 25 March (see 1972.2-3)
    that efforts are afoot to retain in Great Britain important
    Sheridan papers (including "the only prompt copies still
    in this country of The School for Scandal, corrected and
    annotated in the author's handwriting"). Although the
    papers are already purchased from the collection of Mrs.
    Clare Sheridan by an American university, they are

                          253

1972

detained by a stay of export license until 16 April.   A
sum of 6,000 pounds is needed to buy them back.

2   ANON.   "Manuscripts of Sheridan to Stay in Britain."   Times
(London), 14 April, p. 2.
Reports that Sheridan materials scheduled for
exportation to the United States (see 1972.1, 3) have
been saved for retention in Great Britain by an award of
3,955 pounds given by the Rank Organization to the
British Theatre Museum.

3   ANON.   "Sheridan Campaign."   Times (London), 25 March, p. 12.
Announces a campaign headed by the actor Donald Sinden
(in behalf of the British Theatre Museum) to raise 6,000
pounds for the purpose of keeping a major collection of
Sheridan materials (including a manuscript of The School
for Scandal) in Great Britain.   If the money is not
raised by 16 April the materials will be sold to "a
leading American university library."   Other Sheridan
materials sold in November of 1971 at Sotheby's, and, like
these contested materials, part of the collection of Mrs.
Clare Sheridan, were retained in England through the
purchase of Mr. Richard McNutt, an antiquarian bookseller,
of Tunbridge Wells, Kent.

4   BARNES, CLIVE.   "Theater: City Center Company Makes Debut
with 'The School for Scandal.'"   New York Times,
29 September, p. 32.
Takes occasion, while generally admiring a performance
of The School for Scandal given by the newly established
City Center Company in New York, to specify the essential
demands made by the play: (1) a high comedy style
("partly a matter of comic timing, but also partly a
comprehension of time, place and, slightly different from
both, period") and (2) a quality of ensemble.

5   BINGHAM, MADELEINE.   Sheridan: The Track of a Comet.   London:
Allen and Unwin; New York: St. Martin's Press, 383 pp.
Bases a popularized account of Sheridan's life on the
theory that the playwright, like his father and
grandfather, sought recognition as a gentleman and that
the high promise of Sheridan and his forebears failed
because of missteps made at critical moments.   They
"trembled on the edge of gentility, only to fall by
making unfortunate speeches or wrong political decisions,
or by marrying the wrong women" (p. 15).   Reviewed in
Times Literary Supplement, 5 May, p. 520; by Joan H.
Owen in Library Journal 97 (1 November): 3590; also in
1972.13, 20; 1974.7.

6   CROWE, CAROL E. "Sir Philip Francis, 1740-1818: A
    Biography." Dissertation Abstracts International
    32 (April): 5704A-5705A (Georgia).
        Presents the life of Francis as "a microcosm of the
    reign of George III" by virtue of Francis' friendship
    with "George, Prince of Wales, Edmund Burke, Charles
    James Fox, Richard Brinsley Sheridan, and William
    Windham" (p. 5704A).

7   DURANT, JACK D. "The Moral Focus of The School for Scandal."
    South Atlantic Bulletin 31 , no. 4 (November): 44-53.
        Acknowledges the benevolistic base of The School for
    Scandal and argues that the doctrines of Christian
    benevolism, as found in the pulpit theology of the
    latitudinarian divines, help to explain the form and
    meaning of the play. In accord with these doctrines,
    which see vice as an acquisition of discipline and art,
    the play identifies vice with all forms of complexity
    and contrivance. Virtue it identifies with simplicity
    and spontaneity. The outplay of the conflict between
    simplicity and complexity (a conflict culminating in the
    Screen Scene) dramatizes the doctrinal attitude of the
    action.

8   ESCARBELT, BERNARD. "Sheridan's Debt to Ireland." In
    Aspects of the Irish Theatre. Cahiers Irlandais, no. 1.
    Edited by Patrick Rofroidi, Raymonde Popot, and William
    Parker. Paris: Editions Universitaires, Publications
    de 1' Université de Lille, pp. 25-37.
        Sees Sheridan's comic sense as being rooted in the
    Irish spirit of game playing. The disguise scenes in
    his plays attest to this spirit, but the language and
    wit reflect it even more. Mrs. Malaprop's language,
    for example, is a series of games (played more by
    Sheridan than by Mrs. Malaprop herself) exploring the
    possibilities of word sounds; and the construction of
    wit in the plays (cf. Sir Anthony's witty definition
    of a lending library) explores, layer-on-layer, the
    conceptual possibilities of an idea. These practices
    of endowing reality with fantasy appear also in
    Sheridan's personal life (as witness his constant
    practical joking and his quip at the Drury Lane fire
    about taking a glass of wine at his own fireside). They
    are authentic to the Irish tendency of rendering life
    into a game, the better to cope with its trials.
    Sheridan's sentimentalism is an artificial accommodation
    to English tastes and spirits.

9   FRENGUELLI APPOLONIA, CARLA. Il teatro di R. B. Sheridan.

1972

Milano: Celuc, 221 pp.
Places Sheridan's life within the background of his age
and his theater, then provides running commentary on
each of his major plays, including Pizarro. Later chapters
discuss his attitude to his craft, to his actors, and,
eventually, to his political career. Certainly the
components of his professional life show great variety,
but a spirit of vitality unites the whole, a sense of
life as a game to be played. His several careers show
him expanding this attitude ever more broadly upon the
theater of life.

10 HUME, ROBERT D. "Goldsmith and Sheridan and the Supposed
Revolution of 'Laughing' against 'Sentimental' Comedy."
In Studies in Change and Revolution: Aspects of English
Intellectual History, 1640-1800, edited by Paul J.
Korshin. Menston, Yorkshire: Scolar Press, pp. 237-76.
Examines the drama of the 1760s with the purpose of
"judging the climate" (p. 270) in which Goldsmith's "Essay
on the Theatre" appeared in 1773. Suggesting that the
"Essay" is basically ephemeral journalism intended to
promote She Stoops to Conquer, Hume shows that Goldsmith's
comments fail to make "a great deal of sense internally"
and that they make clear reference to only one play, the
Vanbrugh-Cibber Provok'd Husband, a sentimental comedy
admired in the "Essay" by Goldsmith, who is himself
demonstrably a sentimentalist. Theatrical history (as
summarized in detail by Hume) shows that the 1760s did
produce "various sorts of 'sentimental' plays" (p. 271)
but that Goldsmith and Sheridan inherited a tradition of
laughing comedy peopled actively by such playwrights as
Murphy, Foote, Macklin, Colman, and Garrick. In
Goldsmith and Sheridan appear some reactions against
excessive sensibility, but they cannot be credited with
leading a revolution against sentimental comedy or
reviving laughing and satiric comedy, which needed no
"revival" in the 1770s.

11 KALEM, T. E. "Smarmy Aplomb." Time 100 (9 October): 69.
Reviews (favorably but briefly) a production of The
School for Scandal staged by the City Center Acting
Company in New York, admiring the success with which the
actors elude two traps: that of turning comedy of manners
into farce and that of overhumanizing characters "that
are basically stylized commentaries on such moral vices
as slander, hypocrisy and deceit." In such comedies
"style is substance, and the witty gesture counts for
as much as the witty word."

12 KROLL, JACK. "New Rep in Town." Newsweek 80 (9 October): 70.
    Reviews (with reservatons) a production of The School
    for Scandal staged by the City Center Acting Company as
    directed by Gerald Freedman. Especially admires David
    Ogden Stiers, "who plays the hypocritical schemer Joseph
    Surface as a sputtering Catherine wheel of improvised
    mendacities, his falsehoods sticking in his gulping throat
    as he tries to spew them out." Mary Lou Rosato, as Lady
    Sneerwell, turns "the lowly, tacky sneer into something
    positively erotic."

13 LASK, THOMAS. "Caught Between Two Worlds." New York Times,
    29 December, p. 22.
    Characterizes Sheridan, in a review of Madeleine
    Bingham's Sheridan: The Track of a Comet (1972.5), as a
    man "not amenable to reason or persuasion." Not content
    to do what he was best at doing, he dabbled in an
    enterprise in which he could only fail, politics; and,
    as a consequence, he was used by the Whig leadership in
    the way that Harley and Bolingbroke had used Swift. "It
    is painful to follow Sheridan's quixotic and sometimes
    pathetic attempts to assault the haute monde and to
    become a maker and shaker in Parliament."

14 LEFF, LEONARD J. "Sheridan as Playwright, 1751-80."
    Dissertation Abstracts International 32 (January):
    3955A-56A (Northern Illinois).
    Recognizes a deficiency in Sheridan biography, which too
    often favors the man and the politician over the
    playwright, and responds by exploring the biographical
    backgrounds of Sheridan's theatrical career: the familial
    influences, the years of neglect at Harrow, the
    association with Nathaniel Brassey Halhed, the influence
    of Lewis Ker, the playwright's tutor. Sheridan emerges
    from these backgrounds driven by "an almost pathological
    eagerness to please" (3955A). Rejecting his satiric
    bent, he yields in his earlier plays to the popular
    taste for sentiment; and only in his last popular
    comedy, The Critic, does he give free reign to satire,
    attacking "with complete confidence the very institution
    which gave him financial and psychological security--the
    theatre and all its trappings" (3955A).

15 MITCHELL, ELEANOR RETTIG. "Pronouns of Address in English
    1580-1780: A Study of Form Changes as Reflected in
    British Drama." Dissertation Abstracts International
    32 (February): 4593A.
    Describes a study in which plays by Sheridan (and
    twenty-eight other British playwrights) are drawn upon

1972

for an examination of "the changes which took place
in the pronouns of address in British drama during
two hundred years of the Early Modern English period."

16   OLIPHANT, MARGARET. Sheridan. English Men of Letters Series.
     Folcroft, Pa.: Folcroft Library Editions, 207 pp.
     Reprints photographically 1883.7.

17   OLIVER, EDITH. "The Theatre Off Broadway." New Yorker,
     48 (7 October), 100.
        Reviews (favorably) a production of The School for
     Scandal staged by the City Center Acting Company as
     directed by Gerald Freedman. Admires Sir Peter Teazle as
     played by David Schramm, who projects "depth and humor and
     a welcome irony" without pathos. Complains that Patti
     LuPone, however merry and sly her Lady Teazle, allows tears
     in her voice at the end of the Screen Scene, thus
     disallowing the audience's own tears. Of the script: "It
     has such momentum of its own that too much stage business
     can blur or stall it."

18   PRICE, CECIL. "Sheridan at Work on The Stranger." In Studies
     Presented to Tauno F. Mustanoja on the Occasion of His
     Sixtieth Birthday. Neuphilologische Mitteilungen 73
     (June): 315-25.
        Demonstrates that Sheridan "had a much greater share
     in The Stranger than has been generally acknowledged"
     (p. 317). In addressing this subject, Dougald MacMillan
     (1930.6) had seen Sheridan's share as "confined to cutting
     dialogue and introducing the songs and a dance" (p. 315).
     New evidence shows, however, that Sheridan "revised the
     phrasing extensively" (p. 316). This evidence appears in
     a portion of act 5 of The Stranger reproduced
     lithographically in an "early nineteenth-century magazine"
     and showing Sheridan's handwritten interlineations. Price
     authenticates the document and reprints it here.

19   _____. "Thomas Harris and the Covent Garden Theatre." In
     Essays on the Eighteenth-Century English Stage: The
     Proceedings of a Symposium Sponsored by the Manchester
     University Department of Drama, edited by Kenneth Richards
     and Peter Thomson. London: Methuen, pp. 105-22.
        Sketches the career in theatrical management of one of
     the most successful, if "barely remembered" (p. 105),
     members of the Georgian theatrical scene. A committed
     business man, Harris led Covent Garden to financial
     success despite his pedestrian mind and his competition
     with so brilliant a figure as Sheridan, his opposite
     number at Drury Lane. His association with Sheridan

began with The Rivals, with which Harris kept faith despite the first-night failure, and The Duenna, introduced, like The Rivals, at Covent Garden. In theatrical management the two men shared ownership for a time in the Opera House, from which Harris quickly extricated himself; and they cooperated in preventing a third theater in London, a cooperation in which Harris, who owned the dormant Killigrew patent, received compensatory payment from Sheridan, who eventually "bought" the patent for 20,000 pounds. Thought creatively brilliant, Sheridan died penniless. Harris died a rich man.

20   RHODES, RAYMOND CROMPTON. Harlequin Sheridan: The Man and the Legends. New York: B. Blom, 305 pp.
       Reprints photographically 1933.8.

21   WARDLE, IRVING. "Dramatic Hero of a Terrible Fairy Tale." Times (London), 12 March, p. 12.
       Admires Madeleine Bingham's new biography of Sheridan for emphasizing the theatricality of his life but observes that Miss Bingham fails to point out that "Sheridan stopped writing at the moment it ceased to coincide with his life." His best work is directly related to his own life, and he "never closed the gap between writing and private experience."

22   YEARLING, ELIZABETH M. "The Good-Natured Heroes of Cumberland, Goldsmith, and Sheridan." Modern Language Review 67 (July): 490-500.
       Observes that Goldsmith and Sheridan "tried to attack sentimentality on its own ground by presenting their versions of the good-natured hero" (p. 493). They attack not the "sentimentalist philosophy," but the "debased sentimentality" of such plays as The West Indian, which relish overlong sentimental scenes. "The distinction is not between sentimentalism and something other which criticizes the sentimentalist philosophy, but between sentimental drama and a drama which implicitly accepts the basic tenets of sentimental philosophy" (p. 500).

1973

1   ANON. Sheridaniana. Folcroft, Pa.: Folcroft Library Editions.
       Reprints photographically 1826.9.

2   COVE, JOSEPH WALTER. Sheridan: His Life and Theatre.
       Philadelphia: Richard West, 280 pp.
       Reprints photographically 1947.1.

1973

3 DURANT, JACK D. "Sheridan's 'Royal Sanctuary': A Key to
The Rivals." Ball State University Forum 14, no.1
(Winter): 23-30.
Argues that "The Royal Sanctuary," a fragmentary
treatise written by Sheridan between 1772 and 1774, opens
insights into the form and meaning of The Rivals. Like
the epilogue to The Rivals, the "Sanctuary" declares that
men are irresistibly subject to the power of women. It
then sets out a scheme of female education by which
woman's influence can best be utilized. In its indictments
of mindless male vanity, and in the curriculum it proposes,
it reflects the characters of Sir Anthony (the man who
would keep women ignorant), Mrs. Malaprop and Lydia (the
miseducated but still influential woman), Faulkland (the
miseducated gentleman), Jack (the practical-minded man),
and Julia (the properly educated and properly influential
lady). The play dramatizes the influence of women as
properly and improperly directed.

4 FISKE, ROGER. "The Linleys 1775-1780." In English Theatre
Music in the Eighteenth Century. Oxford: Oxford
University Press, pp. 413-21.
Touches upon Sheridan's professional relationship with
the two Thomas Linleys, father and son, especially in
arranging, with the son, the music for The Duenna and in
guiding, with the father, the musical affairs of Drury
Lane during the first three years of the Sheridan
management. Brief references to Sheridan and theatrical
music are scattered throughout the volume.

5 FITZGERALD, PERCY. The Lives of the Sheridans. 2 vols
Philadelphia: Richard West.
Reprints photographically 1886.3.

6 FOSS, KENELM. Here Lies Richard Brinsley Sheridan. Folcroft,
Pa.: Folcroft Library Editions, 390 pp.
Reprints photographically 1939.2.

7 JEFFARES, A. NORMAN., ed. Introductory Note to The Rivals,
by Sheridan. Ilkley, Yorkshire: Scolar Press, 5
unnumbered pages.
Characterizes the play as "a young man's play, written
for the sheer fun of comedy" (p. 4). Its main merit lies
in "that skilful blending of farce with comedy of social
situation, which produces fun as well as humour. It
includes the ever-fresh cross-purposes of youth and age,
the many contrasts of false and genuine, of city and
country, of sentimentality and common sense, of poise
and awkwardness, of the expected and the delightfully

unexpected" (p. 5).

8   JORDAN, THOMAS H. "The Theatrical Craftsmanship of The
     School for Scandal." Dissertation Abstracts International
     33, no. 11 (May): 6314A-15A (Michigan).
          Concludes, from an analysis of the physical, linguistic,
     and dramatic properties of The School for Scandal, that
     Sheridan conceived his play not in abstraction but in
     concrete consideration of his audience, his theater, and
     his actors. He then "set his mind to the matters of
     structure, pace, contrast of character and mood, rise and
     fall of tempo" and "intellectual content" (6315A).

9   KRONENBERGER, LOUIS. "The School for Scandal." In Restoration
     and Eighteenth-Century Comedy, edited by Scott McMillin.
     Norton Critical Editions. New York: Norton, pp. 558-63.
          Reprints a portion (pp. 195-202) of the discussion of
     The School for Scandal in Kronenberger's The Thread of
     Laughter (1952.3): Through its wit and polish the play
     deserves its fame, but "it offers neither a genuine point
     of view, as does all the best Restoration comedy, nor a
     serious criticism of life, as does all important
     literature" (p. 562).

10   LEFF, LEONARD J. "Sheridan and Sentimentalism." Restoration
     and Eighteenth Century Theatre Research 12, no. 1 (May):
     36-48.
          Answers critics and historians who insist that Sheridan
     took up arms against sentimentalism. While showing, in
     his early verse and in the burlesque burletta Ixion, a
     fine gift for social satire, Sheridan chose, in trying
     to win approval and success, to pander to the sentimental
     vogue. Possibly to compensate for the inattention of his
     father, he bent his personal and professional life to a
     search for approving notice. Reflecting this search,
     The Rivals and The School for Scandal are manifestly
     sentimental plays. Through The Critic, at the outset of
     his political career, Sheridan sought to win the notice
     and approval of Charles James Fox. Even after earning
     success, Sheridan could not surrender his obsessive need
     for approval. (See 1972.14)

11   PRICE, CECIL, ed. Introduction to The Dramatic Works of
     Richard Brinsley Sheridan. Oxford English Text Series.
     Oxford: Clarendon Press, I, 1-33.
          Describes Sheridan's methods of work (his ideals of
     perfection complicated by his native indolence and his
     need for society), then provides a history of the
     Sheridan texts (their status at the time of his death,

1973

the efforts of his family to secure for him, in his
widow's phrase, "honor glory and truth," the ascertainment
of his canon). For Price's governing editorial principles,
also explained in this general introduction, see above,
"The Sheridan Texts."

12   RAE, W. FRASER. Sheridan: A Biography.   2 vols.
     Philadelphia: Richard West.
        Reprints photographically 1896.15.

13   STICKNEY, CHARLES JACOB. "The Distorted Word: Word
     Distortion in Modern British and American Literature."
     Dissertation Abstracts International 33 (June): 6933A-34A
     (City University of New York).
        Describes a doctoral study in which The Rivals (as one
     of several literary works) is drawn upon for an analysis
     of "the purposes and processes of word distortions in
     modern British and American literature" (p. 6933A).

                            1974

1   ANON. "Sheridan and the Art of the Burlesque." Times
     Literary Supplement, 22 February, pp. 169-70.
        Focuses, in a review of Cecil Prices's edition of The
     Dramatic Works of Richard Brinsley Sheridan (see 1973.11),
     upon The Critic, which is recognized, through its
     burlesque strategies, as exploding the falseness of
     eighteenth-century tragedy while yet revitalizing the
     heroic conventions of tragedy, a process resulting from
     the delight the play gives in disorder and the humanity
     it reveals in bathos. In the history of English drama,
     tragedy becomes "windy rhetoric"; comedy becomes
     "cynicism." Both present "untrue" views of life. "The
     vacuum between them is filled by the eighteenth century
     genre of the burlesque play" (p. 169).

2   BANKS, R. JEFF. "Modernizing a Toast from Richard Brinsley
     Sheridan." Journal of Popular Culture 8 (Winter): 582.
        Expresses surprise and pleasure at discovering
     Sheridan's ballad "Here's to the Maiden" (from act 3,
     scene 3 of The School for Scandal) prefixed to a Bar and
     Party Guide published in 1973 by the publishers of Knight,
     a magazine for men. Sheridan's term "prove" in line 7 is
     changed to "provide" in the bar guide, and his "quean" in
     line 3 is changed to "queen," but the changes, while doing
     no violence to the original, make the song "a good bit
     more pleasant" than before, more suitable for genial
     up-to-date toasts. It is only to be regretted that the

                            262

bar guide gives Sheridan no credit for his song.

3   BOWMAN, DAVID. "Sheridan's Comedy of Rhetoric."
    Interpretations: Studies in Language and Literature by the
    Department of English, Memphis State University 6, no. 1
    (1974): 31-38.
        Argues that Sheridan, in sharpening the brilliance of
    comedy while yet avoiding the worst symptoms of
    sentimentality, "created a newer and finer rhetorical
    comedy" (p. 37). The language of Sheridan's dialogue
    turns upon innumerable conventional schemes--"epimone"
    (redundant material), "amphora" (identical initial words),
    "ecphonesis" (emotional exclamation), "prosopopeia"
    (personification), etc.--and, while Sheridan "was aware
    of the dangers of rhetorical excesses, he could never
    resist using them for purposes of comedy" (p. 37).

4   CHATEL de BRANCION, FRANÇOISE. R. B. Sheridan: Personnalité,
    Carrière Politique. Études Anglaises, no. 56. Paris:
    Didier, 502 pp.
        Judges the personality of Sheridan to be most closely
    akin to that of his paternal grandfather but sees his
    mother's tenderness and courage and his father's grasp of
    everything theatrical to shape his personality, too, a
    personality compounded of vitality, high spiritedness,
    vanity, and a pervasive charm. A chronological account
    of Sheridan's political career (section 2) provides
    groundwork for an exposition in section 3 of his
    political ideas, domestic and foreign, and a comment
    upon his style as an orator. A champion of freedom and
    human dignity, he set his polemic against all signs of
    tyranny in matters domestic and foreign, and he invested
    his argument in a style charming and spirited, excellent
    in diction, rich in substance and ornament, enlivened by
    apt gestures and firm voice. In the steadiness of his
    principle and the color of his oratory, his personality
    and his political career come into a single perspective.
    Appendixes provide tables setting out the events of
    Sheridan's political career, his political writings and
    speeches, and works relating to his political career.
    Reviewed by Helene Koon in Philological Quarterly 54
    (1975): 1042-43; by Charles Pierce, Jr. in The Eighteenth
    Century: A Current Bibliography, n.s. 1 (1978): 372-73.

5   DARLINGTON, W. A. Sheridan. New York: Haskell House, 144 pp.
        Reprints photographically 1933.5.

6   DURANT, JACK D. "Prudence, Providence, and the Direct Road
    of Wrong: The School for Scandal and Sheridan's Westminster
    Hall Speech." Studies in Burke and His Time 15 (Spring):
    241-51.

1974

Suggests that <u>The School for Scandal and the</u> Westminster Hall Speech are "moral analogues." The terms used to vilify Warren Hastings in the speech are comparable (making allowances for the comic situation) to those used to characterize Joseph Surface in the play. The moral worlds evinced in the two pieces are identical to one another. To study the play in relation to the moral philosophy of the speech is to see it dramatizing the moral imperatives whereby virtue provides its own protection while vice aggravates its own defeat. The destinies of the Surface brothers, which constitute the main interests of the play, reflect these imperatives.

7   _____. "Sheridan, Rowlandson, and Comic Response: A Review Essay." <u>Southern Humanities Review</u> 8 (Fall): 515-24.
Sees conventional biographies of Sheridan, such as that by Madeleine Bingham (1972.5), as being deficient because they fail to read back from Sheridan's work the complex and disillusioned mind of the playwright. Since Sheridan's comic is closely comparable to the comic of Thomas Rowlandson, the study of Sheridan might well profit from the example given by Ronald Paulson in his book <u>Thomas Rowlandson: A New Interpretation</u> (Oxford University Press, 1972) which explores Rowlandson's mind and world through his art. It would likely be discovered that Sheridan, like Rowlandson, perceived in life the harshest lessons of decay and flux and through comic art made bearable to consciousness the harshest realities of experience.

8   FERGUSON, OLIVER W. "Sir Fretful Plagiary and Goldsmith's 'An Essay on the Theatre': The Background of Richard Cumberland's 'Dedication to Detraction.'" In <u>Quick Springs of Sense</u>, edited by Larry S. Champion. Athens: University of Georgia Press, pp. 113-20.
Demonstrates, through discussions of Cumberland's "Dedication to Detraction" (1775) and his <u>Memoirs</u> (1807), that Sheridan's Sir Fretful Plagiary is an accurate rendering of Cumberland's vain, hypersensitive, and petulant character. In answering a supposed attack upon his play <u>The Fashionable Lover</u> (1772), an attack supposed given in Goldsmith's "An Essay on the Theatre" (1773), Cumberland stored up his resentment for two years, at last releasing it in the "Dedication to Detraction." He did not know that Goldsmith was the author of the "Essay," which had been published anonymously; and the same vanity which had caused him to resent a supposed attack obscured his awareness of a real one given subtly in Goldsmith's "Retaliation" (1774).

9   JASON, PHILIP K. "A Twentieth-Century Response to <u>The</u>

Critic." <u>Theatre Survey</u> 15 (1974): 51-58.
   Demonstrates that <u>The Critic</u> is "a play about perception" (p. 57). By opening his action in the home of a
theatrical dangler, by peopling his early scenes with
performers and would-be playwrights, by confronting his
audience with the problems of dramaturgy and the realities
of theatrical production, Sheridan excites innumerable
questions about how experience should be perceived and
judged. "The concentric realities of Puff's play,
Sheridan's play, and our own sense of life promote
tensions and reverberations that are intuitively felt and
demand rational analysis" (p. 57), the kind of analysis
we are led to in Berkeley's <u>Treatise</u>, in Locke's <u>Essay</u>, and
in Sterne's <u>Tristram Shandy</u>.

10   JORDAN, THOMAS H. <u>The Theatrical Craftsmanship of Richard</u>
     <u>Brinsley Sheridan's The School for Scandal</u>. New York:
     Revisionist Press, 193 pp.
        Analyzes Sheridan's craftsmanship in terms of physical
     resources (the actors, the theater, the audience),
     linguistic resources (diction and dialogue), and dramatic
     resources ("tempo, humor, character orchestration,
     climaxes in dialogue, theatrical logic, compressed time,
     and juxtaposition of characters and scenes" [p. ii]).
     The happy effect of the play derives from the interaction
     of these resources. (Cf. 1973.8.)

11   SADLE [I] R, Michael. <u>The Political Career of Richard Brinsley</u>
     <u>Sheridan (The Stanhope Essay for 1912)</u>. Followed by Some
     <u>Hitherto Unpublished Letters of Mrs. Sheridan</u>. Folcroft,
     Pa.: Folcroft Library Editions, 87 pp.
        Reprints photographically 1912.4.

12   SANDERS, LLOYD C. <u>Life of Richard Brinsley Sheridan</u>. Great
     Writers Series. Folcroft, Pa.: Folcroft Library Editions.
     Reprints photographically 1890.2.

13   STAHLKOPF, CAROLE S. "Rhetoric and Comic Technique in
     Richard Brinsley Sheridan's <u>The Rivals</u> and <u>The School for</u>
     <u>Scandal</u>." <u>Dissertation Abstracts International</u> 34, no. 7
     (January): 4219A (University of California, Davis).
        Describes a doctoral study in which the language of
     Sheridan's two most popular comedies undergoes systematic
     analysis. In <u>The Rivals</u>, the schemes and tropes chosen
     by Sheridan assist him in manipulating sentence structure,
     in burlesquing the language of false sentiment, and in
     fitting the diction to the characters. In <u>The School for</u>
     <u>Scandal</u>, schemes and tropes furnish him with a major
     means of exposing as false an entire social code. In

1974

both plays, "Sheridan uses his masterful command of
language and rhetoric to express and reenforce theme,
character, and action; the resulting brilliant synthesis
creates a cumulative comic effect that evokes continual
laughter."

14   WARD, JOHN CHAPMAN. "The Tradition of the Hypocrite in
Eighteenth-Century English Literature." Dissertation
Abstracts International 34 (February): 5128A. (Virginia)
Describes a doctoral study which examines the figure of
the hypocrite in eighteenth-century literature (using The
School for Scandal as one of the paradigms) and notices a
remarkable consistency in portrayals of the hypocrite type.
In all the works studied, "the hypocrite operates under
providential control, serving paradoxically to bolster,
not undermine, the community's moral standards; in his
inevitable downfall many are enlightened and moral and
social order are vindicated." Only with Jane Austen
does the hypocrite start to progress beyond his status as
a mere type to become a personality.

1975

1   AUBURN, MARK S. "The Pleasures of Sheridan's The Rivals:
A Critical Study in the Light of Stage History." Modern
Philology 72, no. 3 (February): 256-71.
Recognizes The Rivals to be a "comedy of character"
by testimony of its American stage history, which shows
it changing forms in such a way as to suppress the more
quiescent characters (viz., Julia and Faulkland) and
amplify the more ebullient ones, chiefly Bob Acres and
Mrs. Malaprop, making them the center of a farcical
action. The pleasures given by The Rivals derive mainly
from "local exposures of characters' foibles and
idiosyncrasies in themselves" (p. 257). The play is
perennially popular, then, because it lends itself to
formal changes (after the character specialties of acting
companies) without sacrificing any of its capacity to
please.

2   _____. Promptscripts of The Rivals: An Annotated
Bibliography." Performing Arts Resources 2 (1975): 41-55.
Lists 28 promptscripts and signed copies of The Rivals,
most of them not cited in NUC. "Their value . . . is to
suggest general trends in the acting tradition, not to
show specific individual innovations appearing for the
first time" (pp. 41-42). Each entry contains four lines:
the first line provides (1) the name of the actor, the

director, and the prompter or stage manager with whom the
book can be associated, (2) the city and theater where the
book was used, if available, and (3) the "earliest
approximate date of first significant use or date
inscribed in the text." The second line gives the current
location of the book. The third line describes the
physical appearance of the book "usually in terms of the
edition from which the promptbook was made." And the
fourth line briefly describes the contents. The
arrangement of entries is chronological, running from
1791 to 1942.

3   DAVIES, ROBERTSON. "Playwrights and Plays 1770-1780." In
    The Revels History of Drama in English. vol 6, 1750-1880.
    New York: Harper & Row, pp. 166-74.
        Rounds out a survey of the decade 1770-1780 in drama
    by commenting on the major comedies of Sheridan and upon
    his major gifts. In form and content The Rivals is highly
    derivative, but it comes to life "by a combination of
    high-bred merriment and a command of language which only
    Goldsmith, in a vein of his own, could rival" (p. 173).
    Its conclusion (projecting the marriages of two oddly
    matched couples) achieves an authentic reconciliation of
    opposites. The School for Scandal "establishes Sheridan
    as the greatest comic writer of his day" and provides, in
    Joseph Surface, not only Sheridan's finest creation but
    "one of the notable figures of English comedy" (p. 174).
    The Critic demonstrates the acuteness and depth of
    Sheridan's vis comica and is "one of the handful of
    great burlesques in our literature" (p. 174).

4   DURANT, JACK D. Richard Brinsley Sheridan. Twayne's
    English Authors Series, no. 183. Boston: G. K. Hall,
    166 pp.
        Offers a descriptive introductory survey of Sheridan's
    literary work (criticism, poetry, theatrical pieces)
    attempting to elucidate the moral substance of Sheridan's
    art: the educational theory informing The Rivals, the
    social irony pervasive in The Duenna, the Christian
    benevolism basic to The School for Scandal, the principles
    of artistic integrity implied in The Critic, the senti-
    mental virtue dramatized in Pizarro. Digests criticism
    and textual commentary so as to provide a handbook for
    beginning students of Sheridan. Reviewed by Joan H. Owen
    in Library Journal 100 (1 September): 1548; in Johnsonian
    Newsletter 35 (December); by Robert D. Hume in Philological
    Quarterly 55 (Fall 1976): 471-72; by Mark S. Auburn in
    Southern Humanities Review 12 (Spring 1978): 163-64; by
    Cynthia Sutherland Matlock in The Eighteenth Century: A

1975

Current Bibliography, n.s. 1 (1978): 373-74.

5   GILL, BRENDAN. "The Theatre Off Broadway." New Yorker 50
    (27 January): 69.
        Reviews a production of The Rivals staged by the
    Roundabout Theatre under the direction of Michael
    Bawtree. Sees virtues in letting Sheridan's wit carry
    itself, without the overmannered inflections and gestures
    given by this cast. Looks upon Mrs. Malaprop as being
    funny "because she is a lady." Calls the role of
    Faulkland "tiresome."

6   LOFTIS, JOHN. "Whig Oratory on Stage: Sheridan's Pizarro."
    Eighteenth Century Studies 8, no. 4 (Summer): 454-72.
        Sees Pizarro not as a decline of Sheridan's powers but
    as an "alteration of his style, his interests, and
    objectives" (p. 455). It is "a Whig play--a play that
    celebrates the social and political philosophy of the
    Opposition to Pitt, even though it includes a pledge of
    loyalty to the king and of opposition to the French"
    (p. 456). That it was viewed as an indictment of what
    Sheridan thought to be the antihumanitarian policy of the
    Pitt administration (especially as regards the slave trade)
    appears in attacks leveled against it (and against other
    German plays) in the Tory press. The amplified
    spectacle in the play is "an emblem of the heroic code of
    conduct by which the virtuous characters . . . regulate
    their lives" (p. 458), and thus it assists the
    dramatization of Sheridan's political themes.

7   MAXWELL-MAHON, W. D. "Sheridan: 'The School for Scandal.'"
    Crux: a Guide to Teaching English Language and Literature
    9, no. 2 (May): 36-43.
        Suggests that The School for Scandal holds its place
    "partly because of Sheridan's vivid portrayal of the
    skirted dandies and fops . . . of Georgian England; partly
    because of his spirited and influential attack on the
    moral sentiment so popular with contemporary novelists and
    playwrights; but mainly because of his scintillating
    dialogue, the like of which is not found again in English
    drama until we come to Oscar Wilde and Shaw" (p. 36).

8   O'CONNOR, JOHN J. "TV: 'School for Scandal.'" New York
    Times, 2 April, p. 79.
        Applauds a television adaptation of The School for
    Scandal performed by the Tyrone Guthrie Theater Company
    for the "Theater in America" series on National Public
    Television. The adaptation sacrifices none of the play's
    integrity as a classic. "The characters are still

268

immediately recognizable--silly, vicious, greedy,
laughable, a collection of 'fiends, vipers and furies'
irrepressibly human."

9   PRICE, CECIL. "The Clare Sheridan MSS. in the British
    Theatre Museum." Theatre Notebook 29 (Winter): 51-56.
        Describes select documents acquired for the British
    Theatre Museum from the estate of Mrs. Clare Sheridan,
    widow of Wilfred Sheridan, a descendant of the playwright.
    Included are references to "Several prompt copies" of
    The School for Scandal, one containing dialogue ultimately
    canceled but significant now in suggesting Sheridan's
    methods of work and his intentions for the character of
    Lady Teazle, letters relating chiefly to managerial
    affairs at Drury Lane Theatre, a document assessing the
    income possibly available to J. P. Kemble should he
    purchase shares in the theater, notes touching the
    promotion and good management of the newly built theater
    in 1795, a report from Samuel Whitbread (dated 9 December
    1812) concerning the rebuilding and reopening of the
    theater after the fire of 1809, brief notes on programs
    and receipts at the theater for the seasons 1747-1762,
    1770-1771, 1776-1782, with receipts only for 1803-1805.
    A catalog of the full collection is available at the
    British Theatre Museum.

10 _____. "Gay, Goldsmith, Sheridan and Other Eighteenth-Century
    Dramatists." In English Drama (Excluding Shakespeare):
    Select Bibliographical Guides, edited by Stanley Wells.
    London: Oxford University Press, pp. 199-212.
        Provides succinct commentary upon the texts of
    Sheridan's major plays and upon criticism and biography.
    Favors, in ascertaining the text of The School for Scandal,
    seven manuscripts containing corrections by Sheridan; for
    The Rivals, the first edition, 1775; for St. Patrick's
    Day, the manuscript licensed by the lord chamberlain; for
    The Duenna, an edition of 1794; for The Critic, the first
    edition, 1779. Selects for brief mention critical studies
    by Dulck (1962.12), Brooks and Heilman (1945.1), Mudrick
    (1955.2), Jackson (1961.7), and Deelman (1962.8), the
    biographies by Moore (1825.9), Rae (1896.15), Sichel
    (1909.5), and Rhodes (1933.8). Pages 201-3 deal
    specifically with Sheridan.

11 _____, ed. Introduction to Sheridan's Plays. Oxford
    Standard Authors Series. London: Oxford University
    Press, pp. viii-xxxi.
        Surveys Sheridan's life and his entire theatrical
    career, providing extracts from contemporary reviews,

1975

comments on Sheridan's practices of revisal, insights
into the meanings of the plays, and assessments of the
playwright's theatrical skills. "Dialogue came easily
to Sheridan once character and situation were fixed in
his mind. . . . Pruning and cutting of the text went on
even after the first performance till every word
counted . . ." (p. xxxi). To Sheridan's mind "What
distinguishes the bad from the good is the degree of
heartlessness in their behaviour. Sheridan wanted this
to be recognized rather than strongly reproved. Good
nature could not cure all the ills of society, but real
generosity of spirit might enhance . . . life . . ."
(p. xxiii).

12   RUDOLPH, VALERIE C. "'Exit Thames between his banks': An
     Emblem of Order in Sheridan's The Critic." Theatre
     Survey 16 (1975): 93-95.
        Suggests that "the Thames within and the Thames without
     its banks" in The Critic "were well-known emblems of
     order and disorder respectively that had already been
     politicized and popularized in such works as Sir John
     Denham's 'Cooper's Hill'" (p. 93). By having Puff
     adjust Thames's relationship to his banks, Sheridan
     dramatizes a facile, ridiculous restoration of political
     order, a restoration not likely to be achieved in fact,
     "given the notorious reluctance of the British Navy to
     engage the enemy fleets in 1779" (p. 94). Through his
     burlesque, Sheridan indicates that true political order
     will come only with a willingness to reassert the spirit
     which had defeated the Spanish Armada.

13   WILLSON, ROBERT F., JR. "The Critic and Theatrical Decline."
     In "Their Form Confounded": Studies in the Burlesque Play
     from Udall to Sheridan. De Proprietatibus Litterarum.
     Series Practica, no. 88. The Hague: Mouton, pp. 138-65.
        Attributes the excellence of The Critic to Sheridan's
     capacity to synthesize the goals of satire and burlesque.
     By burlesquing the "heroi-historical" and patriotic play,
     he satirizes offenses against playwrights (whose work is
     cheapened by facile amateurs), art itself (which is too
     often and too easily prostituted by patriotism and other
     forms of shallow zeal), and criticism (which is too much
     the prey of dilettantes). His extraordinary method
     teaches us not only "how the aims of satire can be made
     to conform to the broader comic aims of burlesque" but
     also "the method by which typical caricatures become
     lively characters" (p. 165).

1976

1 CONOLLY, L[EONARD] W. The Censorship of English Drama,
   1737-1824. San Marino, Cal.: Huntington Library, passim.
      Mentions Sheridan infrequently, but pertinently, in
   discussing a subject very close to his professional life.
   Reference is made to the licensing of A Trip to Scarborough
   and The School for Scandal, and Sheridan is observed as
   holding the conviction, as expressed by him in a letter to
   Samuel Whitbread in 1815, that politics should be kept out
   of the theater.

2 FISKE, ROGER. "The Duenna." Musical Times 117 (March):
   217-19.
      Anticipates a revival of The Duenna at the Camden
   Festival (on 16, 20, 24, and 26 March) by sketching a
   brief history of the libretto and score of the opera.
   The libretto poses no problems, for it is "Sheridan in
   his best form" (p. 217). The score offers problems
   because it is a pastiche. Just over half of it was
   composed by the two Thomas Linleys, father and son: the
   rest of it is a mixture of Scotch popular songs and
   concerted songs by Italian composers. (See 1961.6.)
   Sixteen original orchestrations survive, and Fiske has
   attempted himself to orchestrate the remaining numbers.

3 GOETSCH, PAUL. "Richard Brinsley Sheridan: The School for
   Scandal." In Das englische Drama im 18, und 19.
   Jahrhundert: Interpretationen. Berlin: Schmidt,
   pp. 159-69.
      Places The School for Scandal in historical context as
   a play combining Restoration and sentimental conventions
   and considers why it has endured on the stage while other
   sentimentalized plays have not. The reasons appear in
   its optimistic spirit, its brilliant dialogue, the
   construction of its scenes, and its splendid acting roles.

4 GRATZ, DAVID KENNETH. "Emotion, Modes of Expression and
   Effects on Plot, in Selected Comedies: 1670-1780."
   Dissertation Abstracts International 36 (April):
   6702A-03A (Syracuse).
      Includes plays by Sheridan (and also by Etherege,
   Congreve, Cibber, Vanbrugh, Steele, and Cumberland) in a
   study of the changing attitudes toward expression of
   emotion in English high comedy between 1670 and 1780.
   According to the attitudes evinced, the plays studied
   (not named in this abstract) are categorized as satiric
   or romantic, realistic or sentimental.

1976

5   HALL, ELIZABETH. "Sheridan and the Rev. William Lisle
    Bowles: An Uncollected Bowles Poem and the Dating of Two
    Sheridan Letters." Notes and Queries, n.s. 23 (March):
    106-7.
        Argues that an uncollected poem of Bowles's, "On
    Presenting Mrs. Sheridan with my Purcell to take with
    her to London" (which was printed in the Bath Chronicle
    on 28 January 1802), makes 1802 a more logical date for
    one of Sheridan's letters than the 1806 tentatively
    assigned it in Cecil Price's edition of the Letters of
    Richard Brinsley Sheridan (2: 272). Also argues that
    an implied reference to Bowles's "Song of the Battle of
    the Nile" (1799) makes the phrase "during or after 1799"
    a more logical dating for a second of Sheridan's letters,
    one dated "after 1794" by Price (2: 102-3).

6   LINK, FREDERICK M. "Richard Brinsley Sheridan (1751-1816)."
    In English Drama, 1660-1800. A Guide to Information
    Sources. Gale Information Guide Library: American
    Literature, English Literature, and World Literatures in
    English: An Information Guide Series. Detroit: Gale
    Research, pp. 288-92.
        Lists, within running commentary, studies relating to
    the bibliography, texts, biography, and plays of
    Sheridan. Runs through 1973.

7   MAYER, DAVID. "Fair Royal Exchange." Plays and Players
    24, no. 2 (November): 24-25.
        Remarks, in reviewing a production of The Rivals staged
    at the new Royal Exchange Theatre in Manchester, the
    seriousness lying "just below the almost unbroken comic
    surface" of the play, a seriousness found especially in
    the plight of Lydia Languish (as played by Susan Tracy),
    who is not deluded by sentimental fiction but who turns
    to it for refuge from the fear that she is courted only
    for her estate. Tom Courtenay, as Faulkland, ably
    explores the psychology of masochistic grievance hunting.
    To its credit, the production is not merely a parade of
    eccentrics, as it so often is in dull productions.

8   PRICE, CECIL. "Sheridan and the Drury Lane Theatre,
    1801-1809." Theatre Survey 17 (May): 12-27.
        Surveys the managerial crises suffered by Drury Lane
    Theatre betwen 1801 and 1809, crises including (1) the
    Chancery suit of 1801, which gave to an appointed auditor
    responsibilities for disbursing daily box-office receipts,
    (2) the resignations of John Philip Kemble and Sarah
    Siddons and the subsequent removal of these actors to
    Covent Garden Theatre, (3) the necessity of turning to

spectacle and curiosity in attracting audiences, (4) a
second Chancery suit in 1804, (5) Sheridan's continuing
withdrawal from the artistic life of the enterprise
(especially after he joined the Ministry in 1806 as
Treasurer of the Navy), (6) the fire of 24 February 1809,
from which, because of his indolence, Sheridan failed to
recover and which resulted in his exclusion from further
management. "We see him in the period 1801-09 move
towards his ruin with all the inevitability of a Greek
tragedy, but we know that like the hero of a
Shakespearian tragedy all the causes of his downfall
lay in himself" (p. 25).

9   RHODES, R. CROMPTON. Harlequin Sheridan, the Man and the
     Legends. Folcroft, Pa.: Folcroft Library Editions, 322 pp.
        Reprints photographically 1933.8.

                              1977

1   AHMAD, SULEIMAN M. "Hardy's A Pair of Blue Eyes and
     Sheridan's The School for Scandal." Notes and Queries,
     n.s. 24 (October): 430.
        Suggests that the title of Hardy's novel A Pair of
     Blue Eyes (originally to be titled A Winning Tongue Had
     He) derives from Sir Toby's song in The School for Scandal
     (III, iii), the second stanza of which includes the phrase
     "a pair of blue eyes." Sheridan's play was running in
     London in August of 1872, the time at which Hardy revised
     his title.

2   AUBURN, MARK S. Sheridan's Comedies: Their Contexts and
     Achievements. Lincoln: University of Nebraska Press,
     221 pp.
        Demonstrates that Sheridan shares with other Georgian
     dramatists the main conceptual and moral features of
     comic drama: plots evoking comic anxiety, humor characters
     clearly drawn but not subject to ridicule, little or no
     sexual reference or sexual innuendo. His distinctiveness
     lies, then, not in new departures but in his rare
     instincts for comic pleasure. The Rivals and St. Patrick's
     Day, for example, bring pleasures chiefly through
     characterization, The Duenna through its intricate if
     improbable plot. With his movement from Covent Garden to
     Drury Lane, "Sheridan would show more concern with
     carefully structured plot (as he is doing in The Duenna
     in comparison to The Rivals and St. Patrick's Day), more
     concern with wit, more concern with satire" (p. 80). His
     comedies would be less frivolous and somewhat less amiable

than before. The first of these Drury Lane comedies, A
Trip to Scarborough, is a fine achievement in structural
unity, but it fails artistically because Sheridan failed
to perceive that the beauty of its source, Vanbrugh's The
Relapse, "Lay in its very licentiousness" (p. 103), a
quality sacrificed in A Trip to Scarborough to "innocuous
situation comedy" (p. 103). Such conceptual problems,
however, do not trouble The School for Scandal. It is
successful in plot and in the interplay of several comic
types: punitive comedy of exposure, comedy of self-adjustment, and comedy of merit rewarded. By effecting this
interplay Sheridan created "an amiable comedy whose tone
is representative of the late eighteenth century" (p. 112),
and the sense of this complex tone seems to have governed
his choices as he reworked the early sketches of the play.
Even The School for Scandal, however, does not so fully
answer to his skills as The Critic, for Sheridan was above
all a creator of comic moments, and The Critic, following
the loosest of informing principles (theatrical
burlesque), is a successon of comic moments "into which
Sheridan packed all the comic techniques he had developed
in his earlier works" (p. 166). It rounds off his
achievement among writers of English comedy, an achievement
springing from "complex, fast-moving, amiably comic plots
peopled by probable yet theatrical characters; from a
verbal brilliance dependent not upon wit in the high
Restoration comic sense but upon a full consonance of
expression to character; and from a careful poise of
expectation and surprise in situational comedy" (p. 181).
Reviewed by G. S. Rousseau in Studies in English
Literature 18 (Summer 1978): 577; by Eric Rothstein in
Modern Language Quarterly 39 (December 1978): 418-20;
by Joseph L. Greenberg in Theatre Journal 31 (May 1979):
271-72; by Robert D. Hume in Philological Quarterly 57
(Fall 1978): 461-63.

3   _____. "Two Notes on Sheridan's Compositional Practices."
"Appendix" to 1977.2, pp. 183-86.
    Illustrates, first, a practice whereby Sheridan
occasionally "utilized the wit of others, transforming
a bare suggestion into a coup de maître" (p. 183): A
passage in Fielding's Amelia seems to furnish grist for
his wit in the epilogue to Edward and Eleonora (1775)
and in an early sketch of "The Teazles" (a passage
canceled before it reached The School for Scandal)
wherein, in both cases, the prospect of widowhood leads
the speaker to thoughts of "countermanding" her new
brocade and, in the epilogue, to wondering when she
might hope again to wear such finery. The second note

reads Puff's example of the "puff direct" in The Critic
(I, ii, 168-75) as indeed a "puff preliminary" for a
play forthcoming at Drury Lane, i.e., "Elizabeth Griffith's
dull comedy The Times (DL, December 2 1779), probably just
in rehearsal when The Critic was introduced" (p. 186).

4   LOFTIS, JOHN. Sheridan and the Drama of Georgian England.
Cambridge: Harvard University Press, 174 pp.
Identifies Sheridan as a backward-looking playwright
whose gifts lay not in developing new theories of drama
but in crafting splendid dialogue and in burlesquing
received dramatic practices, practices coming to him
from both Restoration and mid-eighteenth-century plays.
In expressing distaste for sentimental drama, he sought
not to separate himself from his dramatic heritage but
to attack the offenses against it of specific playwrights,
notably Hugh Kelly and Richard Cumberland, whose
characters too often overindulged their sensibilities.
Like other playwrights of the Georgian tradition--Hoadly,
Garrick, Colman, Murphy, Goldsmith and indeed Cumberland
and Kelly in much of their work--Sheridan brought to his
plays (to speak first of the comedies) a spirit
"sentimental" in only a generalized sense and "genial
and optimistic" (p. 31) in rendering the human condition.
While showing his admiration for Restoration dramatists,
his comedies thoroughly reflect their own time. The
Rivals and The Duenna, then, represent "Restoration
Comedy in Georgian Burlesque" (p. 42). In them "Sheridan
played variations on dramatic formulae of the Restoration"
(p. 43), first in The Rivals, developing a "comedy of
character," a play closely similar to those of Congreve
in character types and character relationships, then, in
The Duenna, developing a "comedy of action," a play
subordinating character to plot in the manner of the
Spanish intrigue plays of the Restoration. A Trip to
Scarborough and The School for Scandal recall ideals of
Restoration dramatic theory by reflecting "The Survival of
Neoclassicism" (p. 75). In the first of these plays,
Sheridan adjusted Vanbrugh's The Relapse to classical
standards by observing unities of time, place, and action,
by leveling ambiguities in motivation and event, by
removing indecorous expressions, and by shaping the
denouement to a clear moral purpose. The School for
Scandal adapts these same standards of theme and form
and enriches them by making satire integral to plot, thus
to establish a distinctive tone, a "balance between
sentiment and satire typical of the Age of Johnson at its
best" (p. 99). The Critic again finds Sheridan
participating in established literary traditions, not

only the traditions of theatrical burlesque but also that of the satiric apologia, a tradition best represented in the earlier eighteenth century by Pope's Epistle to Dr. Arbuthnot. In this, his last important play, Sheridan confronts the whole theatrical enterprise, settling scores with his detractors and voicing convictions (however ironically) about dramatic theory, both comic (in the first act) and tragic (in the last two acts). The Critic achieves durability through the complex interplay of many methods and targets of burlesque and through the reconcilement of the "mode of burlesque with the conventions of comedy of manners" (p. 117). By abandoning his extraordinary gift for burlesque, Sheridan gave his last play, Pizarro, up to fustian. But Pizarro does not signal a loss of his theatrical powers. The work of a seasoned statesman, it expresses his feelings about current political issues, especially his opposition to the slave trade and his defiance of Bonaparte. It was "Whig Oratory on the Stage" (p. 124), but it succeeded splendidly as theatre (See 1975.6). Reviewed by Leo Braudy in Studies in English Literature 17 (Summer 1977): 557-58; by Eric Salmon in Queen's Quarterly 85 (March 1978): 522-24; by David V. Erdman in English Language Notes 16, no. 1, supp. (September 1978): 40; by Robert D. Hume in Philological Quarterly 56 (Fall 1977): 454-55. Also reviewed in 1977.6.

5   PAGE, VINCENT, AND HODGART, SUZANNE. "Writing Home."
    Sunday Times Magazine (London), 17 April, p. 76.
        Adapts from the forthcoming Oxford Literary Guide to the British Isles a pictorial survey of the homes of famous British writers and includes among them a pen drawing of Polesden Lacey, the country home bought by Sheridan in 1796 as a "seat of health and happiness" for his new wife. In 1802 (reports the accompanying writeup) he came to regret the purchase when many members of his household (including his wife and son) came down with scarlet fever. "A Regency house now stands on the site, at Great Bookham, in Surrey."

6   PRICE, CECIL. "The Second Congreve." Times Literary
    Supplement, 11 February, p. 143.
        Gives emphasis, within the context of a review of John Loftis's Sheridan and the Drama of Georgian England (1977.4), to Sheridan's general practice of "keeping the theatre out of party politics" despite his willingness to include, on occasion, "social and political references that were usually dropped in performance as soon as they became dated." Admires Loftis's book but finds Loftis

unconvincing in his judgment of The Duenna.

7   RHODES, R. CROMPTON. Harlequin Sheridan, the Man and the
    Legends. Norwood, Pa.: Norwood Editions, 322 pp.
       Reprints photographically 1933.8.

8   SCHULZ, VOLKER. "Die Komik der 'Wandschirm-Szene' in
    Sheridans The School for Scandal." Literatur in
    Wissenschaft und Unterricht 10 (1977): 1-15.
       Discovers the comic force of the Screen Scene to
    derive from several comic modes working together: (1)
    the perfect miniaturization of the five-act comic
    structure: (2) a sustained tension built not upon
    surprise but expectation; (3) an intermingling of the
    favorite conventions of situation comedy--i.e., mistake,
    dilemma, deception, and exposure; (4) careful modulation
    of climax; and (5) a system of ironies in which Joseph
    catches himself in his own noose.

1978

1   DANZIGER, MARLIES K. Oliver Goldsmith and Richard Brinsley
    Sheridan. World Dramatists Series. New York: Frederick
    Ungar, 189 pp.
       Places the two playwrights in their social and
    theatrical milieu, then provides running commentary upon
    their plays, emphasizing tonal and thematic focuses within
    and among the scenes and conventions of character and
    situation recalled by the action. A brief stage history
    follows each analytical discussion. The conclusion
    acknowledges reservations long held by literary
    critics--that the plays flirt with sentimentality and are
    "too healthy" (p. 160) in spirit--but evokes historical
    evidence to indicate that Goldsmith and Sheridan wrote
    for the stage, not for the study. Selective
    bibliographies come at the end. Reviewed by Joseph L.
    Greenberg in Theatre Journal 31 (May 1979): 270-71.

2   MALEK, JAMES S. "Julia as a Comic Character in The Rivals."
    Studies in the Humanities 7, no. 1 (December): 10-13.
       Argues that Julia, in being the butt of Sheridan's
    good-natured ridicule, belongs to laughing comedy and
    that comedy relating to her derives from the "disparity
    between what she says and what she does" (p. 10). It
    also derives from "(1) various speeches in the play in
    which she rationalizes her behavior; (2) Lydia's ability
    to make fun of her; and (3) Sheridan's use of dramatic
    irony to undermine the effectiveness of her somber and

exaggerated diction, which would be out of place if
intended seriously" (p. 10).

3   MOORE, THOMAS. Memoirs of the Life of the Right Honourable
    Richard Brinsley Sheridan. 2 vols. Philadelphia:
    Richard West.
        Reprints 1825.10.

<u>1979</u>

1   BATESON, F. W. "The Application of Thought to an
    Eighteenth-Century Text: The School for Scandal." In
    Evidence in Literary Scholarship. Essays in Memory of
    James Marshall Osborn, edited by René Wellek and Alvaro
    Ribeiro. Oxford: Clarendon Press, pp. 321-35.
        Draws upon texts of The School for Scandal to refute
    the editorial dictum that textual "last" is textual
    "best." "[W]henever an author has offered more than
    one version of a passage a responsible editor will be
    expected to provide in the text whatever after due
    consideration he (the editor) believes the best authorial
    version to be, whether it happens to be early,
    middle-period, or last" (p. 324). In editing The School
    for Scandal, Cecil Price has given too much authority to
    the Crewe MS (Georgetown) as textual "last." Certain
    readings in the John Murray text of 1821, which give
    evidence of Sheridan's own authority, ought better to
    appear in the edited text than their variants in the
    Crewe MS.

2   DARLINGTON, W. A. Sheridan. Great Lives Series, no. 15.
    Darby, Pa.: Arden Library, 144 pp.
        Reprints photographically 1933.5.

3   PRICE, CECIL. "Pursuing Sheridan." In Evidence in Literary
    Scholarship. Essays in Memory of James Marshall Osborn,
    edited by René Wellek and Alvaro Ribeiro. Oxford:
    Clarendon Press, pp. 309-20.
        Recounts the experience of editing Sheridan's letters,
    then prints four of the several letters which have come
    to light since the publication of Sheridan's letters in
    1966. They are among letters "that are peculiarly personal
    in character and that hold our attention even when they
    are almost baffling" (p. 315). The first promises to
    provide the recipient with a new prologue; the next
    speaks distressfully of a miscarriage recently suffered
    by Elizabeth Sheridan; the third, possibly a draft, might
    have been intended for Pamela, the daughter of Madame de

Genlis, and the fourth seems to concern Sir Joshua
Reynolds' representation of Elizabeth Sheridan as St.
Cecilia. These letters suggest aspects of Sheridan's
character nowhere revealed in close detail; and perhaps,
if such letters continue to come to light, "we may put
together eventually a speaking likeness of one of the
most distinguished figures in our theatrical and
political history" (p. 320).

Index

281

Index

Index

Index

"Introduction" to Sheridan's
Plays (Price), 1975.11
"Introduction" to Sheridan's
Plays (Williams), 1926.17
"Introduction" to Sheridan's
Works (Browne), 1873.1
"Introduction" to Six Plays of
Sheridan (Kronenberger),
1957.5
"Introduction" to Eighteenth-
Century English Drama
(Krutch), 1967.11
"Introductory Comment" to The
School for Scandal (Bonazza
and Roy), 1968.1
"Introductory Note" to The Rivals
(Jeffares), 1973.7
"Introduction by Sheridan's
Great-Grandson" (Dufferin),
1896.5
An Introduction to Eighteenth-
Century Drama, 1700-1780,
1953.4
"Invocation to Friendship,"
1816.13
"An Irish Triumvirate," 1936.4
"Irma Is a Lady," 1950.1
"Irresistible Ogle," 1915.2

J., 1826.13
Jackson, J. R. de J., 1961.7
Jacox, Francis, 1864.1
Jaloux, E., 1913.5
James Henry, 1874.4; 1948.5;
1957.3
"Jane Austen's Reading," 1930.12
Jason, Philip K., 1974.9
Jebb, E. M., 1928.8
Jeffares, A. Norman, 1967.9-10;
1973.7
Jefferson, Joseph, 1889.4; 1902.5
Jeffrey, Francis, 1826.14
Jerrald, Walter, 1893.2
Jewish Characters in Eighteenth
Century Fiction and Drama,
1935.5
Johnson, E. G., 1896.12
Johnson, Maurice, 1960.4
Johnson, Philip, 1936.6
Jones, Howard Mumford, 1952.3
(rev.)
Jordan, Thomas H., 1973.8;

1974.10
The Journals of Elizabeth Lady
Holland (1791-1811), 1903.2
"Julia as a Comic Character in
The Rivals," 1978.2

Kalem, T. E., 1972.11
Kaul, A. N., 1970.7
Kelly, Micahel, 1826.15
Kelly, Walter Keating, 1854.2
"Kelly's Memoirs," 1825.3
"Kensington Palace, May 30,"
1962.2
Kernodle, George R., 1946,6
Kerr, Walter, 1970.8
"King's Theatre, Hammersmith.
'The School for Scandal' by
Richard Brinsley Sheridan,"
1953.1
Klapperich, Joseph, 1891.1
Knapp, Mary Etta, 1961.8
Knight, G. Wilson, 1962.14
Knight, Joseph, 1906.1
"Die Komik der 'Wandschirm-Szene
in Sheridans The School for
Scandal," 1977.8
Koon, Helene, 1974.4 (rev.)
Korshin, Paul J., 1972.10
Kotzebue, a Survey of His
Progress in France, and
England, Preceded by a
Consideration of the Attitude
to Him in Germany, 1928.21
Kotzebue in England, 1901.2
Kotzebue und Sheridan, 1888.3
Krause, Gustave, 1896.13
"Kritische Ruckschau," 1961.11
Kroll, Jack, 1972.12
Kronenberger, Louis, 1952.3;
1957.4-5; 1969.4; 1973.9
Krutch, Joseph Wood, 1925.3;
1942.8; 1946.7; 1952.3 (rev.);
1967.11

Lahey, Gerald B., 1958.2-3
Lamb, Charles, 1822.4; 1823.1
Landfield, Jerome B., 1953.9;
1957.6; 1958.4; 1960.10
(rev.); 1961.9; 1962.15
Landre, Louis, 1949.4; 1969.5
Landre-Augier, Germaine, 1963.15
Landstone, Charles, 1951.6
Lane, Margaret, 1960.5 (rev.)

Lanoix, Louis, 1962.12 (rev.)
"The Larpent Manuscript of St. Patrick's Day," 1966.11
Lask, Thomas, 1972.13
"Die Lästerschule" (Gregor), 1957.2
"Die Lästerschüle" (Schaubuhne), 1917.2
"The Late Mr. Sheridan" (Hunt), 1816.15; 1956.5
"A Laugh Analysis of The School for Scandal," 1930.3
"The Laughing Comedy of the Eighteenth Century," 1965.6
Lawrence, W. J., 1928.9; 1933.8 (rev.)
"Lead, Kindly Knights," 1963.14
A Lecture on the Right Honourable R. Brinsley Sheridan Delivered at Constantinople, 1862.1
Lectures on the English Comic Writers, 1819.4
LeFanu, Alicia, 1824.2
LeFanu, William, 1960.5
Leff, Leonard J., 1970.9; 1972.14; 1973.10
Legouis, Pierre, 1934.6
A Letter to T. Moore, Esq. on the Subject of Sheridan's "School for Scandal," 1826.17
"Letters of Sheridan," 1911.1
Lewis, Theophilus, 1967.12
Liars and Fakers, 1925.9
Life of Richard Brinsley Sheridan (Sanders), 1890.2; 1974.12
"Life of Richard Brinsley Sheridan" (Stainforth), 1874.6
"Life of Sheridan," 1817.1
"Life of Sheridan" (Sigmond), 1852.3
The Life of the Right Honourable Richard Brinsley Sheridan, 1816.5
Light, Enoch, 1965.3
"Lines Occasioned by the Medical Attendance on . . . Sheridan," 1816.20

Lines on the Death of ____, 1816.17
Link, Frederick M., 1976.6
The Linleys of Bath, 1911.4; 1926.4
The Linleys of Bath, rev. ed., 1971.2
"The Linleys of Norton," 1929.6
"The Listener on Eloquence, 1750-1800," 1944.3
The Literary Bazaar, 1816.18
"Literary Gossip," 1876.1
A Literary History of England, 1948.8
"Literary Notices. No. 12," 1816.16
"A Little Case of Borrowing," 1891.1
Lives of Eminent and Illustrious Englishmen, 1837.7
"The Lives of the Sheridans" (Saturday Review), 1887.2
"The Lives of the Sheridans. By Percy Fitzgerald" (The Athenaeum), 1887.1
The Lives of the Sheridans, 1886.3; 1973.5
Lives of the Wits, 1962.17
Livingston, L. S., 1906.2
Lloyd, George, 1863.4
Lockhart, John, 1826.16
Lockitt, C. H., 1939.3
Loewenberg, Alfred, 1942.9; 1944.4; 1970.10
Loftis, John, 1966.7; 1975.6; 1977.4
The London Daily Press, 1772-1792, 1963.24
The London Stage 1776-1800, 1968.2
The London Stage, 1776-1800: A Critical Introduction, 1968.3
"The London Theatres, 1776-1800. A Brief Consideration," 1966.5
"The Long and Round 'S,'" 1928.10
"The Long 'S' and "Ye,'" 1928.15
Lonsdale, Roger, 1971.3
"A Look at the London Season: The Rivals," 1957.13

Index

Index

--Plays (Backgrounds of), 1977.4;
(Editorial Problems of),
1928.11; (First Editions of),
1900.5; (Manuscripts of),
1902.7-8; (Receptions of),
1973.11; (Texts of), 1973.11
--Poems, 1819.1, 1874.2,
1904.2, 1914.2-3, 1922.1,
1926.5, 8, 10, 12, 1927.1-2,
5, 7, 1944.4, 1958.5,
1961.8, 1969.1, 1974.2, 1975.4
--Regency Letter, 1928.7
--The Rivals, 1874.7, 1881.2;
(Abridged), 1935.6, 1941.3,
1943.4, 1944.9, 1956.6,
1963.18; (As Source),
1960.8; (As Source of
Walden), 1966.15; (Jane
Austen's Debt to), 1964.2,
8; (Backgrounds of),
1913.4, 1929.7, 1938.4;
(Characters in), 1830.4,
1871.2; [Acres], 1888.1,
1889.4, 1898.1, 1937.5,
1942.1, 7, 1975.1;
[Faulkland], 1864.1, 1926.1,
1929.9, 1937.5, 1957.13,
1970.2, 1976.7; [Julia],
1937.5, 1978.2; [Lydia],
1905.3, 1906.3, 1937.5,
1964.8, 1976.7; [Mrs.
Malaprop], 1930.13, 1933.1,
1937.5, 1942.7, 1946.10,
1961.1, 1970.14, 1972.8,
1975.1, 5; [Sir Anthony],
1957.13 [Sir Lucius],
1884.3; (Criticism of),
1820.1, 1832.2, 1880.3,
1883.8, 1885.1, 1886.1, 2,
1896.2, 1899.4, 1900.1-2, 8,
1905.2, 1910.1, 1913.3-4,
1916.7, 1920.3, 5, 1923.1,
9, 1927.10, 1930.11, 1933.2,
1935.1, 1937.5, 1938.1, 4,
1942.1, 3, 5, 8, 10,
1943.1, 1945.2, 1948.8,
1951.1, 1952.3, 1953.5, 7,
1954.5, 1957.11, 1958.2,
1961.13, 1962.1, 7, 1963.4,
1965.9, 1966.16, 1967.9, 11,
1968.3, 8, 1970.14, 16, 17,

1973.3, 7, 1975.1, 4-5,
1976.7, 1977.2, 4, 1978.1;
(First Edition of), 1911.1,
1929.1; (First Prologue of),
1969.7; (Illustrations of),
1889.1; (Language of),
1973.13, 1974.13; (Larpent
Manuscript of), 1929.4,
1935.4; (Musical Adaptation
of), 1964.1; (Original
Performance of), 1910.2;
(Problems of Performance in),
1895.1; (Prompt Copies of),
1924.1, 1975.2; (Provincial
Performances of), 1943.3;
(Sources of), 1876.1, 1888.4,
1891.1, 1897.1, 1903.1,
1906.3, 1910.1, 1911.2,
1928.6, 1929.7, 1932.3,
1933,7, 1957.10, 1960.9,
1970.2; (Spanish Translation
of), 1952.5; (Stage History
of [German]), 1913.9; (Stage
Setting of), 1925.1; (Text
of), 1910.3, 1927.8, 1929.4,
12, 14, 1930.2, 7, 9, 1939.4;
(Translated by Tieck),
1960.12; (Translation of),
1902.1; (Translation into
Greek), 1937.6
--Robinson Crusoe (Authorship
of), 1944.6; (Provincial
Performances of), 1943.3,
1944.2, 7-8; (Scenario of),
1943.2, 1945.5-6; (Stage
History of), 1949.11
--St. Patrick's Day, 1977.2;
(Criticism of), 1946.1,
1965.11, 1975.4, 1978.1;
(Manuscript of), 1957.12;
(Stage History of), 1949.11;
(Text of), 1966.11; (Early
Edition of), 1924.4
--The School for Scandal,
1874.7; (Adaptation of),
1936.6; (And Royall Tyler's
The Contrast), 1950.3;
(Backgrounds of), 1897.3,
1917.4; (Characters in)
[Charles Surface], 1830.5,
1894.3, 1960.4, 1962.1;

305

Index